Literary Alchemist

Literary Alchemist

The Writing Life of Evan S. Connell

Steve Paul

IIIIII

UNIVERSITY OF MISSOURI PRESS

Columbia

Library of Congress Cataloging-in-Publication Data

Names: Paul, Steve, 1953- author.
Title: Literary alchemist : the writing life of Evan S. Connell / Steve
  Paul.
Description: Columbia : University of Missouri Press, 2021. | Includes
  bibliographical references and index.
Identifiers: LCCN 2021026161 (print) | LCCN 2021026162 (ebook) | ISBN
  9780826222466 (hardcover) | ISBN 9780826274649 (ebook)
Subjects: LCSH: Connell, Evan S., 1924-2013. | Authors, American--20th
  century--Biography.
Classification: LCC PS3553.O5 Z65 2021 (print) | LCC PS3553.O5 (ebook) |
  DDC 813.54--dc23
LC record available at https://lccn.loc.gov/2021026161
LC ebook record available at https://lccn.loc.gov/2021026162

Typeface: Sabon

Contents

Illustrations

Illustrations

Preface

We feel there is within each of us something which will not
ever die.

—Notes from a Bottle Found on the Beach at Carmel

AS A WRITER Evan S. Connell took the long view. In many of his
books and essays, he plunged himself into deep history. In *Son of
the Morning Star*, the book that became his most commercially
successful, he examined the nineteenth-century life and demise of
General George Armstrong Custer. One of his last big projects found
him channeling voices from a millennium ago, during the Christian
crusades. He loved travel and travelers, and he found a resonant
theme in the "long desire," a thought he borrowed from the French
writer Anatole France, in which explorers and seekers follow their
instincts to see what unknown discoveries might appear around the
next bend. Even in his best-known works of fiction, *Mrs. Bridge*
(1959) and *Mr. Bridge* (1969), a pair of paradoxically intimate
novels that lay bare the workings of a middle-American, upper-
middle-class family, there is a distance in his perspective, a cold eye
that presents his subjects' quirks, dysfunctions, disappointments,
and interior lives with a skillful precision; a sharp sense of irony;
and a subtle, arm's-length humor. The lives of India and Walter
Bridge and their three children in the two novels are contained
within the walls they construct, knowingly or unknowingly, for
themselves. India Bridge, especially, lives an almost helpless life
of loneliness within a marriage where romantic love is long lost.
Critics' general conclusions that the Bridge family was probably not

unlike Connell's own are certainly supportable, though he invented many of the facts. Unlike Douglas Bridge, for example, Connell had only one sister, Barbara, not two, and she, he long maintained, was nothing like either Carolyn or Ruth Bridge in the two novels. But there are larger points to be made, especially as one attempts to get closer to Connell's own life, a project he mostly resisted. So many of those who knew him, including those who knew him well and over long periods of time, talk about the walls he put around himself. He was not a social animal. He could enjoy himself at parties but only if accompanied by his closest friends. He didn't talk much, to the point that some people thought of him as mute. He was distant. He didn't look straight at you.

I had been on his trail for nearly three years when an important insight came by way of a longtime friend of his. The writer Anne Lamott had known him since she was a girl of five or six, when he often showed up for dinner at her house in Tiburon, California. Connell and her father, Kenneth Lamott, were compatriots at a literary enterprise, *Contact* magazine, which had been founded in Sausalito, California, in 1958. In later years, especially after Ken Lamott died in 1979, his daughter and Connell maintained a close friendship for the rest of his life. Connell was the quiet one among the *Contact* contingent. While colleagues Calvin Kentfield and publisher Bill Ryan were ever boisterous, Connell—tall, lanky, and reserved—was the one to mull things over, to contemplate, and to hardly speak. As Anne Lamott put it once, he and her father shared a certain gentlemanly aspect: "My father, who had an enormous affection and admiration for Evan, used to call him 'the inscrutable Evan Connell.'"[1]

Annie Lamott remains among only a handful of people still alive who knew Connell well. As we spoke about him over the phone, I was startled by her suggestion that Mrs. Bridge's loneliness was also Connell's loneliness. Once you see the arc of his personal life, however, it all begins to make sense. He loved women, or more accurately, he loved to be with women, yet he never married. And on that matter of love, he struggled in life and in his art with what it meant. He lived sparsely, ascetically. He certainly maintained friendships, though as Lamott told me, those friendships did not usually contain deep emotional bonds. There was one woman in his life whom he might have married. But he seemed to know early on that marriage did not suit him. And the woman, Gale Zoe Garnett, knew that as well. After their early sexual encounters, they carried on a long-distance relationship over many years, both committed more to their own work and their own eccentric ways of being than to what the heart might or might not have desired.

Connell might have cherished his friendships; you can feel that in some of his correspondence. But in essence he lived to write. Webster Schott, who first mentioned Connell in print in 1949 and kept up a friendship for the next six decades, told me much the same thing. "His life was his work," Schott said.[2] That compulsion to write, to engage in the quest for knowledge which consumed Connell, may well explain why he never got married, never had a family. Writing—"this quaint mania" is how he put it once—was far too important to him.[3] It protected him from the intimacy that real relationships require, an intimacy he never saw in his own family and that he very well knew he did not possess. If he possessed something of an outwardly depressive personality or was one of those writers who, as the psychotherapist Anthony Storr has put it, are "disappointing to meet," it is quite possible his true personality only emerged in his work and was "concealed during the ordinary interchanges of social life."[4]

One aspect of Connell's existence never changed. He was forever handsome. Lean and athletic, he possessed a sculpted face with a neatly trimmed mustache or, later, a goatee. His were the proverbial movie-star good looks. He was beautiful, more than one of his woman friends attested. The attraction may well have been enhanced by Connell's leather bomber jacket, a sartorial look he cultivated after his three years in the Naval Air Corps and in his year and a half at the University of Kansas. In the day-to-day archival research that went into the making of this book, two memorable moments affirmed the point. In the writer Max Steele's papers in North Carolina, I found numerous letters from Connell that helped especially to illuminate Connell's creative progress and travels of the 1950s. But the Steele collection also contains that writer's long correspondence with Alice Adams. Adams, a fiction writer of considerable talent, knew Connell in San Francisco and occasionally encountered him at book parties. In one letter from the early 1970s, Adams reported on Connell's presence at one such event, adding an effusion of "Dashing Evan!"[5]

In another library, a young female staffer helped me access a literary reference work and articles from the 1970s and 1980s. As she spotted a photograph in one of those pieces, she offered, without any kind of prompt, "What a suave looking dude." Priceless.

Nevertheless, while looks and outsize talent might well make a formidable package, becoming a literary star—in Connell's time and ours—also requires personality, charm, and a willingness to suffer the indignities of book tours, interviews, promotional appearances, and editorial expectations. Connell mostly eschewed all of that. He never taught and thus never cultivated a devoted coterie of students who would go off into the writing world and carry his banner. He subjected himself to interviews from time to time, several of which have been helpful in the making of this book. But save for the surprising success of *Son of the Morning Star*, his landmark account of Custer and the Battle of the Little Bighorn, Connell and his various publishers never ignited a sustainable publicity campaign to ensure a lasting and well-earned reputation. Other writers have long admired him—it didn't help that he was often labeled a writers' writer—and some readers have long cherished the discoveries and emotional connections they found in the pages of, say, *Mrs. Bridge* or *Son of the Morning Star* or even *Notes from a Bottle Found on the Beach at Carmel*, one of Connell's most startling and challenging works. But for numerous and often unsurprising reasons, Connell has remained a figure lesser known than he deserved.

"My own experience indicates that it is mostly a career of rejection and lost illusions," Connell said decades into his life as a writer.[6] Connell certainly was guilty of sabotaging his prospects by the choices he frequently made and the isolated existence he cultivated. He had his moments in the literary whirl and participated more than once in the machinery of fame. Newspaper and magazine editors often sought him out to write book reviews—I've retrieved nearly four dozen—which often gave him a national platform to discuss ideas of literature, writing, and history. And despite his disregard for the limelight, he cared about the stats—the press runs, the bestseller lists, his publishers' willingness to support a book with advertising dollars.

Still, Connell has long been regarded in terms such as the "best writer you've never heard of." Connell did not amass, like his contemporaries Philip Roth and John Updike, a large stack of novels knitted together by narrative voices and styles that collectively emit the sense of a unified literary consciousness. His works were almost always unpredictable and uncommonly varied. His sixty or so extant short stories include numerous masterpieces as well as minor sketches and the odd curiosity. His choice to veer into historical essays, fragmentary epics, and deep draws from the past left many in the publishing establishment scratching their heads. *Notes from a Bottle*, for example, and a similar volume, *Points for a Compass Rose*, were amalgamations of historical and philosophical nuggets sculpted in the form of book-length poems. Two volumes of essays (later collected as one in *The Aztec Treasure House*) bring to life Connell's penchant for intrepid wandering and long pursuits. One novel (now titled *Alchymic Journals*) channeled the arcane voices of sixteenth-century alchemists, one of whom Connell had referenced in the *Notes* books and also treated to a longer, more conventional essay. His novels caromed in form and subject, from sexual assault (*The Diary of a Rapist*) to the passions of art (*The Connoisseur*) to the Crusades (*Deus lo Volt!*). Connell early on had wanted to be an artist and kept up a long practice of live-model sketching. His last full-length work was a biographical essay of an artist, *Francisco Goya*, which reflected seemingly all of Connell's disparate thematic interests and even included bits from his own life. It's almost as if Connell, nearing eighty, were thinking about his own artistic legacy in disguise.

Although he certainly kept track of the market and the sales details, Connell, it is clear, didn't want to be branded a writer of commercial books and what that typically meant in the literary world. He mainly wanted to write what captured his interest. He wanted, through writing, Web Schott learned late in Connell's life, to understand who he was.

The story of Evan S. Connell is the story of a loner who was born into a life of American privilege and chose a creative path in which to perform a nonstop, absorbing project of literary alchemy. Through Connell, we can get a sense of the bundle of anxieties that beset American men of the latter half of the twentieth century. These range from war to sex, from professional success to idle dreaming, from intellectual advancement to the nature of human love and companionship. All of that frames not only his own life experience but also the thematic scope of his literary work. Connell looked inward to the daily habits and minor struggles of a life and outward to the march of human history, which he saw as miraculous, utterly strange, and frightfully disturbing.

The present volume, I hope, can serve as a reclamation project for Connell and his literary legacy. There are aspects and episodes of his personal life that remain elusive. His longtime editor, Jack Shoemaker, told me, quite skeptically, at the beginning of my quest, "Evan always said he had the dullest life of any writer ever. There was nothing to discover or worry over."[7] On the contrary, examining Connell's life and work, as this book does for the first time in unprecedented detail, has been to discover how a writer wholly commits to his art. Connell had his extracurricular passions but his intellect and his sustained focus drove him to the typewriter, to the page, to the books of the past, and to the ever-bubbling well-spring of his creative mind. Connell made art from borrowed and invented bits. He was a mosaicist, attentive to the tiniest of details, and an alchemist, testing the transformation of matter and soul. In the whole, there are plenty of stories and experiences to help illuminate his life and many aspects and themes of Connell's work that, perhaps touched on in these pages, could be developed into books of their own. Scholarly essays on Connell have been few and far between. However, as I was completing a draft of this book, I was alerted to a new one. It was an essay by David Pickus, who explored an intriguing idea about "social oblivion" in two of

Connell's novels, *Mr. Bridge* and *The Connoisseur*.[8] Perhaps others will follow.

In constructing an account of his commitment to art and to a life of writing, my goal has been to give Connell and his work the attention it warrants, whether he wanted it or not. In a way, this book responds to a challenge I found early on in the quiet page-turning at Stanford University's Green Library, where many of Connell's papers are housed. It came in a letter that Schott wrote to Connell more than twenty years ago. Someone, Schott said, will eventually try to figure out how to reconcile the author of *Mrs. Bridge* with the one who wrote *Deus lo Volt!*, Connell's "Chronicle of the Crusades," and the other works that took him into distant narrative territories. Yes, that's the spirit.

Literary Alchemist

Treasure House

1924–1941

Somberly Otto frowns into the fire; almost adult he is in the
strength of such concentration, though one could not tell
whether he is mulling over the past or the future.

—"Arcturus"

EVAN SHELBY CONNELL Jr. was thirty-four years old, author of
a collection of short stories and his soon-to-be-published first
novel, when he turned out an astounding, life-defining thought.
There it lay on an early page of another work: "I am charged
with excitement! My vision extends! There is no one on earth
who can stop me. Although I am not at ease in this world, there
is no one who can stop me."[1] In the scheme of Connell's entire
body of writing—more than a half-century's production of vivid
fiction and exploratory history—the first-person pronouncement
can well be read as the voice of humanity itself, a reflection on
its long, troubling, and inherently violent existence. It appears in
what turned out to be a rehearsal for a book called *Notes from a
Bottle Found on the Beach at Carmel*, a kaleidoscopic assemblage
of meditations on history that indeed wrestles with the human
dilemma. But I also want to read those lines as a direct message
from Connell himself. It is a note from a bottle deep inside the
writer's brain: "Although I am not at ease in this world, there is
no one who can stop me." How did it come to be that Connell,
product of an outwardly wholesome, middle-class American upbringing, felt ill at ease in the world? And who did he perceive
was trying to stop him? These are obvious questions, of course,

the kind of complications that can propel a narrative. But nothing about Connell is perfectly obvious.

He called himself the frowning boy. To pore over family photos and linger with home-movie footage is to discover the evidence that supports the description. You rarely see Connell with anything approaching a smile. This was as true in his childhood as it was for the rest of his life. Oh, certainly those who knew him well would dispute such an observation. They laughed with him. They saw his happiness up close. But why Connell almost never put on a smile while being photographed is another mystery. "I dislike being photographed," he once told his sister, "and the photographer always says smile, which is ridiculous."[2] A photographer friend he had lined up to deliver an author portrait in the late 1960s described how she had to browbeat him to cooperate.[3] But frowning for photographs is one thing. Greeting the world with a kind of skeptical aloofness is another. It is a way of being, a restless propulsion, a kind of intentional absence from the crowd that certainly shaped Connell's self-made path as a multidimensional writer and artist. He is undoubtedly among the best of recent American writers, one who possessed an extraordinary range of talent and output. Yet, reflecting the characteristic cruelty of the predominant cultural measuring apparatuses, he is also one of the least known.

Connell was born on August 17, 1924, at Research Hospital in Kansas City, Missouri, a fairly prosperous Midwestern burg of more than 325,000 people. Temperatures that day had temporarily settled into the seventies before a typical summer's march toward the nineties, and thunderstorms threatened. Prohibition had gripped the nation in those years, but the powers that be in Kansas City had a reputation for flouting the laws or looking the other way. It was a verdant place, spreading southward from its origins along the unpredictable, more-brown-than-blue Missouri River. It was a noisy and smelly place too. Belching trains; sprawling, bellowing stockyards; streets crowded with trolley cars and automobiles, newsboys and hawkers, grifters and matronly shoppers— Kansas City's urban stew offered something for everyone.

His father, Dr. Evan Shelby Connell Sr., could trace his roots back to colonial America, to the Maryland territory where an Irish immigrant named James O'Connell landed in 1670. Within only one generation the family had dropped the Irish "O" from its name, though it is unclear exactly when and why its members began calling themselves Conn-*ell*, emphasis on the second syllable. A reasonable explanation would involve a verbal way of distancing the family further from their poor Irish origins. It is also unclear how and whether the family is connected to the town of Connellsville in southwestern Pennsylvania, though one of Dr. Connell's ancestors, Colonel John Crawford Connell, was born there in 1768, according to a family tree assembled via Ancestry.com.

The elder Evan Shelby Connell was born in Lexington, Missouri, a town fifty miles east of Kansas City and the site of two Civil War skirmishes won by irregular Confederate forces. His father, William A. Connell, began a medical practice in Kansas City in 1900. Evan Sr. received a degree in medicine from Tulane University in 1913 and continued his medical studies at the University of Vienna until the outbreak of the Great War. Following some logistical difficulty, he managed to leave Austria and landed safely in Montreal on the way home to Kansas City. After the United States entered the war in 1917, Evan Sr. was commissioned as a first lieutenant in the army and served as a surgeon, attached to an evacuation hospital in France. As an eye, ear, nose, and throat specialist, he encountered wounded soldiers who had succumbed to gas attacks and other medical horrors during the last months of the war. Like many veterans of many wars, he rarely, if ever, shared his experiences with his family. Connell Sr., following in his own father's footsteps, established his medical practice in downtown Kansas City, in the Commerce Building at Tenth and Walnut Streets. He also served on the staff of St. Joseph's Hospital. He became renowned as an eye surgeon.

In 1923, the good doctor married Ruth Elton Williamson, a native of Carlyle, Kentucky, with family roots going back to Scottish immigrants and Kentucky settlers. She went by her middle name. As with the opening lines of *Mrs. Bridge*, which addresses the protagonist's unusual given name, India, there was no explanation for the name Elton. ("As a child," Connell would write so meaningfully of India Bridge, "she was often on the point of inquiring, but time passed, and she never did."[4]) The married couple settled into a new frame house at 210 West 66th Street. A year later, Mrs. Connell gave birth to Evan Jr. A year after that, on his first birthday, the infant sat with his mother on the lawn outside their house. A hauntingly characteristic snapshot captured the moment. In it, the baby boy looks off toward some undefined, distant horizon.

As the newborn Connell came into the world, the nation and its allies were on the verge of a final agreement with Germany, after five years of negotiations, over indemnity payments, troop departures, and other business stemming from the Great War. Spain was skirmishing with tribal rebels in Morocco. And the Democratic Party in the United States was angling to defeat the popular and fiscally conservative president Calvin Coolidge in the forthcoming election, perhaps by joining forces, as the political scuttlebutt had it, with Robert M. La Follette's Progressive Party in some Midwestern states. It was also the so-called Jazz Age and the era of the postwar "lost generation," when expatriate American writers in Paris were redefining the language of literature, and artists and musicians were making everything modern and new.

Elton Connell came from a family with some traditional artistic inclinations and strong connections to the community. Her father, John I. Williamson, was a prominent Kansas City attorney who in 1919 was named to serve out an abbreviated term on the state Supreme Court. He was once described as a lawyer of the "rugged, manly type," with "red blood in his veins."[5] Connell once hinted that a drop of that blood might have come from a Native American source, though there is nothing in the family lore or genealogy to verify that. John Williamson was a Missouri native, but true to the family roots, he attended the University of Kentucky and practiced law in that state until moving to Kansas City in 1903. Williamson had a passion for history, which he may well have passed on to his grandson. He was also a poet, though examples of his verse remain elusive. Connell remembered his maternal grandfather fondly. He once felt his grandfather's presence while on a train trip through Scotland. The echoes, thirty years after his grandfather's death, of being called "Lad" finally made sense. As a boy, Connell would often stare at a clay figurine on his grandfather's bookshelf. The object foretold his own future interest in ancient Mexican objects. It also led to a mild disappointment when Connell suspected and confirmed that the piece was a fake and that his sophisticated grandfather had thus been duped into believing in its pre-historicity like any other ill-informed and run-of-the-mill tourist in Oaxaca. As for his grandmother, his mother's mother, Lucy Williamson moved into the Connell household after her husband died of influenza in 1933. She wintered in Sarasota, Florida; collected seashells; and used them to make decorative place-cards for social events. She traveled often to visit relatives. One summer, in 1937, she took her granddaughter, ten-year-old Barbara, on a two-week vacation to a favorite family destination in the 1930s, the Ka Rose Resort on Grand Lake, Colorado. She died in 1951 at age eighty-two.

Connell's other grandfather had been a mining engineer but became a physician. "He seldom spoke," Connell once wrote.[6] But he did sit in a leather armchair and scented Connell's memories with a hint of cigar tobacco. When his paternal grandfather died, Connell inherited a humidor adorned with an image of an Indian chief. Foolishly he discarded a discolored cotton lining—and with it the comforting aroma. Years later, though, Connell himself became fond of the rugged and manly pull of a cigarillo. Curiously, Connell's own reputation, recounted time after time by those who came to know him, was as a man, like his grandfather, who seldom spoke.

Grandmother Martha Young Connell's ancestors were Welsh, and her family tree included the Confederate general Jo Shelby. Shelby happened to be buried at Forest Hill Cemetery, not much more than a mile away from the family home. Connell's grandmother often talked about Shelby on outings to Lexington, where she grew up. As a boy, Connell's father scoured the town's battlefield sites for Civil War minie balls. "I felt proud to be related to General Jo," Evan Jr. confessed, "however distantly, and once dropped his name before an acquaintance who turned out to be directly descended from a rather more celebrated general, Robert E. Lee."[7]

Connell worked some of the family background into his early novel *The Patriot*, about a naval aviation cadet from Kansas City. On a brief leave back home, the central character, Melvin Isaacs, joins his father and a friend on an excursion to Lexington, where the father, Jacob Isaacs, like Connell's own father, had grown up. Connell captures the nearby landscape, after a rain, as they drove to Lexington: "The river ran high, with a deep yellowish sheen, like chocolate or milky coffee, thick with silt. From the bottomlands came an odor of hay and livestock. A few birds soared in the summer wind above the cliff."[8]

Melvin's father shows the two young men where he had played, a stretch of land where a battle between Missouri Guard units and outnumbered Union forces ground out for three days early in the Civil War. He delivers a lecture on local and family history. "My grandfather rode with the great Confederate general, Joseph Shelby," Jacob says. "History books mention Jeb Stuart's cavalry riding around McClellan's army, but General Shelby rode around the entire state of Missouri with only eight hundred men, burning and plundering Union depots, pursued for a month by ten thousand Federal troops who were unable to stop him. It was one of the most amazing military actions of all time."[9] This account closely aligns to the facts as historians understand them today.

Jacob goes on to point out the field where Melvin's great-grandfather had been wounded, "shot in the throat as he crawled over the ramparts with his hunting knife," and where two of the ancestor's brothers had died and another was wounded by a cannon explosion. The visitors receive more background on a tour of a historic home in which bloody warfare had occurred. Before they return to Kansas City, Jacob Isaacs drives by the deserted farmhouse where he was born. As Connell writes, "The windows were broken, the front door stood half-open. The lawn was rankly overgrown."[10] Indeed, he implies, one can't go home again.

If unearthing the lore connected to Connell's middle name, Shelby, sheds light on his identity as something of a southern gentleman, it is possible that he concealed other aspects of his family's Civil War–era heritage. His maternal grandfather, Judge John Williamson, once gave a luncheon talk to the Daughters of the Confederacy in Kansas City in which he paid tribute to the Confederate general Stonewall Jackson. Another member of the Shelby family, Thomas Shelby, was a prominent hemp farmer and slave owner who lived in an opulent brick mansion outside Lexington. And by the time Connell was writing *The Patriot*, an intriguing family story about John Williamson's aunt had been unearthed and circulated. According to the published account, in 1863 Mathilda Williamson left her farm in Carroll County, Missouri, accompanied only by her Black slave, named Shan, to travel on an epic journey. They covered six hundred miles by horse-drawn wagon to retrieve her husband's remains from a Mississippi cemetery. Mathilda had married her second cousin, James Pritchard, a Kansan who shortly after the beginning of the Civil War joined the Confederate Army, became a captain, and died in battle near Coffeyville, Mississippi, in October 1862. After spending several consoling months in Coffeyville, she decided to leave her husband where he lay and return with Shan to Missouri. Mathilda, according to this story, was "a frail melancholy mystic, a writer of obituaries and funereal poems."[11] It is a curious thing that Connell, presuming he had known about his great aunt, would not have seen her as a kind of spirit presence. Then again, of course, he also would have to reckon with the complications of his ancestors' slave-holding realities.

Connell once began an autobiographical essay with his earliest memory, a noiseless scene shaped by his mother's distress. She came running down the stairs aghast as it appeared young Evan was about to pick up his little sister with a pair of brass fireplace tongs: "Her head fitted neatly between the claws, although she must have been too heavy to lift because I had not gotten her off the rug. I believe she might have been screaming, although that fact was not important enough to register."[12] Was Connell being cruel or just coolly studying the mechanical workings of the tongs? He didn't elaborate. But the memory, if true, meant something important to him. The silence—the inability to hear his mother's voice or his sister's screaming—certainly echoes. He may well have seen his mother as a voiceless member of the household, though the memory also depicts her as the protector of her endangered child. As for the other child, the perpetrator, young Evan, bad behavior did not go unnoticed or unremarked upon. Later, we will see the theme arising frequently in the fictional life of Douglas Bridge, the son—and surrogate for the young Connell—in the two Bridge novels.

For most of Connell's childhood, the family lived in a two-story colonial house, painted white with green trim, on a tree-lined street in Armour Hills, a planned, suburban-style development of single-family homes on what was then the southern edge of Kansas City. Neighboring houses generally reflected a similar aesthetic, the look of modest prosperity and social propriety. Southwest High School, Connell's future alma mater, would be built in 1927 on Wornall Road, about a block to the west, and young Evan's grade school, Border Star, was just two blocks north. Armour Hills and adjacent neighborhoods were part of real estate developer J. C. Nichols's vision to create large swaths of gracious and convenient living in the southwest sectors of the city. In the early 1920s, Nichols began building the Country Club Plaza, a shopping district two and a half miles to the north of the Connell family home. In his grand plan for residential neighborhoods built around handsome shopping centers and served by public streets and streetcars, Nichols had already launched the English-country-inspired shops of Brookside, along 63rd Street. The shops were a three-block walk from the Connells' house or a quick bicycle ride in those boyhood summers when Evan bagged groceries or stocked shelves at the Safeway and A&P food stores.

The Nichols neighborhoods catered to the upwardly mobile residents of Kansas City, or more specifically the upwardly mobile white and Christian residents of the city, given the restrictive covenants that prevented home sales to Black people and practices that discouraged Jews and other minorities from moving to the area. When he got around to writing his first Kansas City novel in the 1950s, Connell would not ignore the social atmosphere of his upbringing, including the intertwined subjects of race, class, and upper-crust hypocrisy.

Fig. 1. Elton Connell with
Barbara and Evan, c. 1928.
Courtesy of the Literary Estate
of Evan Shelby Connell Jr.

Fig. 2. Dr. Evan S. Connell Sr.,
late 1920s. Courtesy of the
Literary Estate of Evan Shelby
Connell Jr.

The Connell household was comfortable, measured, and something to be admired. It isn't every day, for instance, that a homemaker's recipe for a sandwich loaf—ham, sardines, olives, cream cheese, the works—is touted by the daily newspaper, but Mrs. Connell surely enjoyed the spotlight in July 1928.[13] The family employed a Black housemaid who could be seen pushing baby Evan's stroller, not an uncommon sight in the neighborhood. Elton Connell was active in social and volunteer circles, hosting teas and bridge parties, chairing luncheons, and taking part in hospital auxiliary events. Evan confessed that generally, as she gardened in floppy slacks or sat quietly looking out a living room window, he never knew what she was thinking. Coming to terms with that—or essentially trying to understand just who his mother was—became the underlying spark for *Mrs. Bridge*.

The young Connell's own inner life is also hard to trace, save for the palimpsest of a psychological map embedded in his works and correspondence. We have his published droll and winsome autobiographical essay. We have the Bridge family novels and numerous short stories and other works to mine for clues. We have photographs that can reveal ephemeral states of mind. It becomes momentarily startling, for instance, to find Connell in full boyish happiness while posed for a formal double portrait with his sister. A photographer at the famous Strauss-Peyton studio in Kansas City captured that outlier photo—and perhaps emphatically prodded the smiling expression—when Connell was six or seven and Barbara three years younger. To complete the polished look, the boy sports short pants, white shirt, and a jaunty neckerchief.

But Connell's "frowning boy," or a visage with a neutral expression, is a much more common sight in family photos. Connell played with that self-image in an early short story, "Arcturus," which presented a domestic scene featuring a man and his young son and daughter around a fireplace awaiting the arrival of guests: "Somberly Otto frowns into the fire; almost adult he is in the strength of such concentration, though one could not tell whether he is mulling over the past or the future. Perhaps if the truth were known he is only seeing how long he can roast his feet, which are practically touching a log."[14]

Family movies captured the joys and frolics of suburban life: Connell's teenaged sister maneuvering on stilts that he had made. Romps with dogs and a pony. Scenes of the good life, with little evidence of disruption as the nation sank into economic calamity.

Connell's grade school, Border Star, presented an encouraging atmosphere for a writer-to-be. Its principal instilled a culture of reading. As the boy entered the lower grades at the school, he became part of the new "A-Book-a-Week" program meant to "develop in the children a taste and inclination for the use of good books." Variety was emphasized: "Nature, folk-lore, history, biography, poetry, geography, hero stories, hand-work, as well as fiction is shown to make a mentally healthy child." By the end of the seventh grade, a student like Connell "will have read something like 300 well chosen books," according to the principal, Miles Thomas, along with "the elements of a general cultural background that will stay with him throughout his life."[15] Of course, not all of Connell's classmates went on to become writers. But the boy certainly found in this reading-oriented environment the seeds for a life of creativity and imaginative expression.

The Great Depression seemed to take a far different course in Kansas City than in other parts of the nation. A civic building boom in the early 1930s, in the wake of the stock market crash of October 1929, produced a slew of government-owned structures—the city hall, a county courthouse, a vast and lavish auditorium and theater. Also built in that era were such significant landmarks as the Nelson Gallery of Art, a legacy of the founding publisher of the *Kansas City Star*, which opened in 1933 when Connell turned nine. These projects kept construction workers busy and—no small matter—produced significant economic sustenance for the likes of Thomas J. Pendergast, the Democratic power broker who also happened to own a cement business among other commercial enterprises.

Dr. Connell's financial holdings apparently did not suffer much in the economic downturn. In 1933, he and his wife took a two-month vacation to Europe. In 1934, he bought a summer home for the family, an historic, ten-room brick house on 160 acres of farmland about twenty miles outside the city. The house, in northeast Jackson County, dated to the 1850s. It cost about $20,000 (or nearly $375,000 in today's dollars). Planned renovations, including a two-story columned portico, would add to the bill. Since Connell's father proved, for the most part, to be a savvy investor, a quality he passed on to his son, he undoubtedly counted on proceeds from the farm acreage to cover at least part of the cost. Somewhat out of character, the elder Connell once shared with his family a story of hitting it big. He and some Kansas City acquaintances had invested in an Oklahoma oil operation, which resulted in a gusher of oil as well as income. The men traveled to the oil field, drank champagne, and were doused in the slick spew of black gold. Dr. Connell's take, however, was capped when the Oklahoma legislature limited oil profits for out-of-staters, but, as his son recounted years later, he was essentially a well-off millionaire during the Depression.[16] In late 1935, Dr. Connell added to his investment properties when he purchased a 215-acre farm in Clay County in the northern reaches of the Kansas City area. Young Evan and his sister, Barbara, shared their own wealth at the time. The newspaper reported that separately and together in the early 1930s, they donated at least four dollars to the Salvation Army's Penny Ice Fund, which benefited the poor.[17]

As an eight-year-old, Connell went to the St. John's summer camp in Wisconsin. The experience surely gave him a feeling of freedom away from his family but also enhanced his affinity for the outdoors and the bracing connections with nature that he would forever express. The modern, manmade world was less to his liking. Witness his adult preferences for living simply and avoiding computers. But it is also a feeling that underlies a line of his fiction, a passage reflecting a character's "benign indifference [that] he used to feel as a child when he considered the world from the gilded saddle of an undulating stallion on a carousel."[18]

In his teens, Connell built model boats and airplanes. Once he stood on the sidelines of the Mirror Pool in the median of the grand, mansion-lined Ward Parkway, amid a cheering crowd, and watched a boat he'd made win first place among the fifteen-inch sloop yachts. In *Mr. Bridge*, Douglas's entry in a similar model-boat race seems to be an embarrassing failure, sitting motionless for much too long in the center of the pond. "Anyhow," Douglas says, "it didn't sink."[19] A younger cousin who lived across the street from the Connells recalled that Evan had a talent for sketching and model-making, and that he had several model planes hanging from the ceiling of his bedroom.[20] A published photograph of the teenager holding one of his model airplanes confirms his interest.[21] An older cousin had been a flyer, and one can certainly imagine that Connell's fascination with aviation was fanned in the moments he gazed on those small craft above his bed in quiet contemplation before sleep.

Any attempt to read Connell's two Bridge novels as the thinly disguised story of his family is met early and often with obfuscation and invention. Just pages into *Mrs. Bridge*, for example, we learn that Walter and India Bridge had three children, each in succession about two years apart—daughters Ruth and Carolyn, followed by the youngest, Douglas. "They had not wanted more than two children," Connell writes, "but because the first two had been girls they had decided to try once more."[22] In reality, Evan Jr. was the first child born to Dr. and Mrs. Connell, followed three years later by Barbara. In interviews Connell often acknowledged that he drew episodes from his own family but also from the lives of friends and certainly from the license granted by his writer's imagination.

As for the fictional family's name, "Bridge," it covered at least two bases. For one, this was a social world where bridge was played around many card tables, including those set up for Connell's mother's parties at their home. Connell might not have remembered it, but when he was five years old a prominent murder case dominated the attention of Kansas City society circles, a lurid tale that began at a bridge game at a Country Club Plaza apartment.[23] So yes, and despite such emotion-fueled rages, bridge was a mark of the good life. Secondly, Connell once said, "There are echoes of the word 'bridge,' meaning that you can cross over anything unpleasant and you can avoid it. This is what people like that do—if you meet something disagreeable, you can pretend it doesn't exist. It just seemed like an appropriate name."[24]

As he told an interviewer years later, the character of Mr. Bridge was founded more on the temperament and mind of his father. He based India Bridge to a lesser degree on his mother. Some things happened, he said; some things were told to him about other kids' parents; other things in the book are fabrications. "The two sisters are inventions, nothing like my sister," he said.[25]

Although he didn't specifically address the foundation for Douglas Bridge, it is logical to regard the character as a stand-in for the young Connell, or a kind of invented memory of his own self-image. And if one were to embrace that kind of reading, then we can be relatively sure of the sense of autobiography that lay in such pronouncements as "Douglas was the most introspective of the three children . . ." and this: "Mr. Bridge had hoped for a brilliant son, and though he had not yet given up that hope he was reluctantly adapting himself to the idea that his son was no prodigy. If Douglas amounted to anything in later life, he concluded, it would be less the result of brilliance than of conscientious effort."[26] Mr. Bridge's regard for his son's intellectual capacity might well be confirmed by Connell's own experience in high school and college. Despite possessing an exceptional IQ of 169, according to school documents contained in his U.S. Navy records, his grades and activities tended to reflect those of an average student. A B-minus in English did not project well.[27]

Connell developed boyhood dreams of travel, the impetus to feed the "long desire," as he would later describe the propensity for self-exploration and voyages into deep spiritual and intellectual mysteries. The local newspaper frequently fueled his imagination. A picture of the Taj Mahal could catch his eye, and like the narrator in one of his last short stories, he might have "pasted it inside one of his schoolbooks and began saving nickels and dimes from his allowance."[28]

On another day, maybe it was the large headline—"All the GOLD in Yucatan"—that caught Connell's attention or maybe it was the fetching photo of Alice LaVarre, the explorer wife of the article's author, William LaVarre. She was pictured sitting on the lap of the Mayan fire god known as Chacmool amid the ruins of Chichén Itzá in Mexico.[29] Connell was twelve and clearly stirred by the images and tales within the layout. Twenty years later he looked back to a revelatory moment like this as he corresponded with a writer friend about their respective travel plans. Mexico was an option. "I tell you," Connell wrote, "ever since I was ten—maybe eleven—whenever it was I learned to read, and saw an article about Chac Mool in Yucatan I've wanted to go there. So, in case you decide you want company on the Mexican visit, we might consider the problems involved, time and life being as they are."[30]

Connell also took note, somewhat painfully, when one of his boyhood heroes, the adventurer Richard Halliburton, went missing and was presumed drowned at sea. Halliburton perished with eleven others aboard the Chinese junk he had built in Hong Kong. They were crossing the Pacific Ocean bound for San Francisco. The trip had been conceived as a stunt to help promote the San Francisco World's Fair. The last communication with Halliburton's vessel, christened the *Sea Dragon*, occurred on March 23, 1939. As a prominent *Kansas City Star* feature noted, Halliburton thus joined Will Rogers and Amelia Earhart as American celebrities who had perished while crossing the Pacific. Halliburton had a special relationship with Connell's hometown. Not only had the *Star* purchased an early article by the young man—about a winter climb of Japan's Mount Fuji—it now carried the syndicated adventure tales that helped turn him into a household name. And Halliburton cherished his friendship with a blue-blood Kansas Citian, Irvine O. Hockaday, with whom he had roomed at Princeton, biked across Germany, and climbed the Matterhorn. As with the William LaVarre tale from Chichén Itzá, Halliburton's 1935 report on "the wickedest cities of the world" (his verdict: Cairo took top honors) were among the illustrated newspaper features that fed the young Connell's roving spirit.[31]

Halliburton was flamboyantly famous. Skeptics questioned the veracity of his stories, if not their purplish prose. But the sway of his influence was undeniable among those caught at the right time of their lives. "Let those who wish have their respectability," Halliburton wrote in *The Royal Road to Romance*, his first book, which Connell eagerly read. "I wanted freedom, freedom to indulge in whatever caprice struck my fancy, freedom to search in the farthermost corners of the earth for the beautiful, the joyous and the romantic."[32] "Whatever was forbidden, that he wanted," Halliburton's father said after his death. "Confidence and courage were his companions: a poet dwelt in his soul, a vagabond in his heart."[33] Walter Cronkite, the prominent television newsman, credited Halliburton for sending him toward journalism. Susan Sontag found him at age seven and pronounced his books essential: Halliburton, she once wrote, "had devised for himself a life of being forever young and on the move. . . . My first vision of what I thought had to be the most privileged of lives, that of a writer."[34]

Connell was similarly attracted to Halliburton's tales. He made a point of giving copies of Halliburton's *Book of Marvels* to his sister's children, and his future travels around the globe and fervent interest in history and marvels undoubtedly can be linked to his early reading. Halliburton "put sand in my shoes," he would eventually write.[35] But Connell also confessed to a sense of disappointment, even betrayal, when the thirty-nine-year-old Halliburton met his fate during that storm in the Pacific. Connell, at fourteen, was a collector of postage stamps. One can infer his passion for "these colorful little saw-toothed government vouchers from all over the world" in a scene he wrote years later.[36] But amid the tragedy of the day, he had sent in what he hoped would be a commemorative postal souvenir, which he now believed to have gone down with Halliburton and the *Sea Dragon*. I can't help but think of Connell's lingering and perhaps subconscious connection to Halliburton in the book design of his 2001 essay collection about travel and exploration, *The Aztec Treasure House*. The book's cover, for one thing, sports an ancient Mexican, turquoise-covered wood rendering of a two-headed serpent, an image repeated on chapter headings inside. Sea dragon. Of course. Reclaiming and repurposing a painful memory, as someone like the psychoanalyst Melanie Klein might put it, can have a beneficial effect on the psyche.

Connell's boyhood reading also included typical juvenile page-turners such as the Hardy Boys mysteries and Zane Grey westerns. He commented later, "I could not get enough of Will James's noble horse Smoky"—from *Smoky the Cowhorse* (1926)—"galloping across the western landscape."[37] He once wrote about the embarrassment of rediscovering an adventure book—not by Halliburton—he had admired as a schoolboy and realizing it was nothing but vapid piffle. See the title essay of *The Aztec Treasure House*, named for the once-cherished book by Thomas Janvier. Janvier's book had also filled the young Connell's imagination with the magical landscape and history of Mexico. Garbed in "corduroy knickers, a sweatshirt, and a felt crown studded with Alf Landon buttons," the young reader—Connell refers here to the Kansas governor and Republican presidential candidate in 1936—was bowled over.[38] And here it was, the very edition he once owned, marked down to $1.49 on a flea market table. He debated whether to revisit the past and waste his time rereading it when he had so many other things to work on, but he succumbed. Alas, his suspicion was confirmed: "Reading what I once considered to be the world's greatest novel becomes a fearful chore."[39] Despite the regret, he writes, one's passions—including his adult obsession with Mexican antiquities and his abiding preference for Mexican food—were not accidental.

Connell might have been thinking of exploration when he took to the backyard with a shovel. The Connell home shared with neighbors a green space nearly a block long, almost like a protected island surrounded by houses on a triangular patch spotted with clumps of trees and shrubs. In *Mrs. Bridge*, Douglas attracts attention and motherly outrage when he builds a tower on a vacant lot out of scrap metal and other found objects. Douglas's friends had dug a cave, but he was scavenging the neighbors' trash and planting a solid structure into a concrete footing. Eventually, India Bridge enlists the Fire Department to demolish it. In *Mr. Bridge*, there is no tower, but Douglas has joined his friends in the underground cave they had dug and turned into a clubhouse. Douglas's father investigates one day but declines to descend for a closer look. Not long thereafter, a bulldozer arrives and destroys the cave and buries its contents. (This, naturally, opens the door to sexual and/or Freudian readings of the episodes, including the embedded gender-specific symbols—the tower, the cave—in each.)

In the Connell household, Evan was known for digging a trench or a cave. His cousin Bill Bolin told me that Evan once dug a trench in the green space out back. Whether it became a clubhouse is unknown. And whether Connell actually built a tower as well is open to debate though family members say it's true.

In the autobiographical essay, written as he approached sixty, Connell reeled off selected memories of his boyhood. Along with his mother's frantic staircase rescue of infant Barbara, there was the annoying chore of clearing the family's steeply sloped driveway of snow and ice. His father would come home late at night, and Evan Jr.'s shoveling ("I detested the job") would allow his father to drive the Reo all the way to the garage. A sense of lingering loss imbued the discovery one day of the limp body of his sheepdog, named Kent, which had been hit by a car.

Connell resented, apparently even years later, moments where he fell victim to adult lying. "I have never forgiven anybody who lied to me," he wrote.[40] Spotting his grandfather hauling a tree into the house the night before Christmas shattered the Santa Claus myth for him, despite adult claims of St. Nick's existence. But more hurtful apparently was the time he spent a few weeks in the hospital with a blood infection. One day his doctor said he would take him to a boxing match that night. Young Evan excitedly awaited the excursion, but to no avail. He felt betrayed. The doctor, he concluded, was merely humoring the ill boy, knowing he shouldn't leave his hospital bed. Connell repurposed the memory in "Arcturus," in which young Otto's doctor promises an outing to the circus. "Then he knew for the first time those pangs that come after one has been lied to," he writes. "But perhaps it was not unjustified; they had thought he would leave them and he did not, and scars on a heart are seldom seen."[41] Connell never forgot the scars of being lied to, of being misled by authority figures. His silences often served to hide his feelings, yet a reader can find his disappointments and his hurts through much of his work.

Connell remembered his father as irritable and not open to questioning. He was "a sensible man, except when infuriated by some incomprehensible wickedness such as Roosevelt." He was totally devoted to his work and whatever it took to provide for his family, which is not to say that he was close to his children: "Like a soldier assigned to guard a camp he held himself apart." And little beyond office and home "could hold his attention very long," though he found some satisfactions in fishing, University of Missouri football games, mystery novels, and, for entertainment when he wanted such a thing, the soothing songs of Nelson Eddy on a Sunday evening. After the oil-field bonanza and the stock market crash, the doctor, narrow-faced and crisply collared, invested conservatively—only blue-chip stocks for him—because he knew that his own father had taken a hit once when chasing gold in Brazil. "Whether his grim routine made him happy, I do not know," Connell wrote. "I think it satisfied him because he felt it was correct."[42] Connell told a Santa Fe friend late in life that he "never saw his father laugh."[43]

Connell recalled accompanying his father to Research Hospital more than once, dressing for surgery and watching the ambidextrous surgeon wield the scalpel: "Tonsillectomies were bloodily unpleasant and the stench of ether exhaled by the victim did not encourage me to become a doctor."[44] When Young Evan offered to try his hand at a cataract surgery, his father did indeed let out a laugh and said he'd have to go to medical school first. That option remained in Connell's future for at least a few more years.

As for his mother, Connell said he had "no idea what she cared about." Maybe Nelson Eddy. She went through the motions of cooking and gardening but without much passion. "I do know that she felt threatened by allusions to sex," he wrote. "I believe she was concerned mostly that nothing outrageous should happen and I suspect that anything passionate, no matter how abstract, made her uncomfortable."[45] In that passage alone, one can find a road map to the consciousness of India Bridge. The repulsion of sex, outrageousness, passion—all become touchstones of Connell's fictional mother figure.

Like many teens in town, Connell once had a weekend job in the *Kansas City Star*'s mailroom, where newspapers coming off the press were sorted and wrapped for distribution. So he had the capacity for building his own relationships as someone who could be relied on. As for his fictional counterpart: "Douglas, who, strangely enough, never actually appeared to be attempting to make trouble; it was just that somehow he *was* trouble. Invariably there was something about him that needed to be corrected or attended to," though he was oblivious to this or unconcerned. "He was hostile to guest towels."[46]

Douglas frequently butts up against his father's stern and oppressive nature: "Jeez, how am I supposed to express myself with nothing but a measly fifty cents a week?" Says Mr. Bridge: "You'll express yourself when I say you can."[47]

If Connell had a particularly distinguished high school career, the evidence is slight. He was a member of the track team, which won a championship in 1940, and the debate club. He appeared on stage in "The Nativity" and had a minor role as "Tie Man" in a production of the Moss and Hart play "Once in a Lifetime." He joined the Engineers Club but none of the literary societies, and in his senior year he did not make the honor roll or the National Honor Society. His graduating class picture reflects even then his old-soul demeanor. There's no hint of a smile, just an arm's-length gaze of thoughtful introspection. More than one fellow high school student remembered him mostly as introverted.

Connell, slender, athletic, and extremely attractive from high school onward, would date girls from Sunset Hill, the high-society private school near the Country Club Plaza. In 1939, the Connell family moved from their Brookside colonial to a six-columned brick mansion on Drury Lane, about a mile and a half away, in the unincorporated Kansas district of Mission Hills. The locale gave him and his family an added air of stable prosperity, though being that much farther from his high school friends and old neighborhood irritated him. Nevertheless, Connell tended to resist the trappings of moneyed Kansas City. While imagining a persona in *Mrs. Bridge*, Connell sets up an awkward confrontation when Douglas's mother finds him on the plaza one day "with the wildest-looking girl in the world." The young woman, named Paquita, happened to be Latina. On another occasion, after earning his driver's license, Douglas rams a car while being distracted by "a singularly voluptuous carhop." Such anxiety over the sexual stirrings of her son causes Mrs. Bridge to come to a brutal understanding: "She had lost his love, she knew not why, as she had forfeited that of Ruth, and the thought of losing her son entirely was more than she could endure." At another moment, "She perceived a change in Douglas's attitude toward her. He was more withdrawn."[48]

Connell's bonds to his own mother would prove fragile, yet here one could project that the emotional tug of war between Douglas Bridge and his mother had some solid grounding in the author's biography.

Connell shared his interest in airplanes and aviation with Douglas Bridge. In March 1939, the Brookside Theater in Connell's old neighborhood featured *The Dawn Patrol,* the hit action movie starring Errol Flynn and Basil Rathbone as British flying aces in the Great War. Connell saw it and absorbed the romance of aviation heroics. As he wrote in *Mr. Bridge*, Douglas did go see *The Dawn Patrol* with friends, and they all were inspired by the derring-do of the air: "It was obvious to them that aviators were in every possible way infinitely superior to other men."[49] Connell would soon enough be able to test that hypothesis on his own.

In early 1941, Connell wondered about joining the Marines, given what he had been learning about "the Nazi maelstrom."[50] Since he was still only sixteen, his father objected and suggested college until the government came calling. Connell interviewed for admission to Dartmouth. The college was known at the time for its pre-med program, a steppingstone to medical schools elsewhere. (Its own doctor of medicine program had been suspended early in the century and was not reinstated until the 1960s.) An alumni interviewer found Connell to be "quite mature, very reserved and sedate in his manners." The recommendation went on to describe the young man's positive attributes: "The applicant is the son of a well qualified, well established, and well thought of physician in this community; his mother has also received a college education. The previous history of the family is very good; the great grandparents having been pioneers in the Middle West."[51] Where one came from, of course, is what counted.

As the hot Kansas City summer wound down that year after high school, Connell was on his way out. "So long, house," he uttered in the yard on Drury Lane. In the moment, his sister took that to understand that, for Evan, "it was the end of an era."[52]

For Connell, it was the beginning of something too. He now had to measure himself against the world in places beyond the relative safety, comfort, mild domestic conflicts, and predictability of home. Something in his life, perhaps something we will never know or can only speculate about, sent Connell into that adult world with a perpetual shroud of loneliness, or perhaps solitude, and a narrow emotional range that almost never would include a true experience of love. One can find him revealing himself, overtly and cryptically, in much of his work—the longings, the disconnections, the "long desires" to learn about the universe and to discover his own identity.

Another book. Another indeterminate speaker. Another fragment, three decades later, from Connell's literary consciousness. Is this invented or autobiographical? "Let me begin my story like all true myths with the statement that I never knew my parents."[53]

In the Air
1942–1945

"It's not that you are not bright. . . . You are a puzzle."

—The Patriot

NOVEMBER 1943. CONNELL sits side by side with a flight instructor inside the cramped cabin of a Taylorcraft dual-control airplane. The plane soars high above a snow-covered mesa west of Albuquerque, New Mexico. The instructor, a Mr. McCarthy, demonstrates a spin. This is Connell's second training flight since arriving in Albuquerque, nearly three months after his induction into the Naval Air Corps. McCarthy points the nose of the plane downward as the craft begins to slowly pivot. The vista of the land below flutters and bends like a subtly colored blanket in the wind. Soon, with the hard surface of the earth speeding ever closer, McCarthy begins to fret. His rudder control is frozen. He looks down toward Connell's pedals and yells. Connell, the tall and lean nineteen-year-old cadet, had stretched out his legs and tucked his feet beneath his pedals. His square-toed brogans are so sturdy he hasn't felt the pressure from McCarthy's stabs at the controls. Connell moves his feet and McCarthy pulls the hurtling craft out of its dive. Merely seconds later, just two more spins, Connell figures, and they would have perished atop the mesa.

Much to his regret, Connell never flew in combat or got anywhere near the Pacific or European theaters where the United States was engaged in the Second World War. Aside from the near-death moment on this Albuquerque training flight, his Naval Air Corps experience was mostly average, though some years later, it became the engine and backdrop of one of his earliest novels.

Before joining the Naval Air Corps, Connell left his Kansas City home in September 1941 to enter the verdant comfort of Dartmouth College's campus in Hanover, New Hampshire. He roomed alone in Wheeler Hall, near the southern edge of town and just blocks from the Connecticut River. He made the freshman track team and then the varsity. He excelled in the high jump. He ran through the New Hampshire countryside but gave up competing as a cross-country runner when he realized that other young men were far more confident and able than he was. When his track team traveled to a collegiate tournament at Madison Square Garden in New York City, Connell got the sense that his athletic skills were nothing special. "Things very often have turned out like that," he once confessed.[1]

Fig. 3. Connell on the Dartmouth track team, spring 1943. Courtesy of the Literary Estate of Evan Shelby Connell Jr. and the Department of Special Collections, Stanford University Libraries.

He also racked up middling grades—C's in art and English and mostly D's in science classes. His pre-med path took a hit when he flunked chemistry that first year. He hated chemistry. "I had a kind of bad-tempered chemistry professor who flunked me," Connell wrote via a fictional character two decades later, "and the thought of taking his course over again was extremely disagreeable so I didn't."[2]

At some point in that academic experience, or perhaps during the makeup drudgery of summer chemistry courses at William Jewell

College outside Kansas City, the idea of joining his father's medical practice, of peering into swollen throats and waxy ears, became repulsive. Connell once said that he began thinking of doing something else near the end of high school and had wondered about writing. His sister confirmed that he had gotten more serious in high school, more reflective and quiet: "I think early on he had a vision of what he wanted to do, but he knew he couldn't do it here in Kansas City."[3]

He wasn't fond of the frigid New England winters, but he survived two of them. He was grateful for the warmth of a Hanover hangout, Fletcher's, which was well stocked with pinball machines. He attributed his middling grades to the time he essentially wasted there.

In his first semester, Connell was invited into a new, elite English class, which required he produce a single essay over the course of the term. Whatever he wrote, however, did not make the grade and he was demoted to a more routine English track. Things did not much improve thereafter. His theme papers in that second semester settled into an unenviable and seemingly inexplicable pattern. One paper got an A, the next one earned a D. This happened over and over—"regular as a metronome."[4] His teacher called him in for an explanation and told Connell he would be getting a C for the class. The teacher closed by recommending a talk with the campus psychologist. It is unclear whether Connell spoke with a counselor, then or ever, but he did learn something useful about himself. He came away from the class understanding that the papers that earned him D's were on assigned, generally tedious topics. When the subject was his choice, he got A's. Looking ahead at Connell's writing and publishing career, one can see how he put that insight to use. Save for numerous book reviews, he almost never wrote anything that wasn't self-assigned.

Near the end of his first semester at Dartmouth, Japanese bombers attacked the U.S. naval base at Pearl Harbor in Hawaii, igniting an ethos of duty and service as America entered the war that had engulfed Europe and now spread throughout the Pacific region. Connell knew he would eventually join up, but for the moment he was only seventeen, and college and pinball remained his primary occupations.

A year later, in December 1942, Connell registered for the draft. By the end of his second school year at Dartmouth the following spring, he had set his sights on the war in the sky. He applied for the U.S. Naval Air Corps. Aviation training "sounded better than marching around with a rifle, eating from a mess kit and throwing hand grenades."[5] For his application, he secured a group of glowing recommendations from family friends. One of those came from Miles C. Thomas, the former Border Star principal who had instituted a rigorous reading program at Connell's grade school. Among the hundreds of boys he had graduated at his schools over twenty years as a principal, Thomas wrote, "I do not know any for whom I could give a higher recommendation for your service than for Evan Connell. He has a high scholarship record. He has been active in school athletics. He has shown unusual mechanical ability in both wood work and in metal work in our school shops."[6] An officer of the aviation selection board described Connell as "tall, neat, quiet and determined" and ranked him a "superior" candidate for officer status, just one step below "outstanding."[7]

Connell had a sense for how his father received the news of his navy application: "My father might have been relieved when the government looked at me with basilisk eyes, because he had spent quite a lot of money on my Dartmouth education and the results were unimpressive. . . . He never did suspect how many nickels went into Fletcher's bonging, chiming, tilting machinery."[8]

Connell, of course, later transformed his life experience into fiction, torquing reality into alternate states as the need arose. By the end of *Mrs. Bridge*, for example, Douglas joins the army and returns home for his father's funeral. In *The Patriot*, Melvin Isaacs, who was drafted at eighteen and eager to serve, defies his father's expectations. As the war in Europe ended, Melvin receives a call from his father, who reiterates a plan that would take the young man through law school and into the firm. "I'm not going to be a lawyer," Melvin interrupts. "You might as well get used to the idea. I'm not sure just what I want to do, I'm thinking over various professions. But I don't want to be a lawyer. I'm sorry—I know you've counted on it—but my mind is made up and I don't feel like discussing it now."[9]

The conflict continues when Melvin is released from the service and returns home to Kansas City. His father has prepared an application for the University of Missouri law school. Melvin announces that he has already applied and been accepted to the University of Kansas, where he will study art. "Fine arts, what kind of a life is that, will you be good enough to explain?" the father comments. "Painting pictures, everyone will think you are too lazy to work!"[10]

Connell indeed gravitated to left-brain creativity, and despite his grades in college classes that exercised that lobe, he began to find solace, or at least a fitting place, in writing and art. His father was furious, or maybe just deeply disappointed. "I understood that," Connell said, "and I am grateful to him that he didn't really keep pushing me in the back with a sharp stick."[11]

In September 1943, just weeks after his nineteenth birthday, Connell was inducted as a cadet into the Naval Air Corps in Mt. Vernon, Iowa, and then began a series of postings as he made his way through flight school and training. Albuquerque, New Mexico. Athens, Georgia. Memphis, Tennessee. A stint of nine months at the naval training base in Pensacola, Florida. In the last months of the war he underwent, much to his surprise, instructor training in New Orleans and finished up training new recruits, having earned the junior-officer rank of ensign, in the fall of 1945 in Glenview, Illinois.

In Iowa, Connell's classroom studies spanning the aviation basics took place on the campus of Cornell College. Of his four roommates, only one made it all the way with him to Pensacola. He was a husky Kansan named Glenn Williams, at some point nicknamed, rather inappropriately, "Blossom." His friendship with Connell would last for years. In Albuquerque over the winter, Connell survived his spiraling, pedal-blocking gaffe in the air without a dressing down as he might have expected. Ground school in Georgia involved exercise and "marching drills conducted by Marine sergeants . . .

Fig. 4. Connell served in the U.S. Navy Air Corps, 1942-45. Courtesy of the Literary Estate of Evan Shelby Connell Jr.

who called out the cadence in a strangely melodic language similar to English." A memorable moment for him involved seeing a line of dark-blue Corsair fighter planes screeching and whistling through the clouds, "leaving the ponderous thunder of engines and a trembling emptiness all around," prompting meditations that someday he and his marching brothers would be up there doing the same thing.[12]

By the time Connell got to Memphis, the War Department was cutting back on cadets, figuring it had plenty to win the campaign in the Pacific. Connell watched as many of his battalion members, perhaps 70 percent or more, were washed out of training programs and sent to relative inaction at the Great Lakes Boot Camp in Chicago. It was happening all over. Yet Connell and Glenn Williams and a handful of their acquaintances got the go-ahead to further their training at the naval complex in Pensacola.

Pensacola gave Connell a change of scenery. His sensory radar was fully engaged, as became clear later when he sat down to capture his memories and turn them into writing. The opening of "Crash Landing," a preliminary piece of *The Patriot* manuscript published in 1958, signaled a strong sense of place and some meaningful brushstrokes of an artist at work: "A cold salt wind blew in from the Gulf of Mexico, carrying a few clouds like puffs of cannon smoke. The wind blew through the pines and swept across the long rows of blue-grey Navy dive bombers, the sturdy Douglas SBD's that had swarmed on the Japanese carriers at Midway, and had sunk the *Shoho* in the Coral Sea. Now the war was almost ended and these planes were old, like the battles of 1942, rusting away in the humid air of Pensacola."[13]

The sprawling Pensacola base provided a sequence of assignments at a series of distinct fields. Cadets progressed from basic training to instrument training to one of several specialties. Forty years later, Connell could still recall his first sighting of an admiral, none other than William "Bull" Halsey, who was leading the air war against Japan in the Pacific. Connell was on foot when a limousine stopped at an intersection, a telltale flag with a star attached to its fender: "Never having observed an admiral, I thought this would be a good opportunity so I bent down a little and peered into the back seat. There sat an old man with tangled yellow eyebrows, staring at me. It was Halsey. I found myself unable to straighten up or look away, and because he chose not to look away we continued staring at each other. I have no idea how long this encounter lasted, possibly fifty years."[14]

Among the new (to him) aircraft Connell flew at Pensacola were the SNV, a "rattling, underpowered" plane, and the SNJ trainer, which performed in a way that made Connell and his fellow cadets "feel like military pilots for the first time." He despised the tedium of instrument school. Unlike the writer he would become, "I hated being unable to see where I was going." Night flights, with no discernible horizon and their "winking dials and trembling needles," drained him and filled him with dread. Still, he graded well enough on instruments to catch a posting as an instructor.[15]

Connell later recalled the purported dangers of flying at Pensacola's Barin Field. The sight of debris in a hangar confirmed the earlier violent sound of a midair collision. He had heard, though doubted, a story that a half-dozen cadets from France once perished in a staccato progression of plunges into the Gulf of Mexico. He well knew that "it is much easier to enter a steep dive than to pull out." Once, Connell was flying nearby when another cadet, one he happened to know, dove into the water. He didn't witness the accident but what he most remembered was the swift disappearance of the young man's belongings, the stripped and folded-back mattress, the emptiness and quiet in the room, the removal of any trace that the dead pilot had been there.[16]

At "Bloody Barin," as everyone called it, Connell posed for a snapshot. He stood on the wing, cockpit open, an elbow resting on the fuselage of one of those sleek flying machines. He looks young and rakish. The dark collar of his flight jacket sets off his confident stare. All the jangly innards are hidden. You don't sense Connell is visualizing a wrecked craft in a field. Instead, you can imagine the pilot, moments later, slipping into his seat and taking up the dicey practice of aerial gunnery, diving, his thumb at the ready on the machine gun, the target a white cloth ribbon tailing from an SNJ in the distance. "It was exciting," Connell would say.[17] And it was dangerous, especially if your wing happened to snatch the cloth target.

It is possible Connell had in mind the extraordinary bravery and skill of Commander David McCampbell, who had earned a Medal of Honor after shooting down in one engagement nine Japanese planes while preventing a single enemy craft from reaching the U.S. fleet. McCampbell already had been credited with downing thirty-four enemy planes and destroying more on the ground. He had been sent on a series of pep talks and war-bond speeches. His gallantry preceded him, and a base auditorium was filled to capacity with cadets on the day he came to inspire and encourage them. Connell listened from the back of the room and was somewhat awed by the presence of a hero, just as he had been speechless in his encounter with Admiral Halsey. McCampbell seemed less physically heroic than Connell expected, and his words failed to register, though the mere fact of his presence was memorable and Connell could sense it among all the gathered cadets. (Connell honored his memory of McCampbell by naming one of his characters after him in *The Patriot*.) For Connell, spurred by the encounter in ways he couldn't fully articulate, his dream remained attached to the Corsair fighters he had watched streaming through the clouds on that earlier, glistening day. And his dream remained deferred.

For a while his next assignment, his last at Pensacola, involved the relative calm of Saufley Field. There, the principal craft were rickety dive-bombers with too many hours or bullet holes in them to continue serving in aerial combat. Connell essentially was biding time and avoiding catastrophe until being commissioned.

So there was time for recreation. On occasion, Connell and buddies would hop a bus to Mobile, Alabama. There was not much going on in Mobile, "except girls, but of course that is why we went there."[18]

One Saturday afternoon, he and a roommate wandered around, killed time at a Walgreens, and booked a cheap hotel room. The prospecting had come up empty. Later, the roommate made a startling discovery: through a crack in a bathroom wall came the sight of two young women in the adjacent room. They were naked, one doing her nails. The young men went into action, grabbed a whisky bottle, and headed out to knock on their unsuspecting neighbors' door. The women weren't buying it. Connell and his friend returned to their room, peeped a while longer, and became resigned to the ridiculous fact "that the situation made no sense."[19]

Connell was assigned to become an instrument instructor at Whiting Airfield, northeast of Pensacola. He had no interest and complained to an officer. What about the Corsair? That's what he wanted. He'd resign if he were forced to teach instruments. The officer came up with a compromise that Connell had not considered: become a primary instructor in the Stearman planes. That would take him to New Orleans. Connell agreed.

The New Orleans Naval Air Station was situated near a beach along Lake Pontchartrain. Unlike Melvin Issacs, who landed in New Orleans as a demoted seaman in uncomfortably tight trousers, Connell remained on course to become a flight instructor and rank as ensign. Still, Connell might have shared the kind of wistful consciousness he gave his protagonist: "Melvin often walked across the road in the evenings and lay down on a stone wall at the edge of the lake. He would lie there for hours, motionless, with his head cradled in his arms, staring up at the constellations, the night birds, and the meteors, and listening to the modest splash of the waves and to the people who waded in the shallow, tepid water in search of prawns or whatever else was edible."[20]

In real life Connell and his roommates "lay awake in the barracks, damp with sweat, waiting listlessly for the next humid day."[21] Connell wondered about his friend Blossom Williams, imagining him co-piloting a patrol bomber over the Pacific and experiencing places whose names would ring with history: Saipan, Iwo Jima, Guadalcanal. "I felt cheated," Connell confessed.[22]

New Orleans offered entertainment and more women than Pensacola and Mobile had supplied. More than one photograph from a family collection shows him with a date. Three photos, three different women. At one affair, with numerous cadets in the background in a restaurant or hotel lounge or the USO club, Connell even is holding hands and nestled up against a woman, his arm around her back. She has more of a smile than he does, but they both look squarely, intently at the camera, their future uncertain, their present alive with possibility.

Not long after American B-29 bombers rained nuclear hellfire on the Japanese cities of Hiroshima and Nagasaki, Connell left New Orleans to become a flight instructor in Glenview, Illinois. There would be no Corsairs in his future. Three months later he took his leave from active duty.

Connell's wartime experience offered a kind of enlightenment, his nephew, Matthew Zimmermann, told me. Connell had shared with him the insight that the war changed everything, especially his outlook and his path in life. "If it hadn't been for World War II,"

Fig. 5. A Navy man's night out in New Orleans, 1945. Courtesy of the Literary Estate of Evan Shelby Connell Jr. and the Department of Special Collections, Stanford University Libraries.

Connell said, "I would have graduated and gotten a job as a banker, and got married."[23] The disruption gave Connell material and a vision that fed his impulse to write.

The following summer, Connell wrote it all down, laying the groundwork for what can be regarded as his most autobiographical work of fiction. "Fortunately," he once recounted, "the summer after being discharged from the Navy, I had sufficient intelligence to write down everything, absolutely everything I was able to recall about Navy life, and these mechanical, ingenuous notations of a 19-year-old"—he would have turned twenty-two in the summer of 1946—"constitute the basis of the *Patriot* story line, though the theme is the result of more recent meditation."[24]

Connell's Melvin Isaacs, the protagonist of *The Patriot*, hardly resembles his creator. On the day he leaves home for naval air training, about a year earlier than Connell did, Melvin is "a tall spindly boy with curling black hair, big feet, bony arms, and a hooked nose, which somehow contrived to give him the appearance of a long-legged, awkward bird, earnest and a little despondent." The "hooked nose" might well suggest Melvin is Jewish, and certainly his name implies that too, though interpreting this is better left for a later moment. Melvin has his father's possibly joking jabs ringing in his ears: "I get things accomplished, why can't you?"[25] He is reminded that his grades in school were something to regret ("It's not that you are not bright. . . . You are a puzzle"), but his parents are proud that Melvin will be fighting for his country and hopeful that the war will not last long.[26]

A dozen years later, *Esquire* magazine gave its readers a glimpse of Connell's formidable talent as a fiction writer on the American landscape. The story, "Crash Landing," also opened the door, in its way, to little-known aspects of Connell's life in the wartime navy. To be sure, the story—about a bomber pilot taking his last flight out of a Pensacola airfield, in an aged, rusting craft—was an act of invention. Clearly, though, it relied on closely observed details of lived experience.

Flying—the whole point of this military experience—was much like writing would very soon become. It gave Connell yet another escape, however fleeting, from the "gilded saddle" of his boyhood as the son of a wealthy doctor living in the luxury of upper-middle-class America.

Anatomy Lesson
1946–1953

"I guess I'll become famous and collect spondulix."

—*Bitter Bird*, Spring 1947

THE LIFE-DRAWING MODEL took a break. She stretched her skunk fur coat over her otherwise unclothed body and headed out the door of the cramped and cluttered art room. Evan Connell put down his chalk and high-tailed it after her, all the way down three flights of stairs. Perhaps, outside the building on the college campus, they shared a cigarette. A fellow student who became a painter has told that story for decades. It's one distinct memory that Gerry Miller still had of a life-drawing class, circa 1946, at the University of Kansas when I visited with her in 2018. She still lived in Lawrence, Kansas, not far from the campus. Another of her memories was how the students lived in fear of the imperious professor, Albert Bloch, a painter of much repute. Connell would in a few years immortalize a version of Bloch and his life-drawing class in a work of short fiction, a closely observed piece of ravishing realism about the meaning of art. But for now, Connell was merely a student again, pursuing a dual identity as a writer and an artist and enjoying the fellowship—and the women—that made up a good part of campus life.

After his active-duty obligations in the Naval Air Corps, Connell returned to Kansas City and entered a period, over six restless years, of self-discovery, geographical wandering, and persistent attempts to join the caravan of writers who filled American magazines and bookshelves with entertainment and human inspiration. Connell in those apprenticeship years encountered incremental progress, frequent failure, some serious mentoring and critical guidance, brief gratification, despair, a bout of depression, and a sense that his life as a writer would be framed by a deep loneliness.

In the postwar atmosphere of American renewal, Connell briefly landed a job as an art editor of an aviation magazine, and he enrolled at the University of Kansas in Lawrence. The campus was located about forty miles west of his family's home in a Kansas suburb just blocks from the Missouri state line. With his head start at Dartmouth and credits earned in his navy training, Connell completed his undergraduate studies in three semesters and a summer term. During that time, he cut quite the figure on campus with his trim physique, leather flight jacket, and neat, movie-star moustache. Gerry Miller, among many, remembered him as handsome.

Fig. 6. After the navy, Connell finished his undergraduate degree at the University of Kansas, 1946-47. Courtesy of the Literary Estate of Evan Shelby Connell Jr.

Connell joined a fraternity, Phi Kappa Psi, and a circle of students who launched a campus humor magazine. His hand, as an art editor, is all over the first half-dozen issues of the *Bitter Bird*— its title a riff on the Kansas mascot, the cartoonish Jayhawk. His illustrations took pride of place on a couple of magazine covers and throughout the inside pages.

One cover expressed a satirical lament about the government and its military veterans. Elsewhere, Connell drew small, atmospheric sketches, some of them featuring female dancers stretching in the air. He drew pointed cartoon panels. He drew portraits of women.

Fig. 7. Connell became illustrator, cartoonist, and writer for the *Bitter Bird*, a campus humor magazine. This is his first cover, 1946. Courtesy of Spencer Research Library, University of Kansas.

A two-page spread in one issue celebrated "Bitter Bird's Week" by featuring seven days of women sketched by Connell: "Share that Blue Monday," read the line under a brunette in profile. "Tuesday's not so bad!" went the smiling blonde in the corner. "Guess what day I'm for?" said the full-length, stylish coquette in the middle of the spread.[1]

Elsewhere, showgirls bantered in cartoons that might have been at home in any men's magazine of the day. "Harmony" was the theme of a drawing of two sailors on the arms of a curvy date, all seen from behind. There was a cartoon showing a nude woman ascending a staircase at the "Club Ritzy" and prompting one of the gazing men below to remark, "She just said conventions were silly and in she went."[2] There was in the Thanksgiving issue for 1946 a full-page portrait of a thinly covered, voluptuous dancer, with a

Fig. 8. Connell's artworks, beginning with his *Bitter Bird* illustrations and carrying on through the years, reflected an obsession with women and their bodies. Courtesy of Spencer Research Library, University of Kansas.

handwritten caption: "For which we give thanks."[3] To look at and read the *Bitter Bird*, Connell was likely not alone in declaring his principal college passions as women and booze. He announced as much in a bit of youthful doggerel. It was titled "Dogface": "The Gover'ment sent me off to war, / But firing a gun my thoughts were afar; / I dreamed of spending some time in a bar, / And following that, a lady's boudoir."[4]

Connell roomed on the third floor of the fraternity's colonial brick house. He wrote in his room and often could be seen pacing a hallway thinking about whatever he had under way in his typewriter. "He never talked about his writing, but I think there was an awareness among us that he took it seriously," one fraternity brother put it. Byron Shutz's unpublished memories of Connell include a description of a muscular, well-tanned, and slender six-footer. His friend's quiet demeanor led Shutz to judge Connell as benignly aloof though not uninterested in those around him. Connell was capable of a restrained, often bemused smile that reflected a general "sense of mirth." "There was a hint of the clown in Evan Connell," Shutz noted, "revealed in subtle, sardonic movements of the mouth, a change of expression in the eyes, and slight, quixotic positioning of the angular body. He liked to play, and did, mostly in company with the other war veterans who lived in the house."[5]

Fig. 9. Connell at a fraternity buffet dinner, March 1946, at the University of Kansas (fourth couple from the left, with Helen Dietzel). Connell's Naval Air Corps buddy "Blossom" Williams is identified with a date, "Dainty" Small, second couple from the left. Photograph by Hank Brown; courtesy of the Estate of Evan Shelby Connell Jr. and the Department of Special Collections, Stanford University Libraries.

From *The Patriot* a reader could be confident in assuming the veracity of Connell's character-shaping description of Melvin Isaacs's few belongings: "books, clothes, some phonograph records, a sea shell he had picked up on the beach at Pensacola, a potted cactus, a box of raisins and one of shredded wheat, for he customarily got hungry at night, a jar of powdered coffee, which tasted watery no matter how it was brewed, a bullfighting poster, and a bottle of sour-mash whisky his father had given him."[6] Melvin had wrapped the whisky bottle in a sweater and hoped he hid it well enough because he didn't want to have to share it.

A short biography of Connell appeared in the last issue of the *Bitter Bird* in which his name appeared. "The Art Editor weighs in at 170 (after a big dinner), has never had a girl, has a scholastic average of 2.3, and is fascinated by beautiful women." His Eagle Scout boyhood was mentioned, his track accomplishments at Dartmouth, and his plan to "pick up master's degrees in Art and English at Stanford and then draw and write." His current interests included "music (cowboy and light opera), Chicago, Shelley, and"—here it comes—"large symetrical [*sic*] blondes." He also boasted of the ability to "reel off 60 verses of *The Rubaiyat* at the tilt of a pinball machine." (There's that collegiate pinball habit again.) When asked about the future, the "mad genius" replied, "I guess I'll become famous and collect spondulix."[7] A column in another issue mentioned Connell's fondness for "football parlays and pretty girls," implying that for some reason he was "always broke." The item also made fun of his skinny frame: "He once won first prize at a costume ball. He drank some wine and went as a thermometer."[8]

Connell published two articles under his own name in the *Bitter Bird* and co-wrote a couple of gossipy columns under the headline "Flaw on the Kaw," "Kaw" being a colloquial and indigenous name for the Kansas River, which flows eastward through Lawrence toward its confluence with the Missouri and the junction of the two Kansas Cities. One article, "On the Avoidance of Work," was a glib and cloying satire about getting by in life as easily as possible. The navy, for instance, had promised less work, mud, and spaghetti than the army.

In the November 1946 issue, a Connell short story, "Medical Ethics," reflected his reading of both Hemingway and O. Henry. A Chicago doctor heads home from his downtown hospital during an ice storm, encounters a wrecked car on a slickened street, and hauls two of its three teenaged occupants back to the emergency room. Meanwhile, the third teen dies at the accident scene. The ending, composed of course by the son of a physician, is a shocker: the young man the doctor left behind was his own son. A Freudian analysis might explore whether Connell was commenting on his own father's feelings after learning that his son had chosen to abandon a medical career for writing and art. A simpler explanation would take it as an illustration of the medical school concept of "equanimity." Facing the injured young man whose carotid artery had been sliced open, the story's doctor explains, "A physician must use his head instead of his heart."[9]

Connell studied with a new creative writing teacher at Kansas, Ray B. West. A native of Utah, West had just earned his Ph.D. in English at what was then known as the State University of Iowa. West became a faculty advisor for the *Bitter Bird*, though as a note indicated in one issue, the student editors had full responsibility and never caused their elders to wield censorship powers. Connell might have found a kindred spirit in West. Some years later, when they met up again in San Francisco, West seemed to encapsulate what Connell was seeking as both a visual artist and a writer: "The geography of the mind is vague, yet known and observable. Its boundaries are the rhythm and shape of verse, the flight of sound, the form and mass of painting and sculpture. Its limits enclose a dream."[10]

While in Lawrence, Connell continued to take to the air in unpaid training flights out of the naval air station in Olathe, Kansas, a county seat about equidistant between Kansas City and Lawrence. He and Blossom Williams, who had also enrolled at the university, would often fly together. One spring day, the pilots took to the air and headed northwest toward Lawrence. In a spirit of bravado, Blossom buzzed the football stadium at a prohibited low altitude. Their naval commanders were not amused. Connell ended up taking the brunt of the heat, a court martial was threatened, and both were banned from flying again. That's how Connell recalled the prank, though his navy records do not document any such disciplinary action. (In *The Patriot*, Melvin joins a visiting friend from the Naval Air Corps for a joy ride out of Olathe. Their campus target was the fraternity house out of which Melvin had moved.)

In addition to *The Patriot*, Connell mined his flight experiences to produce several early short stories. He was still in school when he sold his first story, "A Cross to Bear." It appeared in *Foreign Service*, a magazine for military veterans published in Kansas City, and it earned him thirty-five dollars. The story centered on a gruff navy flier's experiences during a downed-pilot rescue operation in the South Pacific. During his time in the service, Connell never saw that kind of action for himself, though Blossom had. An author ID atop the story announced Connell's intention to put two more years into studying art and journalism in the hope of becoming "successful in both fields."[11] For the moment, however, he was happy to have pocketed his first sale. "Man," he thought, "what a great way to make a living."[12]

Published or not, like many beginning writers Connell had to grow out of certain raw tendencies. He had to absorb the wisdom of his forebears and listen to editors as they tried to wrench youthful missteps and attitudes out of his fiction. Connell, under West's guidance, sent at least two stories to Camelia Uzzell, a literary critic and agent in Oklahoma who had co-authored a book with her husband on narrative technique and literary psychology. Connell's pieces had elements of fantasy and humor, and neither succeeded in Uzzell's judgment. Of one, she wrote, "You have a prankish imagination, and you've let it run along through four thousand words or so of rather trite and very easy invention." Uzzell suggested he read a recent piece of humorous fiction, "The Eternal Duffer" by Willard Temple, from the *Saturday Evening Post*, and stories by Wilbur Schramm, "another writer for popular fantasy." Schramm also happened to be the founding director of the Iowa Writers' Workshop, the first college program committed to training writers, so though his name and work may be forgotten today, he possessed a certain authority at the time. Uzzell was not wholly discouraging: "You ask what you have on the ball. Originality!" Regardless of the story's weaknesses, she said, Connell's "lively imagination" would serve him well in future stories.[13]

Still, the second story Connell sent to Uzzell had even more problems. Most egregiously, it just wasn't as funny as Connell thought it was. For a lesson in humor and satire, Uzzell urged him to read *Alice in Wonderland*. "Every incident, every detail, however fantastic, has its basis in reality," she counseled. "All the items are familiar, it is the use of them that is fantastic."[14]

Connell seemed to have taken that to heart. Not only did he underline the latter sentence in her letter, he summarized it in the margin: "familiar items; fantastic use." Connell, at least, was not a stubborn know-it-all. Fantastical works such as *Alice in Wonderland* or *Gulliver's Travels*, Uzzell explained, achieve their greatness with satire that reminds readers of real life and comments on or criticizes "what goes on in the world." As for Connell's story, "The Reluctant Streetcar," she concluded, "It has no reality and it makes no comment." She went on to advise him to work on the love story embedded in the plotline and to consider that streetcars were on their way out in most American cities, thus raising the likelihood that his setting would seem fatally dated.[15]

Compared with Dartmouth, Connell's grades generally improved at Kansas. He earned B's in the life drawing classes, mostly A's in English and writing; his weakest performances seemed to occur in two psychology courses.[16] After receiving his B.A. degree from Kansas in October 1947, Connell took further advantage of the G.I. Bill, which funded education for millions of veterans of the recent war. On Ray West's recommendation Connell headed to Stanford University in Palo Alto, California, where he received a fellowship to study creative writing with Wallace Stegner. Like West, Stegner had connections to both Iowa—he had roomed there with Wilbur Schramm—and Utah. Stegner's autobiographical novel *The Big Rock Candy Mountain* had appeared in 1943, and he was on his way to becoming an important and influential writer and teacher. He also became a voice of the American West, a regional interest Connell shared since boyhood vacations with his family to Colorado. Connell was among Stegner's first class of fellows in the creative writing program, several of them also veterans.

During Connell's Stanford year, Stegner and the program director, Dick Scowcroft, often turned over the workshop class to visiting writers. One day the visitor was Katherine Anne Porter, whose recent story collections *Pale Horse, Pale Rider,* and *The Leaning Tower* established her reputation as a luminescent talent. Scowcroft handed her one of the best stories he had seen in the class. It was Connell's. Porter was merciless, and Connell was stung. "She was brutal about it," Scowcroft reported, "and she missed that this was really a talented guy and she tore him to pieces."[17] Despite the dressing-down, Connell managed to gain confidence as a Stegner fellow and to discover that if a piece of work were good enough, it would find readers who could appreciate it.

Encouraged by Stegner, Connell moved on from Camelia Uzzell and began sending stories to an agent in New York, Scott Meredith. "Nice going," Meredith told Connell after receiving a story, which he promised to send out. "Remember, to hit the market consistently, you must keep feeding the hungry maw of Meredith with juicy scripts."[18] But Connell's submissions from his typewriter at Stanford soon began to confound Meredith. Some of the writing was wonderful, the agent conceded, but too often Connell reached far beyond the conventions of saleable stories. "I've warned, cajoled, and pleaded with you to stick to the beaten path of commercial fiction writing," Meredith counseled, "but you insisted on doing it the hard way."[19] In at least two letters, Meredith went so far as to instruct Connell in the tried-and-true ingredients of a plot skeleton. In short, he emphasized how the fundamental structure of a story worked: it must include a believable hero or heroine facing an urgent complication, which develops into a crisis before he or she ultimately resolves the situation.

Meredith picked apart in great detail one of Connell's submissions, a story titled "I'll Take You to Tennessee." This very likely was the story Katherine Anne Porter had previously dissected. In it, Connell ventures into the American South of Flannery O'Connor, William Faulkner, and Porter as well. He is trying out the sound of southern voices, the sound of his mother's Kentucky heritage, the sound he had picked up around the region in Memphis, Mobile, and Pensacola while in the Naval Air Corps. A forty-something drifter named Logos Jackson walks west from the Tennessee mountains and winds up living in a shed near a river. He attracts a bevy of youngsters from nearby who badger him to tell his colorful Tennessee stories and to take them fishing. One of the older girls,

Maxine, is sixteen, and on one of those fishing outings she taunts Logos with her blooming womanhood. Logos tells his stories about Tennessee, a kind of reservoir of ancient rituals such as mule parades, "cunjur doctors" (medicine men or snake-oil salesmen), and tent revivals. Maxine asks how she can land a husband. "Sleep with a beef bone under your pillow," Logos replies. The younger kids have no interest in Maxine and her flirtations. Logos says she's got "the Devil in her" and mutters into the campfire that she's "a lamb lost in the wilderness." Maxine wanders off with the feigned intention of looking for her fishing tackle. Logos goes off to find her. By the end of the story, with the rest of the kids bewildered around the campfire, Maxine returns from the woods crying and Logos follows, shirtless. "We thought you'd got lost yourself," one boy says. Logos replies, "I have lost myself, boy." Whatever happened in the woods is left to the reader's imagination, which Connell had stoked with plenty of suggestive details.[20]

Meredith was relentless. The story meandered far too long before Connell presented Maxine as a temptress. "In future work," Meredith wrote, "put the central story-problem plainly before both the reader and the lead character in the first three or four pages, or even earlier." Worse, Connell sprung a crucial fact on the reader way too late. As Meredith put it: "You aren't playing fair with the reader when you wait until page 14 to reveal that Logos is a negro; honest suspense can only be built when the reader knows all the essential facts of the situation right at the beginning." Aside from the structural issues, Meredith concluded that most commercial fiction editors would find "I'll Take You to Tennessee" to be "too hot to handle," given its suggestion of interracial sex or rape. He suggested a rewrite wouldn't be worth the time.[21] Two weeks later Meredith sent back another story, "Sad End of Orville Quixote." "Rereading it," the agent said, "left me with the feeling I'd like to tear my hair out."[22]

Meredith possessed a voice of authority in the publishing world. Around the same time as his correspondence with Connell, he edited a volume of selected stories by the British humorist P. G. Wodehouse, who happened to be Meredith's first client in his agency business. "The best way to sum up the masterworks of Mr. Pelham Grenville Wodehouse," Meredith wrote in his introduction to the book, "is to point out that he is the only writer in the world who can cause other writers to stop raving about their own work and rave about his."[23] In his role as agent, Meredith implored Connell to get back on the trail of proper, plain-old fiction.

Nevertheless, Connell discovered all fiction was a matter of taste. "I'll Take You to Tennessee" found its way to *Harper's* magazine. It wasn't published, but an editor at Harper and Brothers read it and was impressed: "It is artistically and emotionally a most satisfying piece of work," Elizabeth Lawrence wrote to Connell. "If at any time you have a book-length manuscript I should be delighted to see and consider it for Harper's trade list. You unquestionably have a promising future as a writer and novelist if you can continue to convey with such unforced simplicity the emotions of men and women in a world you know."[24] A sliver of encouragement can go a long way to boost a writer's momentum.

Meredith's judgment aside, Connell eventually found a place for "I'll Take You to Tennessee." *Tomorrow* magazine, a venue that leaned to the fantastic and quasi-spiritual but earned respectable literary merit, published the story in February 1949. The issue also included pieces, touted on its cover, by such notables as William Saroyan and George Antheil. Connell listened to Meredith and reacted on at least one point. Logos was no longer identified as a Black man, though some of the Tennessee stories Logos told revolved around African Americans (Connell's character used the N-word). *Tomorrow* emphasized the point in line-drawn illustrations that depicted Logos as a white man.

"I'll Take You to Tennessee" proved to be Connell's most significant early success. It won the five-hundred-dollar Edith Mirrielees Prize, named for a Stanford creative writing professor whose students included John Steinbeck, and a one-hundred-dollar, second-place award from the Midwestern Writers' Conference. Stegner congratulated Connell on the sale to *Tomorrow*. "I'll Take You to Tennessee" also earned a spot in the O. Henry Prize story anthology for 1949. Connell appeared alongside impressive company. William

Faulkner won first prize that year for his story "The Courtship." Among others in the volume were Jean Stafford, Shirley Jackson, and Mark Van Doren. It may or may not have helped that among the three prize judges that year was Connell's former professor at Kansas, Ray West.

Connell felt good enough about the current shape of "I'll Take You to Tennessee" to include it much later in a volume of his collected short works. And in retrospect, the story serves as an early milepost in what would become Connell's long-term project to observe the male condition and the awkwardly shifting boundaries that quiver between men and women. Elizabeth Lawrence had affirmed his ability to capture the emotional lives of men and women. The story also sets out a trope of sexual anxiety that Connell would return to more directly a decade and a half later in his novel *The Diary of a Rapist*.

But the literary jury remained mixed. An editor of the Marxist magazine *Masses and Mainstream* told Connell that he was too talented to waste time on such foolishness as the story in *Tomorrow*. "You'll get a lot of flattery from very smart, charming and irresponsible people," Charles Humboldt wrote to him, "but you'll never say anything that even they will really care about or feel deeply. You will win more prizes and be published in magazines that are only too delighted to find writers who write well about nothing; but the world will leave you behind as you are leaving it."[25]

Stegner certainly liked "I'll Take You to Tennessee." He chose it to lead a volume of Stanford fiction that came out a few months later. And in one way the story might have been too good. Connell applied for a second Stanford fellowship, and though Stegner initially told Connell he would be glad to have the young writer back, he soon had to report that his committee turned him down. Stegner explained that Connell was already on his way to being a writer, and the fellowship was meant for people with potential who had more to gain. Stegner also served as West Coast editor for the Houghton Mifflin Company. He praised the "general upward look of your writing fortunes" and urged Connell to consider Houghton Mifflin when he finished a book-length manuscript, or rather, to consider giving the publisher "a chance to bid on you in the slave market."[26]

An editor at another publishing house sent out a feeler and another word of praise for "I'll Take You to Tennessee." Elaine Shaplen of Alfred A. Knopf was sufficiently impressed to send Connell a note and ask if he had a novel in the works. Connell replied that at the moment he was only writing stories.[27]

Tomorrow magazine was happy enough with Connell's work to buy another story that year. The magazine paid Connell $150 for "The Most Beautiful," a noirish portrait of sexual obsession set in a San Francisco flophouse. The *American Mercury*, the popular magazine co-founded in the 1920s by H. L. Mencken, also published in 1949 "The Color of the World," a Gothic slice of Bible Belt religion, complete with a haunting girl named Faith, that Connell most likely began while under Ray West's tutelage at Kansas.

Fig. 10. Atop Long's Peak, Colorado, summer 1948. Courtesy of the Literary Estate of Evan Shelby Connell Jr.

After Stanford, Connell spent a year at Columbia University in New York. On his way across the country, Connell stopped in Colorado and made a trek up Long's Peak, one of the state's prized fourteen-thousand-foot mountains. No evidence of that journey remains save for a snapshot that emerged out of the belongings of Connell's sister, Barbara. Penciled onto the back of the scallop-edged snapshot are the bare details: Long's Peak, 14,255 feet, July 1948. The image captures Connell sitting on the mountaintop in flight jacket and chinos. His left leg is stretched out, his chin rests on the palm of his right hand, and his eyes gaze off somewhere out of the camera's view. One can only speculate about what he is seeing in reality and in his mind's eye. What will New York do for him and his future? He certainly looked forward to more writing and more ventures into art. One must also wonder who took the photograph and with whose camera. A friend he was traveling with? Unlikely. Another hiker? Had he joined his family at their favorite vacation grounds? All we really know for sure is here he was, a writer in the making, in a meditative pose, contemplating something with a very long view from the summit of a Rocky Mountain peak.

Stegner suggested Connell study at Columbia with Caroline Gordon, a prominent southern stylist. Gordon, however, was away that year, and Connell had to settle for Helen Hull, a prolific story writer and novelist with a background in suffragism and radical politics, and John Humphreys, who had recently founded Columbia's creative writing program. Connell lived in Furnald Hall, a high-rise on the Broadway edge of campus. He spent time in Columbia's art department, learning to make sculptures. The three-dimensional medium appealed to him in a new tactile way. He also attended more life-drawing classes.

The New York experience brought Connell together with a new agent. Elizabeth McKee had sought him out after reading "I'll Take You to Tennessee" in *Tomorrow*. They met for lunch. She told him that some writers knew how to write for "money in a hurry." Others would take a long while to earn their due. Connell told her he had been trying to write like Philip Wylie, a bestselling author of pulp fiction and social essays. Wylie was good, McKee said, "But you don't know how to fake it." Connell once confessed to being "hurt by that because I was trying to fake it."[28] McKee's style was straightforward and tough. Early on, she told him that *Collier's* had returned two stories with the suggestion that Connell "lay off this stuff, and write something 'about himself.'"[29] Connell eventually caught on that McKee had been right. "She never said so, but Elizabeth was terribly embarrassed. I realized I could only write what was real to me."[30]

Connell spent about a year in New York before his G.I. Bill subsidy ran out. Like many an American wanderer, he headed West again. After Columbia and the claustrophobia and density of New York City, Connell found a certain anonymity in sprawling Los Angeles. Living alone appealed to his daily state of mind. He could focus on his mission. He apparently wrote dozens of stories there, all of which came back to his agent having been rejected by one editor or another. Los Angeles, he once said, is both "hideous and, because of the movie industry, fascinating."[31] It's unclear whether he had any success at all trying to write for the movies. "Any luck in Western films yet?" McKee asked in a letter.[32] With nothing much happening, Connell moved north to Santa Cruz, a seaside town where he continued to write in obscurity. For income, he took a job reading gas meters.

Although documentary evidence of Connell's job in Santa Cruz remains elusive, one can turn to his fiction for a taste of the experience. In his search for a purpose after the Naval Air Corps, Melvin Isaacs, protagonist of *The Patriot*, lands a job with the gas company in Lawrence, Kansas. His parents imagine him wearing a suit as some kind of junior executive, but no, he informs them, he's reading meters. He explains to his exasperated father that he'll start work at eight in the morning, and he'll have a notebook, bound in metal, with a page for each property on his route. "Well," Melvin says, "the minute I saw one of those books I thought—I don't quite know what I'm trying to say, but it's sort of a passport, if you know what I mean."[33] The notebook conveys a certain kind of official membership, he surmises, like when he worked on an ice-delivery truck and carried a pick and rubber vest. The conversation with his father devolves into a debate about communism.

While in Santa Cruz, Connell fired up his imagination in at least one unexpected way. One of the most unusual documents along Connell's relatively sparse paper trail is a patent application. His invention? A bicycle mounting device for a toy machine gun. One can only imagine what sparked that creative leap. Walking a quiet residential neighborhood reading meters might well set off productive periods of meditation and daydreaming. Maybe the sight of a boy on a bicycle sent his thoughts back to his own youth. The invention echoed his boyhood penchant for building model airplanes and boats as well as his involvement in the high school engineering club. It resonated with his youthful leanings toward fantastic and alternative worlds and perhaps the "prankish imagination" identified by Camelia Uzzell. As a fanciful weapon, the product also recalled his flight experience in fighter craft along the Gulf Coast. Or perhaps he was thinking of a futuristic action movie that came to mind while poking around Hollywood.

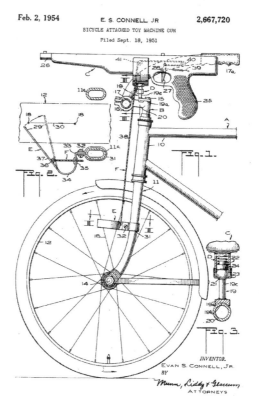

Feb. 2, 1954   E. S. CONNELL, JR   2,667,720

BICYCLE ATTACHED TOY MACHINE GUN

Filed Sept. 18, 1951

Fig. 11. Patent illustration for a "bicycle-mounted machine gun." Courtesy of Santa Cruz, California, Public Library and U.S. Patent Office.

INVENTOR.
Evan S. Connell, Jr.
BY
Munn, Liddy & Glascum
ATTORNEYS

Whatever fiction Connell was writing in Santa Cruz—and none of his unpublished manuscripts from that period have yet turned up—Connell was all business in his patent application. One can visualize him sketching his thoughts with monk-like focus at his simple writing table. "Simulated firing," Connell wrote, "is obtained by moving a spring-like finger into engagement with the spokes of a bicycle wheel during rotation with the latter, producing noises resembling the firing of a machine gun. The device is intended for amusement purposes, the rate and volume of simulated firing being controlled by the cyclist. The device will be particularly appealing to youngsters." He filed the application, apparently with the help of a New York law firm, on September 18, 1951. The government agency granted Connell his patent a few years later, in 1954.[34]

All the rejections aside, Connell got a boost in 1951 when he won a second O. Henry Prize, this one for "I Came from Yonder Mountain." The story had appeared, somewhat incongruously, in *Flair*, a high-toned fashion magazine. And in the annual O. Henry collection he stood alongside such names as John Cheever, Truman Capote, Faulkner again, John Hersey, Carson McCullers, and Eudora Welty. Like "I'll Take You to Tennessee," "I Came from Yonder Mountain" has a southern accent. It centers on a mountain girl trekking to a nearby city and carrying a newborn without realizing until the end that the baby is dead. Although not unusual for its time, readers today might see the story as a stereotypical, privileged view of rural America. Still, despite the honor, Connell was a long way from making a ripple in the literary pond.

The news of Connell's O. Henry Prize in 1951 rated a mention in the *Kansas City Star*. Connell was one of two Kansas Citians in the anthology, the other being Esther Patt (now long forgotten), whom the collection editor Herschel Brickell described as having "exceptional talent."[35] As a result of the publicity, Connell's father invited the article's author, Webster Schott, to meet with him and his son over lunch. Connell, after leaving Santa Cruz and planning to travel to Europe, was back in Kansas City. The setting was the Rendezvous restaurant at the Muehlebach Hotel, one of Kansas City's finest. "I found Dr. Connell to be a courtly man, very attentive, courteous, polite," Schott recalled not quite seventy years later. "I think I was Mr. Schott to him even at the age of 21–22. I was impressed with his civility." Another lasting image for Schott from the meeting was the sense that Evan Jr. respected his father, really seemed to look up to him: "Evan approached his father almost with a reverential distance. He really honored his father."[36] In subsequent years, Schott closely followed Connell's career, and as a freelance book critic would write about Connell's new titles for the *Kansas City Star*, the *New Republic*, *Life* magazine, and others.

Not long after that lunch meeting, in January 1952, Connell, having saved up some money from his gas-company job, packed up his wandering spirit and incipient literary success to make a pilgrimage to Paris.

The French writer André Maurois may well have been sincere when he wrote that Kansas City was one of the most beautiful cities on the planet. Maurois had spent some weeks in Connell's hometown, lecturing at the local university, in 1947. But Connell had no desire to live any longer in the place of his birth and boyhood. After his naval service and the Second World War, after graduating from the University of Kansas the year that Maurois was discovering Kansas City, after graduate schools and trying out California, Connell turned his attention to discovering Europe. To countless American writers, Paris remained the most beautiful city on the planet. Or at least it fed their need to fan the flames of creativity and self-identity. It might be tough to find an apartment, but if you knew the right cafés, you could have a bowl of soup for two cents or a four-course meal for fifty, coffee included. Connell chose Paris that year because he knew it to be "universally renowned as the best place in the world to loiter."[37] His idea of loitering might well be connected to that college humor essay on the "avoidance of work." But writing was his work. And in Paris Connell could not only envision himself a writer, he could write in a place that, unlike Kansas City and Santa Cruz, loved and fostered writers and writing. He could enter the world of writers who once again made the City of Light a singular destination for a cultured class of dreamers and doers, lost souls and visionaries.

William Styron had also arrived there in early 1952 and quickly determined that "Paris is the nuts." He would have been happy to hang around for a long time but, as Styron told his agent (who happened to be Connell's agent, Elizabeth McKee), the "perpetual *joie de vivre* in the air precludes the writing of a long tragic novel."[38]

Styron was one of the current American émigrés with a novel already under his belt (*Lie Down in Darkness*), and he took on a role as an advisory editor to a new literary journal being planned by a group of Americans now in Paris. It would be called the *Paris Review*.

After touching down in Paris, Connell spent the summer of 1952 traveling: a month or two in Spain; a few days in the French sector of Morocco; northern Italy; Salzburg, Austria. And then back in Paris, where he could be enthralled by views of the Eiffel Tower and revel in the atmosphere of Left Bank watering holes, such as Le Dôme, made famous by writers before him.

One day at the American Club, where Benjamin Franklin famously presided over meals while wooing French support for American independence, Connell met a young southerner who had already registered a literary triumph. He and Max Steele, a South Carolina native, drank tea and noshed on chocolate cake. "He'd been to the flea market," Connell once recalled, "and had bought a European fountain pen, which was leaking ink into his shirt pocket the whole time. I decided not to mention it."[39]

Steele had come to Paris on the G.I. Bill to study French and literature at the Sorbonne and the Académie Julian. He told Connell about the fellowship he had won from the Eugene F. Saxton Memorial Trust to complete his novel *Debby* and the Harper and Brothers competition that brought him $10,000 and publication in 1950. *Debby*, the story of an intellectually stunted World War I widow, travels territory not far removed from Connell's early fictional explorations of mothers and children. It earned a rave in the *Washington Post* as "a compassionate and deeply moving first novel . . . tragic and tender . . . never sentimental."[40] Steele hoped to write and publish another novel. Steele was the sort of southern gentleman who wrote his mother every week or two. (Connell apparently did not.) By the fall of 1952, Steele had signed on, like Styron, as an advisory editor to the *Paris Review*, which Peter Matthiessen, George Plimpton, and their friends and funders were planning to launch by the following spring.

Steele got to know Connell as much as almost anyone got to know him. They had long talks about writing and literature. They

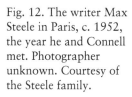

Fig. 12. The writer Max Steele in Paris, c. 1952, the year he and Connell met. Photographer unknown. Courtesy of the Steele family.

shared meals. They lamented the shallow American way of materialism. It took some time for Steele to take the measure of his new friend: "He's a strange, extremely quiet guy," Steele told his mother in a letter home, "and it has taken months of patient friendliness to get to know him, but it is worth the trouble to be able to talk with some one who has so much respect for a craft and literary integrity. He has, I suspect, enough money not ever to have to worry about making a living so can write as slowly and carefully as he pleases. In addition though he is extremely ambitious and competitive, which makes knowing him a challenge and a drive."[41] A few months later, Steele distilled his evaluation into a single sentence, a kind of stamp on Connell's being that anyone who knew him over the next sixty years would recognize: "He's a strange, silent, extremely lonesome person who can write like no one else."[42]

Connell had started writing a novel that sprung at least in part from his student experience in Kansas. Encouraged by Steele, he applied for and won a Saxton Fellowship. He submitted seven chapters of *The Anatomy Lesson* to the program in July, and by the end of 1952 he gave a progress report. He had been working on the book all year, he wrote, and had shifted the focus more pointedly toward the old professor, named Andrev Andraukov, who was emerging as the central character. Connell evidently conflated his art-studio experiences in Kansas and New York. He was partly inspired by a Columbia class in anatomy for artists taught by Robert Hale, who memorably noted that a woman's kneecap looked like a map of the Bronx.[43] "I have shown pieces of the manuscript to several people," Connell said, adding that they all believed that "the work is progressing satisfactorily."[44] He had compiled about two hundred pages of manuscript and expected to finish the book in the spring. Steele had read the draft and was convinced that Connell would win, as he had, the Harper Prize.

In early 1953, Connell wrote again to the Saxton Trust to announce that he had completed his promised novel. Connell had sent the manuscript to Elizabeth McKee, and an editor at Harper and Brothers was reading it. He reported that he was still fiddling with the manuscript, deleting one chapter, breaking up others, and so "the book is temporarily fragmentary."[45] He promised to send the revised manuscript within two months, once he finished putting it back together.

Over the winter, Connell traveled through northern Europe—the Netherlands, Germany, Scandinavia. By March 1953, as he was reconfiguring his manuscript, he settled in Barcelona, a city that Steele before him had found to be both stimulating and inexpensive. "I was enjoying life on the Left Bank so much that I felt obligated to leave," Connell later wrote. "Those nurtured in the Protestant midwest of America will understand this, otherwise it cannot possibly be explained because it makes no sense."[46] One can't allow oneself too much fun, Connell seemed to be saying. This was surely ironic, given that the sentiment reflected his parents' demeanors

Fig. 13. Sketch of
Connell by Roger
Barr, Barcelona, 1953.
Courtesy of Michael
B. Barr and the Barr
family; Department
of Special Collections,
Stanford University
Libraries.

somewhat more than his own. In Barcelona, a chance encounter
at the American Express office led Connell to a room in a board-
inghouse and a friendship with an American painter named Roger
Barr. The room, on the Paseo de Gracia, was sparsely furnished and
unheated, but he managed to get through the spring by wrapping
himself up "in a shirt, sweater, muffler, and leather jacket" while
writing short stories and "holding one foot and then the other
above my hot plate."[47]

Connell acknowledged his experience sounded like the cliché of
a Bohemian *artiste*, but it worked for a while. Soon, though, Barr,
who had made a portrait sketch of his new friend, left Barcelona
for the islands, and Connell succumbed to the lonely life of a writer in isolation. He walked eight blocks every morning to sit in a

café and sip a cup of hot chocolate. He imagined that the waiter was becoming his closest friend. He looked in shop windows and thought about buying some "wonderful pieces of junk," he told Steele, including "a bas relief Last Supper in aluminum where Judas looks somewhat bored by the whole affair as if the food was not well-cooked." He had a way of turning the sights and sounds of daily life into moments of poetic self-reflection: "Followed a two-wheel cart, drawn by three horses, clear across the city last night listening to hooves on stones. It sometimes seems those carts are the most pleasing thing I've seen in Europe." He noticed the many "exotic prostitutes" but kept his distance in fear of the rampant venereal disease.[48]

Connell's Barcelona experience descended into a kind of compulsive, moody self-analysis:

> I made a little calendar with a numbered square for each day of the month, and at night before going to bed I would shade one square with a pencil according to how I had felt: light gray if the day was not too bad, darker if I had felt bitterly depressed, sometimes very dark indeed. I would compare them, noting that Wednesday had not been as bad as Thursday. This was satisfying. The calendar proved that I was able to survive, and I could hardly wait for each day to end so that I might evaluate it. The suspense finally became intolerable. Across each square I drew a horizontal line, dividing the day into morning and afternoon, which meant that at twelve o'clock noon I could assess the morning. Yet even this began to seem too long. I divided each morning and each afternoon. Then, four times a day, I could judge the hours.[49]

Connell's malaise seems inexplicable. He had freely chosen his independence, his path. Yet he wobbled. He suffered a moment of sidewalk humiliation one day, Easter Sunday, when a passing woman, in the absence of her husband, asked him to tie her son's necktie. He tried, first by facing the child, then from behind. "At last I stood up and said I was sorry, I could not do it." Connell had a sense that he was "disintegrating" and wondered if he had become incapable of managing "the simplest domestic task. That day became as black as my pencil could color it."[50] One can sense that Connell contained his moodiness and possible bouts of depression throughout his life within the framework of his defining, mostly introverted demeanor.

Connell's mood in Barcelona would not have been brightened by the news from New York about his novel. McKee was lukewarm about *The Anatomy Lesson*. She told Connell she thought the characters felt more like symbols than people. And the word from Simon Michael Bessie at Harper and Brothers was also not good. "I find it difficult to understand," Bessie wrote in a memo to McKee's agency, "how anybody who can—from time to time at least—write as well as he does can do such a bad job of putting what he wants to say into the form of a living novel." Bessie found the book "pretentious" and the characters often "forcibly bizarre." Andrev was unsympathetic and never really comes to life, he wrote. "Since this is the only thing of Mr. Connell's I have read, I can only say that I think he's got talent and imagination and that he ought to put them to better use."[51]

Connell took the pounding somewhat in stride. "Bessie not only was infuriated by the badness of the book," he told Steele. "I think he could not bear to be in the same room with the paper on which it was written."[52]

Bessie did have one encouraging bit of analysis. One late scene in the book had promise, he said, the one involving the art professor's anatomy lesson. And, indeed, as Connell grappled with the novel—"the book gets shorter and shorter," he told Steele, "there is still so much rubbish in it"—he turned that scene into a standalone story and sent it out.[53] In the story, Connell displays a mastery of vivid, scene-setting detail while presenting Andraukov, his fictionalized amalgamation of Albert Bloch and one or two other art teachers, as a tyrant professor who lived only for art. "Nothing interested Andraukov except paint."[54] His life-drawing class takes place in the stuffy attic of a small campus building that turns into a torture chamber as he taunts students with questions about art and the human body. By the end of the class he enhances his figure-study lesson by drawing chalk lines on the nude model and pushing a thimble into her navel to indicate how that bodily feature was no mere one-dimensional disc. It had depth. Andraukov pauses to reflect, telling a story of a class years earlier when a timid student portrayed the nude model in a bathing suit. The artist, he says at the peak of his lecture, "shall hear at times the voice of God, at times the shriek of each dwarf in the heart and in the soul, and shall obey those voices."[55] Bessie was right. In Connell's hands, Andraukov is not exactly sympathetic, but he certainly is unforgettable.

"The Anatomy Lesson" found a place in the third issue of *New World Writing*, a paperback American journal of fiction, nonfiction, poetry, and criticism. An Iowa journalist happened to read it that summer and gave Connell another fleeting public notice as a writer, if ever so slight. Grouping "The Anatomy Lesson" with two other stories in the collection—by Louis Auchincloss and Gene Baro—the books columnist suggested they collectively "are tense, sensitive, consciously restrained sketches of aesthetically frustrated persons. Their special brand of bitter-sweet poignancy is characteristic of much American avant-garde fiction."[56] That achievement aside, the novel as a whole apparently fell by the wayside. In that year, 1953, Connell also had his eye on the new Paris literature venture. On a letter to Steele that season, he penciled in an afterthought: "What did Paris Review have to say?"[57]

In retrospect, Connell came to conclude that the utter isolation of Barcelona, when he was not yet thirty, did not help his writing. Whatever he worked on there—specifically his *Anatomy Lesson* manuscript—proved to be a waste. He realized that in order to succeed he needed a certain amount of social stimulus from time to time to help broaden and humanize his perspective.

Connell left Barcelona in May for more travels—through northern Africa then Italy, writing just about everywhere he went. He spent a few days with a Paris friend, known only in his letters as Minette, in a fishing village on Mallorca. Minette, or sometimes Minnette, evidently was an American teacher who would show up eventually in San Francisco during Connell's time there later in the 1950s. She earned mentions in numerous letters Connell wrote to Steele and others. Once he reported she was pregnant and followed quickly with "not mine."[58] In 1960, he learned that she was taking a fiction class with Harvey Swados at San Francisco State. Connell employed Minnette, or at least her name, in his short story "The Walls of Ávila," written just a couple of years after their trip to Mallorca: "J.D. had been in love, moderately, in the abstract, with a long legged sloe-eyed girl named Minnette whose voice should have been poured into a glass and drunk."[59] That moment represents a motif about uncertain love and lack of marriage that readers eventually will find regularly in Connell's fiction.

On Mallorca, Connell lamented only the one night that he got sick eating squid. Minette returned to Paris and Connell took off on his own. After he landed in Algiers, someone tried to steal his type-writer. He liked what he saw of Tunis but then moved on to Italy, flying to Palermo before taking the train to Rome. He found Italy to be more expensive than Spain, and he was less comfortable with the language. "Italian sounds like Spanish spoken with a mouthful of toothpaste," he told Steele.[60] It rained too much in Rome, and Connell escaped into the American library. He told Steele he had been thinking about a character for another novel, "a girl I once knew who was married six times at the age of 22." There was more: "She was a beautiful girl whose last husband packed a revolver and once put out a cigarette on her cheek. I think it happened after she read a story and at the end saw my name and let out a squeal. She and he were in bed at the time."[61] If Connell ever expanded on that yarn, the results remain lost.

In Florence, Connell spent his days in a *pensione* with a window overlooking the Arno River, much like E. M. Forster's "room with a view." He augmented the inn's light meals with pizza from nearby vendors. He patronized the library of the U.S. Information Service, the postwar cultural unit of the State Department that served to promote American values and ideas abroad. He reveled in the qui-et there and read its books, one day finding inspiration—"a few hints"—in the work of Stephen Crane. Italy was okay, Connell decided, though he wasn't fond of seeing children swimming amid the garbage dumped into the Arno. He wandered through art galleries, though he never saw much of interest except a Venus of Cyrene and a Jackson Pollock. And there was the odd night when he was served a glass of whiskey and water, "shown a set of 16th century Chinese obscenities, and then propositioned ('Can I be honest with you?') by a plump balding journalist," he told Steele. "He took the bad news gracefully and is not a bad fellow really. We got to talking about Frenchmen; he was brought up in Paris and told an awful story about his aunt taking care of a pair of French domestics, sending their children through excellent schools, etc. etc. and when the war came the domestics immediately sold everything in the house and turned over the keys to the Germans."[62]

Connell planned to return to Paris by late July and asked Steele to recommend a place to stay. He didn't want to lodge in a hotel again. He was looking forward to renewing their dinner arguments about "everything from Eisenhower to Steinbeck." As it turned out, Steele was going to take a trip back to the States so he offered his apartment, a relatively comfortable place on the Avenue Ségur in the 15th *arrondissement*. The two writers exchanged news about various wild friends and incidents in Paris, prompting Connell to spin out what sounded like a piece of fiction in the making: "The last place I can recall meeting so many diverse personalities was in Port-au-Prince where the hotel manager was an ex-Nazi sadist. There was also a Spanish general who had opposed Franco, a pair of abstract-abstract sculptors from NY, a Canadian college student (who I bumped into several months ago in a bar in Barcelona) and a houseboy named Espère who was married to a goddess every Thursday night. All this served up with voodoo drums."[63]

Over the summer, Connell was still wondering whether the *Paris Review* might publish a story of his. He had submitted another piece of the novel that Bessie hated but hadn't yet heard a word and didn't even know whether he'd be paid, he told Steele. "If not, no matter; I'll be glad to have the chapter published anyway."[64]

"Itty-Bitty Details"

1954–1958

"I don't suppose it will ever sell, but if I hung on sales, I would have quit long ago."

—Connell to Max Steele, 1954

IT IS TEMPTING and entirely reasonable to consider the notion that Evan Connell's literary career essentially began over a lunch with George Plimpton in Paris. Up until then, Connell had served a drawn-out and free-form apprenticeship, punctuated by travel and a postwar, post-college search for identity. Along with some extracurricular schooling from brutally honest editors and agents, Connell had scored a handful of small literary and commercial successes, including the publication of his story "The Anatomy Lesson" in *New World Writing*. But Plimpton—here was someone in a position to wield what felt like genuine literary power. Plimpton and his coterie of writer friends had launched the *Paris Review* in the spring of 1953. The gangly and well-spoken easterner served to affirm Connell's chosen place in life. Connell, who had just turned twenty-nine, had come to Paris to write. That's what he'd put on his passport. Occupation: "Writer." The *Paris Review*'s first issue had arrived with the announcement, from co-founder William Styron, that it would showcase "the good writers and good poets, the non-drumbeaters and non-axe-grinders."[1] That made Connell a "good writer," because Plimpton could tell him that, yes, a story he had submitted would appear in the third issue of the magazine, coming out soon.

Fig. 14. With George Plimpton (left) and William Pène du Bois, the *Paris Review*'s art editor, in Paris, c. 1953. Photographer unknown; published in the *Kansas City Times*, 1955. Courtesy of the *Kansas City Star*.

A few weeks after his return to Paris in early September 1953, Connell found himself sitting across a café table from the magazine editor. Lunch with Plimpton nearly always took place in the smoky bustle of Café Tournon. Three decades after Jazz Age Paris sizzled with the previous postwar migration of writers and artists, café culture on the Left Bank abounded again with Americans, and Tournon had become one of the favored gathering places for ex-pat creatives—Black, white, Bohemian, sophisticated, and, like Connell, eager to excel and succeed with a sense of artistic freedom. The café, a block away from the Luxembourg Gardens, operated around the corner from the office the *Paris Review* shared with *La Table Ronde*, its French literary collaborator and publisher. The editors and their friends gathered at Tournon nightly for "animated conversations, occasional arguments, proclamations of various sorts." Eugene Walter, an advisory editor of the review, described Tournon as a "literary salon, permanent editorial board meeting, message center, short order eatery, debating club, study hall . . . who knows how many books and other works springing forth from this noisy, smokey, clattery, raunchy, beat-up café."[2] At lunch Plimpton and Connell talked about—what else?—their writer friends, Connell's own work, and Plimpton's publishing vision. "We didn't want to be esoteric and we didn't want to startle anybody," Plimpton explained about the review not much later. "Among other things, it just seemed to us that there were too many literary reviews devoted to nothing but criticism, to a lot of talk about writing. So we decided there was a place for a magazine that had some actual writing in it; well-written short fiction, articles and poetry, with criticism coming in its proper place at the back of the book, following actual creative work."[3]

Plimpton was eager to share a developing idea to publish a special issue featuring Ernest Hemingway. Plimpton had recently met the "outrageous old man" at the Ritz Hotel bar, and Hemingway's agreement to sit for an interview had set off a plan among the *Paris Review* editors to craft an issue around him.[4] After all the upbeat gab, Connell winced when Plimpton told him that Max Steele would be returning to Paris after two months away in South Carolina and would want his apartment back. "He is furious that you are coming back," Plimpton told Steele in a letter the next day.[5] As for Connell, Plimpton thought of him as "a shadowy figure" who would pop up seemingly from nowhere. He was a "wonderful looking man, looked like an Indian, with sort of a western black mustache. Always looking at the ground it seems to me." And as a writer he "is always a keen observer."[6]

With its blossoming cachet of literary credibility enhanced by its historically fertile location, the *Paris Review* indeed was becoming a significant voice in American writing. "It looks like the first really promising development in youthful, advance-guard, or experimental writing in a long time," *Newsweek* declared.[7] So the appearance of Connell's "Cocoa Party" in the fall 1953 issue served to announce his arrival in the midst of this postwar literary renaissance.

"Cocoa Party" was another standalone chapter of Connell's Saxton-sponsored novel, which was otherwise going nowhere. Steele had brought the story to the magazine's attention in the spring. Little happens in the tale except for a gathering of students and a conversation dominated by a professor. The central character spends a few minutes meditating on a small Gothic gargoyle made of soapstone. Cups of cocoa are indeed served. Professor Locke (recall Albert Bloch of Kansas) continually presses another man, a laconic art teacher and musician, to speak. We know this other professor; it's Andraukov from "The Anatomy Lesson." Finally Locke suggests, "There is a certain poetic unity about you, Mr. Andraukov. What a pity it cannot communicate itself to others. As it is, you are only a type. Still, after a time we do become types, I suppose, sad parodies of all we have striven to be."[8] Connell may well have found such types on the campuses he knew. The young man, not yet out of his twenties, seems to have absorbed a jaded view of fate, as Locke goes on to express it: "With what desperate speed do we rush into our lives and later, bewildered, behold them recede rather like some wave."[9] Connell's life of independence and writing had barely begun. And this story had a retrograde European pace to it, not unlike, say, a piece of fiction by Thomas Mann, whose work Connell admired. Connell had written "Cocoa Party" before reaching Paris. With its rural setting in the "great Kaw valley," the story, like "The Anatomy Lesson," draws from the Kansas college landscape Connell had experienced and was now in the process of escaping.

For his part, as midwife to Connell's writing career, Plimpton would maintain their connection for years to come.

One night after coffee at Tournon, Connell stopped by another Paris café for a drink. A singer launched into a popular mariachi song, "Guadalajara," which set Connell's mind racing back to a bar in Santa Cruz. The memory fueled a late-night effusion at his (or Steele's) apartment. About 3 a.m., he rolled out the last page of "The Fisherman from Chihuahua." The story is set in a Mexican restaurant during the winter doldrums along Santa Cruz's municipal pier. Each night a Mexican man arrives after work to eat dinner and play pinball. Eventually he is joined by a strange companion. Dressed in a silk shirt with an open collar, the tall and dark-skinned man of mysterious origins wears a crucifix. It hangs from his neck, and because of his luxuriant chest hair, Connell writes, it never touches his skin. After meals of "mostly greens and beans and fried meat made arrogant with pepper," the man raises his head and emits a deafening yowl.[10] This happens almost every night. It's either a song or a demonic yawp, but word spreads and the sleepy restaurant begins to fill up each night with diners hoping to experience the spectacle. With its hyper-real vision and a near mystical feeling, the story represented a stylistic advance for Connell. He hoped once again that Plimpton and the *Paris Review* would want it.

Connell found another story in Paris just by listening to Max Steele. "The Short Happy Life of Henrietta," first published a few years later, involves a naive young woman from Nebraska who encounters "two jolly little men from Algiers."[11] As its title echoes Hemingway's "Short Happy Life of Francis Macomber," a reader might well expect tragedy to ensue. And, indeed, Connell's story has an O. Henry–style, rather brutal twist at the end of its brief, ironic narrative. Steele supposedly heard the story from another friend. "It was supposed to have happened," Connell once said. "I told Max that if he didn't write it, I was going to. I gave him a year. He didn't use it, and I did. Ever since, he's been threatening to sue me."[12] Steele's source happened to be the American writer Theodora Keogh (née Roosevelt), whose first novel, *Meg*, announced her as a formidable talent capable of exploring the dark side of human behavior. One could reasonably draw a connecting line from Keogh's book to Connell's story of Henrietta to a later story by Steele, "A Caracole in Paris," which, with its single-woman-in-danger story line, seemed to be his own attempt to return to the subject. Keogh, in fact, might have complained years later that Connell had ripped her off. Connell dismissed the thought and said he had never read her.

Nevertheless, Connell gathered material wherever he sensed it. He became a masterful borrower. A character named Max appears in "Madame Broulard," another Paris story, in which the narrator rents an apartment from the eponymous landlady. It was no easy thing to land a Paris apartment, as Steele discovered when he moved from the Latin Quarter to his nicer quarters closer to the Eiffel Tower. In Connell's story, the narrator's occasional encounters with Madame Broulard provide a cross-cultural education. And certain small moments give Connell a chance to paint vivid imagery. A party scene at Max's, where everyone is sitting on the floor, presents "a collage of plaid shirts, hairy arms, sandals, girls' legs, and many blue packs of Gauloises cigarettes."[13] The narrator, an American student, and his friend Max take occasional swipes at tourists, the kinds of people who pick up knickknacks at the Clignancourt flea market and take them home to Kansas City or New York. The fictional Max says their like—he doesn't necessarily exclude himself or his friend—have turned postwar Paris into an occupied city again, dominated by "the Americans with their purple nylon shirts and chewing gum and three-hundred-dollar cameras and American Express tours."[14] Connell, Steele, and other Americans were constantly struggling with their conflicted feelings about the French and their temporarily adopted city. In the story, Connell briefly references the recent war as well as the global dilemma of the atom bomb and the French propensity for insulting American intelligence. Still, all Madame Broulard wants from the narrator as he prepares to wind up his stay and return home is a photograph of him at the Statue of Liberty. As she tells him, "It is from us to you, this statue."[15] Civility at last—or was it more a final pinch of arrogance at a time when Americans in Paris too often tested the patience of the locals?

In addition to his fateful lunch with Plimpton, Connell had another influential meeting in Paris. He shared a meal with Christopher Logue, a British poet two years his junior. Most likely they met at the Tournon. "The Tournon," Logue once recalled, "was cheaper than the Flore and the Deux Magots in St. Germain-des-Pres."[16] Logue was in the early stages of becoming a poet, long before he became most known for his reimagined versions of *The Iliad*. "Logue taught me more about English prose than anybody before or since," Connell recalled about three decades later. Logue had no money whatsoever, less than everyone else in the penurious writer's circle. But he was proud and wouldn't take a free meal. Connell consulted with Steele, who suggested offering Logue lunch in exchange for reading a story. That worked. Connell handed over a short manuscript and expected Logue to skim it and chat for a few minutes before eating. "Not so," Connell recalled. "He took my story apart: paragraph by paragraph, sentence by sentence, phrase by phrase, word by word. He talked for nearly an hour while I listened in shocked silence. It never had occurred to me that prose could be of such importance."[17] In another version of this recollection, Connell said, "For better or worse Christopher has affected the style I use more than anybody else."[18]

A few weeks after Connell's meeting with Plimpton, Steele returned from the States, and Connell prepared to wind up the European chapter of his apprenticeship. Connell sent Steele four thousand francs to cover his utility bills. He also mentioned that a theatrical group in New York, the Circle in the Square, was exploring the possibility of making a film version of "The Anatomy Lesson." He had just signed a contract on the deal.[19]

Connell spent most of October and November in Madrid and elsewhere in Spain. "The cooking is bad, the women exotic," he told Steele.[20] Eventually he got to Portugal and left Lisbon bound for New York on November 25, 1953, aboard an Italian ocean liner, the *Vulcania*. After a few weeks in New York, where, among other things, he tried to shop a collection of Christopher Logue's poetry, he spent the holidays with his family in Kansas City. Such visits home were rarely joyful. His mother was ailing, though she and her husband had lifted their spirits in recent cruises to Hawaii, South America, and Cairo. Connell, though, might have been seething about a slight he suffered at his mother's hands. As the story goes, a female friend from New York called the house one day. She was in town and wanted to see Connell. Mrs. Connell never passed on the message—deliberately. By her reckoning, a young woman who would call a young man out of the blue couldn't be proper material for her own son. Whenever he told that story to his niece, she recalled, he would still shake with anger and get red in the face.

By early 1954, Connell settled in San Francisco, a city he first encountered during his year at Stanford. He didn't intend to stay long, but he liked the light and the air and the views from the hilltops and from his attic room at the Victorian Hotel on Eddy Street.

He was feeling antsy about the United States, discouraged by the current Cold War hysteria ("bomb shelters and air raid wardens every few blocks") and by its "morality drive," emblemized, he told Steele, by a recent crackdown in San Francisco on prostitutes and bookies. "I have lost a good bit of sympathy for America," Connell wrote. "I recall you saying that it seemed so alive here; that Europe seemed to you to be living in a back alley; I feel almost the opposite."[21] On another day, he reframed his political stance: "America is still outlawing everything from Communism to fornication and if they continue to do so I may be converted to both."[22] With little regular income to speak of, he took a job as a shipyard clerk, logging "the number of condensers, resistors, machine gun barrels and 3000 other such items that the yard receives" in the process of building minesweepers for the Dutch Navy.[23] Several nights a week he fed his artistic cravings, if not his adoration for the female body, by attending life-drawing classes. On Sundays, he often spent the afternoon in Palo Alto, visiting with old Stanford roommates and friends. It was the kind of habitual relief and leisure time he allowed himself in Paris, akin to stopping for a cup of coffee in the Dôme after live-model sketching in a drawing class.[24]

Partly fueled by his stop in Kansas City, Connell focused intently on another novel. This one involved a Kansas City matron from a time and place not unlike Connell's own boyhood. The name he gave her was India Bridge, a woman with a first name as unusual and inexplicable as the one Connell's mother went by, Elton. Connell had tried to make the character's story fit inside the form of a conventional narrative, but he always said he didn't know how to write it; he couldn't figure out a structure.[25] After a while, Connell hit on something. The woman's life kept insisting itself in paragraphs or brief scenes that he could not imagine stretching out into a typical, novelistic chapter: "It seemed to me that the lives I was writing about were best captured in the itty-bitty details, and I finally started to write it that way."[26] He had worked out the scheme while still in Paris, churning out as many as one hundred pages of "story-sketches," the term he used to describe them to Steele: "As I read over the sketches they seem a bit peculiar; perhaps, if they continue to pour out on paper at the present rate they will make up a book something like 'Portrait of Mrs. Bridge in 114 Frames.'"[27]

It took only a few months to complete a draft. And by April he had sent the three-hundred-page manuscript to his agent. He described some of its contents to Steele: it amounted to 185 chapters and had enough characters "to sink Tolstoy." And he was thoroughly self-deprecating about its fate: "It is a totally worthless book."[28] That summer Connell sent five short, raw sections—"an idle sample" of the manuscript—to Eugene Walter, a *Paris Review* gatekeeper.[29] Connell told him that Harcourt had already turned the book down. He was calling it *The Beau Monde of Mrs. Bridge.*

As Connell soon learned, the experimental approach was not an easy sell.

Elizabeth McKee liked what she saw of it. "Although India is a 'type,' she really exists in the book for me—in other words she is not just a symbol," she told Connell. "And to me she is so valid for, alas, I know so many women like her. The novel has humor and pathos, too—and I think it's a tragic book in the best sense of the word."[30]

Nevertheless, the response from many of New York's top editors—almost all of them men, as it happened—was quite different. Joe Fox at Knopf was typically unconvinced: "There is no doubt that Mr. Connell has talent, but I don't think he has used it properly in this very unconventional approach. He has presented us with a series of rather blurry snapshots of a very unattractive marriage. . . . I will say for the author that he has made Mrs. Bridge more interesting than I thought possible. He has done nobly with a very thin type." A handwritten comment in the margin of Fox's letter, probably made by Connell on the copy McKee had forwarded to him, revealed a learning moment: "In actuality, the marriage *is* attractive in some respects—point them out."[31]

Peter Davison at Harcourt turned down the novel but said it represented an advance over the previous manuscript he had seen, *The Anatomy Lesson.* He thought the short chapters were "very effective," but he and his colleagues couldn't get past the feeling that Connell failed to generate any sympathy for India Bridge.

India Bridge

But where is what I started for so long ago?
And why is it yet unfound?
                    ...Walt Whitman

1
love and marriage

India Stasts had been a plump, helpless girl with affectionate eyes
and an anxious manner as though she were afraid of being thought disagreeable.
When she was young she vowed never to marry and for a while it seemed to her
parents that she never would. But finally, well along in her 20s, she
submitted to the annoyed insistence of a hard-featured young lawyer with
red hair named Walter Governor Bridge, who said to her with chilling intensity
that the world would hear more of him.
    So it was that a few months after her father died she married Walter Bridge,
founded a home in Kansas City and set about her destiny without much meditation
except deep in the night when as hour upon hour they lay drowsily clutching
each other in anticipation of the dawn, the following day, and another night
which might prove them immortal, she sometimes started in wakefulness. Then
she would lie in his arms staring up at the ceiling or at his strangely
helpless face with an uneasy expression.
    For a while after their marriage she was in such demand that it was
not unpleasant when he went to sleep, but presently he began sleeping all
night. She often lay awake then for long periods of time looking up into
the darkness, wondering about the ways of men, and at last there came a night
when she shook him awake and spoke of her desire. Affably he put one of
his slender white arms across her waist but that was all -- he feigned
drowsing off. She knew he was awake, still he pretended. Thus she concluded
that while marriage might be an equitable affair, love was not.

2
Ruth born

    Her first child, whom they named Ruth Anne, was born easily when they
had been married a little over 3 years. After the delivery Mrs. Bridge's
first conscious words were: "Is she normal?"

3
with her family

    Two years later -- Mrs. Bridge was just 31 -- Carolyn appeared and was
immediately nicknamed 'Corky'. Then about a month and two years after Corky
there arrived a crowning little boy named Douglas who almost refused the
world. They had only wanted two children but as the first two had been girls
they decided to try once more. If the last had also been a girl they would
have let it go at that because there would have been no sense in continuing
what would shortly become amusing to other people.

80
from another world

    Carolyn, endlessly buying sloppy sweaters and phonograph records of
sugar-and-water love ballads, was more extravagant than her older sister,
but it did seem at times that Ruth might manage to spend that much on

Fig. 15. The earliest extant pieces of Connell's India Bridge novel appear in
a 1954 letter (detail reproduced here) to Eugene Walter, who was reading
manuscripts for the *Paris Review*. Excerpts from the novel ran in the *Paris
Review* a year later under the title "The Beau Monde of Mrs. Bridge." Courtesy
of Eugene Walter Collection, Harry Ransom Center, the University of Texas at
Austin.

Davison quoted a fellow editor: "What emerges is the picture of a person trapped in a life whose absurdity is so elaborated as to be intolerable—but the life is all the reader will see; the person inside it, whom the author loves and forgives, is pretty well lost."[32] Davison remained encouraging and expressed hope to see more of Connell's work in the future. Over the next year Robert Loomis at Rinehart and Cass Canfield Jr. at Coward-McCann also took a pass, as did editors at Little, Brown and Harper and Brothers. Loomis and his colleagues "were forced to the conclusion that he has written a book that was not *quite* worth writing."[33] Canfield called the book "a study not a story," adding, "Mrs. Bridge is interesting to view but tiresome to follow." Connell annotated more of those letters, vowing, in his small, tightly written hand, to "turn the 'liability' into an asset."[34]

Connell's shipyard job ended in August 1954 and he set out on a weeklong drive through the West and Northwest. The desert. The mountains. The forests. All made up "the fairest part of this land." To Steele, Connell also extolled the attractions of the gambling parlors of Las Vegas and Reno: "Nowhere else are there so many libertines in tight cowboy britches dealing blackjack. The atmosphere is electric." Shortly after he returned, he was drawn into a disturbing scene. His attic neighbor at the Victorian Hotel, an "exotic redhead," jumped off the roof, apparently despondent over her marriage. As police gathered evidence around her bloodied body on the street and in her apartment, Connell made note of the details. Her reading material included Oscar Wilde and a biology textbook.[35]

Meanwhile, the Plimpton connection continued to pay dividends, even if the *Paris Review*'s checks—$12.50 for "Cocoa Party"—were slow in coming. Plimpton and his fellow editors were duly impressed by the more pronounced, dark aura of Connell's Santa Cruz story "The Fisherman from Chihuahua." They published it in the fall-winter issue of 1954, and being a journal that also valued visual art, even included two sketches that Connell, the onetime art student, provided. As much as people liked the story, the line drawings of elongated, aching figures also sparked interest, Plimpton told Connell. Connell's stock rose further when Martha Foley chose the story for inclusion in *Best American Short Stories 1955*.

Connell continued to polish stories and other magazines continued to reject him. The *New Yorker* turned down "The Walls of Ávila," a forty-five-page manuscript about a world traveler returning home after ten years abroad. Another long story he produced in this period, "Arcturus," was Connell's rewrite, as he put it, of Thomas Mann's "Disorder and Early Sorrow." Connell's story introduced the mild-mannered Muhlbach, a figure who would return in several more of his works. As for the Bridge novel, "I don't suppose it will ever sell," Connell told Steele, "but if I hung on sales, I would have quit long ago."[36] Over the Christmas holiday season that year in San Francisco, Connell spent a few weeks working the overnight shift at a post office.

Soon, Plimpton came through again. Despite the judgment of the New York publishing houses, Plimpton sensed the innovative brilliance that Connell had crafted in the novel about India Bridge. He told Connell that the *Paris Review* would publish excerpts in its summer 1955 issue, number 10. Plimpton also elevated Connell's stature as contributor to a new level. He placed Connell's name on the cover, just below the top headline touting an interview with James Thurber and just above that of the boisterous voice of another American who had spent time in Paris, Henry Miller.

Six years after the publication of "I'll Take You to Tennessee," four years after the second O. Henry Prize, less than two years after he left the creative cauldron of Paris and opted for the relative quiet of San Francisco, Connell's literary arrival surely felt sweet. And for readers, the cover status really paid off. Inside the quarterly were pieces of what appeared to be a startlingly fresh novel with which Connell and his agent had been struggling. The work bore the title "The Beau Monde of Mrs. Bridge" and presented a distinctly American portrait of fragile innocence, delusion, and Midwestern repression.

Plimpton and Connell went back and forth over which vignettes to include and settled on a sequence of a dozen. There was an account of Mrs. Bridge's tentative driving skills behind the wheel of the Lincoln automobile her husband had given her. There were episodes involving her encounter with books—a local minister's collection of essays and a volume of Joseph Conrad. The latter caused a moment's reflection on the possibility of living life to the fullest. There were cocktail parties and embarrassing moments that spotlighted India Bridge's discomfort over matters of manners, social propriety, and race. Plimpton thought the story, in the midst of the journal's usual "gloomy clutch of fiction," would be a welcome light addition.[37] "I'm sure the stories will be well thought of," Plimpton said by letter. "We're all very fond of them here."[38]

In the spring of 1955, Connell left San Francisco for another road trip, eventually planning to visit his parents in Kansas City, "where I do not know anyone anymore."[39] On the way, he stopped in Las Vegas and other notable sites around the West, including the Black Hills of South Dakota and Mount Rushmore. He spent an afternoon at the battlefield site in Montana where General George Armstrong Custer met his fate in his famous last stand, "going over the maps and routes and almost felt my two drops of Indian blood. What a pageant that must have been that day."[40] This, of course, was an experience and a sensation that would become all-consuming for Connell a quarter of a century later.

After Kansas City, he spent two months in Denver, satisfying an urge to see the mountains that had entranced him on boyhood vacations to Colorado. His father and brother-in-law joined him for a few days of fishing. There is no record that Connell spoke with his father about the recent publication of "The Beau Monde of Mrs. Bridge" or shared it with his family while at home. Why stir it up? The elder Connell's daily work schedule hardly left room for reading something as frivolous, to him, as the *Paris Review*. In Denver, Connell also reunited with his navy friend Blossom Williams. Blossom, "a swarthy, hairy, muscular boy from southern Kansas," was the pilot who got Connell in trouble by buzzing the Kansas campus during a flying exercise. He also provided Connell the foundation for one of his starkest early stories. As Connell once recounted, Blossom, after their training years, had gone on to serve on patrol bombers in the South Pacific. On one mission his crew spotted a missing pilot's yellow raft in the ocean, spiraled downward for a closer a look, and, following protocol to prevent the Japanese from finding it, blew up the empty craft. In school at Kansas, Williams had written a love story that somehow incorporated the incident—Connell called it "tedious, disorganized, sentimental."[41] Connell told him that if he couldn't place it—he never did—Connell would write his own version of the story. Connell dated "The Yellow Raft" to 1954, in the period he was turning out story after story in San Francisco. Yet he never disclosed whether he shared the short story with Williams on that visit a year later. By September 1955, the fearless traveler got in his car to leave Denver and took the long way back to San Francisco, via New Orleans.

Not long after the India Bridge excerpt got its launch in Paris, Connell's earlier novel hit a wall. Joe Fox, the Knopf editor who had rejected the Bridge novel, dismissed *The Anatomy Lesson* because of Connell's "artless plotting" and "sloppiness in the treatment of his subsidiary character." Nevertheless, Fox added, "there is no doubt in my mind that Connell is going to be a writer. He has an unusual mind, he can express himself and he has something to say—though I must admit that he lost me on this one."[42]

Connell turned back to another novel in progress, this one loosely based on his navy flight training and his family's roots in Confederate-era Missouri. While back in Kansas City, he had visited the nearby town of Lexington where he remembered seeing as a child a famous remnant of the Civil War—a cannonball stuck in a pillar at the antebellum Lafayette County Courthouse. Seeing the remnant again, lodged near the column's capital, seemed to be all it took to spark the literary tinder. He worked in a scene of the main character on a fishing trip with his father and brother-in-law, transplanted to Ontario from its real-life occurrence that summer.[43] Connell had high hopes for the book. He thought that New York would be more impressed with it than it had been with *The Anatomy Lesson*—or at least greet him with "less hostility."[44]

Connell submitted the navy novel, *The Patriot*, to the Harper Prize contest, and McKee sent it to Harper and Brothers in the spring of 1956. When it came back, she told Connell: "I think that the novel, Evan, because it is unconventional in both subject and structure will be a difficult one to place. But you do have a large and devoted group of editors throughout publishing who have asked to see anything which you write."[45]

With the fate of *The Anatomy Lesson* seemingly sealed and the number of Connell's published and unpublished stories on the rise, he and McKee envisioned a collection of short fiction coming together in addition to the hard-to-sell novels, *The Patriot* and *India Bridge* (as it was being shopped).

Despite his outward comments that sales didn't matter, Connell internalized a kind of burden over the long odds of being published. "I realized long ago," he told Eugene Walter, "that writing would be principally a matter of being rejected." But he had tethered himself to writing and settled for the consequences. "I should have been a sculptor, you know," he wrote, "but had not the guts to abandon fiction."[46] He had made the choice. He did what he later advised in an essay meant to caution aspiring writers: "Find out what you are."[47] Still, he had to steel himself whenever he opened a letter from his agent or a publishing house. So he surely felt a moment of relief when he read a letter in October 1956 from Candida Donadio at the McIntosh-McKee Agency and came to this line: "Viking wants to publish you." Connell underlined the words "wants to publish you" in ink and added four exclamation points.[48]

Viking was as yet unsure which of his books it wanted to publish first. A week later Elizabeth McKee reported to Connell on her meeting with Viking editors Tom Guinzburg, Helen Taylor, and Keith Jennison. In play were the story collection, now titled *The Anatomy Lesson* and including the eponymous story, and *The Patriot*. For the former, Viking offered an advance of $750. The latter involved a smaller, provisional advance, pending revisions. Slyly, McKee withheld the *India Bridge* manuscript. "This can be shown to them later as I don't want to upset the balance now."[49]

McKee also had relayed to Connell a spirit-boosting appraisal: "Rose Styron who is now reading for *The Paris Review* (and who is no fool) told me that she thinks you're the most talented person they have published."[50]

The longer Connell stayed in San Francisco, the more he became enthralled with it. He had been all over and concluded that San Francisco was the best city in the United States. He could sit at his desk—a three-dollar find at the Salvation Army store—and look over rooftops and out toward Oakland and the bay and marvel at how the fog could appear one moment and then disappear and how the whole character of the cityscape could change throughout the day. "It is as though one's sense of time had slowed down and the alterations of fifty years occur every few hours," he wrote.[51] The climate and atmosphere were absolutely right for writing, "neither bourgeois nor bohemian." He didn't mind putting on a wool flannel shirt on cool August nights, and if he felt starved for female companionship, well, so it goes. He had heard that Max Steele had possibly married, and he inquired: "If so, does she have a sister, because I'm getting on in years and find the nights are long. Something's got to be done."[52]

Another attraction of San Francisco was the presence of the writer Walter Van Tilburg Clark. Connell admired Clark's best-known book, *The Ox-Bow Incident*, a novel of the frontier West that Hollywood had converted into a successful movie in the early 1940s. And he thought that two or three of Clark's short stories stood among America's best. In an accounting of his recent reading, he once mentioned Clark's "The Wind and the Snow of Winter," a story about a goldminer returning to his remote town, which won an O. Henry Prize in 1944. "What a splendid thing it is," Connell told Steele.[53] Ray West, Connell's teacher at Kansas, had recently joined the San Francisco State College faculty, and Clark followed in 1956. Connell registered for one of Clark's classes. He only heard one lecture, about Henry James, but mostly Connell submitted manuscripts that Clark and he would discuss over coffee.

"I listened attentively," Connell said, "but if we did not agree on the treatment, I would do it my way."[54]

Many of Clark's regular students were enthralled by his style, not only because he was the first faculty member to show up without wearing a tie. He led them deeply into great works of fiction, whether it be Flaubert or Hemingway, and emphasized symbols, myth, and understatement. "In analyzing a piece of fiction or in drawing our insights into the creative act, he was superb," Charles Breshear told a Clark biographer, "and our admiration for him was little short of idolatry. Among ourselves, we called him 'The Younger Brother of God.'" After one class session, a discussion dominated by students, Breshear said, "As we left, we felt brilliant—felt we had grappled with a story's essence and pinned it to the backsides of our foreheads."[55] Don Carpenter, who earned a master's degree in 1961, eventually worked Clark into a novel: "He was the most respected of the writer-teachers at State."[56]

Connell assured McKee that he could count on Clark to help advise him on his story collection and the revisions to his novels. The Viking editors were high on Clark, McKee responded, and happy to hear he would weigh in on the manuscripts.

To Connell, Clark was as much of a mentor as Stegner had been. Most people mistakenly thought of Clark only as the author responsible for that movie about vigilante justice, "The Ox-Bow Incident," starring Anthony Quinn. How unfair. Clark and Stegner both expended much energy working with students so perhaps they didn't write as much as they might have. And they both felt something strong about the West; Clark even had the look of a westerner, a "tall, gray face" and piercing blue eyes that made Connell think he "belonged outside, not in a classroom."[57] (In fact, Clark was a New Englander by birth.) As Connell once wrote in a review of a book of Stegner's essays: "Walter Clark was a bit of a mystic, which Stegner is not, yet these two shared a common response to that vast territory they called home." In the review, Connell quoted Stegner on the matter: "Almost as much as he"—Clark—"but later in my life, I grew to hate the profane Western culture, the economics and psychology of a rapacious society. I disliked it as reality and

I distrusted it when it elevated itself into the western myths that aggrandized arrogance, machismo, vigilante or sidearm justice, and the oversimplified good-guy/bad-guy moralities."[58] It's not difficult to imagine Connell identifying with that outlook. At the time he read Stegner's essays in the early 1990s, he had long transplanted himself to the western landscape where such matters remained fully alive and debated. Nevertheless, he also found it difficult to identify himself as a western writer. As he told an interviewer near the end of his life, he never really escaped his Midwestern roots: "I don't know the West the way I know the Midwest. You grow up in a place and it's in your bones. . . . Whatever West I've known is rather superficial."[59]

Viking chose to introduce its new author with his short stories. All that remained of Connell's first planned novel were the two previously published standalone stories, "The Anatomy Lesson" and "Cocoa Party." The former now took the lead position in the new book, titled *The Anatomy Lesson and Other Stories*. The collection would include some of his earliest published pieces, such as "The Fisherman from Chihuahua," and some ("Arcturus," "The Yellow Raft") that had appeared in journals only recently. Viking announced the book in early 1957 with an ad in *Publisher's Weekly*: "A publishing 'first' we're proud of! Mr. Connell's short stories have won attention wherever they have appeared in magazines and some of the annual 'Best' volumes. Now, in book form, they demonstrate an amazing versatility and maturity, and signal the beginning of a remarkable career."[60] In its jacket copy, the publisher touted Connell's award-winning status and his reputation among in-the-know readers of short fiction. (Oddly, the tout erred in placing the title story in Stegner's volume of *Stanford Short Fiction*; it was "I'll Take You to Tennessee" which earned that honor and also appeared in this new book.) Connell was proud of the fact that Viking incorporated his suggestion for a cover illustration. It was a study sketch for Michelangelo's *Libyan Sibyl,* not only reflecting the content of the title story but also offering a nuanced nod to his own passion for drawing.

Fig. 16. Connell's family gathered at the Mission Hills Country Club in Kansas City, 1957, to celebrate the publication of his first book, *The Anatomy Lesson and Other Stories*. From left: Connell, sister Barbara Zimmermann, Dr. Evan S. Connell Sr., Elton Connell, and Barbara's husband, Matthew Zimmermann. Photograph by Ken Taylor, originally published in the *Independent*, Kansas City. Courtesy of the *Independent* and the Literary Estate of Evan Shelby Connell Jr.

To readers encountering Connell for the first time, "The Anatomy Lesson" and its companion stories delivered evidence of the writer's keen eye for humanity and exquisite sensory detail. Some hinterlands critics gave him mixed responses, but the *New York Times* was generally positive. Its reviewer found in the title story "character portraiture of a kind that qualifies 33-year-old Connell as one of our most noteworthy contemporary short-story writers." And of the stories in general the critic ultimately concluded, "Mr. Connell is no raconteur, no shock applier, no morbid ruminator in childhood's dark corners; instead he is a craftsman who can evoke, sustain and dignify the 'small' tragedy that is often hidden from view."[61] With his first book, Connell the craftsman had arrived.

While waiting for Viking to respond to his *Patriot* manuscript, Connell continued to work on the Bridge novel, and he gave Clark a chunk of his manuscript. In a note he told Clark what he'd been hearing from editors: "a study rather than a story. Events take place but nothing really happens. She is interesting to view but tiresome to follow." Editors had called India Bridge boring, uninteresting, and too thinly developed to support a whole book. "These criticisms are what I'm trying to overcome in the present draft," Connell wrote. He asked Clark specifically to look for the weakest, "least effective sequences" and help him eject repetitious moments and the like. "I suspect that in order for the book to be acceptable," he concluded, "every incident must be satisfying."[62]

Clark replied in a two-page analysis, which he wrote by hand on Connell's letter. Clark's tiny script contained some opening praise for Connell but soon ventured into a tough critique.[63] To Clark, Mrs. Bridge was not yet a fully developed character and Connell would do well to heighten the voices of her children as a way to reflect the "outer world" beyond what seemed like her internal emptiness. Clark thought the world of the children seemed more interesting than that of the adults. In one section of the manuscript, Clark wrote, "She practically vanishes here, her predictability, already dangerously spent in the world of the children, becomes absolute here." Another big problem: Mrs. Bridge's husband was not well conceived. Clark doubted that the emptiness of Mrs. Bridge could sustain a novel of the length Connell intended. His suggested remedies included getting much closer to the character and giving her "at least some potential for drama . . . at least the possibility of worry and a growing sense of futility," and allowing the children's voices and viewpoints of other, more interesting characters to emerge more consistently.[64] Connell clearly took Clark's criticisms seriously and continued to revise.

On another front, a standalone piece from *The Patriot,* a story titled "Graduation at Pensacola," came back from the *New Yorker,* where the feelings about it ranged from amusing to "a bit too familiar and dated" as a war story.[65] Still, Connell had a sense that things were beginning to turn around for him. *Harper's Bazaar* wanted to see a story it had rejected once before. And Ray West, now editing the *Western Review* in San Francisco, published two of his stories.

The editors at Viking still had problems with *The Patriot*. Helen Taylor, a senior editor, crossed the continent to spend a weekend with Connell going over the book. Connell lamented to Steele that the publisher liked an earlier draft while he preferred a later one. Steele also had sent a quick opinion—he didn't much like the book, though Connell pressed him for details. Then again, Connell conceded, Walter Clark had read an early draft and thought it was a mess. After meeting with Taylor, Connell felt somewhat bewildered and sensed that *The Patriot* would drag out much longer than he had hoped. And it soon became clear that Viking put a priority on the India Bridge novel. A couple of months after her visit, Taylor wrote to Connell, starting with a brief discussion of *The Patriot* but spending more effort on her concerns with "a few problems with MRS. BRIDGE."[66]

Taylor assured Connell that the novel would be on Viking's fall list, so the pressure would be on to fix a series of problems soon, before the book went into production. She suggested there needed to be some rearrangements and possibly some tightening and cuts, but more important at first was an issue of time. Although the novel was not written with a strict chronology, she and her colleagues had identified a dozen or more places with anachronistic references or inconsistencies, several involving the ages of the three Bridge children. Among other things, she questioned whether Mr. and Mrs. Bridge, whom Connell depicted on a trip to Europe in the late summer of 1939, on the verge of Hitler's invasion of Poland, would have gone to Spain so soon after the conclusion of its civil war. Taylor soon followed up with more "nitpicks and suggested cuts."[67] Connell was undeterred. By the summer, he told Max Steele that Viking remained interested in *The Patriot*, even as he worked on the sixth draft. And as for the novel now called *Mrs.*

Bridge, "they are all quite enthusiastic about the mad matron of Mission Hills."[68]

Connell's connection to Walter Clark extended to the pages of a magazine launched in the latter half of 1958. Clark became an advisory editor of *Contact*, subtitled "The San Francisco Journal of New Writing, Art and Ideas" (or sometimes "The San Francisco Collection . . ."). Co-founded and published by William H. Ryan, the journal operated above the Tides bookstore in Sausalito, a quiet, colorful, and steeply sloped waterfront village across the bay from San Francisco. Connell gravitated toward that world and its circle of writers and artists, and he made a splash in *Contact*'s very first issue. It contained ten additional fragmentary excerpts from the Bridge novel, pieces that hadn't been published in the *Paris Review* or reprinted in *The Anatomy Lesson*. The excerpts appeared under the overall headline "Mademoiselle from Kansas City." Connell's name appeared on the *Contact* cover and a photo of him—suave, mustachioed, nearly expressionless—on the back, alongside such well-known writers as Ray Bradbury, S. I. Hayakawa, and Alan Watts. Another name in the issue: Van Gogh, who was represented by a suite of drawings selected from a huge exhibit then showing at the M. H. De Young Memorial Museum in San Francisco. *Contact*'s inaugural edition was dedicated to the poet William Carlos Williams, who turned seventy-five that year and who had edited a journal of the same name in the 1920s and 1930s: "We hope, too, to regenerate in these pages some of the vital spirit that he instilled into the old *Contact* magazine which he and Robert McAlmon first edited in 1922."[69] Williams appeared in the issue with a brief account of the origins of that earlier *Contact* and its publication program. "One of *Contact Editions'* most distinguished publications," he wrote, "was Gertrude Stein's monumental *The Making of Americans*. Without the backing of the *Contact* name I doubt that it would ever have been printed." Williams stood for "the American idiom" and lamented T. S. Eliot's counterweight, which took verse "back on our heels" for decades. "Only today are we beginning to get our feet under us again, finally rid of the Eliot influence," he writes. "Now is the time for the name *Contact* to appear among us again, making its way among a heap of impedimenta which clutter the path about the feet of our young writers."[70] If Connell were negotiating his way around that "heap of impedimenta," the issue's excerpts from *Mrs. Bridge* announced him as a partisan of Williams's "American idiom." There was a lot to be proud of, including the *Contact* editors' prediction that Connell's novel would be "among the outstanding fiction works of 1959."[71]

The excerpts in *Contact*, rather smartly selected, all revolve around the eldest of the Bridge children, Ruth. Curiously, not all of the anecdotes appear in the published novel. Ruth is in her late teens and always running up against her mother's propriety. The first segment opens with Mrs. Bridge's discovery of a dirty comb in a wastebasket and her confrontation with Ruth:

"Do you think we're made of money?" Mrs. Bridge demanded. "When a comb gets dirty you don't throw it away, you wash it young lady."

"It cost a nickel," Ruth said angrily. She flung her books onto the bed and stripped off her sweater.

"Nickels don't grow on trees," replied Mrs. Bridge, irritated by her manner.

"Nickels don't grow on trees," Ruth echoed.[72]

Elton Connell's descendants, including two granddaughters—the daughters of her only daughter, Barbara Zimmermann—insist that the comb episode is straight from real life. Other segments of the book find Mrs. Bridge at a loss to understand how her daughters, Ruth and Carolyn, were so different. And when Ruth finally graduates from high school—after five years, perilously close to six—she goes off to New York where she works for a fashion magazine and befriends a colleague who is homosexual. She relates this latter fact on a visit back home. Her mother is quizzical: "Why, he's gay, Mother. Queer. You know." Mrs. Bridge replies, "I'm afraid I don't know."[73]

It's curious that Connell, when interviewed about the novel over the years, almost never referenced the poignant timing of its release.

Elton Connell, his mother, died in July 1958, not long before the *Contact* publication and just six months before Viking published his first novel, the book that she had at least in part inspired. She was only sixty. Connell never really deflected the suggestion that to create the lives that populate *Mrs. Bridge* he had drawn quite a bit from his own family. His portrait of India Bridge certainly contained elements of Elton Connell's life and experience. As her obituary in the *Kansas City Star* recounted, she was active in civic and church affairs, perhaps more active than we ever see India Bridge.[74] But Connell never weighed in on how Mrs. Connell might have felt, or how, in fact, she did feel, if she had read or heard of the excerpts published a few years earlier in the *Paris Review*. (He once said she'd never read them.) Connell acknowledged that "my sister was angry and hurt, I believe"—though the qualification there, *I believe*, could make one wonder if they ever even talked about it.[75] Sure there might have been wounded feelings, but this was how writers went about their business, drawing from life as they knew it. Connell told one interviewer that he remembered a woman writer, a name he couldn't recall, who lamented that she had held back from writing about one of her friends. Connell also never addressed a sly irony embedded in the novel. By naming Mrs. Bridge's first and most rebellious daughter Ruth, he had borrowed his own mother's given name, though one she didn't use. It seemed to be a way of imagining a woman asserting her own identity, one who was wholly unlike his mother. In one sense Elton Connell could be considered a woman who was not there, while Ruth Bridge, her fictional daughter, served to show us what was missing.

If Barbara Zimmermann had hard feelings about her brother's novel, she didn't exactly reveal them in an interview three decades later. "The shoe fit pretty tight," she said. "Our mother was gone by the time it came out, but I remember a friend of hers who had a . . . sense of humor. She asked Evan to sign it for her, 'To a friend of Mrs. Bridge.'"[76] Barbara Zimmermann, or Bobbie (Bobs to her brother), recalled the day when the new book came in the mail, just before its public release: "Everyone was excited. The house was full of people. Someone called out, 'Have you read the dedication?' I hadn't, and I found out it was dedicated to me and my husband. We were so thrilled." If soon enough Bobbie felt she was reading about herself in some of the scenes about Ruth and Carolyn, she didn't say so: "Not everyone fit the mold Evan wrote about, but still some people did. And people will always try to see someone in it. The only person definitely there was Evan. He was Douglas."[77]

There is, to me, an aching moment in Connell's correspondence where he comes closest to revealing something meaningful relating to his submerged emotions about his mother—even if it is a moment of silence. In late July 1958, Connell began a letter to Max Steele with the news: "I returned only last night from Kansas City where I'd gone because of my mother's illness; she had cancer for five or six years, and died recently. There's not much that can be said about it, if anything."[78]

End of discussion. And hardly ever discussed again.

Mrs. Bridge Arrives
1959

"This may get me beyond the 'little magazine' audience."

—Connell to Max Steele, 1958

BEFORE THE END of the year, and before Viking's public release of *Mrs. Bridge*, Connell sent a proof copy to his early mentor Wallace Stegner. The response was encouraging. "When I began it," Stegner wrote back, just before Christmas 1958, "and had got fifteen pages along, I wondered if the pointilliste method would hold up, if the book could manage to have *draft*. I needn't have worried. It does. And I imagine that the reviewers and readers, who I hope are numerous, will be talking a good deal about the method, which you handle very surely and with the constant effect of a straightarm." But beyond the form, Stegner emphasized, he admired the depth of understanding and coolness that Connell displayed in his character studies. India Bridge was "real" and "pathetic" and "sad," and as the object of literary portrait-making she made Stegner think of no less a figure than Flaubert's Emma Bovary. "Maybe you aren't that good," he assured Connell, "but as I finished your book that's the way I felt."[1] Connell also shared an advance copy with Helen Hull, one of his Columbia writing professors. "Your book," she told him, "should remind writers that selection, not total recall, is an artist's job."[2]

Connell was heading back to Kansas City for the holidays—sure to involve a depressing family gathering in the absence of his mother. His editor, Helen Taylor, encouraged Connell to sit down for an interview with the *Kansas City Star*'s book-page editor, Thorpe Menn, who had already expressed enthusiasm for the novel. "I wonder," she wrote to Connell, "if you object to our suggesting a real live interview while you are home? We have a notion that Kansas City will really support this book." Taylor suggested that many popular books got an initial boost from the authors' local communities, so Connell should get on board and "take advantage of your presence as much as is not distasteful to you."[3] Emphasizing the hometown advantage, Viking gave Menn permission to publish his review in the *Star* a week ahead of the official release date in January. Bennett Schneider, one of Kansas City's leading bookstores, which was situated in India Bridge's familiar shopping territory, the Country Club Plaza, had already reordered "a very sizable quantity" of the book.[4] Menn soon reported, however, that the "modest author . . . declined to participate in any fanfare announcement" of the book's publication.[5]

Connell was a bit anxious in the prepublication limbo. "I have the sensation of having dropped a coin in the slot and am now watching, absolutely helpless, the wheels beginning to turn," he told Steele. He knew the people at Viking were optimistic about the novel's potential reception, but the birth of a book is ever unpredictable.[6]

Connell could do nothing more about it now except watch its progress. All those rejections and all those publishers' fears about its form meant nothing. Yet, his instincts were confirmed. He had originally imagined the book as a conventional novel, and its modernist, fragmentary structure had emerged sometime around his departure from Paris five years earlier. As a Viking copywriter distilled the book in its prepublication campaign, "Mrs. Bridge's life is made not in the grand design of heroic tragedy, but of particles of this and that, and her tragedies could be said to be generally lost in the roar of the vacuum cleaner."[7] Connell's strategy to corral "particles of this and that" would prove to be a brilliant stroke, a technique that eventually also underpinned his approach to writing historical narratives in the years ahead. One could think of it as positively atomic. Connell told Steele that the gesture of titling the paragraphs emerged as he arranged them. Maybe it was the manifestation of a latent

Fig. 17. *Mrs. Bridge* book jacket, January 1959. Courtesy of the Department of Special Collections, Stanford University Libraries.

influence from *Moby-Dick*. A critic for the *New York Times* cited another likely model. Charles Poore thought *Mrs. Bridge*'s segmented style owed something to Machado de Assis, a nineteenth-century Brazilian superstar whose influence on South American writers and others extended far beyond his own time.[8] (For starters, see Gabriel García Márquez, Jorge Luis Borges, and John Barth.) This was not an idle comparison. One of Machado's novels happened to be in the literary air in the early 1950s as Connell began working on *Mrs. Bridge*. Machado's *Memórias Póstumas de Brás Cubas* dates to 1881 but its first English translation appeared in the summer of 1952, not long after Connell joined the expatriate literati in Paris. Connell, the avid reader, surely would have caught wind of the novel, titled in the English edition *Epitaph of a Small Winner*. And, as a writer eagerly hoping to make his way in the literary world on his own terms, he would have taken note of the book's unusual form—a series of 160 disconnected short chapters, each numbered and titled. The *New York Times* reviewed Machado's novel under the headline "A Masterpiece from Brazil," a judgment that sticks.[9] Although Machado's novel is more pointedly satirical and more first-person meta-fictional than *Mrs. Bridge*, the two books share, along with their distinctive and highly functional episodic template, a subtext of disillusion.[10]

Early signs for *Mrs. Bridge* were good. Viking sales reps had blanketed the San Francisco Bay area and book-signing parties were on the schedule. Magazine mentions began to arrive. A Berkeley radio station, KPFA, wanted Connell to read an excerpt over the air.[11] He demurred—"I don't have the proper inflection for Mrs. B"—and suggested that a Palo Alto friend of his could read it.[12] Helen Taylor reported a second printing of the novel was in the works even before January 19, 1959. By the end of the month, Connell hinted to a friend there'd be a third.

As it reached the reading public, *Mrs. Bridge* was competing in the publishing marketplace with such bestsellers as Boris Pasternak's *Dr. Zhivago* and Vladimir Nabokov's *Lolita*. Connell learned from Thorpe Menn in Kansas City that *Mrs. Bridge* was flying off the shelves as fast as *Dr. Zhivago*. The Russian novelist had just been awarded the Nobel Prize in literature in October 1958, though in a defensive, Soviet-era political move he announced he would not accept it. Each of these popular novels, of course, was built on deep and indelible passions. And Nabokov's wicked little book, incorporating a theme of pedophilia, offered sensibilities and sensuality only hinted at in Connell's novel. India Bridge's relationship to the sensual life seems to be summed up in Connell's published memory of his mother, who always appeared threatened when the subject turned to sex.

Connell had no problem injecting the subject into his novel. Sexual anxiety pervades the book, from the opening chapter's melancholy reflection on sex and marriage to Mrs. Bridge's fears about the dating habits of her two daughters and son Douglas's girlie magazine. When Walter Bridge stops to stare at a black-lace, tipless bra in a

Fig. 18. Connell, in a rare publicity appearance, at the Richmond, California, Book Fair, March 1959. Courtesy of the Literary Estate of Evan Shelby Connell Jr. and the Department of Special Collections, Stanford University Libraries.

Paris shop window, readers might well recognize the mystery, the longing, and the connubial void the moment is meant to contain.

In one defining chapter it is hard to miss the symbolism when Douglas's mother calls the fire department to dismantle the tower he had built in a vacant lot—an assemblage of scrap metal, wood, and found objects planted solidly in a bed of concrete. How else to read the episode but as an emasculation, a wound that the sensitive teenager wouldn't soon, or ever, get over? India Bridge did not exactly know what she wanted, but she knew what she wanted to avoid.

If Max Steele were correct seven years earlier when he sized up Connell's competitiveness, the latter didn't seem to wear it in the open. But he did pay attention to the details—tracking press runs, noticing ad campaigns, reading reviews. Connell was certainly pleased and sensed that his career was about to take a major step in the right direction. "This," he told Steele, "may get me beyond the 'little magazine' audience."[13]

January 19, 1959. Connell had taken the long way back from Kansas City, piloting his ten-year-old Plymouth through Oklahoma City, the Southwest, and into Juárez and Tijuana, Mexico, before heading up the California coast. Within days of his return, publication day arrived, and Luther Nichols, a critic for the *San Francisco Examiner*, compared Connell with the likes of James Agee and Carson McCullers. Nichols put the spiritual emptiness of the novel's central character in the same realm as a painting by Edward Hopper and Arthur Miller's play *Death of a Salesman*. Connell "writes of the troubles of the ordinary human heart as if he were its right ventricle."[14] William Hogan of the *San Francisco Chronicle* reminded readers that when he wrote about *The Anatomy Lesson* two years earlier he had predicted great things to come from Connell, and now the novel delivered even more than he had expected. *Mrs. Bridge*, Hogan wrote, brought with it the "shock of recognition" that Edmund Wilson once ascribed to emergent literary talents. Hogan compared the novel to the realism of Sinclair Lewis but declared Connell "an original."[15] And, beyond the pages of the newspaper, Hogan informed Elizabeth McKee that he intended to nominate *Mrs. Bridge* for a National Book Award and the Pulitzer Prize. When Connell learned of this, he hadn't a clue as to how those prizes worked but knew they came with big money and an easier future. "I suppose there's no harm speculating," he told Steele, "provided you don't feel outraged when the awards go to someone else."[16]

His hometown champions at the *Kansas City Star* were equally absorbed by his achievement. The paper's review began on the front page. Webster Schott, a freelance critic who would write about Connell and his books for decades, attributed the novel's power to "its almost terrifying reality" rather than its "technical virtuosity and Connell's sensitivity and concern." He continued, "If in its humor and sadness and sense of loss Mrs. Bridge seems like a 20th century tragedy, the tragedy is so moving because the people in this novel are so believably human." Schott found deep sadness in the book, a tone much tempered by "delightful humor." He had little to complain about and predicted Connell's novel would be one of the best of the year: "Mrs. Bridge belongs in spirit and genre to that select company which includes J. D. Salinger's *The Catcher in the Rye* and John Cheever's *The Wapshot Chronicle*." India Bridge, that "pathetically funny and tragically lost woman," was in effect a close fictional relative of Holden Caulfield and Leander Wapshot.[17]

Not everyone was won over by Connell's effort. Florence Crowther, reviewing *Mrs. Bridge* for the *New York Times*, called it a "wistful little book." She found "a touch of humor" and "sometimes mild pathos," but essentially it was all "unconvincing." She concluded, "It's hard to believe that a lady from Kansas City with a house in the best residential section, one full-time maid, one mink coat and a Lincoln for her very own, should finish up as timorous and ephemeral as a lunar moth on the outside of a window."[18]

In his *Times* review a few days later, Charles Poore was far more impressed, pronouncing the novel "a searching and memorable portrait of a lost lady." Although his review contained mostly plot summary and character analysis, Poore suggested that, in addition to the footprint of Machado de Assis, there were echoes of "Booth Tarkington's midland America."[19] From today's vantage, one can be fairly certain that this example was more a reference point than a lasting asset.

Fanny Butcher, the *Chicago Tribune*'s influential literary critic, endorsed *Mrs. Bridge* in a brief piece that captured what may well be the reason for the book's everlasting appeal: "The author's method of telling the story is touching, funny, and deeply convincing. This is a book in which somewhere nearly any woman would find at least a fleeting image of herself."[20]

Dorothy Parker devoted the tail end of her bimonthly books column in the March *Esquire* to Connell. After a resounding pan of two sex-laden novels, now long forgotten ("Lord, Lord, if I have to read any more about moist thighs . . ."), Parker turned her attention to what she sensed was "a highly important book":

This is the story, step by step, of a middle-class American wife and mother, living on the skirts of a small city. She is an occasional visitor of country clubs, she assists at charitable displays, she has the conventional two girls and a boy, and a husband devoted to his business. But *Mrs. Bridge* is no tale of Westport extramarital pavannes. Mr. Connell writes of his woman without patronage, without snickers, without, indeed, any comment whatever on what he sets down of her life. He tells her story, less in sketches than in paragraphs, and how it is done I only wish I knew, but he makes Mrs. Bridge, her husband and her children and her neighbors understandable, moving, in his few taut words.

Parker went off on a stylistically interesting digression. At first she thought there was one episode in the book that didn't feel quite so real—the European vacation that Walter and India take in the late 1930s. Parker felt Connell had "gone a little overboard, a little Sinclair Lewis." Then she recalled a recent gathering among some "International Set" friends who were visited by a southern couple just back from their first trip overseas. The travelers "told us all about their expressions and experiences." For Parker, this was a re-velatory moment in retrospect: "No, Mr. Connell did not exagger-ate. In *Mrs. Bridge*, he never did anything that was not perfect."[21] Connell beamed, "God bless Dorothy Parker."[22]

Parker's review served to square accounts in a way with *Esquire*, the men's interest magazine edited by Arnold Gingrich. The maga-zine's fiction editor, L. Rust Hills, had wanted to publish a cutting from the novel, but Gingrich objected. In Hills's telling, the ex-change went like this:

"It's bland as junket and totally offensive," Gingrich said.
"But Arnold, how can a thing be bland as junket and totally offensive?"
"I don't want to discuss it," said Gingrich.[23]

It is unclear whether Gingrich harbored ill feelings for Connell or just had, perhaps, unresolved feelings for his own mother. He had, recall, published Connell's "Crash Landing" not long before. And in subsequent years Hills successfully shepherded more of Connell's work into the magazine.

More printings. More reviews. More publicity in popular media. The book climbed up the *New York Times* bestseller list, then stalled at No. 9 or 10. Connell kept track. He equated the practice with following the stock market—"up two points, down one, what will happen next week?" The first six weeks of a San Francisco bestseller list produced this performance, he noted: "3, 2, 4, 4, 5, 3."[24] A British edition was in the works. "Apparently they have some matrons too."[25] So was a German translation. Connell's sister, Barbara, heard that one discussed on a television show. There was talk of a Broadway adaptation, but Connell was skeptical. When a ten-page contract arrived from the team of David Shaber and William Snyder—Shaber would produce, Snyder would write—Connell recounted some of its crucial details in a letter to Steele. He wondered if he'd be signing away too much of the future revenue of the book and other possible properties, in which the producers would share. A month later, he signed the contract. In July 1961, Connell learned from his agent that Claudette Colbert had turned down the role of India Bridge. Beyond that the play never materialized.[26]

Connell welcomed the note, handwritten, that arrived in March from John Updike. He had finished reading *Mrs. Bridge* the night before and was haunted by it for hours. Updike had read the excerpt "Mademoiselle from Kansas City," which had appeared in *Contact* a few months earlier and eagerly awaited the book. "And that scene in the country club with the tornado coming—etc. etc." Updike said he missed a scene that had appeared in *Contact* and noticed a change or two. He wondered if Connell had cut the novel—"I could have read twice as much," he wrote. Like Connell, Updike had only recently emerged as a promising American writer, known for short stories published in the *New Yorker* and his first collection. Updike's first novel, *Rabbit, Run*, with its portrayal of average American lives, would appear a year after *Mrs. Bridge*. In a brotherly gesture, he said of Connell's book, "it's all frighteningly good."[27]

After five years in San Francisco, Connell always seemed to be comforted by the views beyond his writing desk. He could rhapsodize about such scenes, as if meditating on the weather were a natural condition of the writer's life. And certainly it added to San Francisco's "magical" qualities. "At eight this morning," he wrote to Steele, "the sky was brilliant cerulean; by nine it was a milky opalescent blue because of a high, thin fog; now it is a little after ten and the fog is rolling thickly backward across the hills to the ocean, only the tops of one or two apartment houses on Nob Hill are indistinct." Later the buildings would turn pastel and he could see the low mountains past Berkeley and Oakland. "Well, it's for this and other such things that I live here, and the fact that some August days are so cool you need a wool shirt and a jacket."[28] San Francisco was the best American city, he told Steele. And after the launch of *Mrs. Bridge*, the waitresses at the Buena Vista restaurant, "who have ignored me for three years now appear pleased to see me, what next?"[29]

Connell, in fact, was trying to tempt the restless Steele into moving to San Francisco. Steele had stopped teaching and was talking of traveling to Mexico and relocating. Maybe New Orleans. Maybe the Bay Area. Connell talked him up in book circles. And more scenery: "The bay sparkles in the sun, the pastel buildings not unlike Miami Beach, there will be many sailboats under and around the Gate and Alcatraz and the beaches redolent with female bodies, or from, or of. And you can't beat that, so to speak."[30]

When he wasn't revising *The Patriot* or writing letters, Connell worked out regularly at a YMCA, spent time at the beach, loitered around the city, sketched and painted nude models, flirted with women in art museums. He listened to baseball games on the radio and occasionally attended them, though he preferred going to Stanford football games down in Palo Alto. He also read widely. He might have taken particular interest in Nathanael West's *The Day of the Locust* (1939) because of his own brief dalliance in Hollywood, but he wasn't much impressed. He figured West's novel had been "tossed off one weekend" and found it "entertaining, incisive in a superficial way."[31] At the same time, he also happened to be reading the recently published *Great Cases of Psychoanalysis*, particularly an article by Carl Jung. "He writes like a teacher explaining the elements of geometry to a roomful of average students."[32] The workings of the mind, of course, serve as essential prime territory for writers. The influence of Sigmund Freud on American culture and conversation had become well ingrained, though his ideas were still controversial by the late 1950s. Connell had actually considered psychiatry as an emphasis when he was studying at Dartmouth and expecting to gravitate to medical school. Yet he was ever the autodidact, and his reading here is reminiscent of the advice the young Ernest Hemingway once received from a friend that to be a writer he didn't need to go to college, just arm himself with a good textbook in psychology.

Connell had good words to say about Janet Lewis's "lovely short novel," *The Wife of Martin Guerre* (1941), a book he would later tout in an essay. Nevertheless, he told one correspondent that the novels he read were often classics that most people had gotten to before he did. He tried to get into *War and Peace* but failed for the third time. He also conceded defeat, if not boredom, at the hands of Henry James and William Faulkner. And even Chekhov, whom he acknowledged as an influence, was capable of producing "some rank and foolish things." Overall, he wrote, "I do a fair amount of miscellaneous reading—from De Sade to the Viking explorations in America and the Muybridge experiments in photography, and quite a few story collections."[33]

One day Connell shared an event stage in San Francisco—and a meal of chicken, peas, and raspberry sherbet—with a lineup of prominent writers. He listed them in a letter to Steele: Elizabeth Bowen, Stephen Spender, Niven Busch, Janet Lewis, Barnaby Conrad, Lady Carolyn Freud, and Christopher Herold, recent winner of a National Book Award for his biography of Madame de Staël. Connell was fine with appearances, he said, because they might sell a few books, but he regretted accepting speaking engagements and essentially stuck with that policy for the rest of his career.

Connell also shared a lunch table one day with Pascal Covici, an esteemed editor at Viking. Covici gossiped about some of his writers, including Max Bodenheim and John Steinbeck. And in the evenings, Connell was hanging out with a young, ponytailed painter named Jill Strohn. On one outing they bundled up in the San Francisco chill to watch July 4 fireworks on the Marina Green.

Connell appreciated a letter he got from an editor at the *Nation*, who asked if he would like to write something. He didn't have any ideas at the moment, but he was happy to be asked. George Plimpton asked Connell to interview Aldous Huxley for the *Paris Review*, but Connell declined that opportunity as well: "I wouldn't know how to go about it and am afraid I would feel a bit uncomfortable, which, in turn, might make him so."[34] Connell had sometimes identified himself as a journalist, but the thought of conducting one of those intensive interviews for the *Paris Review* did not square with the typical methods in his writer's toolbox. Connell suggested that Plimpton ask Steele to do it. (The Huxley interview appeared a year later under the byline of Raymond Fraser and George Wickes.)

Plimpton also was planning an anthology of *Paris Review* stories and successfully sought permission to include one of Connell's.

Over the summer of 1959, Elizabeth McKee expressed concern about Connell's finances and hoped he could hold on until receiving his first royalty check from *Mrs. Bridge*, which was scheduled to land in his mailbox in late August. He did. And his fortunes rose considerably when he pocketed nearly $6,000 from Viking (more than $50,000 in today's currency). In turn, that fall he frequently offered Steele financial aid, as his friend had left teaching to write. Steele declined the help.

Late that year, Connell's work appeared in at least two more books. One was *Fiction of the Fifties*, an anthology, edited by Herbert Gold, intending to represent the literary pulse of the day. Writers weren't so different than those of other times, Gold acknowledged in his introduction, but "a special kind of light has been focused, a direction marked out, and when we look at the contemporary writers who mean much to us at this end of the decade we may see how they have responded as a group to the particular disasters and challenges of our time."[35]

James Baldwin, represented by "Sonny's Blues," offered this perspective: "What the times demand, and in an unprecedented fashion, is that one be—not seem—outrageous, independent, anarchical."[36]

Connell was impressed by Baldwin's statement and by his story, and he also took note of one by Anatole Broyard. Connell was not so fond of his own contribution, "The Condor and the Guests," an early (1948) farce imbued with social satire and environmentalist reverberations set in Kansas. Yet, he could feel some satisfaction in being highlighted alongside the likes of Saul Bellow and Flannery O'Connor.

In response to Gold's request to comment on the state of writing at the time, Connell offered a typical parry: "Any sort of response would necessarily be so speculative that I am rather hesitant to attempt any reply. This age makes demands on us all; perhaps more than ever before, our very lives depend on the capacity of our nerves to withstand the thought of instantaneous annihilation, and no doubt this condition reflects itself with greater or lesser subtlety in every action, most profoundly in such action as we term creative."[37] To write, in other words, is to survive.

A reviewer for *Kirkus* called Baldwin's contribution outstanding and noted that Bellow's story, "A Sermon by Doctor Pep," matched Gold's vision for writing that "expresses most clearly the philosophical and religious quest necessarily contained within all abiding sense for passing things." The critic concluded, "A few of Mr. Gold's selections are disappointing (perhaps stories about suburbia have become too commonplace in recent fiction to be appealing or vital any more), but they are all consistent in their attempt to give coherent expression to a wide range of contemporary American experience and to avoid the label of 'beat' or 'angry.'"[38]

It is hard to know whether the critic was thinking of Connell's story when honing that judgment—too much suburbia?—though on certain levels one can agree that for the most part Connell clearly did avoid associating with the literary qualities attributed to the angry writers and the Beats.[39]

After the British edition of *Mrs. Bridge* appeared in early 1960, the *Guardian* weighed in with kind words for the "quietly skillful" novel. Connell managed to bring India Bridge to life "with a technique that employs numerous snapshots taken from shrewdly selected angles." Critic Roy Perrott admired the book's "satire and sympathy" and called the title character "as irrational as any coconut islander, though less instinctive."[40] Connell already had some coconut island experience under his belt, so it's likely he recognized the comparison.

Connell was pleased though realistic when *Mrs. Bridge* reached the long list for the National Book Award in fiction for 1960. There it stood, an ego-boosting affirmation alongside such prominent titles as Saul Bellow's *Henderson the Rain King*, Shirley Jackson's *The Haunting of Hill House*, and William Faulkner's *The Mansion*, and, in hindsight, long-forgotten novels by Hamilton Basso, Louis Auchincloss, James Jones, Mark Harris and, again, John Hersey (*The War Lover*). Connell and the rest became also-rans when Philip Roth landed the prize for his debut story collection, *Goodbye, Columbus*. Helen Taylor had predicted that Connell would not win, and he understood. As for Roth, Connell had read some of his stories, and as a result, "I'd judge he was good."[41]

A paperback edition gave *Mrs. Bridge* continued life and every now and then he'd hear from friends, especially writer friends who correctly predicted that the novel had lasting value. "I have read *Mrs. Bridge*, and I wanted to tell you that I think it is one hell of a fine book," William Styron wrote. "It has all the earmarks of a classic, and I am certain (or as certain as one can be in this chancy world) that it will be read many years hence. If, finally, there is any truth in Proust's dictum to the effect that all that matters is the respect of one's fellow writers, well, for what little it may be worth, you have mine, believe me. Excuse my presumption in writing you, but I have come to think that these things matter."[42] Styron went public with his praise for Connell around the same time, referring to his "sharp, remarkably observant talent" in the introduction to the *Paris Review* story collection that Plimpton put together. "The Fisherman from Chihuahua," Connell's Santa Cruz story, appeared first in the lineup.[43]

As a book of its moment, *Mrs. Bridge* attracted, despite some critical nippers, a wide and adoring audience. But few ephemeral bestsellers survive, year after year, decade after decade, as certified American classics. It is useful to look closer at some of the qualities of Connell's novel that helped it live on as essential literature— qualities that speak to the evolution and maturity of his writing and to the transcendent vision which shaped it. Start with the epigraph. Connell did not choose such scene-setters lightly for his books. Almost anyone can identify with the sense of yearning evoked by the quote from Walt Whitman: "But where is what I started for so long ago? And why is it yet unfound?" Life is a quest—a long desire, a wrestle with time—and we are not always sure to where or why. Even Connell, as he states over and over. Where do I belong? What is home? How can I find a sense of satisfaction? Such longing can be felt throughout *Mrs. Bridge*. Each character possesses a piece of it in her or his own way.

From scene to scene, moments of deep insight accompany many of its small motions. "I believe it was Chekhov who observed that people do not go to the North Pole, or whatever; they eat cabbage soup and fall off stepladders," Connell once said. "I think he was right, which is why there is no extraordinary event in the life of Mrs. Bridge."[44] Throughout this and subsequent works, Connell operated with the sense promoted by Plutarch that "a slight thing like a phrase or a jest often makes a greater revelation of character than battles when thousands fall."[45]

Connell delivers this quotidian wisdom lightly but assuredly. Very late in the novel, dwelling on the coming of war, on anxious thoughts about her three grown children, India Bridge is "lost in confusion." She lies down to rest, she tries to think about a happier past, but all she can determine is that these things happen. Why?

"One day, while shopping on the Plaza, she had recognized someone who used to live next door to her when she was a child. The woman was now evidently verging on old age, and Mrs. Bridge, counting down the years as she observed, from a distance, the conclusion of the youth which was her own, felt a drowning sense of despair and futility, and ever after that day she felt herself moved a little more slowly."[46] Time certainly can be cruel.

Connell earned a close, midcareer reading by a writer he had once met and who later became a good friend. Gus Blaisdell, a poet and editor in Albuquerque, published his assessment of Connell's first six books in 1966, in an essay in *New Mexico Quarterly*. Yes, he agreed, *Mrs. Bridge* was a masterpiece, but given where Connell was headed, Blaisdell wrote, "in comparison with the breadth of Connell's later work, it is a very small masterpiece."[47]

More detail on this later, but as for *Mrs. Bridge*, Blaisdell made several points that attest to its lasting reputation. For one: "India Bridge is the mother of most Americans, a fact that makes her pitiful, real, and worthy of compassion, as evidenced by Douglas' behavior during his father's funeral—he immediately becomes the man of the house because he understands his mother's inability to cope, finding it both natural and sad."[48]

To excavate some of Connell's most exactingly inspired achievements, Blaisdell highlights a subtle but crucial episode one night when Mrs. Bridge notices a flash of lightning. Walter Bridge looks up from his paper and wonders if he'd heard the clock strike. Connell writes, "She never forgot this moment when she had almost apprehended the very meaning of life, and of the stars and the planets, yes, and the flight of the earth."[49] As Blaisdell sees it, "The key to this passage is Matsuo Basho's famous haiku about the person who, seeing summer lightning flash, does not feel that life is fleeting. With a few deft strokes Connell establishes a basic difference between India and Walter Bridge." To that, he adds, "*Mrs. Bridge* is a singular formal achievement. It is circumspect and gracious in style, oblique but always with the center in view."[50]

Four decades later, another critic, Mark Oppenheimer, pronounced Connell's portrait of his mother figure as "one of the truest in modern literature": "India Bridge is a decent woman, hopefully naïve, willfully unliberated, cursed with a brain she is afraid to use and time that she cannot manage to fill."[51] So *Mrs. Bridge* has maintained a long reach on American bookshelves.

Meg Wolitzer, a novelist born in the year that *Mrs. Bridge* was published, fondly recalls growing up surrounded by her parents' books, including several marked-up copies of the novel. Her father was a therapist, her mother a writer and teacher, and both were avid readers. Wolitzer still recalls the pink and gold accents of the book's original jacket as a totemic presence. Even more, the novel became a touchstone of American literature, one she publicly extolled in 2018, nearly fifty years after its appearance. "It's just a daring book," she told me a year later, when she visited Connell's hometown for a lecture. "It remains that to me. . . . What you learn from your parents, either you reject it or accept it. I was of the opinion that this was a classic novel, because my mother and father loved it. . . . And when I entered the world of writers, I realized that book occupied a very special place."[52]

In her essay about the novel, Wolitzer highlighted the sensation of being inside it as one reads, a quality shared by only the best of books and one she did not attribute to *Mr. Bridge* or the 1990 movie that drew from both of them:

> It's not just that the novel is formally unconventional, about a supremely conventional person, or has much to say about repression, subjugation and emptiness. Its tone—knowing, droll, plaintive, shuttling rapidly between pain and hilarity— elevates it to its own kind of specialness. When Mrs. Bridge's former art instructor appears at the door in bad shape, selling magazines, out of pity she agrees to buy a subscription to *The Doberman*, despite not owning a dog. "Gadbury raised his head and looked at her in grave astonishment." As do we, repeatedly.[53]

Wolitzer credits the humor—that understated, dark, sometimes tragic hilarity—Connell gently injects into the narrative as one of the book's defining qualities. She also appreciates the honest and deep reflection of a woman's consciousness that was so original for its day, given the many male writers who came to dominate the literary scene—Updike, Roth, and Heller among them. Years before our conversation, Wolitzer had taught the book in an adult-education class in New York and was confronted with a reading that valorized India Bridge as some kind of pre-feminist goddess. "To read it purely that she would've been a different person if born a little later is perhaps missing the point," Wolitzer told me. "It's more complicated than that, because she is defined not only by the limitations imposed on her by her era, but also by her own specific qualities. The class certainly loved the book. And I think some of them were older and interested in the ways that possibilities for women had changed over time. But one person expressly saw her as a feminist heroine, and I guess if I'm going to look at Mrs. Bridge through that lens, I see her more as a feminist cautionary tale."[54]

While *Mrs. Bridge* might or might not represent a piece of proto-feminism—maybe more so if one were to compare and contrast the behaviors of the mother and her daughters—the novel, according to Mark Oppenheimer, "exploded the feminine mystique four years before Betty Friedan invented the term."[55]

Gender consciousness and the anxious interplay of men and women would continue as one of Connell's important themes in fiction. While *Mrs. Bridge* announced Connell's certain arrival as a top-tier writer, it by no means freed him from creative struggle. *The Patriot* would clarify for him the risks and obstacles of trying to make successful fiction. And, following that, his next major project, along with others in the years ahead, found him engaged in journeys that took him in wildly different directions.

Fragments of History, Fragments of Mind
1960–1962

"Within you there is something more powerful than
yourself."

—Connell to Max Steele, October 27, 1959

AS MUCH AS he wanted to move on with his work, Connell was
stuck in the past. *The Patriot* manuscript remained a mess. The
book hewed closely to his own life experience, even more so than
Mrs. Bridge. The central character of *The Patriot*, Melvin Isaacs,
like Douglas Bridge, was an introverted rebel. But he joined the
Naval Air Corps and trained as a pilot during World War II, as
had Connell. It was intended to be Connell's first book, but Viking
chose to go with the story collection and then *Mrs. Bridge.* In a
way, with its rather more conventional structure, *The Patriot*
would look and feel and read like a step backward. But it was a
step to which he—and Viking—had committed. With *Mrs. Bridge*
running its course in the marketplace—foreign editions were appearing, a U.S. paperback was on deck—it was time to wrestle the
bigger novel to the ground.

Connell submitted yet another draft of *The Patriot* to Viking in
the fall of 1959. The reaction, the waiting, the demands for change
had been so frustrating he felt he couldn't work on other things. So
he idled away the days in a little park on the beach, in view of the
Golden Gate Bridge, "reading miscellaneous detritus. Casanova's
memoirs, recollections of Whitehead, the conquest of Peru and
why the dodo lost its wings."[1] Connell also read a long essay by
Norman Mailer in *Esquire*, an extraordinary self-examination and

play-by-play experience about his troubles revising and publishing his third novel, *The Deer Park*. What Mailer had to say sounded much like the script going through Connell's head: "Taking The Deer Park into the nervous system of eight publishing houses was not so very good for my own nervous system, nor was it good for getting to work on my new novel. . . . I squandered the careful energy I had been hoarding for months."[2]

Connell could identify: "He should hear my sad story," he told Steele. Unlike Mailer, Connell had ceded some of that energy to his agent, but he had paid close attention to her every move. Now, a half-dozen Viking editors were all over his manuscript, and Helen Taylor was planning to visit Connell early in the new year to talk about the book. "I feel exasperated and truculent and somewhat befuddled," he had told Steele during his struggle with an earlier draft. He was comfortable with the state of the novel, "and it doesn't seem formless," as one of the Viking readers had put it. Another said he couldn't tell which way the novel was going. Someone had sent Connell a copy of John Hersey's *War Lover*, a novel about a World War II pilot that Knopf had published that year, hoping he'd find a sense of direction. Despite its eventual status as a National Book Award finalist, Connell found Hersey's novel to be "at best mediocre" and "obviously manufactured."[3] And its sense of flight never approached that which Connell admired in "St. X," or Antoine de Saint-Exupéry, who was something of a standard-setter for those in thrall with aviation. Connell knew Viking would publish his book, but he didn't want to sign a contract until he was convinced they were satisfied with it. He was tired of the hassle yet he sent off a copy of the latest draft to Steele, along with some of the Viking criticisms. Steele had already read two earlier versions of the novel. Perhaps his advice could help.

Among other things, Steele had earlier thought the secondary characters, including the father and many women, were shallow. The novel, he said, was unpublishable at that point, though he knew Connell had the talent to make it good. Of version number three, Steele delivered a full and frank critique. He recognized *The*

Patriot's theme from earlier Connell stories—the artist against the world, in which Melvin the son is the artist and his father, Jacob, is the conventional American. Steele correctly judged that the climactic "suicide dive" chapter, a version of which had appeared in *Esquire*, verged on greatness. Still, he thought the subsequent chapters meandered and the whole scheme needed to be rearranged.[4]

Connell shared Steele's critique with Helen Taylor when she arrived in San Francisco for their meeting in February, and she took Steele's points seriously. Nevertheless, Connell had expected more of a clash in his conference with Taylor. In the end, he came away from it with only a long list of relatively minor revisions and a planned publication date in the fall. Afterward, he told Steele, he feverishly rewrote day and night and hoped to send off the manuscript of *The Patriot* "for the leventy-leventh time" in a few weeks.[5]

The second issue of *Contact* reflects—unfortunately, from today's perspective—a truth of midcentury American literature. Every one of the eight contributors whose photographs appeared on the rear cover was a white man. All but a couple of the names on the masthead belonged to white men, the exceptions including the linguist S. I. Hayakawa, an advisory editor, and an art director, Barney Wan. This was the reality of Connell's emergence into the hallowed hall of literary recognition. A local critic enabled the male dominance of the journal when he lauded its "breadth of taste . . . [and] rugged masculinity."[6] One is left only to speculate how the few female contributors to that issue—the poet Joanne de Longchamps and five or six street photographers in a portfolio on "The Human Condition"—felt about the characterization.

A *Contact* advertisement at the back of the new edition touted its earlier contributors, including Connell. The ad quoted from Dorothy Parker's rave review of *Mrs. Bridge*: "A highly important book."

One of Connell's earliest mentors, Wallace Stegner, took up half the second issue with a novella that presented a deep reflection on that sense of rugged masculinity. His story, "Genesis," encompassed a boy's education on an early twentieth-century cattle ranch in the high plains of western Canada.

By the third issue, in fall 1959, *Contact* managed to weave in more women's voices, including the poets Denise Levertov and Maxine Kumin, fiction by Mary Lee Settle, and an interview with the playwright Lillian Hellman. Walter Van Tilburg Clark, one of *Contact*'s advisory editors, had a byline, in an article announcing a new development for the magazine. It had merged with the *Western Review* and took on its editor, Ray B. West, Connell's former Kansas writing teacher, now at San Francisco State. Clark recounted the evolution of West's project from its Utah beginnings through three years in Kansas and a decade at the Iowa writers' workshop. Both journals were in the business of scouring the vast region beyond New York, beyond the Rocky Mountains, for fine literature. As Connell told Steele, perhaps with a healthy dose of wishful thinking, "This area seems to be growing into the new literary center of the country."[7] Still, Clark recognized a "ferment" in the writing world of the day, one much like that of the fertile 1920s. Writers now, especially those in the West and those reflected in the pages of *Contact*, represented "another questing for values and for the forms that can embody them effectively."[8]

Connell, in the same issue, seemed very much like a writer in search of deep values. And those values happened to be wrapped in an effective, if also experimental, form. The magazine included a ten-page piece of another current project, one that represented a wholly new direction for the author of *Mrs. Bridge* and *The Patriot*. Titled "Notes from a Bottle Found on the Beach at Carmel," the article or story or whatever it was presented meditations on history that looked like a long prose poem. Connell called it "a bizarre little bit of poesy."[9]

Someone sent a copy of *Contact 3* to Thorpe Menn at the *Kansas City Star*, who praised the journal as refreshing evidence of a so-called San Francisco Renaissance. As for *Contact*'s presentation of a kind of artistic experiment and modernism, Menn wrote, "It's as if a modern Mark Twain had appeared to replace pretentiousness with the lusty vigor of the Old West—as American literature should be." And then, commenting specifically on Connell's unusual piece, Menn found it fascinating, obscure at times but stimulating. He quoted Connell's odd introductory note in the journal, which, judging from a letter to Steele, Connell never intended to be used: "It has, for me a curious fascination. I look on it as I would someone dancing a queer and private dance, thinking himself unobserved. . . . Truly, I don't know what it is."[10] One thing Connell did not say about the work was that, as a piece of writing, it was perhaps 180 degrees the opposite of *Mrs. Bridge*. It shared certain properties of a fragmentary consciousness, but its nonlinear qualities would not necessarily win the hearts of editors or satisfy a market looking for a proper follow-up to Connell's debut novel.

The "Notes" project looked like poetry but it read like an assemblage of strange tidbits of history and philosophy, a commonplace book, if you will, with running commentary. Connell shaped it with an uncanny sense of forward momentum and propelled readers to unexpected and uncertain places. From the outside, Menn recognized Connell's Euripedean theme of searching for mystery and meaning in the vast unknown. In his fragments of history, Connell could write what others could only think about, Menn suggested in his *Star* column.

Connell's project prompted a somewhat different evaluation from an editor at the *Atlantic Monthly*, who had returned a submission sent by his agent: "Here's the Connell, which we have all read without extracting the slightest meaning from it. What, may I ask, do you think is going on there? Thanks anyway—wouldn't have missed it—broadening experience."[11]

The excerpt in *Contact* opened (as does the later book) with a scene from the gruesome public execution of Robert-François Damiens, the ne'er-do-well servant who had made a failed attempt, with a knife, on the life of King Louis XV. After the flesh-searing attacks on Damiens's bound body, "Four horses were not enough to draw him apart."[12]

From there we read of the dreams of Mexican peasants in a valley of the Sierra Madres who come to believe that a random orange coursing down the river portends their discovery of a fabled silver mine.

Wanderers, explorers, men of God and faith, and believers in the certainty of death, or Death, make appearances in Connell's procession of discrete shards. He is very much self-conscious about the kaleidoscopic appearance of his enterprise, as he declares in a one-line segment: "Whenever the barrel is turned the crystal tumbles."[13] Connell, of course, was an avid reader, and one can imagine him with his pencil marking or copying anecdotes that struck him as odd or pertinent or particularly startling.[14] One can also imagine him being absorbed and very likely inspired by an earlier book of meditative fragments, *The Unquiet Grave* by the British writer, editor, and critic Cyril Connolly. Published in 1944, Connolly's book has been a literary touchstone ever since, though Connell evidently never mentioned it in print.[15]

If some remained in the dark after ten pages of Connell's curious meditations in the magazine, the performance made other readers clamor for more. Connell initially had no plan to keep the project going. But an inquiry from the poet and playwright George Hitchcock prompted Connell to think about expanding it: "I decided that I'd see if I could carry on with it for a book-length manuscript."[16] And, indeed, the magazine eventually would publish Connell's "bizarre bit of poesy" in its entirety, several months before *Notes from a Bottle* appeared as a book.

It would be undocumented folly to directly connect Connell's historical mash-ups with his introduction to psychotropic drugs. But the coincidence begs for at least a brief discussion. In 1959, through a physician friend in Los Angeles, Connell met Dr. Oscar Janiger, who was among a group of psychotherapists conducting experiments with lysergic acid diethylamide (LSD). The drug had been discovered and developed in Switzerland. It attracted the attention of brain scientists as well as the CIA for its hallucinogenic properties and what might be learned about the human mind under its influence. Connell became one of hundreds of subjects in Janiger's experiments. He was lesser known than, say, Cary Grant.

The Hollywood star's public rave about the psychedelic experience opened the door to Timothy Leary's cheerleading at Harvard, if not to the ultimate government crackdown on psychedelics and those who used them.

Connell, who tried it in 1959, found LSD to be "extraordinary." The experiment took place at Janiger's summer house on Big Bear Lake outside Los Angeles. He didn't feel sexually stimulated, but at one point when he tried to visualize a female image, all he got was a pattern of figures like those of a water ballet, or again like something seen through a kaleidoscope. "I was mostly absorbed, as is everyone during the initial experience, by insignificant items such as one's fingernail or skin texture," he wrote. He was riveted by his discovery "that within you there is something more powerful than yourself."[17] He wanted to try it again, in a stronger dose, though he was aware of the potential for losing control. He wouldn't be so stupid, he told Steele, to just abandon himself to enjoying the drug.

Connell went public with his experience a couple of years later: "I can clearly recall clutching the edge of a table with both hands in a desperate and futile attempt to hold on to reality, or what we assume to be real." His platform was a book review, written for the Kansas City newspaper. Under consideration were two new books, one by a Hollywood actress using a pseudonym, the other by Alan Watts, the philosopher and popularizer of Zen Buddhism in the West. An introductory editor's note announced that Connell had participated in research experiments with hallucinogens. In the review's opening paragraphs, Connell helpfully aimed to describe the indescribable: "Those who have taken LSD report almost without exception that it is their most overwhelming single experience to such a degree that many who have tried the drug are reluctant even to discuss it. The happening is scarcely communicable in words, at least to the uninitiated. One does not, for example, merely remember past experiences; one re-experiences them." He went on to describe Dr. Janiger's own recovery of boyhood sensations of kicking up dust and feeling the sun while walking on a country road. And Connell mentioned an LSD episode related by another Los Angeles friend, Dr. J. R. Bueno, who was plunged into a terrifying "reliving" of a journey down the Amazon. In his review, Connell complains about the melodramatic account of "Constance A. Newland" (*My Self and I*) but heaps praise on Watts's "brief, poetic essay" (*The Joyous Cosmology*). He quotes at length Watts's anecdote about a summer afternoon on a garden terrace when "the people with me are no longer the humdrum and harassed little personalities with names, addresses and social security numbers, the specifically dated mortals we are all pretending to be. They appear rather as immortal archetypes of themselves without, however, losing their humanity."[18]

Connell's LSD experience gave him something in common with Richard Alpert (the future Baba Ram Das), who had experimented with the drug as a doctoral student at Stanford before going on to Harvard and teaming up with Leary. The connection came to light in a memoir by Alice Denham, a curious witness to midcentury modern literature. Denham was a southern transplant to New York who modeled for a living and desperately wanted to write. Hugh Hefner, the publisher of *Playboy*, featured her in one issue with both a short story and a nude centerfold. Denham's passion for literature nearly equaled her sexual prowess, and as a result she logged encounters, not all of them happy, with numerous esteemed literati. "Evan was the most strikingly handsome writer I'd ever met," she wrote. Her one-night stand with Connell followed a party hosted by Alpert in Palo Alto, though her timeline is fuzzy and Connell later questioned many of her details.[19] Both of them fortified by tequila, Denham and Connell made merry. The next day, on a drive along the coast, Denham ran into the Connell conundrum—after all her chattering about the people she knew, the men she'd rebuffed, the writing she was trying to do, he had nothing to say. They sat in silence for an hour: "I couldn't get through to him."[20]

Connell's fascination with the transformative properties of LSD did not apparently last, even as the psychedelic 1960s unfolded in San Francisco like a kaleidoscopic, ever-expanding blossom. By one friend's account, he did not return to the drug later in the 1960s. And he even expressed displeasure over her use of marijuana. Another friend, Anne Lamott, said Connell never discussed taking acid and added that he would have stayed away from it for fear of losing control. Still, Connell's experience along the multitudinal "doors of perception" (in the phrase of Aldous Huxley, of whose experiments Connell was well aware) can be sensed from time to time as he himself went off to explore immortal archetypes, to find within that "something more powerful than yourself," and to invoke the "long desire" that shaped many of his intellectual quests.[21]

The editors of *Contact*, a group that soon included Connell, took up the subject of mind-altering drugs not long thereafter. They presented a first-person account of a psilocybin mushroom experience in Mexico alongside an essay on hallucinogens and the mind by a pediatric psychiatrist.[22]

With *The Patriot* revisions in the mail and off his shoulders, Connell could breathe, at least until the galleys came back in a couple of months. He considered taking a road trip to Reno—code for a bout of blackjack—and maybe Mexico. And he offered his volunteer services to *Contact*, as a preliminary reader and rejectionist. He picked up a bundle of manuscripts, all of it "wretched material."[23]

Connell encouraged Steele to submit his work to the magazine. He was also amused by *Contact*'s leaders' plans to expand into book publishing even as they claimed continued tight finances. No matter the foolishness of it, Connell was involved in the first two books to come from the Contact Editions imprint of Angel Island Publications. One was a collection of San Francisco photographs by Jerry Stoll. His pictures from the streets and from behind the cultural scenes reflected the city's bohemian and artistic pulse. Titled *I Am a Lover* (1961), the book included an absurdist introductory note by Connell: "So here is a book of photography, about which nothing will be said."[24] His point was that the photographs spoke for themselves. But Connell also provided a series of atmospheric quotations meant to echo the grainy realism of the photos and serve as a kind of meditative counterpoint. The book's title, for instance, came from a resonant line by Sherwood Anderson—"I am a lover and have not found my thing to love." That one happened to appear opposite a night scene which included Connell's friend Jill

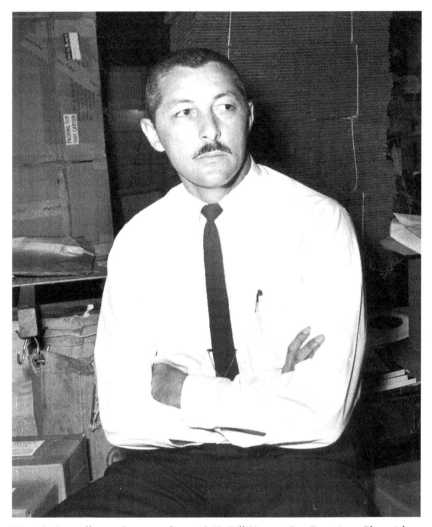

Fig. 19. Connell as a *Contact* editor, 1962. Bill Young, *San Francisco Chronicle*; courtesy of Polaris Images.

Strohn. She is wearing a long patterned coat, capri slacks, and flip-flop sandals, her cigarette being lit by a suited man in the vicinity of the lighted Coit Tower.[25] Connell supposedly mined many of the texts by reading an entire volume of *Bartlett's Familiar Quotations*.

The second Contact Editions book would be a fiction collection edited by Ray West. *A Country in the Mind* (1962), featuring work that had appeared in West's *Western Review*, includes Connell's long story "Arcturus" as well as pieces by Walter Van Tilburg Clark and Wallace Stegner.

Connell also contributed to another budget-busting Contact Editions project, *The Artists' and Writers' Cookbook*. The book was beautifully designed by Nicolas Sidjakov, one of Connell's frequent chess partners at the No Name Bar in Sausalito, and published in a slipcase. Connell offered a recipe for paella, which he'd gotten from a Barcelona restaurant in hopes that a girlfriend would make it. He never was known to cook, even for himself. "Usually it's very good," Connell writes of the dish, "though, of course, there are times when the *paella* doesn't turn out just right for one reason or another, but if you have plenty of wine nobody will care."[26]

Connell did not have much hope for *The Patriot*. He just wanted to get past it. As he told Steele after finishing revisions, "some copy readers find it 'strange' and 'baffling' and by now I say the hell with it." He wasn't expecting good reviews. If it didn't sell, he wouldn't care. But one thing was clear to him: he would never "spend that much time on a book again, not unless I know what I'm doing."[27]

It was wholly within style for Connell that when *The Patriot* appeared in print, the book's jacket bore an art historian's delight. Rather than picturing some twentieth-century pilot, the design presented a drawing by Albrecht Dürer—charging warriors on horseback, their weapons held high, and an angel above. The angel's outstretched forefinger could be interpreted as either pointing the way or expressing judgment. Connell's take on war and patriotism woven within the novel's pages certainly seems to parallel the latter position on the presence and meaning of Dürer's angel. If nothing else, after all the anguish over finishing the book, the cover was one thing Connell liked about it.

Connell's fictional portrait of a young man's rite of passage, his rebellion against the world, offers a many-sided view of male anxieties. From the outset, the rather bumbling Melvin can't seem to help himself. He is the first of his new class of cadets to be publicly chastised—ten demerits and four hours of extra duty. His crime? He turned his head during formation in order to watch a shapely woman pass by. Later, in Iowa, he scores a girlfriend for languid walks on Saturday night leave, but when sent out to Albuquerque, he can't manage to answer her plaintive, lovelorn letter. He can't decide what to do: "He thought he should write to her, but he did not want to. Finally he put the letter in the bottom of his locker, hoping it might somehow disappear."[28] Then, no sooner has Melvin fallen for a lovely girl on a train than she is talking his ear off on the phone at the naval base and he's hitting up his buddy for three hundred dollars to pay for her abortion: "She accepted the check as nonchalantly as though it were a potato chip, and he was taken aback once more by the incredible equanimity of women."[29]

Although there's no evidence that Connell paid for a girlfriend's abortion, much of the novel drew from Connell's own experiences, including the wholly convincing sections within the cockpit. Melvin's experience as an art student in Kansas—first embracing abstraction with "flamboyant assaults on canvas," invoking the spirit of Jackson Pollock, then denouncing it—might not have been Connell's, but they shared the search for life's meaning in the act of creation.[30] Beyond that, Connell's ventures into political satire and outright absurdity, while momentarily entertaining, feel somewhat forced and disconnected. Still, one might sense the spirit those sections share with Joseph Heller's military satire *Catch-22*, which would be published just a year later.

Connell did not limit his sensibilities to the character of Melvin. As one critic has noted, Connell portrays fellow flyer Patrick Cole as "an extremely skeptical and aloof young man who had learned too much from his study of history to be gulled by war-effort propaganda." He sets Cole up as a counterweight to "simple-minded patriotism" and "the hypocrisy which that patriotism so often breeds."[31] Indeed, in the middle of the book, Cole serves as a kind of philosophical conscience, feeding Melvin a lecture on untrustworthy governments and "the aphasia of the moral man."[32] It should also not be lost on us that Connell did not wash out of the Naval Air Corps, as Melvin Isaacs did. And though we know very little of what personal history Connell and Roger Barr, his artist friend from Barcelona, shared with each other, it's intriguing to learn that Barr himself washed out of his naval air service for a misstep aboard an aircraft carrier in the Pacific.[33]

About the novel's intimations of Melvin's Jewishness: Connell, of course, was writing in a period when Jewish writers were ascending on the American scene—Bellow, Mailer, Malamud, Roth, and Heller among them. Connell never comments on that or on whether he consciously sought to have Melvin Isaacs's story resonate alongside the others. Still, well into the novel, Connell depicts the Jewish wedding of Melvin's sister, Leah, and, almost near the end, readers learn that Melvin's mother had cousins who not only were Yiddish-speaking, Eastern European Jewish immigrants but also had survived the concentration camp at Auschwitz. Their arrival in the story gives Connell a topical plot point regarding World War II and the age of anxiety that followed, though it's one of the novel's more awkward sections as well.

By the fall of 1960 when *The Patriot* came out, the reviews were indeed mixed, though one critical blurb declared it "a highly original work of art." A Midwestern paper noted that "the perceptive author's examples of our society's absurdities are like the ground glass of a camera coming into focus."[34]

The book sold "all right," Connell told Steele, "though nothing spectacular."[35] Given all the work he'd put into it, the experience was mostly disappointing. He knew his old hometown newspaper planned to serialize *The Patriot*, but Granville Hicks's pan in the *Saturday Review of Literature* ("unfortunately it is a long step backward"), and another one in the *Star* by his Kansas City booster, Webster Schott, stung.[36] While *Mrs. Bridge* was nearly perfect, Schott wrote, *The Patriot* hardly did justice to Connell's vast talent.[37] It is clear from reading his review that Schott had been briefed by Connell on the torturous year of revisions. Schott even took the unusual step of writing to Connell's father, explaining his criticism in hopes that it wouldn't be taken personally.

Connell was not surprised or too much taken aback by the experience. As he put it to Steele, "Tant pis."[38] Viking remaindered the novel in 1962, barely eighteen months after its appearance.

Holiday magazine, a slick and popular monthly devoted to travel and the high life, put out a special San Francisco issue in April 1961. The offerings included a love letter to the Golden Gate Bridge by Connell. In addition to his reporting about fatal leaps—197 suicides, or 0.162 incidents per week, had been recorded since the bridge opened in 1937—Connell recounted the colorful, and sometimes tragic, history of the bridge's planning and construction. But he framed the straight-ahead details within some typically elegant evocations of San Francisco's sensual attractions: "The rectilinear red bridge is both a functioning structure and an element of the landscape, as if an Oriental artist had stamped his signature onto the scene." As a gateway to the Pacific Ocean and the lands beyond, one could imagine, looking westward as the sun went down, that it was possible to "step off the bridge and travel this golden road to Yokohama."[39]

Later in the piece, he delivers what feels like a defining account of the essence of a city to which he clearly remained attached:

Endlessly the light changes. A Southern California haze gives way to the full wash of Mediterranean color; an hour later the city stands forth in Nordic clarity.

This light draws artists from around the world and keeps them here, baffled and fascinated, whether they paint the city, the Bridge, the Bay or, as abstract expressionist Franz Kline says, "not the things that I see but the feelings that they arouse in me."

Traveling across the bridge is like finding yourself within a prism, witnessing the spectrum. From south to north the traveler curves through the viridian foliage and dark brick buildings of the Presidio to the main span of the bridge, rust-red despite the name of the paint; over the water (luminous, murky, opalescent, altering by the minute) from which the light seems refracted everywhere; through an electric-blue sky where white and dusty brown gulls hang suspended like paper birds dangling from strings, tilting, skidding and slipping in the Pacific wind that whines through the cables; then on down the ramp between the sienna hills of Marin County.

And at night, returning by way of Sausalito (a hotbed of dangerous, vehemently dissident individuals with un-American beards), traveling from north to south, across the Golden Gate, you behold a dream: there wink the vitreous topaz lights of San Francisco like the holy city of Byzantium.

There is a lot to unpack here—from Connell's heightened sensory impressions to his learned nods to ancient history, European vistas, and modern art. The mention of Byzantium loops back to the beginning of the piece, when he quoted General John Frémont on naming the channel: "I gave [it] the name *Chrysopylae*, or Golden Gate, for the same reason that the harbor of Byzantium was called *Chrysoceras*, or Golden Horn."[40] And near the end, the wicked little comment on the dangerous creatures of Sausalito. No doubt that was an ironic bit of inside baseball, an embrace of his friends, the barflies, and other locals he encountered on his frequent trips across the bay.

As if representing the Sausalito team, two of Connell's *Contact* colleagues also appeared in this *Holiday* issue. Kenneth Lamott profiled the San Quentin State Prison, the subject of a book he published the same year. Lamott captured the sense of civic pride that surrounded the prison's prime location on the bay and its colorful, crime-centered history.[41] Calvin Kentfield, the onetime merchant seaman, covered the waterfront: "In the beginning," he wrote, "San Francisco rose from the sea not like the sparkling Venus it is today, but more like some underwater satyr or naked leering demon from the grottoes of Poseidon."[42] Such literary color flowed thickly in the social circles Connell had come to know so well.

The Guggenheim Foundation in 1962 granted a creative writing fellowship to Connell—$3,600—to support publication of the *Notes from a Bottle* book. The category was fiction, which is another way to regard the work, given its poetic form, philosophical mediations, and floating narrative voice. Thorpe Menn, in Kansas

City, eventually summarized it this way: "The book consists of cryptic jottings by a lonely voyager of all times, reflecting a lament that Western civilization, given 2,000 years, could not rise to the grandeur of its ideals."[43] So, fiction. Why not? Then again, as one critic would put it, "This is not a novel. It is a philosophic extravaganza."[44]

In December 1962, *Contact 13* devoted eighty-five pages, just about the entire issue, to the full text of Connell's hybrid work. Connell had been sheepish about doing that. He feared it would look like a vanity project. Bill Ryan, who had published the original segments of the work in *Contact 3*, asked to see the finished product. Connell said he'd only agree to it if his fellow editors, Kenneth Lamott and Calvin Kentfield, signed on. They did. Lamott introduced the piece with a kind of awe. Connell, he wrote, "emerges as a cartographer of the darkest continent of all, the spirit of man." And he summarized Connell's historical journeys as a litany of time-traveling mystery, misery, and wonder: "the explorers of Vineland, the warriors of World War II, the ancient Etruscans, the perpetrators of the Hiroshima bomb, medieval alchemists, the saints, martyrs, and great heretics of the church, the builders of Chichén Itzá, the conquistadores, the composers of the Vedas, and the operators and victims of the gas chambers."[45] What Lamott, or even his introspective friend, didn't know at the time was that Connell would return to many of those same subjects in the years to come in more fully explored essays on travel and history.

By contrast, Connell's editors at Viking were unenthusiastic. Some of them loved his bravura and the occasional beauty of his lines. But they knew the book would be a tough sell. They concluded it lacked the surety and skill of, say, Ezra Pound's *Cantos*, and they urged Connell to shelve it until he had built a firmer reputation. "Again, the fame of your name is not enough to command waving of banners," Helen Taylor told him.[46] The text's appearance in *Contact* might well have been Connell's defiant response to Viking's resistance. He certainly did not want to deny contemporary readers the chance to absorb his historical perspectives on the global anxieties of the day. Viking soon enough gave in and brought out *Notes* five months later, in May 1963. Sales and income expectations were low. Viking knew it would lose money and had threatened Connell with a ten-dollar retail cover price, as if it were meant for an audience of elite poetry readers. In the end, the book was issued at six dollars (or fifty dollars in recent currency).

As his editors predicted, reviews were few and decidedly mixed. A San Francisco critic pounced on the book as pretentious, bloated, and frequently trite. Richard Barker seemed to want to read the book as poetry—yes, a mistake—and he found it wanting, especially in comparison with its apparent experimental progenitors, including Pound and Charles Olson. The latter, Barker wrote, "would have reduced Connell's 243 pages to 30."[47] A Los Angeles critic was among those who savored Connell's experiment and moral vision. Richard G. Hubler observed, "It is a brilliant, bravura piece of work. . . . What is notable is the optimistic view of the human dilemma which repeats itself so regularly—like the slow beat of a gigantic heart—throughout history. It is this upbeatnik quality that gives the book coherence and purpose."[48]

Kenneth Rexroth gushed about the book on his San Francisco radio show. By one account, perhaps hyperbolized, he called it the "best book by an American perhaps ever."[49] By the time Rexroth's praise appeared as a blurb some years later, the judgment had cooled down to "I think it's one of the most remarkable books that I have read in a long time."

Connell clearly had established a working method for his explorations in history. He read widely and he gathered shiny and intriguing nuggets wherever he ventured, like a pan-wielding prospector in the wilderness. He later explained to his critic friend Gus Blaisdell that he had not been inspired by any "major sources of influences." Connell used a recurring device of geographical locales (compass points, or latitude and longitude readings), suggesting that his ghostly narrator—could this have been his nod to Cyril Connolly's Palinurus?—was traveling the world in his search for meaning. Connell told Blaisdell that Lamott had plotted all the narrator's locales and determined that they were meaningless, "which is correct. I simply liked the sense of space and overtones of travel and search and anguish that the points imply. A painter may feel the need of a certain color without there being a reason." Connell followed his instincts, sometimes against reason, often with an inner gyroscope tuned to a higher plane. A key to understanding his overarching concern—in this book and books to come, it would turn out—is Connell's statement that "the only conscious design is toward catastrophe."[50] The weight of the world had descended on Connell's shoulders. As a writer and a human it never seemed to lift.

Future critics would deliver more admiration for the book and a follow-up volume a decade later. Nevertheless, after the *Notes* experience, Viking and Connell parted ways.

A Girl Walks into a Bar

1963–1965

"I am not threatened in any way, unless it is by the
knowledge of how quickly time passes."

—Connell, "The Mountains of Guatemala"

ONE PERSON WHO came to know Connell as well as—perhaps
better—than anyone entered his closely managed orbit circa 1964,
probably late in the year. Gale Garnett, a dark-haired, dark-eyed
beauty, walked into the No Name Bar in Sausalito with impunity.
She may or may not have been of legal drinking age, though no
one seemed to care. When she tells the story, she says she was sixteen years old and hid that from Connell, who was forty or so, for
some time.

Yet it's impossible to reconcile that detail with other facts of
Garnett's rather mysterious and coyly preserved life. The internet
has perhaps five different birth dates for her, Garnett told me in
one of our first face-to-face meetings, though she declined to verify which was accurate. She was a free-spirited actress and singer.
She proved over many years to be independent-minded, strong-
willed, and driven to creative achievement. Born Galina Garnett in
Auckland, New Zealand (or possibly in Hawaii, according to two
news accounts), she was taken by her parents to England and then
to Canada at about age eleven, or maybe ended up in New York at
the age of nine. Her English (or maybe Italian) father, Lani Garnett,
was a performer and pianist, but he died when she was twelve.
Little is known of her mother, who was partly Russian, though one
account suggests she left the picture after a mental breakdown. As

127

Garnett's usual story goes, she ran away from home, ended up in New York, enrolled at the performing arts high school, and had her first legitimate, off-Broadway stage role at the age of fifteen.

So far so good. But here the story breaks down a bit and becomes dependent on other sources, including slivers of press accounts. As early as 1957—maybe she was fifteen at that time, more likely a bit older—Garnett had become a topic of conversation for New York gossip columnists. The news ticker can be summarized like this:

> An impressive singer, once heard on Art Ford's radio show. The actor Rod Steiger paid for her acting lessons. She was Elizabeth Taylor's stand-in during the making of *Raintree County* and served as arm candy at a society event for Taylor's ex, Nicky Hilton. She expects her future would be in European films because "they appreciate hips over there." "Born on Maui" and "now a precocious 19 and going places as an actress," Earl Wilson wrote in late 1958, adding, "oh that 36-23-37 figure." Lived alone in Greenwich Village and appeared in *Poverty Alley,* a TV movie made on New York streets in 1958. Was a regular for a brief time as the "Coca-Cola girl" on the *Eddie Fisher Show,* Fisher, coincidentally, being a future husband of Liz Taylor.[1]

The High School for the Performing Arts, indeed, has a record of Garnett as a member of the class of 1959 (her first name possibly misspelled as Gayle), though it had no confirmation that she graduated. One entertainment writer in the early 1960s quoted Garnett as saying that she served as an understudy at a New York theater but mainly pushed a broom as a janitor. In his 1958 interview with Garnett, Earl Wilson reported her much in demand off-Broadway and seemed to confirm her appearance that year as understudy for all the female roles in a double-bill of Eugène Ionesco one-acts, *Jack* and *The Bald Soprano,* at the Sullivan Street Theater.[2] "In a couple of years you would have heard about me," she told Wilson.[3]

The only explanation that comes close to aligning with Garnett's contention that she was sixteen when she met Connell is this: Garnett told me she was "in a show" at the time, and indeed her name appears in a cast listing for a touring production of an elaborate Broadway hit, *The World of Suzie Wong*. After a two-month run in Las Vegas, the show, with its more than forty players, settled into San Francisco for a month in the summer of 1960. But sixteen? More likely Garnett was eighteen, maybe even twenty, probably born circa 1940 or 1942. She may well have found her way to the No Name Bar in Sausalito—it had a reputation among actors and writers—and seen Connell for the first time that year. But the ensuing love affair probably did not erupt until more than four years later.

After San Francisco, *The World of Suzie Wong,* the story of an American artist in Hong Kong and the "bar girl" he came to love, played in Los Angeles for a short run at the Biltmore Theatre. (A Hollywood movie production was underway about the same time, though Garnett had no role in that.) Garnett performed in the Biltmore run and apparently got an appetite for Los Angeles. Along with a role in a local staging of *Spring Awakening,* she began landing minor acting parts in television series over the next three years (*Hawaiian Eye, 77 Sunset Strip, Bonanza, The Real McCoys*) and making connections with the movie business. "I arrived in Hollywood with an Oriental show," she told Mary Campbell of the Associated Press, "and I became a resident Polynesian–Indian–Mexican. Occasionally they would get very daring and I would play a Greek."[4] Notably, her voice stands in for the Italian actress Claudia Cardinale in the first *Pink Panther* film in 1963. She also stretched out into singing, landing coffeehouse gigs, then bona fide clubs such as the Troubadour.

In early 1964, Garnett's singing career took off when, riding the wave of the folk music revival, she signed a contract with RCA Records, which released her first album, *My Kind of Folk Songs.* The record included her versions of some traditional songs ("I Know You Rider," for one), leaning toward the blues and British Isles ballads. But front and center were several of her own songs,

Fig. 20. Gale Garnett publicity photo, 1964. Courtesy of RCA Victor Records.

including "We'll Sing in the Sunshine," a bouncy anthem "to personal independence," as she put it in the liner notes. The song got well drilled into the ears of American radio listeners, as RCA soon issued the tune as a single and made Garnett a star. She won a Grammy Award for the song that year. She played concerts with Jimmie Rodgers. She toured nine cities with the Four Seasons and Roy Orbison. One wire service review identified her as twenty-one and said she possessed the deep voice of someone much older. "She sings," the review went, "with the sincerity of Odetta," referring to one of the most prominent female folk singers of the day.[5] Garnett also identified herself as twenty-one and as having been an actor and singer for nine years. (Perhaps Connell never read her liner notes. If he had, he would've learned much of her struggle toward a career by reading the letter from Pernell Roberts, star of television's *Gunsmoke,* which dominates the back of her second album, *The Many Faces of Gale Garnett.* Roberts clearly had been with her in Los Angeles at the time of her first club dates and observed "the determined face of a young girl who refused to be defeated" and "a wise face that sang and spoke an understanding of life far beyond your years.")

By this time, it is possible she had heard about "the bar with no name," as it was identified in *Contact* ads, from John Huston, the film director. She had made his acquaintance in Los Angeles and maintained it as he took up residence at St. Clerans, a manor he had restored in County Cork, Ireland, and to which he settled in 1964. Eventually, to read some of Garnett's letters to Huston, he apparently offered to adopt her as a way of providing support, but she apparently declined.[6]

Garnett said she'd been in the No Name Bar enough to recognize Don Carpenter and some of the other writer and artist regulars. But it was Connell who caught her eye for real. "I walked in, and I thought he was beautiful," she said. More than a half-century later, Garnett paused as we chatted in a Toronto restaurant, her eyes going dreamy as she looked off to the side, perhaps to recreate the image in her mind. "He was one of the best looking men I'd ever seen." The sexy mustache. The elegant demeanor. She thought Connell looked like Zachary Scott, the Texan who had starred in *Mildred Pierce* and less-remembered movies. "I used to go in there fairly regularly because all my friends were adults," Garnett said. She boldly walked over to their table and asked to join. There was no objection. Connell perked up. He took interest. He asked about her and her work. She told him about her acting career and song writing. Eventually, Connell quietly delivered what she perceived as his usual pickup line. "Wanna get a hamburger?" As she related this, Garnett dropped her voice to imitate his quiet, velvety baritone. "Evan," she said, "had this peculiar habit of talking without moving his lips." "As long as it isn't a hamburger," she replied. She didn't eat beef, pork, or lamb, but fish and fowl were okay, and they agreed to leave the bar and cross the street to Ondine, the onetime historic yacht club now operated as a swank, celebrity-filled restaurant on the Sausalito waterfront.[7]

The timing for this affair, late 1964, is supported by Connell's papers at Stanford. The first letter from Garnett that is preserved there dates to January 1965 and refers fondly to their recent intimacies. Even later came this secondhand testimony from the owner of the Tides book shop: "I always know when Evan has a new girl, as she always comes in the next day and buys one of each of his books."[8] If the evening at the No Name and Ondine represented a first date, it also was the beginning of a beautiful friendship, one that deepened and evolved over great time and distance and lasted for the rest of Connell's life.

Connell was spending more time in Sausalito since joining *Contact*'s staff as a senior editor in late 1960. He drove over the bridge almost every day after writing to read manuscripts and hobnob. *Contact* had increased its frequency from quarterly to every other month. The magazine's offices, the Tides bookshop downstairs, and the nearby bar offered most of the companionship he desired. His circle clearly felt that they were helping to develop a vibrant literary culture in the Bay Area despite their isolation from the New York publishing scene. Connell bristled at the condescension that typically emanated from New York. *Contact*'s book arm had submitted Ray West's *Western Review* anthology, *A Country in the Mind*, in expectation of a notice in the *Kirkus* publishing newsletter. In return came this reply from its principal, Virginia Kirkus: "Unfortunately, we cannot review the titles of isolated publishers." Connell went public with this complaint in a newspaper article about *Contact* and its book-publishing efforts: "The industry is centered in New York, and with that parochial attitude for which New York is celebrated, anything west of Buffalo, excepting Detroit autos, is unworthy of consideration."[9] Still, the experience grated and confirmed Connell's sense of being on the margins of literary success. For his own part, Connell's name alone, as Helen Taylor had warned, still could not ensure a sale of his own work.

The *New Yorker* rejected yet another Connell story around this time while professing a standing interest in what he was up to. Fiction editor C. M. Newman found "Song Heard on a Starry

Night" to be only somewhat effective and mostly pretentious. Still, he held out hope that eventually Connell would come through.[10]

Max Steele did move to Connell's San Francisco in late 1962. Connell shepherded Steele and his wife, Diana, around the city for a couple of days and helped them find an apartment not far from his. Steele took a teaching position at San Francisco State, alongside Connell's mentors Ray West and Walter Clark. One year he taught a creative writing workshop through the University of California Extension Center. Diana Steele went to work for the California Division of Employment, where Connell once took a job screening incoming applicants for unemployment benefits.

Connell encouraged Steele to contribute stories to *Contact*. None appear in its pages, but it is quite possible Steele was responsible for one or more segments of a periodic culture column. The column ran four times under the pseudonymous byline of Chacmool. This, of course, was the name of a Mexican prehistoric site of great interest to both Steele and Connell. The columns, including a pan of the San Francisco Film Festival and reviews of both movies and books, read less like Connell than someone a bit more glib. Even a review of two new editions of the eighteenth-century porn classic *Fanny Hill* did not sound as if it came from Connell's typewriter. It did appear, however, with a nude portrait, from the rear, by the photographer Ruth Bernhard, who had other photos in the issue. Given Connell's long experience in sketching nudes and the author publicity photo Bernhard shot for *Notes from a Bottle*, his editorial hand was likely involved. Internal evidence, including the sound of two different voices, suggests that if Steele in fact contributed anonymous reviews, so too did Kenneth Lamott.

Whether or not Steele wrote for *Contact*, he clearly was aware of the magazine's eventual struggles and occasionally traded observations with his and Connell's agent, Elizabeth McKee. "Evan still comes by fairly frequently," Steele wrote in the summer of 1963, "and looks very tired sometimes because he is accepting now the full responsibility for Contact's continuation and is dealing with printers, lawyers, and the sometimes mean heckling of [publisher Bill] Ryan whom I never cared for. I believe if he gets this issue out on time and the next one underway, he will be able to reorganize a staff that can carry on without his full time help and that he can get back to his typewriter where he of course belongs."[11]

Five years after Elton Connell's death, Connell's father remarried in February 1963. It was the second marriage for both him and his new wife, Emily Fitch, the former Mrs. Frederick Bliss. The ceremony, uniting two high-society figures, took place at St. Andrew's Episcopal Church in Connell's old Kansas City neighborhood. Connell did not attend the affair, though later that year, he hosted his father and stepmother for a few days in San Francisco as they stopped on the way to a vacation in Hawaii. Connell's connection to his hometown remained rare, though he heard from the principal of Southwest High School that his name had been eternalized in the school's Hall of Fame. Did a faint smile emerge?

If so, the smile relating to his hometown soon disappeared. At least, if one can take a cue from an editorial comment in *Contact*. Connell—this is a presumption about a commentary signed by "The Editors," but who else had the Kansas City connection?—found a cautionary tale in a disturbing story of civil rights injustice that emanated from back home. This was the case of a Black Kansas City, Kansas, couple who, ten years after the Supreme Court's decision in *Brown v. Board of Education*, were not allowed to enroll their children in a white public school. "In Kansas City," the piece begins, "where everything is up to date, except cognizance of United States Supreme Court rulings, a Negro couple, Hugh and Lela Shanks, refused to register their children in a segregated school, whereupon they were arrested, tried, convicted, and fined for abetting truancy." The editorial goes on to tweak the media, including a prominent broadcast personality who, "on first learning of the case, announced that he would interview the couple, but after some reflection failed to keep his appointment." Connell did not spare the newspaper that had treated him so well: "The most influential paper in that part of the Midwest, *The Kansas City Star*, maintained almost total silence. Discretion, cowardice or apathy? Take your pick." The piece noted that Mrs. Shanks was home-schooling her children and others from her neighborhood:

> "Every time the doorbell rings," she says, "the children ask a little more matter-of-factly each day: 'Is it the police?'" And she continues, "One morning as we recited the pledge of allegiance to the flag of the United States of America and to the Republic for which it stands, one nation under God, indivisible, with blank and blank for blank.' When I scolded her, she said, 'Well, that couldn't mean us.' I told her some day this would all be a memory and she would know it meant her from a living experience."

The editorial was conscious of two other essays that appeared in the same issue. In one, George P. Elliott dwelt on a series of irrational incidents in the age of the Cold War and nuclear anxiety.[12] In the other, Ken Lamott addressed the inadequacies and myths embedded in recent reports of California's demographic ascendancy in three national magazines (*Life*, *Look*, and *Newsweek*). He noted especially how none of them recognized the lives of Black Californians, a curious "avoidance of skin color."[13] Like those, the *Contact* editorial does not reflect an optimistic attitude toward the state of the nation, and certainly aligns with Connell's voice: "What good is school anyway? What are American children learning? . . . A poll of student attitudes in sixteen universities showed that a majority regard Communism as a greater danger than nuclear war. A preference for death is implicit. One begins to wonder, with Mr. Elliott what this country is all about. Just what is it all about?"[14]

Lela Shanks and her husband soon left the disappointments of Kansas City and moved to Nebraska, where she built a long career as a civil rights and peace activist. And for Connell, the chilly feelings about his Midwestern origins only hardened.[15]

Before Gale Garnett captured Connell's full-time fancy, there was Anita Clay Johnson in Kansas City, a divorced mother of three. Connell lured the blue-eyed, dark-haired, and statuesque Johnson to San Francisco in the summer of 1963. He had gotten to know her during a holiday visit to Kansas City. She was an aspiring writer and through family connections had sought him out. She had published short stories in 1958 and 1960, and had attended a weeklong New York City Writers Conference under the tutelage of Saul Bellow, Robert Lowell, and Edward Albee. You've got too much talent for Missouri, Connell told her.[16] After her divorce from Dr. John E. Johnson, she thought her publishing prospects would be greater in the emerging western capital of American literature, San Francisco.

Connell helped her find an apartment, first on Alma Street, near Golden Gate Park, then a year later in Sausalito. He introduced her to Max and Diana Steele, and she got to know Connell's circle of writer friends, including Herbert Gold, Calvin Kentfield, and Don Carpenter. Connell may or may not have helped her with her writing, though he did connect her with his agent, Elizabeth McKee. That first summer, Johnson contributed an article to the *Kansas City Star* stemming from the Monterey Jazz Festival. She wondered why musicians such as the great horn player Carmell Jones were forced to abandon her former hometown.[17] Her first novel, *In a Bluebird's Eye*, about a girl growing up in east Tennessee who discovers the realities of race relations, didn't appear until more than a decade later, long after she had moved on from Connell and remarried. She met her next husband, the concert promoter John Kornfeld, in 1964 at a literary party thrown at Kay Boyle's home.

According to her two daughters, Anita Kornfeld maintained her friendship with Connell long after their affair, if indeed there was something more than a casual, chaste attachment. Connell once attended a literary event at the Kornfeld home in Napa Valley wine country, the setting for her three-generation saga *Vintage*, and he inscribed and sent to her and her husband a copy of his 1980 essay collection *The White Lantern*. Eventually she began writing a novel, intending to draw from her life in San Francisco and the Connell crowd in Sausalito, though she never completed the project. It's evident that at some point early on Anita Kornfeld discovered what many women learned about Connell. After the opening round of intimacy, he had little to say or insufficient emotional matter through which they could connect.

In addition to supplying anonymous reviews as a contributor to the Chacmool column, Ken Lamott also wrote under his own name in *Contact*, delivering smartly observant journalistic essays and pointed and entertaining book reviews. Of the latter, for example, he once did a number on the critic Leslie Fiedler, first offering grudging admiration for his provocative pronouncements on sex and literature, then hoisting him on his own petard via a new collection of short stories. Lamott judged Fiedler's fiction to be occasionally "appalling" and generally dismaying in the realization that "a writer who is so useful as a critic should be so insensitive when it comes to his own work."[18] In another issue Lamott lamented the mostly deboned state of book reviewing in newspapers and magazines, a topic he undoubtedly shared in conversation with Connell. Lamott declared the best book reviews could be found in some of the science magazines, especially *Natural History* and *Scientific American*. He illustrated his argument with lengthy examples comparing reviews of a handful of current titles in one or the other of those magazines with the flabby soft-pedaling he found in the *New York Times* and elsewhere. Given Connell's opinions on book reviews delivered over the years, even as he was writing his own for the *Times* and other outlets, he and Lamott seemed to be on the same page. They also seemed to feed off one another's interests and self-reflection. In late 1963, Lamott ventured an essay on war, young men, and identity prompted by a recent book, *The Warriors* by J. Glenn Gray. In the book Gray, a philosopher, examines his own experience and what he learned of human nature during World War II, when he served as an intelligence officer interrogating suspected Nazi functionaries and collaborators near Allied lines in Europe. Lamott had served a similar role in the war, questioning Japanese prisoners in the Pacific. Connell had shared his copy of the book with Lamott, and they undoubtedly talked about their respective reactions. Like Connell, Lamott recognized that it spoke directly to their generation of veterans, "not because it awakens nostalgia—it is not by any means an intellectuals' Legion convention—but because it revives a whole world of morality that almost all of us have shiftily, furtively, and guiltily put behind us, abandoning much of our concern as moral individuals in the face of our preoccupation with the mathematical probabilities of death that are now offered us by various bombs."[19] Connell wrote his own appreciation of Gray's revealing and disturbing book, for the *New York Times*, five years later.

If the publishing establishment were less than interested in the San Francisco literary scene, a popular magazine found reason to look in on Connell's world. *Cosmopolitan* captured a group portrait of the creative doings in Sausalito, calling it "Bohemia on the Bay." Reporter Richard Harrity spent several hours with Connell. Connell, he wrote, "looks like the half back on a freshwater college football team." Harrity couldn't fail to encounter the quintessentially nonsocial Connell: "I was forced to do practically all the talking, for he is a young man who, according to one of his friends, 'lives in a world of vast silences.'" Harrity praised *Notes from a Bottle Found on the Beach at Carmel*, which gave him a sense that Connell had "the seed of greatness in his soul" and put him in mind, quite astutely, of James Joyce's post-Dublin working motto: "silence, exile, and cunning."[20]

Cosmopolitan's spread included one of the most unusual photographs of Connell I've turned up. First, some background: The scene was a party thrown by the artist Jean Varda on the occasion of his seventieth birthday. Varda was a free-spirited collagist, friend of Picasso, pal of such notable California talents as Henry Miller and Anaïs Nin, and cousin of the esteemed French film director Agnes Varda. He lived on a converted ferryboat in Sausalito, and on this day he took some of his guests out on his handmade, two-masted sailboat. About ten revelers are visible on board. *Contact*'s publisher Bill Ryan was one of them. Flo Allen, a well-known artist's model, was another.

The photograph, to me, is a modern equivalent of Renoir's *Boating Party,* the Impressionist masterpiece filled with social codes and deep content. What mostly draws my eye to the tableau is the space occupied by two adjacent figures. One is Connell. The other is Allen Ginsberg. A couple of years younger than Connell, Ginsberg at the time was the leading poet of the Beat brigade. With full black beard and flowing locks, Ginsberg is shoeless and dangles a leg over the side of the boat. He's wearing a white T-shirt and looking toward the camera rather jauntily in the sun. Connell, seated just behind Ginsberg's right shoulder, appears somewhat bemused, and there's no hint of a smile beneath the thick arc of his mustache. Maybe he is wondering how he landed on this crazy craft among a bevy of Bohemians while he was decked out in a proper suit and tie. It figures.

Aesthetically, the two writers couldn't be further apart. Yet there they are, two distinctive literary voices sharing an odd space at a moment in time. To me, the photograph from the early 1960s remains both a mystery and a delight.

Connell was no fan of the Beat writers, who had gained so much attention in those days. Their transgressive abandon just wasn't his style. Bill Ryan, perhaps putting a retrospective spin on the matter, once said that they'd started their literary journal "so the Beats could be shown how to write proper prose."[21] But Connell had lived in San Francisco for nearly a decade and certainly knew Lawrence Ferlinghetti's bookstore—City Lights, ground zero for Beat sensitivities—the North Beach scene, and the reputation of Ginsberg and his fellow "angel-headed hipsters." It's likely he had even read John Clellon Holmes's article in *Esquire* a few years earlier on "The Philosophy of the Beat Generation," which had appeared in the same issue as Connell's "Crash Landing." Holmes had emphasized Ginsberg's achievement in the explosive and controversial poem "Howl": "It contains a good many expressions and experiences that have never been in a poem before; nevertheless, its aim is so clearly a defense of the human spirit in the face of a civilization intent on destroying it that the effect is purifying."[22] Connell may well have recognized that theme as a distinctive thread of his own foray into epic verse (of a sort), *Notes from a Bottle*, which by the time of Varda's party was already on the market. Yes, they could meet on that intellectual ground on which ancient philosophy and modern anxiety collided. And they could have shared their relative experiences with LSD. After all, according to one Connell letter, Ginsberg and Dr. Oscar Janiger, the Los Angeles LSD researcher, were cousins.[23]

It remains unclear whether the boating party occasioned the first meeting of these two decidedly antipodal figures of late twentieth-century American literature. I know it wasn't the last. For the *Cosmopolitan* photo shoot, the party also gathered at Vesuvio, the North Beach Bohemian haunt owned by Henri Lenoir. Ferlinghetti and co-author Nancy Peters included a photo of that gathering in a pictorial history of literary San Francisco. And once again, Connell and Ginsberg are shoulder to shoulder. This time they are standing at the bar, front and center in a lineup of celebrities that also included Lenoir, Varda, and Flo Allen.

Connell and Ginsberg at least crossed figurative paths, curiously, in 1974. Ginsberg that year won a National Book Award in poetry, and Connell was a poetry finalist for *Points for a Compass Rose*, his non-poetic follow-up volume to *Notes from a Bottle*.

And in the late 1980s, Connell and Ginsberg shared not only some literary space but a meal. Connell was elected to the American Academy of Arts and Letters. (Ginsberg had preceded him by fifteen years.) Connell's then-editor Jack Shoemaker threw a dinner party in New York, and they both were at the table, along with William and Rose Styron, John Updike, James Dickey, and Ginsberg's companion Peter Orlovsky.

The record of any conversation between Connell and Ginsberg is, unfortunately, lost to history. But symbolic of Connell's epic quietude in many social situations, it is immensely revealing that Shoemaker, when I asked him about the dinner party, remembered Ginsberg being there but struggled mightily to recall his own author's presence at the table.

For his part, Connell years later recalled Ginsberg as a photo hog, someone who would rush over whenever a camera appeared.[24]

Gale Garnett, back in New York from her Los Angeles television stints and her concert tours, wrote to Connell in January 1965. Her letter is effusive. It's flirty. She laments sleeping alone again, and to emphasize the point she draws a self-portrait, stretched out on her side, unclothed, her head on a pillow. She cherishes the week, "a perfect week," they'd spent together. She'd never had such feelings, she says. "We are both hard working," she tells him, "and rather committed to living and I'm glad we took the time for each other and hope we can take it again."[25] They may well have taken up together only a few weeks later, when Garnett scored a gig at the hungry i in San Francisco, the first of two appearances at the North Beach basement club that year.

Fig. 21. Along with her singing career, Gale Garnett became a local celebrity in Sausalito, here appearing in a poster collage for a radio station. Courtesy of Neil Davis.

Garnett traveled to Paris in the spring of 1965 for a concert at the Olympia Theater and to record an album. In November, she returned to San Francisco for a month-long stint at the hungry i, which was a hotbed for folk musicians and political comedians. During the span of the show, Garnett took up residence on a houseboat in Sausalito. There would be more gatherings with Connell and his friends at the No Name Bar. There would be outings in the city. She reported buying two pre-Columbian objects at the San Francisco gallery owned by Billy Pearson, a former jockey, bon vivant, and friend and beneficiary of John Huston.[26] Garnett had been intrigued by Huston's collection of global antiquities, and she got Connell started down a similar pre-Columbian path.

Along with his developing relationship with Garnett, this was also the year that Connell underwent what proved to be the financial nightmare of *Contact*. There had been hints in the past. A belt-tightening but image-burnishing format change. A promise to go monthly that was never fulfilled. A missed issue. An appeal for funds. In July 1963, an editors' note recounted the many successes *Contact* had achieved in its first five years, especially in getting recognized on the literary scene. Still, "our financial situation, while not precisely desperate, is not a happy one." New York publishers would scoff at the magazine's budget, the editors noted. "Our monthly payroll would not pay the tab of a literary tea." But the business is cruel and trying, and "we have recently found ourselves wondering if the game was worth it." No, the magazine was not folding, nor will it, they said. But more subscriptions would help save it, and if anyone were interested in investing, well the staff was ready to listen.[27] It's unclear how well the appeal worked. One thing did change: Ryan, the thirty-five-year-old publisher, gave it up.

Ryan had put up more than $30,000 of his own money, according to a retrospective article. He said that five years earlier, *Contact*'s first issue sold 11,000 copies but the numbers had declined ever since. When he enlarged *Contact*'s dimensions to the size of popular magazines, beginning in 1962, it was an attempt to change its status beyond the "little magazine" category. In typically boisterous Ryan fashion, he announced that resizing with an all-out literary party. Max Steele recounted the event in an article a year and a half later. The venue was Juanita's Galley, a raucous Mexican restaurant in Sausalito that operated on a decommissioned paddlewheel ferryboat. More than three hundred "West Coast intellectuals"— journalists, professors, writers, and their entourages—dined on chicken, prawns, seafood casserole, and beer. Max Steele reported on the boat party and the magazine's transition for one of the San Francisco newspapers: "And there was a general feeling aboard that Ryan—that driven, ambitious Irishman, that ex-swimming champion, ex-advertising man, ex-bookstore owner, that magnificent generous host—was really going to hit it big." The feeling had been that *Contact* was about to become a truly national magazine, giving San Francisco something to crow about. "Only a beautiful blonde on the arm of critic Irving Howe was heard to say as she surveyed with boredom the feast and feasters: 'But it's all so terribly local.'"[28]

Ryan soon left Sausalito for spells in publishing and other media in New York. With a new owner, the journal's leadership fell primarily on Connell, Kentfield, and Lamott. "What can we do but publish the best manuscripts we have on hand," Connell told Steele in what seems like typical understatement. "That's all we've ever done and that's all we can do. . . . I see no reason the magazine can't go on and on."[29] Connell said he would cover expenses. But no more lavish parties. No more Dictaphone. Not so much color on the covers. "My God," he told a contributor, "the Paris Review has been going 12 years and they've yet to buy anybody a cup of coffee."[30] The magazine also moved to office space on the second deck of the historic *Berkeley* ferryboat docked in the Sausalito harbor. Steele pronounced the new issue, polished and beautifully designed under the care of a new art director, to be "good and sometimes brilliant" and perhaps "the most handsome magazine currently on the stands."[31] There was lots of wishful thinking all around.

Contact hung on for five more issues over the next two years. Near the end, Connell and his colleagues investigated the possibility of forming a nonprofit organization to run what was in essence a no-profit business. Connell demurred when Gordon Lish apparently suggested combining efforts with the journal he edited, the *Golden West Review*.[32] By early 1965, owner Nicholas Cox turned off the spigot and Connell and his colleagues started beating the bushes for "a couple of thousand dollars to insure the May/June issue," and if possible "a Foundation or a group of sponsors, or something, so that we don't run into this situation every three months."[33] They had no illusions about their limited-audience mission. Lamott called publishing "economic insanity," and Connell acknowledged that *Contact* was "not commercially oriented."[34] One reporter seemed surprised by the casual approach Connell and his friends took to putting together the magazine. If they liked something, it would run. "We don't work consciously for the readers," Connell said. Four months after issuing *Contact 21*, in February 1965, the magazine suspended publication. The editors and directors took the "melancholy opportunity" to send a note of gratitude to those who had supported the literary venture over the previous eight years.[35] Lamott informed Gordon Lish of the decision "to kill the old girl" and of the "look of relief on Connell's face."[36]

Some years later, Connell memorialized the idealism of Sausalito's literary publishing heritage in a short story titled "Octopus, the Sausalito Quarterly of New Writing, Art and Ideas." The story satirizes the origins of *Contact* (or its fictional counterpart, *Octopus*), its seat-of-the-pants operations, and its questionable finances. The narrator has been talked into becoming the associate editor, which, of course, was a non-salaried position: "Octopus would not be doctrinaire; nothing would be predetermined, nor would its embrace be limited. All that mattered was quality." There was a constant struggle between the publisher (a character named Willie Stumpf, a comic stand-in for Bill Ryan), whose content and promotional ideas bordered on suicide, and the editor (called Bowen, a cockeyed version of Kentfield). "On the one hand, Bowen was serious about publishing a respectable literary magazine and I thought that with two hundred and fifty million people in the United States there might be more than two or three thousand who wanted more than drivel. On the other hand, there was Willie." Connell furthered his *Contact* reflections in a second story, "Bowen," a farcical but often affectionate portrait of an ill-fated writer inspired at least in part by Kentfield. ("What animated Bowen to write at a level beyond understanding was the mythic quality of life at sea.") Stumpf, Connell writes, "thought more copies could be sold if the magazine had more cartoons and Bowen told him he should be marketing codfish instead of literature. As a result, the next issue was indefinitely postponed."[37]

The character Karl Muhlbach first appeared in Connell's long story "Arcturus," which he crafted as early as 1954. Connell wrote it under the influence of Thomas Mann's social satire *Disorder and Early Sorrow.* Mann's novella dates from 1925, the year after Connell's birth. It presents a day in the lives of a German family after the Great War, with a pallor of melancholy and an emphasis on the contrast between the earnest professor-patriarch and his modern children. As Connell wrote, he had Mann's "little masterpiece on the desk beside me." He aimed to model Muhlbach on Mann's stuffy Dr. Cornelius, "a figure almost impossible to like or completely dislike."[38] George Plimpton at the *Paris Review* once rejected it because it seemed too obviously an imitation of the Mann story. (Connell felt flattered by that.) But Ray West bought it for the *Western Review,* and it appeared in Connell's first story collection, *The Anatomy Lesson,* as well as the anthology West edited for Contact Editions. The story also landed in Martha Foley's *Best American Short Stories 1957*, alongside entries by Nelson Algren, Flannery O'Connor, and another emerging Bay Area writer of note, Gina Berriault.

By the early 1960s, Connell had returned to Muhlbach. Three more stories centering on the character appear among a dozen pieces in *At the Crossroads*, published in mid-1965. By this time Muhlbach was a widower. It's reasonable to imagine Connell meditating on his own father's solitude after Elton Connell died in 1958. Muhlbach's wife's illness had been palpable in "Arcturus" and now was contained within the fictional memories of Karl and his children, Otto and Donna.

Critics found Muhlbach to be a formidable and intriguing character. "The stories of this disenchanted man, who looks for a new fulfillment and meets only fallout shelters and an amorous divorcee, are perfect," Harold Gratzmacher wrote in the *Chicago Tribune*.[39] Irwin Gold in the *Los Angeles Times*: "superb tales of wit, insight, and impeccable style."[40] Of Muhlbach in "Saint Augustine's Pigeon," one San Francisco reviewer stated that "this improbable hero is realized as perfectly as any figure in recent fiction." The local critic found Connell's writing comparable to Saul Bellow's and thought "Muhlbach should be recognized, along with *Herzog*, as two of the most trenchant creations of the times."[41] At the *New York Times*, Orville Prescott concluded that the three Muhlbach stories "are all satirical comedies written with cool humor, suave irony and great verbal aplomb," though he found most of the rest of the book to be far too clever, uneven, and "dismally disappointing."[42]

In "Saint Augustine's Pigeon," the lead story in *At the Crossroads*, Muhlbach, an insurance executive, sets out to treat his loneliness on the exotic end of the female-companionship scale. The story becomes a satire of classically bourgeois male fantasy, anxiety, and emotional turmoil. "I don't want a receptionist or a secretary or a teacher or a female executive," Muhlbach muses. "What I require is something in spangled tights." Or as he put it more definitively: "A young lady experienced in each conceivable depravity, totally intemperate, unbuttoned, debauched, gluttonous, uncorked, crapulous, self-indulgent, drunken and preferably insatiable." There's a lost-in-New York quality to the story that echoes with any number of later film treatments from John Cassavetes's improvisations to Martin Scorsese's *After Hours* to Natasha Lyonne's recent Netflix series *Russian Doll*. It's real, it's absurd, it's ultimately human as Muhlbach recognizes the indignity of a pigeon's heavenly plopped message and the sad fact of his own identity: "Knowing this was not meant to be, does not, nor ever shall diminish the yearning."[43] (Connell was reading Saint Augustine at the time, hence the story's title.) Yearning, of course, is another aspect of the long desire: the search for meaning amid the chaos. And yearning also speaks to the vast unknown in Connell's own lonely life. His own experience with a pigeon's rude dropping on his shoulder did not go to waste.

Desire is also a theme in the Muhlbach-centered story "The Mountains of Guatemala." The title comes from a promotional brochure Muhlbach pockets about a resort hotel in Guatemala. It seems to be a lovely and pleasant place, and Muhlbach would like to go. But that's a mere symbolic digression in a story about a winter night when the ostensibly repressed manager from Metropolitan Mutual heads out to a party. "I'm well off," he muses, "in good health. I am not threatened in any way, unless it is by the knowledge of how quickly time passes." He waits for a bus, which is late in the snow. He reflects on last night's dinner party and obsesses over the hosts' soiled tablecloth as if he were heir to India Bridge's propriety. On the bus, a young woman in a raccoon coat steps up to shatter his quiet reveries. She returns his gaze with a searing glare and moves to a seat closer to the driver. Muhlbach, in a flash of male anxiety that prefigures the #MeToo movement of a half-century later, takes it as a slap: "The humiliation is poisonous; it clings like a roach crawling up his sleeve. What have I done? He asks himself. . . . All my life I have represented civilization, now I am threatened. I have been touched and warned. She has ordered me to hold my eyes averted; if I do not, I risk a serious penalty. One word to the keeper of the bus: this man has been molesting me. Must it balance on the equanimity of each strange woman?"[44] Equanimity. There's an echo of an observation about women Connell made in the mind of Melvin Isaacs in *The Patriot*.

Of course, as it turns out, the pink-lipsticked young woman and Muhlbach arrive at the same building, the same party. Although others assume they have come together, they never speak, never resolve the distance between them.

In the third Muhlbach story in the volume, "Otto and the Magi," Connell appears to make another run at a climactic scene from *The Patriot*, in the aura of Cold War American anxiety. Muhlbach has built an underground bomb shelter in the backyard of his suburban New York home. These were all the urgent rage in the 1950s and early 1960s as Americans were led to fear the potential of an attack by the Soviet Union, which had developed its own nuclear weapons. The poet Sylvia Plath, from her perch in England, expressed concerns about the drift of Strontium 90, a radioactive isotope, faint clouds of which were spread by American bomb tests. She opined on the subject in a letter to her mother: "The fallout shelter craze in America sounds mad."[45] Orville Prescott counted "Otto and the Magi," with its contemporary context, among the high points of the story collection: "Mr. Connell's mockery of the cozy, playful, cheerful guide to family togetherness during atomic extinction is savage."[46]

At the Crossroads also presents a pair of comic figures, Leon and Bébert, who star in several stories here and later as kindred fools. Their patter descends from Beckett perhaps, from Abbott and Costello, from any number of other comic duos in the entertainment business. They might be seen as precursors too, though somewhat less idiotic, of the *Dumb and Dumber* routines of the Farrelly Brothers movies starring Jim Carrey and Jeff Daniels. Leon and Bébert move in more sophisticated circles, but their absent-minded concerns and predicaments, like those of *Dumb and Dumber*, prove to be surprisingly effective. Tracing the Beckett thread would not be so far-fetched. *Waiting for Godot,* which premiered on stage in 1953, had a run by the San Francisco Actors Theater in 1957, including, notably, a one-night performance at San Quentin State Prison. Ken Lamott was teaching part-time at the prison and published a brief history of the penal institution in 1961 as well as a piece in *Contact.* Connell introduced Leon and Bébert, literary cousins of Beckett's Vladimir and Estragon, in "The Suicide," which first ran in the pages of the *Saturday Review* in 1963. Another way to read the characters, especially in "The Suicide," is as two sides of the author's persona struggling to understand how to think and live.

Writing about *At the Crossroads* in the *New York Review of Books,* Eve Auchincloss found Connell to be a complex and complicated talent. She sensed his cold, distant eye and the surprising comic voice: "Connell is an uncomfortable writer. Though a miniaturist, he has much intelligence, wit, a ghoulish sense of the absurd, a nice ear for speech. He is certainly not unaware of the cost of failing to live through the heart; but he dwells on the alternative with so ruthless and cool a sense of consequence that it is hard to tell which side he is on."[47]

Connell had some early exposure to journalism training at the University of Kansas, but his nonfiction writing almost always took the form of essays, book reviews, fragments, and historical narratives. Articles he wrote for the San Francisco newspapers in the early 1960s seemed more like press releases for *Contact* than pieces of reported journalism. Given Connell's limited experience with Hollywood by the mid-1960s, and the mixed feelings he already had about the movie world, he was tantalized by an opportunity to perform an act of journalism for *Esquire* magazine. The assignment: write a profile of Rita Hayworth, a symbol of Hollywood glamour. His response, according to a later account: "I countered with Kim Novak. Did you ever see her in 'Picnic'?"[48] In the end, he produced a slyly satirical but straight-faced romp titled "A Brief Essay on the Subject of Celebrity with Numerous Digressions and Particular Attention to the Actress, Rita Hayworth."[49] One way to look at the piece is as the answer to the question, what does an entertainment journalist do when the subject of his or her piece is an uninspiring, empty-vessel stiff? Connell does find himself sitting in a Hollywood mansion having tea with Hayworth, the "love goddess" of Tinsel Town legend. He has read the five-page resumé supplied by her publicist and finds it wanting of anything resembling a human being. But before he even gets to her, Connell begins with a meditation on fame and memory triggered by a visit to Inscription Rock, a sandstone bluff outside Gallup, New Mexico, where travelers going back centuries stopped and carved their names and messages to the future. ("I'd always wanted to write about Inscription Rock," Connell said. "My agent had shopped the idea around New York, but no one cared. I saw a way to link the two."[50]) We mark our territory and some of us are remembered. Then comes California, where all our prayers will be answered, where we may linger by a "private pool in the shade of imported palms, while a vulgar public clusters outside the gate." And here is Hayworth, "the subject of poems, technicolor dreams, threats, grotesque fantasies, memories and speculation, the warm brown eyes telling much of what she is not—mendacious, spiteful, conniving, treacherous—but little of what she is."[51] She has nothing really to say, so Connell notices what's around the room (he was a master of details): a stone statue, a painting by Derain, copies of *House Beautiful* and *Harper's Bazaar*, a volume of Millay. In the end, it's a brilliant rebuff to the publicity machine that assaults us, even more these days, by the minute. Fame exists only because Connell was here to witness it. And fame, no matter how much he actively avoided it, was really a secret desire and would become the cause of no small amount of frustration and regret. He likely understood what the poet Karl Shapiro wrote on the matter: "Once I kissed Fame (mouth like an ass hole)."[52]

Despite the disappointment over *Contact*'s demise, Connell's personal finances took a turn for the better in 1965. In the fiscal year ending March 31, he earned nearly $20,000, equivalent of more than $155,000 in today's dollars.[53] And soon, according to some literary gossip from Max Steele, Connell received a $30,000 advance for his next novel. The forthcoming book would be another shattering departure for Connell, yet more proof that he had no interest in repeating himself or becoming comfortably understood in a heartless publishing world that thrived on meeting expectations.

Of Crime and Men

1966

"I knew what I was doing—writing a novel. Not everybody
understood. Two old women who lived in a nearby
apartment heard about it and quickly moved out."

—*Bookforum* interview, 2001

DONNA MAY SCHURR, an eighteen-year-old junior college student
in Garden Grove, competed as Miss California in the 1955 Miss
Universe pageant. Several months later her fame took a tragic turn
when a shaggy-haired automobile upholsterer assaulted her in her
home, dragged her outdoors and into his car at knifepoint, drove
off, and soon raped her. In the subsequent chaos of the episode, her
fiancé pulled up to her home as she left her assailant's car, setting
off a high-speed chase that reached more than one hundred miles
an hour. The fiancé, Lloyd Brett, had a loaded pistol in his car, but
before he could use it, police arrived and apprehended the six-foot,
two-hundred-pound rapist, Jack James Walker. Walker confessed
not only to the crime of that evening but also to raping Miss Schurr
nine months earlier. Walker, married and father of a child, was an
obsessive creep. "I knew when I went out to Donna's house that I
was going to get caught," Walker told police. "I had that feeling
but I couldn't help it. I had to go through with it anyhow."[1]

Connell followed newspaper accounts of the case, and by 1965,
almost a decade later, he began transforming its essence into another novel built on fragments. He centered the story not on the
victim but on the perpetrator. The episodes unfold as daily diary
entries, projections of a central character troubled by love and life.

In the novel, Earl Summerfield works as a drudge in the state unemployment office, a dreary place Connell got to know for a while in real life. Unlike Connell, and more like Jack James Walker, Earl is stuck in an unhappy marriage and saddled with increasingly bizarre fantasies. The title leaves little to the imagination: *The Diary of a Rapist*. Connell didn't much like the line, but he couldn't think of anything better.

Robert Gottlieb, a well-connected literary editor, bought the novel for Simon and Schuster. Gottlieb was best known at the time for having acquired Joseph Heller's *Catch-22*. He had also edited *At the Crossroads*, Connell's second story collection. He would oversee three more of Connell's titles over the next decade, though their relationship eventually withered and, as Gottlieb once put it, they drifted apart.

The Diary of a Rapist might have been a shocking title for its time, though sexual assault, kidnapping, and similar crimes of abuse were not uncommon fodder for the daily newspapers. *Contact*, in its drive for topical and provocative surprise, had devoted an issue in October 1960, Connell's first as an editor on the masthead, to "The Criminal Man." Defining what they meant was open for discussion and interpretation. There were mentions of political prisoners (Alvah Bessie, one of the Hollywood Ten filmmakers who had declined to discuss their alleged communist affiliations before a congressional committee) and there were writings and artwork by prison inmates. Nelson Algren had an essay in the issue, reflecting on the dark inner heart of his native Chicago. And there was an opening epigraph from Blaise Pascal's *Pensées*, which reads, in part, "The embarrassment wherein he finds himself produces in him the most unjust and criminal passions imaginable."[2] The intellectual attraction to depravity could be seen elsewhere in the high-brow fascination with noir genres in print and in Hollywood movies of the 1940s and 1950s.

Connell clearly wanted to further explore the dark recesses of the male mind. He had opened the door in "Saint Augustine's Pigeon." Karl Muhlbach in fact briefly meditates on sexual assault. As an exotic dancer performs at a club, he wonders, "like an evil flower blooms," if he were capable of such a dangerous act of violence, but ultimately he is repulsed even by the thought. "He tries to remember if some previous thought has brought up such a criminal idea from the depths of himself, or if he has overheard or seen anything that nourished it. Nothing. Nothing." Still, he is no different than anyone and "but for the grace of some inherent power go I—good God! Good God, are we so near the precipice, each one of us?"[3] Connell's intentional reading of Saint Augustine, of course, informs Muhlbach's journey of male desire.

Connell told an interviewer that the beauty-queen case had indeed got him going on *Diary of a Rapist.* "It all seemed to fit in," he said. "All the people I see going to work, they have a kind of security, but there's an unbelievable romanticism going on in this country. What I've tried to do as a writer is get behind this romanticism and into people's fantasies—and show them as they are."[4]

Connell was baffled that no fiction writer yet had taken up the Miss California case. To him, the story elements were powerful:

> He was caught the second time because he drove her home instead of running away, which meant to me that during the interim (some months) he had not only fallen in love with her but had convinced himself that she might learn to care for him, provided he drove her home and thanked her for a lovely evening, so to speak, and later they would live happily ever after. I couldn't (and still can't) find a better explanation for the fact that he wanted to see her safely home. The death-wish, however hackneyed, probably is part of the complex. At any rate, these were the principal factors in starting this book.[5]

For added verisimilitude—Connell was, after all, inventing a character only partly based on Jack James Walker—he consulted with Oscar Janiger, the Los Angeles psychiatrist who had directed his LSD experiments. Connell gave Janiger the information he'd gathered about Donna Schurr, including police files. He also talked with women who had been raped "and tried to get as much information as possible on how the man behaved and what he said and the impression he made on them."[6] Ken Lamott offered to line up interviews with convicted rapists at San Quentin, but Connell declined.

Connell borrows from reality to convey Summerfield's stalking and attacks. His victim, like Donna Schurr, is a beauty queen, though Summerfield's nighttime meanderings also involve stealthy entries and defilements in strangers' homes. What we don't know of Jack James Walker's home life, Connell imagines in scenes from Earl's marriage. Connell's main strategy is to channel Earl's consciousness in sometimes Joycean internal monologues. We learn from his second sentence how Earl feels about his wife, Bianca, a teacher seven years his senior: "Nothing gives her more satisfaction than to humiliate me."[7] Day after day, the narrative grows darker and the character becomes more fully rounded. He stews. He plots. He questions himself. He prowls. The novel represents what Thomas Hardy once understood, that "if a way to the better there be, it exacts a full look at the worst."[8]

Some readers found a wealth of empathy in the novel. "Earl is a wonderful character," Gale Garnett told me, "and I think that's a brilliant book. It's about a man who's tyrannized by his wife and has a secret life." Garnett said it was one of her favorites among Connell's books. "I always thought they would make an interesting film out of *Diary of a Rapist*. I still think that."[9] No film ever materialized. But it's possible to think of Connell's novel as a precursor to the hotly debated horror satire *American Psycho* (1991) by Bret Easton Ellis, which did get the Hollywood treatment a generation or so later.

As Connell awaited publication of *The Diary*, he got another glimpse of the criminal mind by way of a fellow writer. The *San Francisco Chronicle* had asked him to review a sensational new book by Truman Capote, the southern stylist who turned from short stories to the true account of a family's murder in rural Kansas. Capote's book, *In Cold Blood*, had been serialized in the *New Yorker* in the fall of 1965. Now the page-turning work of narrative nonfiction, what Capote called a "non-fiction novel," arrived with a thump and a publicity roar—an eighteen-page spread in *Life*, a *Newsweek* cover story, a George Plimpton interview of Capote for the *New York Times*, and much more. Connell was one of the very few dissenters (Stanley Kauffman at the *New Republic* was another). The *New York Times* noticed his "wounded outcry" critique in a story about Capote's book, quoting Connell's line: "It goes down the gullet like custard."[10]

Even today, Connell's review is withering. Capote's effort was ill-conceived, poorly written, and unjustifiably praised, Connell stated. He announced his position from the very start: "Under certain conditions," he wrote, "an artist can become as powerless as a dead snake." Connell allowed that Capote clearly was capable of better writing than the banalities of prose he committed here. Capote had no sense of the real lives and language of the people he encountered, and obviously despised, in Kansas. He wondered even whether Capote's first mistake was following the editorial instincts of the *New Yorker*'s William Shawn, whose judgment the author had praised. "What a terrible indictment," Connell retorted.[11] This was not an example of the genteel, log-rolling tradition of book reviewing. Connell might have been wrong to invoke Somerset Maugham's suggestion that a writer's weaker works would be forgotten. For *In Cold Blood* remained, despite its many faults, a touchstone of the so-called New Journalism for decades to come. A reader can detect in the review Connell's resentment over the arrogance of New York publishing. One might also conclude that it added to Connell's reputation as something of a bitter bird, even as it burnished his credentials as an uncommon writer with unshakable standards.

The Diary of a Rapist was greeted with a wild range of reviews and nothing like the publicity treatment Capote received. Marjorie Driscoll in the *Los Angeles Times* called Connell's book "a convincing, profoundly disturbing and magnificent novel."[12] Roger Shattuck, in the *New York Review of Books*, paid grudging respect to Connell's track record but quarreled with some of his structural strategies.[13]

Despite Connell's overt disregard for the consequences of publishing, he was ever cognizant of the results. *The Diary* was neither a huge success nor a flop, he told Steele. The early count was 6,500 copies sold. He was pleased that foreign publishers had acquired the rights in the United Kingdom, Italy, Germany, and the Netherlands. The reviews were generally good, and he heard from his agent that Hollywood was sniffing around. (An option eventually was sold for $10,000 but expired.) To capitalize on the publicity, William Hogan at the *Chronicle* asked Steele to write a piece about his friendship with Connell, but Steele demurred, explaining to a friend that "it seemed either too personal or too silly."[14]

Connell clearly retained mixed feelings about the book. He once expressed concern when he heard it was showing up in X-rated bookshops. "I imagine the customers felt swindled when they discovered it has very little to do with sex." And he took note when "two old women who lived in a nearby apartment heard about it and quickly moved out."[15] That, of course, might be apocryphal. Another thing we don't know for sure is whether Connell saw in Earl Summerfield and his diaries any connection to Nabokov's rapist and murderer Humbert Humbert and the character's journal entries in *Lolita*.

Almost forty years later, A. M. Homes, a novelist who often traces dark themes of American culture, was invited to introduce a new edition of *The Diary of a Rapist*. "It is," she wrote, "as modern and terrifying a novel now as it was in 1966."[16]

Gale Garnett rode her musical fame to concerts in New Zealand in February 1966, followed by television appearances in Australia. By spring, shortly after *The Diary of a Rapist* hit the market, she accompanied Connell on a trip to Europe. They arrived in Lisbon then spent six weeks in Spain and a couple more in Paris. Connell saw parts of Spain he had missed in the early 1950s, including the historic cliff-top city of Ronda and Malaga on the southern coast. He missed San Francisco, he told Steele, and he had an odd insight about traveling: "I think I take more pleasure in remembering that I have been through the alleys of Seville than in the actuality of being there."[17] In Paris, Garnett dragged her reluctant boyfriend to a series of discotheques. They toured a flea market, had dinner with the literary critic and poet John Crowe Ransom, and spent time with Connell's old friend the artist Roger Barr. Not much had changed in Paris—Wadja's café remained a favorite haunt, though he knew no one now at the Dôme—except that the prices were higher and the streets were clogged with more cars.

Connell and Garnett left France after Bastille Day and visited John Huston at his Galway manse. Soon, Garnett went back to the United States—she had a concert at the Sonoma County Fair in California—and Connell returned to Paris before setting off on what turned out to be a journey around the globe.

Connell was still overseas when he received word of a critical assessment of his work to date that went deeper than he could have imagined. It came from Gus Blaisdell, a poet, editor, and philosopher in Albuquerque. The Stanford graduate, a voluble polymath, clearly saw in Connell a formidable talent and perhaps one whose intellect was not fully appreciated by the literary world or readers in general. Blaisdell set out to correct that in an essay published in the *New Mexico Quarterly* in the fall of 1966. More than a half-century later, Blaisdell's "After Ground Zero" remains one of the most serious and exhaustive considerations of Connell's writing by a literary critic or scholar.

Blaisdell began with a sense of the zeitgeist, as his title implied, a nod to nuclear catastrophe and its affects on civil society: "The comforts of a peace based upon arsenal rattling, gnawing anxieties over impending annihilation, and a terse skepticism of human rationality are dubious and precarious when the possibility of that peace rests on the poker-hand of policy backed by ICBMs."[18] Blaisdell suggested that Connell was not obsessed with annihilation, though as with any writer it informed his portrayal of the times and his outlook on the arc of human history.

Blaisdell presented a deep reading of Connell's first six books. Connell's short fiction reflects the influence of Mann, of course, but also Proust, Chekhov, and Joyce, yet has distinctive New World qualities: "The tone of a Connell story is unmistakably American; the perception is European. . . . Avoiding the beginning-middle-end artifice of narrative fiction, Connell creates the illusion that his stories are nothing more than textures or surfaces. . . . Shunning any realistic imitation of life, he unerringly achieves intense verisimilitude. With Joyce's godlike author, Connell remains aloof from his creations, completely outside them, in apotheosis, paring his fingernails."[19]

Blaisdell lamented the limp critical reception given to *The Patriot*. He found its writing and details to be top-notch and its vision and comments on "war, the machines of war, and the men trained to operate those machines" to be "without parallel." When taking up *Notes from a Bottle*, Blaisdell launched into a philosophical discussion of what he termed "vatic" literature, or poetry that served as prophesy. Fair enough. "It is only a bold or foolish writer who would undertake a work that is in direct opposition to the inherent skepticism of the American temper." Of course, Connell knew he was taking that risk, and not only did he accept the consequences, though sometimes regretfully, he doubled down when he returned to the format a few years later. Blaisdell served up a treatise on Muhlbach, a character who "accepts the madness of our time" and whose enriched inner life stands in contrast to his public blandness.[20] The inner life of Earl Summerfield presents something altogether more challenging.

Blaisdell found a resonance between *The Diary* and an unabashedly soul- and flesh-baring memoir by the French writer Michel Leiris. Titled *Manhood*, the book dates from the 1930s but had just appeared in its first English translation, by Richard Howard, in 1964. Leiris, a surrealist poet and anthropologist, would have been known to the American literati during Connell's period of loitering in Paris in the early 1950s. Blaisdell cited Leiris's book in passing but suggested that *The Diary* shared "conceptual similarities" with *Manhood* along with Djuna Barnes's modernist (and gay-lit) classic *Nightwood*. (This relationship—a ménage à trois of books, as it were—seems worthy of an essay of its own. And, again, there's no mention of *Lolita*.) From Barnes, Blaisdell extracted an underlying point, the one Connell poses with both Muhlbach and Earl Summerfield: "There is not one of us who, given an eternal incognito, a thumbprint set nowhere against our souls, would not commit rape, murder, and all abominations."[21]

Manhood, indeed, is a cauldron of male anxieties—about identity, sexuality, death, and leaving childhood for the "fierce order of virility." Leiris meditates on literature, mythology, religion, art, family, bullfighting, women's breasts, and his own wounds, desires, and debaucheries. At one point, he recalls his discovery of key lines from Apollinaire (in translation): "That woman was so lovely / She terrified me."[22]

Connell did not read *Manhood* while conceptualizing and writing *The Diary of a Rapist*. In fact, Connell told Blaisdell that he was unaware of Leiris and he hadn't read Barnes. But he clearly would have recognized the metaphysical signals emanating from *Manhood*. "Like many men," Leiris writes, "I have made my descent into Hell, and like some, I have more or less returned from it."[23] Leiris acts as a kind of voyeur of his own life and actions; Connell portrays Earl Summerfield as a voyeur in action, imagined from a real life, though Earl's introspection pales against the depths of Leiris's self-reflections.

Literary analogies aside, Blaisdell considered *The Diary of a Rapist* as Connell's masterpiece, more consequential in literary terms than the smaller though still masterly achievement of *Mrs. Bridge*. (I would not go that far.) Connell's portrait of a deeply flawed man contains, like *Mrs. Bridge*, an inner light of something like grace. Writes Blaisdell, "One can and must weep for Earl Summerfield, which is a reason for the stature of Connell as an artist."[24]

Connell wrote to Blaisdell with an understated note of thanks: "It's very carefully done, and of course I was most interested in reading it."[25] He asked Blaisdell to send copies of the quarterly to his father and to the book critics in Kansas City and San Francisco. Dr. Connell thanked Blaisdell for the "fine evaluation" of his son's writing. "I find great pleasure," he wrote, "in a communication from someone with sufficient intelligence to appreciate his work."[26]

Clearly, the good doctor knew by now that Evan Jr. was operating in an elevated sphere.

Despite Blaisdell's careful work, Connell also wanted to offer a series of small corrections and expansions. He hadn't actually been a pre-med student at Dartmouth. He thought Blaisdell's emphasis on characters' thoughts of suicide seemed out of proportion to his own intentions. Third, the tortured being at the beginning of *Notes* was not a saint, as Blaisdell had it. "The fact," Connell wrote "that the victim of some such atrocity may have been a splendid man is of less consequence than the fact that the atrocity occurred."[27]

Blaisdell had made much of the near-suicide scene in *The Patriot*, where Melvin Isaacs watches his hand, in something like an out-of-body experience, in the act of stopping the aircraft's precipitous dive. Connell elaborates by recounting the story that triggered it. He recalled reading a review of a published diary kept by a Japanese soldier on a small island. The soldier and a companion, both starving, made a pact that when one died the other would be free to eat him: "The companion died and the diarist immediately took out a knife and prepared to cut up the body and eat, but just as he was about to cut into the body he observed his left hand catch hold of his knife-hand and prevent it from doing as he intended. This is one of the most shocking things I have ever read."[28] In another letter, Connell requested that copies of Blaisdell's article be sent to Wallace Stegner, Walter Clark (now teaching at the University of Nevada-Reno), Max Steele, and John Kendrick, his old Stanford roommate now working as an editor at the University of Chicago Press. Blaisdell had solicited a story from Connell for the *New Mexico Quarterly*, and Connell replied that Elizabeth McKee had another Muhlbach piece in hand, called "Puig's Wife."[29]

Connell left Paris in late September 1966 and continued traveling eastward. His *Paris Review* friend Peter Matthiessen might have captured the spirit under which Connell operated. "So long as he kept moving he would be all right," Matthiessen writes in *At Play in the Field of the Lord*, which was published the year before. "For men like himself the ends of the earth had this great allure: That one was never asked about a past or future but could live as freely as an animal, close to the gut, and day by day by day."[30]

Connell stopped in Dubrovnik and spent a few weeks in Greece. Cairo. Tehran. Istanbul. The mysteries of the Near East added to Connell's storehouse of sensory stimuli. He spent some time in Tel Aviv and Haifa in Israel and paid an Arab guide to take him to Petra, the famed archaeological site in Jordan. As his wanderings wore on, he couldn't shake off a germinating thought. The seed of his next book was forming.

Walter Bridge Returns
1967–1969

"Consciously I was trying to say how a group of people
lives—and that's it."

—*New York Times* interview, 1969

THE ANCIENT QUARTER of Famagusta had innumerable attractions
that could speak to Connell's soul. With its fourteenth-century ca-
thedral and the remnants of its Venetian-era walls, this seaside city
on the island of Cyprus boasted long sand beaches and hotels with
enough luxurious appointments to make it a celebrity playground.
When Connell looked out at the Mediterranean from a café table,
he wasn't so much enamored of stargazing. He had been traveling
since May, first with his friend Gale Garnett, then on his own. After
leaving Paris, his extended journey would continue south and eastward, ever eastward around the globe. But here, on November 29,
1966, in the glorious light and the rich blue of the sea, Connell's
inner writing eye caught a glimmer of a long simmering thought.
This idea had recurred and expanded and churned all through this
wandering adventure. *Walter Bridge.* It was time to tell his side of
the story. Connell tasted his drink and made some notes.

Often he said to himself: my life did not begin until I met her.
Connell numbered it "1," and penciled a circle around the figure.
He knew she would like to hear this but he could not tell her.

The point of this paragraph was Walter Bridge's inability to express his love for his wife, India Bridge, the mother of his three
children. Connell's initial notes for *Mr. Bridge* cover a page and
a half of paper. "Use 'Mrs. B' episodes from Mr. B's pt. of view,"

he wrote. "Dislikes psychiatrists but best friend is one." He refers to a family scrapbook on his mother's side, the Williamsons, with southern roots and "eccentric great-uncle Hugh." Connell projected an ending that does not square with the finished book. And there's a snippet of dialogue, as Walter argues with his son about communism: "'I'd just as soon you didn't mention this to your mother.' 'Don't worry,' said Douglas in a voice that was almost friendly." You can sense Connell dredging up an exchange just like one with his own father, a reverberation that also rang through *The Patriot*. One full paragraph has Mr. Bridge dwelling on his legal work and how his wife just would not understand if he talked about his cases when he got home every day. And here is Connell thinking about his characters: "Carolyn + Mr B are at times dislikeable [sic]." Same goes for Ruth, Douglas, and Mrs. Bridge, each of whom should be dislikable at one point or another.[1]

Thoughts and notations on the second Bridge novel accompanied Connell to Tehran, Karachi, and Bombay (now Mumbai) through Christmas and into the new year. He was itching to get home to work on it. "I was piling up some odds and ends, scraps of paper and stuffing them in the suitcase," he said two decades later. "And at that point I became anxious to finish traveling and settling down to the usual dreary routine where I could work nine to five so to speak and get to work on it."[2] Still, he kept traveling. His itinerary combined moments of pleasure and meditation with anxious episodes and spells of despair. He once described a period in India when he said he nearly went mad. His little-known autobiographical essay goes into much detail about a shouting match with an incessant rickshaw tout. For general consumption he condensed his experience in the preface to his last published book, the story collection whose title echoes his state of mind— *Lost in Uttar Pradesh*:

I have seen the Taj by moonlight and at noonday under a blistering Indian sun have plodded up a dusty slope to the Ajanta caves, trusting Vishnu to guard my laundry bag and suitcase. I have walked across the bridge of lepers at Hyderabad, trying to conceal the pity and disgust I felt, lost my wits during a furious argument with a crazed rickshaw boy, quarreled stupidly about a chocolate fudge sundae in a hotel dining room, dodged rocks during a soccer riot, got myself poisoned by a doctor at the Calcutta public health service, shared a park bench with a foul-smelling Australian hooker in the muggy twilight.

Beyond doubt, India is a special place. Westerners who stay long enough begin to go mad and think the Western world insane. Late at night I saw a man with a blanket over his head sitting beside a little fire in a courtyard next to a pyramid of bones, an allegorical scene. And in a cluttered Delhi shop I uncovered a bunch of seventeenth-century Mughal drawings.[3]

Connell's lyrical response to the magic and madness of India may well convince a reader of his special feelings for that vast and variegated nation. Indeed, after a lifetime of travel, he told a friend that India was his favorite destination. "Why India?" she asked. "It surprised me."[4]

Connell finally got home by March 1967. After all the sights and sounds of the past year, he couldn't help but feel grateful to be back in the comforting light of San Francisco. "This is really the best place of all," he told another writer.[5] Unlike Walter Bridge's uptight and homogenous Kansas City, San Francisco was looser, more embracing of difference and variety. "I live here," he told one of the local papers, "because it is a city of beautiful nuts."[6] He got to work, gathering all those loose papers and making sense of the novel that was forming in his head: "I worked six and a half days a week for a year on it. I don't think I took ten days off the entire time. I rewrote the entire book three or four times and some sections twice that."[7]

Connell had long intended to return to the Bridges but resisted at least in part because people had been clamoring for it in the wake of *Mrs. Bridge*'s success. He just didn't want to perform like a puppet. He didn't want people to think he'd found a formula or could succeed just by repeating himself. His wildly different books of the

1960s may have defied his editors' and readers' expectations, but they satisfied his own. When people asked whether he was writing a sequel to *Mrs. Bridge*, Connell said no, it was "a companion volume." It would echo the style of the earlier novel and cover a time period that was roughly the same.[8]

Still, despite the hard work and intricate revisions that went into it, Connell considered *Mr. Bridge* a relatively easy book to write. He told his editor that he thought it was a stronger book than its predecessor, or "technically better," and that "the character is more complex."[9] He used the vignette template of *Mrs. Bridge* and compiled a total of 141 numbered chapters, two dozen more than in the first book. He found himself needing to consult a map of Kansas City, given that he had lost touch with his hometown geography. But shaping the emotional geography of the Bridge family and the consciousness of its patriarch needed no such external tools.

The portrait of Walter Bridge is not pretty. He is a man of his world—a prosperous white lawyer in 1930s and early 1940s America. Part of what had made *Mrs. Bridge* such a timeless account of midcentury society was Connell's radar for themes of race and class. Now, as he worked on the sequel, the nation had experienced enormous upheavals. There was the gut-punch of the Kennedy assassination. There were the struggles for civil rights— the marches, the legislative advancements, the culture of protest. While all of that lay in the future for the Bridge family of fiction, those present-day realities undoubtedly helped Connell craft the family's retrospective story. Connell's keen awareness of the racial landscape of his hometown, as emphasized by the *Contact* editorial of a few years earlier, surely added to the thematic urgency of this new novel.

Race is something like an exposed nerve in the body of Mr. Bridge, both the character and the book. It echoes even a half-century later. In one scene, India Bridge has come across a magazine news story with a photograph of a lynching. She points this out to her husband. His answer could have come out of the mouth of any tone-deaf plutocrat of his day or ours: "There are many fine people in the South. . . . What did this fellow do?"[10] This assertion blames the victim, of course, and speaks to the tortured logic employed by those who enjoy a privileged status in the face of fundamental challenges to their existence. When asked whether he was aiming for something universal in the novel, Connell said he wasn't, at least not consciously, "though it's certainly true that some of Mr. Bridge's bigotry can be found everywhere in America—everywhere in the world, for that matter. Consciously I was trying to say how a group of people lives—and that's it. What you call 'universally applicable' belongs to the critics, not the writers."[11]

Despite his soft-shoe rejection of the idea, Connell certainly intended for race and racism to be an important subtheme of *Mr. Bridge*. He emphasized the point two months after he submitted his manuscript by sending in two more race-oriented chapters, titled "Harriet and Carolyn" and "ground glass." In the former, a minor crisis and upset ensue when Carolyn Bridge orders the family's Black maid to sweep some leaves from the back steps. In "ground glass," Walter Bridge wonders who is killing the neighborhood dogs by adulterating their food. His mind settles on some of the Black men who work nearby. "I think both add somewhat to the relationship between Mr. B and Negroes," Connell told his contact at Knopf, "which I think is one of the significant lines of his character. And the ground glass chapter fills out what seemed to me to be a lack in the previous book about this family—that is, the absence of pets."[12] Connell did not overtly state what had to have been on his mind. He offered up these two new vignettes about race in a letter of June 21, 1968, two and a half months after the assassination of Martin Luther King Jr. and the resultant riots in Kansas City and elsewhere and barely two weeks after the killing of Robert F. Kennedy, who was in the midst of a presidential campaign based at least in part on a theme of racial healing.

Connell recognized that readers could certainly identify with many other aspects of Walter Bridge's life and circumstances: "What's really intriguing about him is that he's going through experiences which many people go through—losing his children to their own lives, for example. . . . It seems there will always be some sort of conflict between generations, some sort of rebellion by children against the hypocrisy of their parents. But it wasn't my intention to draw morals. All I was getting at was that this is how that experience happened to one man, Mr. Bridge."[13]

Connell reveals that Walter Bridge's bigotry extends beyond race to religion and ethnicity, specifically Jews. In the Bridges' Kansas City (and Connell's), Jews were prominent in social and political circles though they were unwelcome for membership in the "exclusive" country clubs, and they endured the often unspoken prejudices and subtle cues of disrespect that emanated from their white, Christian friends and acquaintances.[14] With daughter Ruth exploring her new creative life in New York, Mr. Bridge has a revelation: "When anything having to do with art or music was announced there were Jews involved. Why this was, he did not know, but he faintly resented it." Near the end of the novel, as the war approaches and Douglas and his father argue over his desire to join the Marines, Walter Bridge's attitude comes into sharp focus. "Hitler was insane," he thinks, "and this was unfortunate because some of his ideas were sensible." Douglas has overheard a comment his father had made to friends and delivers a stinging verdict, which Walter finds difficult to defend: "You hate Jews."[15]

Walter Bridge's own self-image amounts to a mantra of mainstream, middle-class America. He wants son Douglas to think about his future in the same terms that served him so well, the important things he had accomplished: "financial security, independence, and self-respect. In his mind these were of supreme importance. They stood together like the points of the fleur-de-lis."[16] One needn't stretch too far to imagine how those points applied to Connell himself.

Focused and patient at his neat desktop, near the living-room window overlooking the Golden Gate Bridge, Connell typed, read, and wrote revisions by hand as he went. He finished the first draft of *Mr. Bridge* by June 1967. He left a paper trail of manuscript drafts, which provides an opportunity to inspect or divine his process as a writer and reviser. He once said that he knew he was done revising when he found himself putting back commas that he had earlier taken out. In his papers, for example, in addition to the first notes he made in Cyprus, we have at least three pencil-scratched pages, each with another version of the first episode of *Mr. Bridge*, titled "love." One manuscript page, very likely the first draft version, has the title word capitalized; the others and the finished book make it lowercase "l."[17]

One significant transformation occurs on that same page. In the scene, Walter Bridge is struggling internally with his inability to express love for his wife. Connell moved this operative line from the middle of the paragraph to the end: "After all, he reflected, she could not expect me to behave like some poet and of course I can't pretend to be what I am not." Connell eventually dispelled with the first-person reflection and in the subsequent versions, which lasted through to the published book, the line appears like so: "After all he was an attorney rather than a poet; he could never pretend to be what he was not." As a reader, I regret the loss of "behave like some poet," though I can understand that perhaps Connell did not want to sound disparaging at this point. But the relocation of the line makes logical sense and serves to end the paragraph with psychological force.[18]

Connell would become a meticulous participant in the design of his own books, sometimes to the point of frustration. His penciled notes on one of these manuscript pages includes typesetting specs and the thought that the first episode should fit entirely on the book's first page. It did.

The second draft rolled off his typewriter four months later, and perhaps in an expression of relief he planned to spend Thanksgiving with Gale Garnett on a visit to Max and Diana Steele's home in Chapel Hill, North Carolina.

Garnett had issued five or six more LP records by that time, showing off her sultry voice and versatility with other people's songs as well as her own. She wrote ten of the dozen songs on *New Adventures,* for example, most of them about love lost, love found, and a sense of poetic longing.[19] Although she never regained the acclaim she'd received for "We'll Sing in the Sunshine," a listener can fairly wonder whether Connell served as Garnett's muse, as she

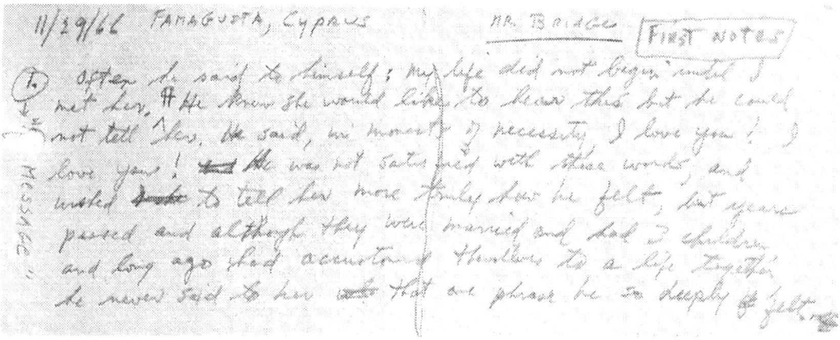

11/29/66 Famagusta, Cyprus — Mr. Bridge — First Notes

1. Often he said to himself: My life did not begin until I met her. # He knew she would like to hear this but he could not tell her. He said, in moments of necessity, I love you! I love you! He was not satisfied with these words, and wished to tell her more truly how he felt, but years passed and although they were married and had 3 children and long ago had accustomed themselves to a life together he never said to her that one phrase he so deeply felt.

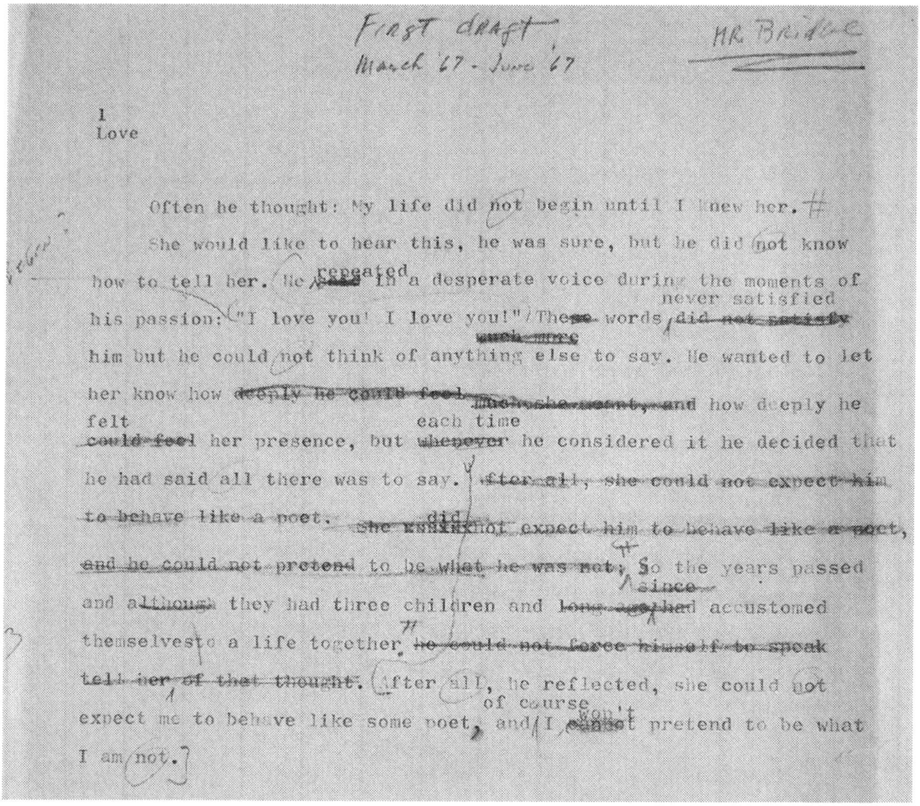

First draft — March '67 - June '67 — Mr. Bridge

1
Love

Often he thought: My life did not begin until I knew her. #

She would like to hear this, he was sure, but he did not know how to tell her. He [repeated] ~~said~~ in a desperate voice during the moments of his passion: "I love you! I love you!" These words [never satisfied] ~~did not satisfy~~ ~~such more~~ him but he could not think of anything else to say. He wanted to let her know how ~~deeply he could feel~~ ~~the...~~ and how deeply he [felt] ~~could feel~~ her presence, but [each time] ~~whenever~~ he considered it he decided that he had said all there was to say. ~~After all, she could not expect him to behave like a poet.~~ ~~She~~ ~~[did]~~ ~~not expect him to behave like a poet, and he could not pretend to be what he was not;~~ So the years passed and although they had three children and [since] ~~long ago had~~ accustomed themselves to a life together, ~~he could not force himself to speak tell her of that thought.~~ After all, he reflected, she could not expect me to behave like some poet, [of course,] and I [won't] ~~cannot~~ pretend to be what I am not.

Figs. 22 and 23. Connell first jotted notes for *Mr. Bridge* while on a round-the-world journey in 1966-67. A page from his subsequent manuscript draft illustrates his incessant revisions. Courtesy of the Department of Special Collections, Stanford University Libraries. Copyright, and used by permission of, the Literary Estate of Evan Shelby Connell Jr.

clearly inspired him from time to time in his fiction. Connell once told his editor Bob Gottlieb that Garnett asked about him every now and then: "I judge you made some sort of impression. I do not speculate whether good or bad."[20] Garnett also repeatedly told Connell, after Gottlieb moved from Simon and Schuster to Alfred A. Knopf in 1968, as Connell was completing *Mr. Bridge*, that he should "go with Gottlieb!"[21]

Connell once was asked to write a brief personal essay about love. It gave him an opening to hint at the playfulness he found with Garnett. He began by recalling, probably fancifully, two schoolboy crushes. Then this:

> Long after Winifred and Mary Jane there came a wacky actress/singer. We went around together doing this and that here and there and eventually she gave me an album she recorded. She inscribed it: "With fond memories of that strange night on the beach at Ensenada with the pineapple, the machine & the palomino pony." That's a very nice inscription. We didn't visit Ensenada, I myself have never laid a hand on a palomino, and although I like pineapple well enough I detest machinery. However, the sentiment is touching. For the past five or six years I've been trying to think of the right response.[22]

Whatever bond they had formed, it was possibly indescribable. Connell and Garnett clearly harbored a deep affection and carried it for decades. Much later—much too late—Connell confessed he'd been in love.

Karl Muhlbach made another appearance in print as Connell worked on Walter Bridge. Gus Blaisdell, co-editor of the *New Mexico Quarterly*, published Connell's story "Puig's Wife" in the summer of 1967. (This is the same issue of the quarterly that includes Max Steele's story "A Caracole in Paris," the one with true-story DNA related to Connell's "The Short Happy Life of Henrietta.") "Puig's Wife" is another glimpse of temptation and desire. Muhlbach is summoned by the wife of a longtime friend.

Her husband, his old college roommate, will arrive at their hotel later in the evening, but Huguette Puig insists that Muhlbach join her early. This sets off a major round of anxious introspection. "I'm cursed," he thinks, much as Walter Bridge would think, "with this Protestant conscience that forces me to do what I say I will do, and I hate it." Muhlbach wonders whether he's being set up for a seduction or something more sinister. His mind races. Through every emotion, every conceivable male impulse, every possible play that could unfold in this hotel room between him and her. Huguette's husband, Puig, finally arrives. Sure he's suspicious, but the meeting also dredges up old and disturbing memories. Huguette's suppressed seduction continues behind a bathroom door, partly open and in Muhlbach's view. Ultimately, "for an instant she gazes at him. Then as though he did not exist she turns her back, the worst and oldest insult."[23] The high comedy of Muhlbach's predicament all of a sudden collapses into a tragic male epiphany. The temptation, the desire, the reality, the unknown and unspoken emotions—Muhlbach's existence begins to merge with Walter Bridge's, if not Connell's as well.

Connell found time to review a book for the *New York Times*. It was a wildly unconventional novel by Nicholas Delbanco titled *Grasse 3/23/66*. Connell quarrels with the book's jacket copy, which states the novel draws from mythological sources. "Does it matter that 'Grasse' may be founded on Orphic mysteries? What matters more is that in the village of Grasse in 1966 a man and his wife found they could not live together any longer. That ought to be enough. There should be plenty to say about just that. Scholarship is best left to scholars; much of it fungles the brain of a writer." Connell would eventually, in his books of history and travel, put on the cloak of a scholar though not the airs. He took his history generally without theory. When he wrestles with Delbanco's strategy of unspooling a monologue "drenched with allusion, alliteration, philosophical speculation, endless word-games and quite vivid sensory recollections and evocations," the description, except for the pun-heavy word play, sounds a bit like *Notes from a Bottle*.[24]

Connell took another assignment from the *New York Times* a few months later. He was beginning to like the opportunity for "sounding off occasionally."[25] He complained that the *Times* failed to send him a copy of the Delbanco review, so he never saw it in print. Now, he was tasked with reading the Irish American author Brian Moore's novel *I Am Mary Dunne*, presumably because of his past experience as a male writer imagining the life of a woman. (Moore failed in this case, Connell wrote, where, by implication, he had succeeded.)[26] This was not a small thing for Connell. Reviewing for the *Times* gave him a national platform to expand his status as a literary figure. For all his disdain of the New York machine—"New York and the publishing world seem very distant and very hard to comprehend at this distance"—he did yearn for a certain success.[27] He did want attention, at least on his own terms. And sitting in judgment of other writers (the following year he took on Sherwood Anderson), or at least having a seat at the table to contribute to literary conversations, gave him another outlet for his writing compulsion. Reading, after all, is another way of living a life alone.

Connell completed two more drafts of *Mr. Bridge* in early 1968. And he did, indeed, follow Gottlieb to Knopf. Connell sent Elizabeth McKee the manuscript in April, and she sent it on to Gottlieb with a clear sense of optimism: "Here is MR. BRIDGE. I need say nothing more."[28] A few days later McKee informed Connell by telegram that Gottlieb loved it.

While waiting to hear from Gottlieb directly, Connell felt at a loss. He told Steele that his "loitering" amounted to doing laundry, swimming at a motel pool in Marin County, thinking about travel, watching movies (the newly released *In Cold Blood,* though he offered no comment), and playing chess.[29] He still attended life-drawing classes, sketching and painting nudes.

He was happy that *The Diary of a Rapist* had been published in Italy (*Diario di un strupratore*) though felt a bit odd that a photograph of him appeared on the cover, "apparently because no Italian was willing to pose as a rapist." He was also displeased by the

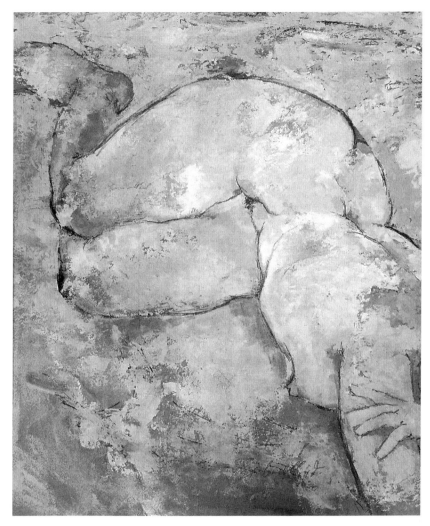

Fig. 24. Connell, the former art student, kept up a sideline of live-model sketching and painting in the 1950s and 1960s in San Francisco. The painting, c. 1965, is from the author's collection. Photograph by the author.

Italian publisher's comparison of his book to Capote's *A sangue freddo*, which, of course, he had soundly panned (in English).[30]

One more thing kept him occupied, he told Steele: "Reminding myself it's time to get married. But how, and to whom?"[31] This was not the first time Connell dropped a hint about his interest, whether genuine or not, in marriage. That the subject had lately been on his mind could be excavated from a passage in his story "The Caribbean Provedor," in which a stranger berates the central character for being unmarried and childless.[32] Connell's on-again, off-again relationship with Garnett was filled with real ardor but it remained unclear where it was heading. To hear Garnett tell it, as she did years later, she scared Connell off when in a feverishly passionate moment she bit his lip and drew blood. She was into it; he was not.[33] In her chronology of events the bloodletting would have happened before now, "now" being the months that Connell was finishing *Mr. Bridge*. But his feelings for Garnett remained and he trusted her enough to pass some of her thoughts about his novel on to Gottlieb. At this point, Garnett also had gone full hippie in style and substance as she recorded two albums with her new Sausalito band, the Gentle Reign. She was comfortable performing amid the psychedelic aura that infused the Bay Area in the years between the Summer of Love (1967) and the ugly scene—including the horrendous beating and stabbing death of a Black teenager by Hell's Angels gang members—that defined the huge rock concert at the Altamont Speedway in December 1969. San Francisco newspaper columnist Herb Caen caught her in the fickle reality of the groovy spirit: "Gale Garnett, that excellent Sausalito singer, explaining why one of her recent recordings failed to click: 'It was a grass-acid song in a speed-smack year.'"[34] Connell, of course, was not much into the grass-acid thing, let alone the speed-smack alternative.

Connell too had an ongoing inability to connect with women, beyond the pleasant occurrences in bed. He had installed some kind of emotional wall around himself that was mostly impossible to penetrate. In my conversations with her, Garnett never quite described him that way, but she was insistent on avoiding any discussion of what felt to her like the privacy of their own story. Other women, including Anne Lamott, a close friend who knew Connell well for nearly half a century, have testified to his failure to connect. Blanche Streeter, who got to know Connell at the No Name Bar, "had a fling" with him around this time, she told me. ("Everyone had a fling with Evan," Lamott added, by way of context.)[35] Streeter worked in San Francisco in advertising at the *Chronicle*. Every Friday after work, she headed to Sausalito and the bar. The more they got together, she said, the more she realized Connell would only reveal so much of himself to her before shutting down. Then came a *Life* magazine spread in October 1969, which held Connell up as "The Roundest Square in U.S. Letters." You didn't even have to read the story to see the electricity in the air. There was a photograph of a smiling Connell and a sexy, apparently braless Garnett. Blanche Streeter read the apparent joy in that photo as a sign to back away.

Fig. 25. Connell with Gale Garnett, 1969, from a *Life* magazine profile. *Ralph Crane/The LIFE Picture Collection/Shutterstock.*

That same year, when Connell learned that Gottlieb was getting married, Connell told him, "I envy you."[36] Assuming he was sincere, at the age of forty-five, Connell, the son of his emotionally distant father, was facing the consequences of being the lonely writer. Yet, he had much earlier expressed his likely feelings about marital bliss in a line from the traveling character J. D. in "The Walls of Ávila":

"Neither of us wanted to get married," he said. "We had a good summer. Why should we ruin it?"[37]

Yet, one hardly knows what to believe. "I think I'm about ready for marriage," the bachelor told a local reporter.[38] Webster Schott, who wrote that *Life* profile in 1969, reported that Connell didn't think marriage was for him. "Press the matter and he says he is 'waiting for an exotic dancer.'"[39] Shades of Karl Muhlbach in "Saint Augustine's Pigeon" and a point to be explored further in the next chapter. In private, years later, Schott told me that Connell "had a little difficulty caring about his sex partners" and once rued out loud "the lies you have to tell in order to have a sex life."[40]

Before responding directly to Connell about the *Mr. Bridge* manuscript, Gottlieb melded his own thoughts with memos received from junior editors at Knopf. They detailed some confusion over the chronology, especially regarding the background of the Second World War—when the American entry began, for example, when the Germans invaded Russia, and when Douglas Bridge would have been of draft age. One reader wondered whether Connell at times seemed unfairly harsh toward Walter Bridge. At one point the character sounded out of his time, more like Barry Goldwater, the conservative Arizona senator and presidential candidate in the 1960s.[41]

Gottlieb's detailed response to *Mr. Bridge* arrived on May 22, 1968. A contract was still making its way through the Knopf legal department, he wrote. Most of his editorial points were minor, and Connell dutifully check-marked each one as he pored over the three-page letter. He highlighted the chronological concerns and possible anachronisms. One episode—only one—seemed identical to its parallel in *Mrs. Bridge*, and Gottlieb urged Connell to avoid the repetition and hone in better on Walter Bridge's point of view. A couple of episodes caused Gottlieb to question Connell's portrayal of Walter's behavior. Next to one, which involved Douglas having gotten a girl pregnant, Connell penciled a decisive comment: "cut."[42]

In his initial response, Connell was typically laconic: "Some of your criticism is unquestionably right and the rest of it probably is. I'll send along revisions as soon as can be."[43] In early June, Connell responded with about six pages of corrections and alterations. He agreed that he could do without the chapter about Douglas and a pregnancy. Gottlieb had wondered whether Ruth Bridge would really have gone to a bowling alley. Said Connell: "I changed this to a football game because it doesn't make any difference. Although (Dept. of Useless Information) bowling alleys were perfectly acceptable for school kids in Kansas City in the 30s. Pool halls were suspect. Bowling was very big."[44]

According to Connell's contract, he received a $15,000 advance (more than $100,000 today) and a royalty rate of 15 percent. He was pleased that Knopf seemed happy with the book. And he perked up when Gottlieb told him that a colleague, after reading both Bridge novels, "now wants Ruth Bridge. I think what I want is Douglas grown up."[45] I doubt that Connell sent Gottlieb a copy of *The Patriot*, but a grown-up Douglas? Connell's next Muhlbach project might qualify. As for Ruth Bridge, Connell may have taken the bait, though he never produced a novel. Sometime in the mid-1960s he sketched out two more episodes that the Dartmouth alumni magazine published under the collective title "Mademoiselle from Kansas City." More than a decade later, when he republished those pieces in the story collection *Saint Augustine's Pigeon*, he added a third, rather squalid though poignant and revelatory episode, which appeared to be the last we would hear of Ruth Bridge.[46]

When Connell chose an epigraph with which to begin *Mr. Bridge*, it seemed to reflect his own consciousness at the time. The source was Wallace Stevens: "I was the world in which I walked, and what I saw / Or heard or felt came not but from myself, / And there I found myself more truly and more strange." The lines come from "Tea at the Palaz of Hoon," published in Stevens's first book.[47] Connell certainly identified with the poem's assertion of a self-created existence. Although a reader is led to reflect on its connection to Walter Bridge, one can also see in the novel the self-created emergence of

Douglas Bridge, the rebellious creature who ultimately is set free of his father's influence.

For Connell, the world in which he walked was increasingly disturbing. At the beginning of 1968, he lamented to Gottlieb, "All would be well, I guess, if our government was not insane."[48] By the end of the year, after the assassinations of Martin Luther King Jr. and Robert F. Kennedy; after the chaos and teargas surrounding the Democratic National Convention in Chicago; in the midst of a corrosive student strike at San Francisco State; after the revived, law-and-order Republican Richard M. Nixon defeated Hubert Humphrey in the presidential election; and as the war in Vietnam dragged on, Connell delivered a book-related essay to the *New York Times*, one imbued with a deep strain of political pessimism. Connell was writing about a volume of military history that he had read a decade earlier and urged Ken Lamott to read—*The Warriors* by J. Glenn Gray. (Lamott had reflected on it for *Contact*.) Gray's six chapters drew from his service in Europe as a counterintelligence officer during World War II, his return a decade later to talk with war survivors, including many Germans, and his thoughts, as a Ph.D. in philosophy, on the future of war. From Gray's reflections, Connell extracts the idea that "nothing corrupts the soul more surely and more subtly than the consciousness of others who fear and hate us." As Connell suggests, in Gray's assessments of the past, "a reader may discover the present and the future."[49]

Connell was eager to make sure readers got the notion that the authoritarian horrors of Nazi Germany could indeed happen here, in the United States, or anywhere that "conceals in itself violent criminal forces, waiting only for an opportunity to appear in daylight." As Connell emphasized, "he pointed straight at America when he said that if, during the passion of war, we grant full authority to men who are committed to total victory, we invite moral chaos. It is as if he foresaw Gen. Curtis LeMay offering to remove Vietnam from the map." In Gray's book, Connell found themes he had explored in *Notes from a Bottle*, had hinted at in *The Diary of a Rapist*, and would come back to time and again in his work—the human capacity for recklessness, "which has been the regnant mood of America," and our impulse for destructiveness. If more people don't read Gray's book, Connell's message went, we are doubly doomed.[50] Connell also signaled that he was wading deeper into this "shadow stream" when Gus Blaisdell published sections from his new "Notes 2" project: "Just now I heard the explosion of the cannon across the bay. / Sundown, and I shall withdraw / the black Knight."[51] Many more games of chess at the No Name would ensue before that book arrived with a chess game embedded in its pages.

Editors at the *New Yorker* read the *Mr. Bridge* manuscript and opted not to run an excerpt: "Though the character of Mr. Bridge is very clearly drawn, his views are for the most part familiar and tend to become predictable."[52] Connell's agent found a more welcoming reception at *Esquire*, which bought several sections and planned to publish them in the spring before the book's publication in May.

As the Knopf staff prepared to bring *Mr. Bridge* to market, Connell shared some thoughts. Send books to his posse of supporters—Stegner, Clark, West, and Steele. Thorpe Menn, the *Kansas City Star*'s literary editor, had proven useful in the past, especially when he got front-page treatment for *Mrs. Bridge*. Blaisdell was chomping at the bit to read it, perhaps with the idea of expanding his comprehensive essay on Connell into book form. Webster Schott writes for *Life* magazine and other publications. And with a bit of a twinkle Connell had another suggestion about his hometown media outlets: "Now you will not believe a word of what follows, but Kansas City has a Society Magazine. Yes, ma'am. It is called *The Independent*, comes out every week, and the country club matrons gobble it up. I'm not sure about the address because I have only a 10-year-old copy, but it would be worthwhile to get a copy of the book to the *Independent*. Possibly with a note pointing out that everything happens in Kansas City."[53] It is of course notable that Connell would have retained a ten-year-old copy of the *Independent*, most likely because it had something about *Mrs. Bridge*. Kansas City was currently on his mind, as he was planning for a brief holiday trip there in December.

The first months of 1969 presented Connell a career boost on several small fronts. Along with Knopf's generous advance, there were new small-press reprints of three of his books, and Hollywood producer Tony Bill optioned *The Patriot*.

Another book of photography, to which he contributed a collection of quotations, appeared from a California imprint. Called *Woman by Three*, it featured portfolios by a trio of photographers (two women and a man) who cast their eyes, in portraits and street photography, on the lives of women. Connell's thread of texts reflected not only what he sensed in the photographs but what spoke somewhat lyrically to his own state of mind as well. Yes, he might have agreed that although he could not figure out how to be married, he was hopelessly in love with women. "I am very fond of the company of ladies," writes Samuel Johnson on one page. "I like their beauty, I like their delicacy, I like their vivacity, and I like their silence." Or this, from Simone de Beauvoir: "Body and soul, it is by taking her to his heart that man finds his roots in the earth and thereby finds fulfillment."[54] Beauvoir went on to say that men and women are destined for attachment. Connell certainly understood that. He had just completed a novel that dwelt on the absence of true attachment. His vision may well have been to close the void of his loneliness with meaningful attachment, but, as he put it, how and with whom?

Connell was pleased to get the news that Knopf had upped its initial print run of *Mr. Bridge* before publication. Like most authors, he was eager to hear about what the publisher was doing to turn his book into a success. He asked, for example, to see a schedule of advertising so he could look for ads. "One works on a book a long time and naturally becomes unnaturally interested in every item," he told Gottlieb's assistant, Toinette Rees.[55] He told Gottlieb that he knew how publishers regarded authors who demanded advertising for their books, but he wasn't one of those people, he just wanted the information.

Blair Fuller, the garrulous co-owner of Minerva's Owl bookstore on Union Street, threw Connell a book-signing party in April as reviews of *Mr. Bridge* began to appear. Fuller poured the Chablis and Connell forced himself to socialize. As one journalist noted that season, Connell was extremely private ("that's your word for it, not mine," he responded) and famously "rejects public appearances and campus appointments." He didn't even own a telephone until recently ("I can't stand the noise," he said).[56] But Connell wasn't so shy or dismissive of attention that he'd skip a party in his honor.

In the spring of 1969, as *Mr. Bridge* was making its way to print, Connell found a new female interest, at least temporarily. Amy Burk happened to be the writer Raymond Carver's sister-in-law, and her husband had just gone to Europe with another woman. No matter, Burk had a thing for married men, often older types, and once dated the writer James Dickey. She was something of a wounded bird. Abused as a child, she was possibly bipolar. In 1961, her affair with a police detective named Harry Olliffe ended when Olliffe's wife, the other blonde in his life, shot him to death with his own revolver. The episode informs Carver's later story "Harry's Death."[57] But Connell, in his crisp shirts and that leather bomber jacket, was certainly an attraction. Connell likely knew none of Burk's history when he invited her to ride shotgun in his old Rambler American and take a road trip with him to Santa Fe. Details are hard to pin down, but Connell's journey with Burk to New Mexico didn't go well: "Everyone had hoped this would be a respite for her, but after a week, she suffered a nervous collapse—it would turn out to be her first of several manic episodes—and was hospitalized in San Jose."[58] Further testimony about Burk comes from a piece of autobiographical fiction by the novelist Douglas Unger, who married her a few years later: "She *was* crazy, and she was irresistible. She radiated a bold quality that was both sensual and a challenge, like a slap, then there was another, harder slap if she were ignored, and that drew her lovers to her."[59] Connell was briefly drawn to her, but even after their foreshortened trip, they kept in touch and not long thereafter he had lunch with Burk and her sister, Carver's wife, in New York. Burk, at least in part, would serve as character-shaping fodder for Connell's novel *Double Honeymoon*, which would come along in the mid-1970s.

As for Gale Garnett, she was about to make another trip to Paris and soon decided to leave San Francisco and take up residence, as well as Canadian citizenship, in Toronto. Garnett had been present for at least part of the *Life* magazine photo shoot that took place along with Schott's interview with Connell in early May. (The resulting article, and its unabashed image of the couple in Garnett's "pad," wouldn't appear until early October.)

Connell's *Mr. Bridge* received mixed reviews from the *New York Times*. "Strung together," wrote Christopher Lehmann-Haupt, "the vignettes begin to add up to a compassionate, funny, but ultimately devastating portrait of the kind of person our children are now warning us about." Still, the critic suggested, the novel lacked the kind of epiphany experienced in its predecessor, and instead of "a major social portrait" readers are left with "a satirical miniature."[60] As expected, Guy Davenport's review appeared on the cover of the *Times*'s Sunday book section. It was perceptive and intelligently rendered. Gottlieb was thrilled that Davenport took Connell as seriously as if he were dissecting Proust. Davenport, though, subtly deflated the book as an exercise in mere realism. Echoing Nietzsche, he wrote, *Mr. Bridge* lacked the complexities and spirit of true comedy or tragedy. The Bridge novels, he concluded, were "triumphs of realism," adding, "Mr. Connell's art is one of restrained and perfect mimicry. . . . Alongside all this enameled charm, we soon discover, there is a slyness of implication that is more puckish than serious. Rarely has a satirist damned his subject with such good humor."[61] Still, Davenport's argument was rather subtle and most general readers might have slid past his elevated quibbles. Gottlieb and Connell could hardly have complained about the treatment, which was bolstered by a separate, featured interview that ran in the same section.

Among other critics, Webster Schott came through in *Life* (his review appeared six months before his profile piece) and Herbert Gold in *Playboy*. "He has penetrated the monotony barrier of suburban

Kansas City—and Minneapolis or Evanston—to lay open the quietly desperate, secret life of Midwestern noninvolvement," Schott wrote, adding, "Had Sinclair Lewis possessed compassion equal to his anger, discipline to complement his energy, he might have written *Mr. Bridge*."[62] Blair Fuller parlayed his association with Connell into a rave in *San Francisco Magazine*. Connell thought William Hogan's take in the *Chronicle* was tepid. Richard Rhodes, a Kansas City writer who well knew the Bridges' turf, cast a wary eye in the *Chicago Tribune*. Rather than dispassionate, Rhodes argued, Connell's portrait of Walter Bridge "is charged with the wry irony and covert indignation of a grand jury indictment." Rhodes felt that Connell was motivated by a hatred toward his subject and failed to inject a sense of humanness that Rhodes would have preferred to see, given, notably, that Mr. Bridge, or a Mr. Bridge type, lived on his own block and he had gotten to know him well: "I suppose my dilemma is personal. I found the book repellent and fascinating at the same time, like an autopsy I once attended."[63]

In general, Connell seemed "quite pleased with the things that are happening to and with *Mr. Bridge*," Steele reported in a letter to the agent they shared.[64] The feeling sank somewhat in the fall when Connell learned from a Knopf staffer that despite having four printings of *Mr. Bridge*, returns had mounted up and took a bite out of the book's success. To add insult to injury, Ken Lamott reported that he'd tried to call Connell at the No Name Bar and a new bartender didn't happen to recognize the name.

Connell surely was moved by Schott's article in *Life* that fall, though he was also somewhat deflated when he learned that the piece had only appeared in San Francisco and European editions of the magazine. From its environmental portrait of the long-legged writer ascending the steep Russian Hill near his apartment to Schott's complimentary words, the prominent package was a full-on stroke of the writer's ego. The photograph of Connell and Garnett, her face mostly obscured by her long dark hair but her plunging neckline quite visible, was clearly a talker. It contained details rarely seen in photographs of Connell: he's smiling quite broadly—the kind of smile he reserved mostly for precious and private occasions—and he's got a slim cigar in his hand (she's holding a cigarette). Outtakes from the photo session, viewed in *Life* archives online, document what clearly seemed to be a warm, relaxed, and lively relationship.

Buried deep in his article, Schott quoted Connell on a point that today would be considered not only unflattering but utterly deflating (or "canceling," in the jargon of hyper-sensitive identity culture). The only thing Connell did not like about San Francisco was "the flock of homosexuals." As he put it: "offensive people."[65] Some readers have been inclined to sense in Connell a kind of repressed or closeted self-hatred. Some who know little to nothing about him wonder if he himself were gay, as if that really mattered. Yet, his outward attitude expressed in that moment certainly coincides with Walter Bridge's, especially as depicted in *Mr. Bridge*.

Connell heard from Garnett, in a letter from Toronto, a few weeks after the magazine article appeared. She'd had dinner with John Huston in Los Angeles, who told her that *The Diary of a Rapist* was "truly excellent." She explained her dissatisfaction with the United States and San Francisco and her reasons for moving to Canada: "Police occupation, crooked mayor, violence, middle class white kids irrationally obsessed with Che guevara, etc." And she had a few thoughts about "*Life*'s coverage of your Art and my Tit": "Is your father still speaking to me? To you? I thought the article was O.k. but you are a dangerous man to quote out of context. Or do you think all homosexuals are offensive people? I hope you don't but it doesn't really matter I guess. Nor do I think of you as a sexual prude, as was suggested by the article. Au contraire, if thoughts were deeds. Don't you think?"[66]

Garnett brought up the subject of Connell and homosexuality, unprompted, when I met with her for the first time in Toronto. She insisted Connell was not gay. Connell, she said, was such a good-looking man, but he couldn't stand getting hit on by men. This was the period when the gay liberation movement was stirring, especially on both coasts. (The Schott interview occurred just weeks before the riot at the Stonewall Inn in New York, which is often cited as the beginning of the gay rights movement.) Garnett said she scolded him about it: "He had a big bad temper about this. And finally I said okay I can't take this. You're being a big baby. Let me talk to you. Women have lived with this all of our lives. People hit on you. And if they're reasonably sane, and that's most of them, and you're not interested, they walk on. But what they are saying is they think you're beautiful. And if that bothers you, you're a silly person. . . . But you take such pride in your lack of racism and your lack of ethnophobia."[67]

Garnett told me that Connell had gotten her point and eventually improved on the matter. And it's not as if she'd broken anything off entirely. Just weeks later, Garnett, who had landed a lead role in the Toronto production of the Broadway hippie-happy hit musical *Hair,* beckoned Connell to come see her naked on stage. Of course, he'd already seen her naked, she allowed, so why not come see the twenty-nine other naked actors?[68]

It is not clear how to take a moment a half-century later recalled by the writer Blake Bailey, who had spoken with Connell during research for his biography of John Cheever. Bailey asked Connell about his friend Calvin Kentfield, who, Bailey reported, had had a brief, drunken dalliance with Cheever in Los Angeles in the early 1960s. This was during the period when Connell and Kentfield were editing *Contact.* Connell seemed stunned if not shaken "to learn that Calvin staggered along both sides of the street," Bailey told me.[69] Had Connell never known of Kentfield's experience with Cheever? Bailey says he had not. Was he disturbed by the revelation four decades later or disturbed that he was unaware? Was he processing distant, foggy memories of the Sausalito scene? Were there other secrets to be learned? We'll apparently never know for certain.

Connell inscribed a copy of *Mr. Bridge* to his father, who by now was living with his second wife back on the Missouri side of the state line. In blue ink on the flyleaf Connell wrote, "Dad, Hope you enjoy the book. Any resemblance to anybody you know is purely coincidence. Evan." Connell's niece Janet Zimmermann was fairly certain that Dr. Connell, her grandfather, never read it, though, according to Schott's *Life* piece, Connell's father said he had. He told Schott that he thought the book was "well written." He acknowledged that some episodes were about him, "but the whole thing isn't."[70]

Schott had known Connell for nearly two decades by that point. His observations about Connell were savvy and well-reasoned. He had revelations about Connell's reticence, his writing philosophy (he had none, just keep on working), and his wardrobe (one suit, two pairs of shoes, including sneakers, in which he ran around Marina Green a few times a week). Among the several insights he shared about Connell and *Mr. Bridge* was the notion that his straightlaced friend was in fact a version of Walter Bridge himself, without perhaps Walter's most grating qualities. He was "Mr. Bridge de-Bridged," Schott wrote. "The form has been preserved, but the contents changed. Evan Connell's character and habits come straight from the Midwestern soil that grew Walter Bridge. Connell is as stable as the Kansas wheat crop. He eats slowly. He drives carefully. He is exactly on time. His manners are perfect."[71]

Here, all this time, we had been thinking of Connell as some model for the rebellious Douglas Bridge, or vice-versa. Now, little did Bob Gottlieb realize, his author had indeed given him what he wanted, the grown-up Douglas in the guise, at least partly and surprisingly, of Walter Bridge.

The Muhlbach Mask

1970–1976

"He feels unable to answer the nebulous questions that leap out of nowhere and vanish like poodles jumping through a hoop."

—*The Connoisseur*

IT WAS A typical August day in Kansas City, a muggy afternoon with temperatures in the nineties. Connell, with a new, neatly trimmed goatee framing his mouth, was back in his hometown, accompanied by a guest from Hollywood. Abby Mann, the accomplished screenwriter of Stanley Kramer's Oscar-winning *Judgment at Nuremberg*, was eager to write and produce a movie version of the two Bridge novels. He was thinking about George C. Scott as Walter Bridge, Joanne Woodward as India, and even Katharine Hepburn as the tragic Grace Barron. But first things first. A script had to be completed, and Mann didn't know how long it would take. He would write it and Connell would consult. Maybe a few months, maybe a year. In any case, Mann expected that location shooting would begin the following year, in 1972. They stopped to look at Connell's boyhood home on 66th Street, with its sloping driveway and big, shared backyard, and the high school nearby. Southwest High, once the jewel of Kansas City's public school system, had begun to register a momentum turn as prosperous white families migrated to the Kansas suburbs, creating a seismic shift in the racially segregated city and its schools. Connell's radar had been attuned to racial disharmony in Kansas City as elsewhere and undoubtedly he was brought up to date regarding the current situation.

Fig. 26. Connell and Hollywood producer Abby Mann scouted Kansas City in 1971 for a planned production based on the Bridge novels. The project dissolved within a year. Courtesy of the *Kansas City Star*.

Connell and Mann toured the quaint Brookside neighborhood with the grocery stores and movie theater that the young Connell knew so well. "Kansas City keeps growing," he told the local newspaper, "but in many ways it seems much the same. Downtown is much the way it was when I was a kid." They visited Connell's sister, Barbara, and her husband, Matt Zimmermann, who now lived in the expansive house that Dr. Connell had had built on a corner lot on Drury Lane in Mission Hills, the exclusive Kansas-side suburb. Just being in that place, with its architectural echoes of Mount Vernon, its tree-shade, trimmed lawns, and winding roads, reminded Connell what it was about his hometown that bothered him. "If I go to a party in San Francisco, I will meet all kinds of people. If I go to a party in Mission Hills, I will meet only Mission Hills people."[1]

Connell's visit back home coincided with a period of turmoil in his family. His niece Janet Zimmermann, who had followed her mother down a path of evangelical Christianity, had recently become involved in a commune. She went to a house in a midtown neighborhood for Bible studies and just to hang out. When she decided that she would move in, her grandfather Connell strongly disapproved and, in her telling, essentially disowned her. The young woman, then in her late teens, was so distraught that after her uncle heard about the spat he offered her a refuge. She could move out to San Francisco and live with him. She was flabbergasted by his suggestion. "I feel sure Evan knew I felt trapped and offered me a way out," she told me. "Being who he was it was one of the kindest acts I have ever experienced." Although she stayed where she was and wound up in an unhappy marriage to the commune's leader, in retrospect she said the episode typified the family's inability "to discuss feelings without being cut off" while also creating a cherished bond with her uncle.[2]

It's unclear how long Abby Mann's interest in the Bridges' story lasted or when he and Connell parted ways. They had a contract, but, as Connell told an acquaintance, "such an unstable business."[3] By the end of 1972, the year that shooting in Kansas City had been envisioned, Mann was writing the script for *The Marcus-Nelson Murders*, a high-profile project based on a true wrongful-conviction case in New York. That led Mann directly to a television series reprising the role actor Telly Savalas played in the movie as a New York police detective named Kojak. Mann was frying fish that turned out to be bigger and hotter than the emotional chill of the Bridge family. But the author of the Bridge novels had moved on to other projects as well.

Three books appeared in relatively quick succession in the early 1970s. Connell kept up his penchant for long-distance travel and the quests for meditative and sensory experiences that fed both his self-directed loneliness and his ever-widening basket of writing fodder. And Connell's arm's-length relationship with the literary establishment took one or two surprising turns.

Even before *Mr. Bridge*'s appearance, Connell had returned to the "Notes" project, his fragmented explorations of human history, violence, and enlightenment. Gus Blaisdell had run a segment in the *New Mexico Quarterly*, and the escalation of the Vietnam War kept a fire under Connell's simmering rage. The odd, irony-filled fact turns up everywhere in the piece: "The contract for the construction of the first guillotine / was awarded to a German harpsichord maker, Tobias Schmidt, / who was the low bidder, and who explained that sometimes he set aside the practice of his art in order to assist the realization of discoveries that would benefit humanity."[4] If such a passage didn't scan as poetry, it added periodic ballast—something solid and graspable for the reader—to the seemingly random wanderings of the work's mystical narrator.

The working title was an unimaginative *Notes 2*, but Connell's editor, Bob Gottlieb, knowing the first book's uncommercial history, objected. Connell returned with a somewhat more evocative title, *Points for a Compass Rose*. By late 1972, the manuscript had grown to four hundred pages. Connell suffered from what he felt was total neglect from Gottlieb and Knopf and decried the "worst ever" experience in publishing one of his books: "It's just the old story about NY people utterly forgetting the existence of book writers who live in the provinces."[5]

In the midst of multiple book projects and the dalliance with Hollywood, Connell left his longtime perch on San Francisco's Russian Hill and took up residence in Sausalito. He packed up his spare possessions—the books, the ancient ceramics, the sexy Sophia Loren poster that hung above his stove—and carted them just over the Golden Gate Bridge to the onetime fishing village. As Don Carpenter wrote, "Sausalito had its waterfront, boat yards, yacht harbors, bars, restaurants, incredible views of the bay and San Francisco, everything you could ask for if you had your afternoons off."[6] For a while Connell shared a gaudy, Spanish-style villa atop a hill that overlooked the bay. It was just up the hill from the Tides bookshop, which operated in the building that had housed *Contact*, and the No Name Bar, just a two-minute walk away. A steep stone staircase still rises from a nearby alley off Bridgeway. The climb presented no big deal to the fit runner who'd had plenty of experience navigating the challenging slopes of San Francisco.

One of Connell's downstairs neighbors was Neil Davis, the No Name's owner. Davis recalled Connell fondly as a frequent customer who mostly hung around to play chess. It was over the chessboard one day that Connell suggested to Davis the lights in the No Name were too bright. Davis responded by replacing them all with warmer bulbs.

Connell didn't stay very long in the villa, moving out when it was slated for renovation. Sausalito's housing market was tight, and he wound up relocating farther north, in Mill Valley, where Carpenter lived. It was a less vibrant town but Connell landed in something like "a swingers place complex with tiny swimming pool, airline stewardi, etc."[7] Along with writing he filled his suburban time with running, swimming, and chess at the No Name. It was a "flat time," he told Blaisdell, "but I don't get sick and the car doesn't break down."[8]

Connell's next book, a novel, began to germinate during a journey he took to South and Central America in 1969. Gale Garnett had helped to spark Connell's interest in collecting ancient objects. "She had quite a collection," Connell said. "Which surprised me. Because at that time she was in her early twenties. You just don't expect girls in their early twenties to be collecting 2,000-year-old ceramics. I'd be over at her place staring at these things for long periods of time, and it increased my interest in them."[9] He was most impressed by Garnett's savvy and the fact that instead of squandering her music earnings she invested them in art.[10] Now, Connell was intent on seeing what he could find on his own in the world of pre-Columbian artifacts. At one point he hoped to track down "a big Olmec jade in British Honduras" (now Belize).[11] He was also eager to make the trek to the ancient site of Machu Picchu in Peru. And though he spent a few days in Manaus, in northern Brazil, he later regretted not going into the Amazon jungle. Writing once about a travel narrative he admired caused him "to remember a humid settlement beside a languid tawny river, the aerial circus of mosquitoes, preternatural crawling specimens, suffocating heat, lethargic days, identical nights—tomorrow and tomorrow and tomorrow."[12]

Connell's stopover in Guatemala toward the end of his journey might have been prefigured by the travel brochure Muhlbach carried in his pocket in "The Mountains of Guatemala." While the promotional material promised luxury, in reality Connell found something a little less appealing: more mosquitoes. When a noisy DC-3 prop plane deposited him near the Mayan ruins of Tikal, he was greeted by swarms of insects. The flying hordes stuck around and tried to get on board when he got back to the plane to leave. "I don't think they enjoy living there very much either." Of the places he visited in about seven weeks that season, Connell was unimpressed with La Paz and Managua and checked off what appear to be routine visits to Quito, Buenos Aires, Montevideo, and Rio. He didn't think he would ever return. He was dazzled, though, by the anthropology museum in Mexico City, drawn there for two days by its ceramic and stone treasures. His personal collection expanded—a variety of clay figurines, a couple of turquoise Chimú pendants, an ancient Nazca bowl, and a contemporary carved turquoise piece "in the Olmec style."[13]

Connell's dabbling in pre-Columbian objects became Muhlbach's own obsession as well, another sign of the shape-shifting personae that Connell was creating in fiction. As he entered middle age, he recognized he had not fallen far from the proverbial family tree. He worried that he had become too much like his father and would have known by now that the emotional range he'd walled within himself could not ever change. Like his father, he cultivated some financial security by carefully selecting, with professional advice, corporate stocks to invest in. Occidental Petroleum was a winner! (Web Schott begged to differ. He said he got that tip from Connell and lost money.) Connell also traded stock tips with Herbert

Figs. 27 and 28. In the late 1960s, Connell began acquiring ancient Mexican and pre-Columbian artworks. This terra cotta Mayan figure inspired his novel *The Connoisseur*. Questions of authenticity about this greenstone Olmec mask became a plot line. Object image courtesy of Janet Zimmermann; mask photograph by the author, courtesy of Matthew Zimmermann.

Gold. Connell's passion for art and collecting, though an echo of his maternal grandfather's interest, was all his own. Dr. Connell would never have given himself over to the soft enterprise of art. So Muhlbach, insurance executive, widowed father of two, became a compromise character, or rather a composite or chameleon. A bit of the two Evan Connells, a bit of Walter Bridge and Douglas grown up, a bit of the writer's projections of what a mature widower in late twentieth-century America ought to be. Occasionally, Connell invests Muhlbach with thoughts or qualities that may well be his own as when he thinks that, as he tests the waters for a female companion, it's not his looks that get in the way, it's something else: "I'm not ugly, it's just that I look uncommunicative, as though I had a briefcase full of government secrets. I wish I didn't always look so stiff, my teeth aren't bad. Well—step right up, ladies!"[14] It's fair to read in Muhlbach some of Connell's own consciousness, desires, and awkward social behaviors.

Connell intended to give Muhlbach another star turn in a short story, but it grew into a novel about the man immersed in his new passion. From its opening moment—Muhlbach is struck instantly by the imperious aura of a ceramic figure on a shop's shelf—Connell and his character are in search of their own identities. What drew Muhlbach to this little nobleman? Did he see himself in its form, its being? Why did he have to own it? There you have the launch of a story about obsession, possession, art, and a quest for knowledge.

Muhlbach's lightning-bolt experience was, in fact, a direct transformation of Connell's epiphany one day in a Santa Fe shop, circa 1969. And Muhlbach's subsequent journeys through the bogs of shady dealers, fraud, fakes, scholarship, and personal desire frequently match Connell's growing obsession and experience, as he recounted it in a magazine essay some years later.[15] "That initial scene in *The Connoisseur* . . . is really the central thrill for Evan," a friend, the cartoonist William Hamilton, once said. "He doesn't really care much for material things. He likes those ancient things, which are clues of some kind to the great world that he explores." Gale Garnett recognized the novel as a kind of self-portrait of

Connell's inner being, "as this person suddenly found he was addicted."[16]

In late 1972, Connell was invited to serve as a juror for the National Book Award (NBA) in fiction. The task put him in something like a lion's den of literary argument, the kind of New York publishing ritual that he typically avoided. Yet, coming off the mild success of *Mr. Bridge*, it gave him an opportunity not only to see how the machinery worked but to contribute his voice and create a ripple. The proceedings began in early January 1973 and stretched over the next three months.

Jonathan Yardley, the *Washington Post*'s book critic, chaired the panel, which also included Leslie Fiedler, William H. Gass, and Walker Percy. They were esteemed writers and critics all, representing a wide variety of tastes and authoritative and contrarian opinions, if not a full spectrum of cultural demographics. Fiedler, known for his provocative essay collection *Love and Death in the American Novel*, had a distinctive reputation. As the critic Roger Sale once put it, "For Fiedler the important task has always been to be abrasive, to say 'No! in Thunder,' and in as many different ways as he can."[17] So the table was set for a donnybrook.

Yardley launched their discussions by sending around a list of books on his mind as contenders. The committee sought to nominate ten books on the way to choosing finalists and the ultimate winner. Yardley offered eight suggestions. Among them were Eudora Welty's *The Optimist's Daughter*, Don DeLillo's *End Zone*, and *The Sunlight Dialogues* by John Gardner. The other judges followed suit. Gass, for example, seconded Yardley's suggestion of Steven Millhauser's first novel, *Edwin Mullhouse*, and also had John Barth's novel *Chimera* on his list. Connell's initial nominees were typically eclectic: a story collection by John Updike and novels by Barry Hannah, Alix Kate Shulman, R. M. Koster, Merle Miller, Isaac Bashevis Singer, and John Williams, whose fourth novel, *Augustus*, appealed to Connell's interest in ancient history in a way that Barth's meta-fictional romp did not.[18]

Six weeks later, Connell and his colleagues spent three hours hashing it out in a meeting room at One Park Avenue in New York. They whittled a list of more than one hundred books down to twenty-five initial contenders. Soon they were down to nineteen, but after a few rounds in their systematic voting process, Yardley concluded, "It was pretty obvious that we had some very basic differences in taste." A month later, the committee announced a list of twelve finalists, though given the obvious strong feelings, they had already begun to discuss the possibility of choosing two books to share the prize. Fiedler, who, like Gass, championed the new, the bold, and the restless, noted that it would be better to name two winners than none, which would represent "cowardice." Connell and the others concurred.[19]

Connell's clear favorite was Williams's *Augustus*. He had taken more looks at it as the weeks went on and thought it was "genuinely distinguished" and could compete not only with any of the nominees that year but with any book in any other year. The novel is an extraordinary recreation of the hearts, minds, and intrigues of Romans, told in a series of letters and memoirs. Connell's argument for the book, which he expressed in a note to Yardley, is instructive in that we find Connell defining the elements of great literature: "I find it superior in several ways—in the richness of language, in the tremendous deliberation that went into its making, in the manifest intelligence and skill of its author, in the startling life of the characters, in its meaning to our own society, in its complexity, and also in a curious moral elevation which altogether separates this book from any of the others."[20] By comparison, every other finalist, even the very good ones, were much smaller achievements or hardly measured up. If he had to pick a second book to share the award, it would be Singer's.

Then came a dinner meeting in April at the Algonquin Hotel, one of New York's coziest and famed literary landmarks. The balloting began with a list of five books, those by Singer, Williams, Thomas Rogers (*The Confession of a Child of the Century*), Welty, and Barth. Williams's novel remained Connell's clear favorite. Percy

pushed the Welty, and Gass and Fiedler teamed up to argue strongly for Barth. *New York Times* critic John Leonard later expressed
bafflement that the panel rejected DeLillo, Gardner, Millhauser,
and Donald Barthelme. But as he noted, during a season of awards,
"Tonys, Oscars and roundball get more publicity, the values of this
culture being what they are; the National Book Awards get more
complaints, the values of writers being what they are."[21] In the
end, the committee reached a compromise and landed on Williams
and Barth. They were "two serious books by two serious writers,"
Yardley said judiciously, "and though they are very different books,
they reflect the different ways in which the art of fiction can be
practiced."[22]

For his part, Connell came away relatively unscathed by the experience, though it gave him further ammunition for his occasional
satirical spoofs in stories about literary and publishing bombast.
Connell had a good time: "Was rather fascinated by NY insiders
telling me who would win the fiction award. I blandly suggested
to Gordon Lish that maybe *Augustus* . . . but Gordon dismissed
that idea."[23] Connell also thanked Yardley for that "long drunken
Algonquin supper" and offered hope that it could become an annual gathering.[24] Nearly three decades later, a reminder came out
of the blue when Connell got a note from John Barth. Barth, at a
vacation rental in Florida, found a copy of *Mr. Bridge* and read it
for the first time. His note was just to say how much he admired
the novel. In Connell's memory, he feared that Barth had carried
a grudge because of something critical Connell might have said
during the judging. In a letter to Yardley, he had indeed referred to
Barth's novel and two others as "dreadful." But by this time, the
year 2000, Barth said he could not remember such a thing.[25]

Connell's next experience with the NBA came just a year later. *Points for a Compass Rose* was named a finalist in poetry for
1974. Connell regretted the category, continuing to insist he knew
nothing of poetry and never intended the "Notes" books to be read
that way. Among his competition that year was his old acquaintance Allen Ginsberg, who by then had cemented his standing as

the best-known poet in America. Once again, an NBA jury panel arrived at an impasse. Its members passed over Connell's book and settled on two others—Ginsberg's *Fall of America* and Adrienne Rich's collection *Driving into the Wreck*.

Connell often managed to be somewhere else when one of his books appeared in print. *Points for a Compass Rose* came out in May 1973 while he was in Paris. Connell had finished a draft of his Muhlbach novel, *The Connoisseur*, and the NBA business was over. Now he took a break to spend time in Madrid, Copenhagen, and then Paris, where he revisited his Left Bank haunts and shopped for collectibles. The city, he told Blaisdell, was crowded with traffic but "remains lovely and incomparable, especially mornings on the back streets."[26]

Back home, reviews of *Points for a Compass Rose* were all over the map, as it were. Brilliant and puzzling, demanding, wry, fascinating. Connell was perturbed by Paul West's review in the *Times*.[27] West admired the book in some ways, but the feeling was lost among his many recommended remedies. The review wasn't bad, Connell told Blaisdell, "he just sounded somewhat baffled."[28] Another *Times* critic, Herbert Mitgang, thought Connell would have benefited from some judicious trimming but essentially was moved to applaud, "It is a cockeyed vision for a cockeyed world with the added force of a fascinating structure."[29]

Although once again the book proved to be a hard sell, Connell found what feels like the perfect reader in a young writer just emerging as an essayist of note in her own right. Annie Dillard had published a book of poetry and was a contributing editor at *Harper*'s. There she worked for managing editor Lewis Lapham, the former San Francisco journalist who had already enlisted as a Connell acolyte. Lapham, in fact, had suggested that Dillard take Connell on, and she was astounded by the opportunity. Dillard's first book of prose, *Pilgrim at Tinker Creek*, was not yet out, but it soon would announce her as a sensitive observer of life and the natural world. For *Harper*'s she delivered an extraordinarily thoughtful and skillfully detailed essay about Connell's two "Notes" books. It was, in short, a rave, a levitation: "We have here on the planet with us a man of such courage and strength of spirit that he has not lost what Alfred Adler calls the 'nerve for excellence.' He has kept it despite the burden of an awareness not only of the enormity of his project and of the limitations of his own human understanding, but also of the abject ignorance and indifference of his audience." Dillard embraced the two books as the apex of epic poetry, dense with meaning, with spiritual quest, with dazzling detail, and with brain-challenging complexity. "Somehow Connell makes you care," she wrote. "And you understand at last that these notes are not tentative explorations, and far less are they 'expressions'; they are instead the magnificent artifices of a giant intellect."[30]

Dillard perceptively noticed that the speaker of *Points for a Compass Rose* was not the same wandering and self-reflective sailor as in the previous book. This one—"overbearing, stringent, sarcastic, nourished by hatred"—has taken it upon himself to record and remember atrocities and to sound "apocalyptic trumpets," though not without some glimmer of hope. Dillard was unabashed about the book's mind-blowing effects.[31]

Connell was grateful though slightly embarrassed by Dillard's remarkable essay. "You mentioned a number of things that I had hoped others might mention—about not forgetting the guilty, for instance—so I was at least doubly pleased."[32] Two months later, after he learned that *Points for a Compass Rose* had been nominated for the National Book Award, Connell told Dillard he suspected her review helped. Dillard answered him with a self-effacing confession of "ignorance and . . . abysmal inadequacy"; she wondered if she hadn't overstated his theme of penance, which had sparked her interest.[33]

Connell's book had a long-lasting effect on Dillard. Twenty-five years later, after ten books of fiction, prose, and memoir, Dillard issued what she called a "personal narrative," *For the Time Being.* Much like Connell's two exploratory projects and later works, Dillard's book interweaves threads of history, science, contemporary witness, and spiritual questing. She emphasized the homage with an epigraph consisting of three brief quotes from *Notes from a Bottle*.

Not long after the 1973 NBA debates and the launch of *Points for a Compass Rose*, Connell returned to his Muhlbach novel and finished a second draft. The manuscript had grown to 216 pages, he told Blaisdell, and he'd probably spend another two months on it. By the fall, he was ready to go through the meat grinder once again. Connell agreed to a $12,500 advance from Knopf, which he hoped would be paid swiftly given that he still owed a Los Angeles gallery for a collectible. And the feedback began to roll in. Elizabeth McKee, for example, made a comment about the book's momentum, questioning whether Muhlbach's accumulation of pre-Columbian scholarship was happening too quickly. Soon he got a detailed letter from Gottlieb, who, after two times through the manuscript, was utterly pleased. He made a couple of minor suggestions. For one, he and his colleague Nina Bourne were certain that someone with Muhlbach's interests would not be living in Queens. It just didn't feel right. Brooklyn Heights maybe, or certainly Manhattan. Gottlieb's main critical issue had to do with pacing, an echo of McKee's complaint. The book felt like one long and frenzied action. He suggested heightening the moments where time passed, using space breaks and more emphatic transitions to delineate each action in the story. All that would make Muhlbach's evolving obsession feel more real, Gottlieb said. "Otherwise, hurrah."[34]

Gottlieb enclosed a memo from Bourne that spoke directly to Connell's ego. "I love it so much I literally hugged myself while I was reading it," she wrote. "If what you read novels for is to get into somebody else's head & pulse, this does it. It is a small gleaming piece of almost perfection." Bourne had worked with Gottlieb at Simon and Schuster and left with him for Knopf in 1968. She was well known for having created an effective marketing campaign for Joseph Heller's *Catch-22*. So she was realistic and understood they'd have some work to do to sell *The Connoisseur*. In an afterthought Bourne said she was ever charmed by Connell—by the

Bridge books, by *Compass Rose*, and now by this. And her conclusion was perceptive, certainly meaningful coming from someone who had already spent more than three decades in book publishing: "This is the two Connells beginning to come together. He seems to me to have a kind of shining control of what he is doing."[35]

Connell responded to Gottlieb with a series of edits and some fresh insertions about settings in Albuquerque and Taos prompted by a recent trip to New Mexico. He offered an epigraph from Saint Thomas Aquinas, a comment on visual beauty, though Connell didn't have a satisfying translation: *Id quod visum placet* (that which pleases just by being seen). And in gratitude, despite the experience with *Points for a Compass Rose*, he said he wanted to dedicate the book to Gottlieb, who was touched and accepted. Gottlieb said that watching what Connell brought to the editing process was a revelation: "It's sparer now, and stronger, without having sacrificed its goodness and generosity of spirit. I wish I knew what its secret source of virtue was—so I could recommend it to others."[36]

Connell undoubtedly was pleased by the editorial reaction and other early responses. He told Max Steele, "People sound genuinely eager to read it, as opposed to sounding politely eager."[37] That exacting difference speaks to Connell's hypersensitive nature. His radar for appreciation and rejection was well calibrated. He was ready to give Muhlbach a longer life. Before the year was out, and nine months before *The Connoisseur* would see print, he had already begun another Muhlbach story. This one would return to the scene of Connell's short story "Mountains of Guatemala." And speaking of self-esteem, Annie Dillard's piece in the January 1974 *Harper's* got to the Knopf office in December, prompting much excitement. Connell jokingly suggested that maybe he should begin "Notes III," though Gottlieb likely heard that as a threat.

Connell gives Muhlbach very little to do in *The Connoisseur* save for looking at objects, reading up on the field, going to an auction, buying a fake, chasing down experts, and finally becoming lost in reverie. In his personal life, he is usually late for dinner, to the quiet displeasure of his housekeeper, the aptly named Mrs. Grunthe;

neglectful of his two children, Otto and Donna; and consistently eluding the advances of the talkative Eula Cunningham. Muhlbach's new obsession certainly has parallels in the work-first characteristics of both Walter Bridge and Dr. Evan Connell. But it also reflects Connell's own modus operandi. Yes, he had become something of an obsessive about collecting. He was still anxious about paying off the enormous debt he had taken on for that Xochopitl Olmec piece in Los Angeles. But more than that, Muhlbach's energized pursuit of knowledge and understanding of what he'd stumbled into in that shop mirrors Connell's own working method as a writer. A thought, a seed of a story idea, stopped him in his tracks and sent him on an intellectual journey, a quest for revelation, for alchemical transformation and fertile discovery. He read. He visited libraries and read some more. His writing was all about understanding not only his subject but also himself. Connell never had much use for Freudian analysis in his work—he was partial to Jung anyway— but more than any of his books, *The Connoisseur* feels much like a self-portrait at middle age. It certainly contributes to the notion that Muhlbach as an ongoing project in Connell's mind amounted to as much of an alter-ego in Connell's mature years as Douglas Bridge was in relation to his youth.

One passage in *The Connoisseur* explains Muhlbach's attraction, Connell's attraction, to possessing these messages from ancient craftsmen. As a dealer emphasizes to Muhlbach, "Originals attract us for another reason, which goes all the way back to prehistoric belief in magical properties. If we own something original, whether it's a skull or a lock of hair or an autograph or a drawing, we think maybe we acquire a little of the strength or substance of whoever it belonged to or whoever made it."[38] Connell had an almost ritualistic connection to the pieces he collected. He drew wisdom from their presence on his shelves. Although he was not overtly an occultist, Connell appreciated that these figures were conversation pieces in all senses of the phrase. He could sense the nobility in facial expressions. Unlike those who think of these figures as barbaric, he found them eminently human both in their representations and in

Fig. 29. A self-portrait sketch, from the early 1970s, appeared in *Self-Portrait: Book People Picture Themselves, From the Collection of Burt Britton* (New York: Random House, 1976). Courtesy of the Literary Estate of Evan Shelby Connell Jr.

the evidence of their making. "It's still possible to obtain a sense of being in contact with a remote past," he once explained to a journalist inspecting his collection.[39]

The run-up to publication of *The Connoisseur* was interrupted by the death of Connell's father. Connell, who had traveled to New York for the National Book Awards ceremony in April, also made a quick trip to Kansas City, where his father, at age eighty-three, lay dying at St. Luke's Hospital. Connell said goodbye to him, sat quietly in a moment of mutual self-respect, but told family members he wouldn't come back for the funeral. A graveside service preceded Dr. Connell's burial at Mount Moriah Cemetery. Connell's letters to Gottlieb and others from that period make no mention of his father's death. As with Connell's near silence attending the death of his mother, the absence of comment about his father, the internalization of his private feelings, seems wholly within character. It would be decades before Connell offered small utterances that shed light on the emotional voids in his family. There were never expressions of love, he told one interviewer. Gale Garnett once offered a plausible insight into their relationship: "I didn't get the idea that he either loved or hated his father, but simply that he admired him, respected him, and to some extent feared him."[40] Stunningly, Connell revealed late in his life that he believed his father felt guilty over his wife's death. In a minor car accident in the 1940s, she had been bruised in the breast that later developed a cancer. Connell said his father never spoke of the guilt, so it's unclear how he knew it.[41] And this, from a local columnist's interview: "My father never praised me for my work as a writer. The only time I can remember him ever appreciating anything I did was when I was 12 and I made a footstool in school. He put his feet on the stool and commented that it was very comfortable."[42] Resentment dies hard, perhaps especially when it involves one's parents and an emotionally starved upbringing.

Connell may well have ritualized his conflicted feelings for his father two months later. He loved the mountains and western landscapes and fondly remembered family vacation trips to Colorado, and now he spent a couple of weeks on a rejuvenating rafting trip down the Colorado River and through the Grand Canyon. You ought to try it, he told Gottlieb.

Connell supplied Knopf staffers with names of writers and gallery owners in New York and Los Angeles who should receive early copies of *The Connoisseur*. The recipients included Philip Roth and, somewhat surprisingly, Alice Denham, the literary aspirant who had bedded both Roth and Connell fifteen years earlier, back when they were emerging talents.

Reviews began to appear in August. The *Atlantic Monthly* weighed in with one of the first ("a deft, sophisticated, and pleasurable story").[43] In Kansas City, Thorpe Menn compared Connell's admirable confidence and restraint as a writer to a passage reflecting Muhlbach's thoughts about a master potter who refrained from decoration in order to let the ceramic piece speak quietly but assuredly for itself.

Guy Davenport reviewed Connell for a second time: "The real hero of the novel is an idea. We watch it enter a man's mind and after much discomfort and hesitation take root like a stubborn weed. Thought, said Wittgenstein, is a disease. The virus can be anything."[44]

To hear Connell's friends Max Steele and Alice Adams discuss the book, as they did in letters to each other, they were unimpressed at best. Bored was more like it. "It is carefully & beautifully written," Steele wrote, "& except for the Book of the Month Club will find few readers. I can not imagine a non-writer reading it."[45] Adams, who had loved *Points for a Compass Rose*, replied, "Skillful and dry and ultimately disappointing, I thought. Should have been left as a short story."[46] Their reactions might have been more realistic, or more reflective of the merciless market, than the positive reviews.

Even as *The Connoisseur* slowly simmered on bookstore shelves and as reviews continued to roll in—a lukewarm appraisal in the *New York Review of Books*, for instance—Connell was finishing another draft of the next novel centered on Muhlbach. Connell got it going by repositioning "The Mountains of Guatemala" to become the opening chapter of *Double Honeymoon*. The novel put Muhlbach in a turbulent *pas de trois* with two characters from that earlier story, the young and free-spirited Lambeth Brent and the fiery diplomat Rafael López y Fuentes.

Gottlieb was unconvinced by Connell's portrayals, especially of Muhlbach's swooning, immediate attraction to the impulsive Lambeth. Muhlbach's passion for ancient objects was fresh and believable in *The Connoisseur*. In *Double Honeymoon*, which seems to be set chronologically before the collecting obsession, Muhlbach felt divorced from the previous portrayal, and the older man's passion for a younger woman—partly Gale Garnett, partly Amy Burk, partly made up—was so much more of a cliché. Just how old was Muhlbach supposed to be, Gottlieb wondered in his two-page, initial critique. Even Connell's big fan Nina Bourne was distressed by the manuscript. As her memo to Gottlieb began, "Oh dear." That "shining control" she'd noticed in the previous novel had dissipated, it seems.[47] Gottlieb discussed many of their points in a phone call with Connell. Connell soon sat at his typewriter and responded. Sure, he could take another look at one moment or another. But some of Gottlieb's observations were confusing or contradictory. What Connell was trying to do, he said, was not to have Muhlbach wrestle with Lambeth's tragic down-spiral but to have him "passing through the periphery" of her tragedy, as most people experience such episodes.[48]

Connell was willing to make another go at it. He would get a revision back to his agent in a month or two. But he surely felt Knopf's relative lack of interest and told Gottlieb he had noticed a declining amount of advertising for each successive book: "I have never minded revising as long as I think the project is being improved. On the other hand, after laboring in the mines for lo these 25 years I've decided that win or lose I must depend ultimately on my own judgment."[49] Gottlieb ultimately conceded that, while Knopf would publish the novel, it would do so with not much enthusiasm. Connell decided to take it elsewhere, and it landed at Putnam. The novel essentially was doomed. Connell knew it, recalling a few years later, "I didn't realize how it should have ended until after the book was published."[50]

Four decades later, Connell earned a mere two sentences in Gottlieb's memoir of publishing and not even a mention in the Wikipedia account of the notable writers Gottlieb once handled. "I very much liked Evan Connell's *Mr. Bridge*, and Evan, too," Gottlieb writes, "a laconic man who seemed to me both intensely moral and naturally elegant." As a formidable man of letters, Gottlieb is worth listening to and his description of Connell's legacy—"his career was an odd one"—carries some weight.[51] Nevertheless, it very much leaves open the possibility that Connell's oddness—whatever that meant—is a virtue worth examining.

After *Double Honeymoon*, Connell essentially left Muhlbach behind. Although the novel's sexual anxieties reflect a part of

Connell's own persona, for further explorations of his alter-ego in fiction one could turn to subsequent short stories, several written in the early 1990s, and a recurring character named Koerner. (Another Germanic name, another nod to Thomas Mann.) But the unsatisfactory experiences of his two Muhlbach novels sent Connell on a much different writing road altogether.

Among the Wanderers

1977–1980

"The legend of the Traveler appears in every civilization,
perpetually assuming new forms, afflictions, powers,
and symbols. Through every age he walks in utter solitude
toward penance and redemption."

—*Notes from a Bottle Found on the Beach at Carmel*

CONNELL'S TRAVELS TO Central and South America, and just about everywhere else, began to find their way to his front burner in the gaps around the Muhlbach novels. Book publishing usually produces a period of limbo between edits and production, and there the writer's mind begins to get anxious. *What will I do next?* One book comes out, another is expected. Connell never seemed to be at a loss. "If you go to Bogotá," he began writing one day, "and visit the Banco de la República you will see, in the bank's Museo del Oro, nearly 10,000 pre-Columbian gold artifacts."[1] Connell, of course, did go to Bogotá. He also pored over historic volumes in the Columbian Library in Seville, Spain. And he immersed himself in relics of the Middle Ages at the dank Cluny Museum in Paris. He began crafting a series of essays that reached far back in history. He wrote of traveling and travelers, of mystics, plunderers, and, as it happened, more about pre-Columbian people and their cultural legacies, which had consumed Muhlbach and himself over the last several years.

After the two Muhlbach novels, Connell consciously took a break from fiction. There would be no more short stories for a while; no novel came to mind. "I must say," he declared, "it certainly is easier to write essays than stories, mostly because one doesn't have to think."[2] Lewis Lapham, having become editor at *Harper*'s, asked Connell to do some writing. Connell produced book reviews and offered a few of the essays he'd turned out. "And technically," he emphasized, "it is infinitely easier to write an essay than a story because you need very little imagination. After the research all you have to do is organize it and present it. With a story, though, you always fail; it is never as good as it should have been."[3] Connell habitually second-guessed his fiction. He often thought about how he might have made *Mrs. Bridge* better. He tinkered with stories every time they came up for reprinting. He never seemed satisfied.

Now, Connell tapped into a lode of historical figures and ideas that had interested him since childhood. He recounted the disappointment—resentment even—he felt when Richard Halliburton's junk went down in the Pacific. He grieved not only for his adventurous hero but also for the journey's souvenir stamped envelope that sank with Halliburton's boat. He spun out the story of Halliburton's fatal Sea Dragon adventure of 1939 and his role as "the last great traveler."[4] But Halliburton was just one of many historical travelers Connell referenced as he developed a theme that tied the essays together. He borrowed an idea, from Anatole France, about *un long désir*, the sensual impulse to be consumed by a quest for something unreachable. As the essays accumulated, Connell planned a book he called "El Dorado and Other Pursuits." By the time Holt, Rinehart and Winston published it in 1979, it became *A Long Desire*.

"I've never tried this sort of thing before," he told an interviewer not long thereafter, "and the research turned up so much extraordinary information. Those maniacal conquistadores jacking around in the jungle, and Prester John, and Henry Hudson, and the Etruscans, and the alchemists, and the Vikings, and so forth. All in pursuit of something, no matter how insane."[5]

Connell was venturing once again into history, thinking about singular characters who fearlessly blazed into the unknown. Some of them—Paracelsus, Prester John—had previously found their way into *Notes* and *Points* so they continued to tug at him for attention. He admired Mary Kingsley, the Victorian explorer who made remarkable journeys through Africa. He was discovering what Lapham later determined about the nature of history, a thought shaped in part by reading Connell. History was not something that happened in the past, Lapham once wrote. It is a story about what had happened. And Connell set out to master his own stories of the past. What could he know? How was his own identity formed by the vast pool of human consciousness? As in *Notes from a Bottle*, he knew these essays could very well illuminate the present and shine a light on the future. "He understands that history is composed of objective fact but also subjective experience," Lapham said of Connell. "Connell is asking himself what Montaigne asked of himself, What do I know?"[6]

Connell, coincidentally, had called on Montaigne to make an appearance in *Mrs. Bridge*. India Bridge comes across a random quote from the Frenchman in a magazine: "I have always observed a singular accord between super-celestial ideas and subterranean behavior." India reflects on this: "In less crystalline style she had observed somewhat the same thing and was puzzled by it." She goes on to conclude "that if super-celestial ideas were necessarily accompanied by subterranean behavior it might be better to forego them both."[7] Rather than forgo the two activities, Connell, in his own works of history, gleefully embraced them.

His approach in this series of essays was less fragmented than *Notes* and *Points*, more focused and sustained in a linear prose structure, though not without startling turns and surprisingly humorous interjections.

After nearly two years in Mill Valley, California, Connell finally found a suitable place to settle again in Sausalito in 1975. The small apartment in a newish complex at 232 Eden Roc sat along a quiet cul-de-sac, just off Bridgeway and near the harbor. It was two miles from the bar with no name, but for Connell that was an easy walk when, after a day of writing, a game of chess was in order. As elsewhere, the new place had only the essentials. He wrote in his bedroom. With his Olympia typewriter atop his simple desk, his mind wandered all over. He was, after all, doing exactly what he wanted to do. "I've been at it so long that it's become a way of life, like almost any other, sometimes enjoyable and gratifying, sometimes exasperating and frustrating," he said. "I can choose my subjects, work when and how I please, without being supervised or directed." And then the second-guessing, the feeling of inadequacy, of knowing "that the best I can do this morning will probably look defective tomorrow."[8]

After Mill Valley, being in Sausalito gave him a chance to get into the city more often. There were the usual writer gatherings at Enrico's, with Don Carpenter, Herbert Gold, and Blair Fuller, and visits to the Discovery and other bookshops. Connell drove a few times a week up to the Tamalpais High School track to get in a three-mile run. There was a mysterious blonde, and likely other women, who occupied Connell's time on occasion. One fling came to an end when the woman became too eager to get married, "which unfortunately would drive me berserk."[9]

A Long Desire, Connell's essay collection, speaks to Antoine de Saint-Exupéry's idea that "to travel, above all, is to change one's skin." Connell was a traveler of fewer extremes than those he wrote about. By contrast, when Graham Greene traveled, he poured himself into the plight of each society's marginalized class. Greene filled his novels with social struggle. He looked outward. Connell's gaze was more often turned inward. His travels, beyond his geographical journeys, were also intellectual, mind-expanding adventures into history and musty books. As he wrote in *Notes*, "Sea-gold and marble columns never have been what I sought, nor shards of broken amphorae; but the slightest measure of myself, and of those who have preceded us across this desolate shore."[10]

In one of Connell's essays, a meditation on gold and money, he brings up memories of his late father. There was the story of the Oklahoma oil strike of which the elder Evan had had a stake. On reflection, Connell found a distinction between his father and himself:

As he told me this story, I thought about the black mist in the air, the dangerous black column of spouting oil, and the pools in the field. I don't remember thinking about anything else. Nor do I recall what questions I asked. Maybe I asked if he had to take a bath afterward, or if they were still drinking champagne, or whether anybody slipped and fell. But now, if I had the chance, I would ask what went through his mind when he learned that the Oklahoma legislature had seized his fortune. Although, because he was my father and I knew him so well, I think I could answer for him. He would have been angry. He would have felt that he was being cheated.

At first I would have felt the same, I suppose. And yet, unlike my father, I would have decided very soon that what occurred was inevitable. I doubt if we are meant to get our hands on unreasonable wealth.[11]

That personal conclusion provided a clever transition into the next anecdote, one about the mountain villagers in Mexico we first met in *Notes from a Bottle*. When they spy an orange floating down their river, they wonder about the vast riches surely contained in a long hidden gold mine called El Naranjo.

After Evan Sr.'s death, Connell's family ties ran mostly through his sister, Barbara. He sent Christmas packages to her and her husband with books and other gifts for his two nieces and his nephew, all by now young adults and off on their own. His journeys back to Kansas City tailed off, but he and Barbara wrote to each other regularly. The earliest extant letter to his sister dates from late 1978. His letters to Barbara, or "Bobs," as he addressed her in each and every one, amount to something like a diary of his life and work from that point onward. His typical letter contained reports on his career, daily events, news of friends, and occasional barbs about politics and religion that he knew would irk his politically conservative, religiously born-again sister. She would soon receive a copy of the dust jacket for *A Long Desire*, he told her in that earliest letter. The book would be coming out in late spring. There evidently had been an ongoing conversation about what Connell's agent was or was not doing for him, and he told Bobs in this letter that given their long relationship he couldn't imagine changing agents. McKee, in fact, had suggested replacing the Hollywood agent who had done little or nothing for Connell. Occasionally there was a mention of a trust fund, which in Connell's case in some years yielded a quarterly draw of about $3,000. Despite or maybe because of his relatively simple lifestyle and the roller-coaster rewards from his books, Connell did not suffer poverty.

Connell enjoyed the annual Christmas party thrown by his writer friend Curt Gentry. Gentry, he explained to Barbara, co-wrote a major book (*Helter-Skelter*) about the Charles Manson murders with Vincent Bugliosi, a prosecutor in the case. Connell brought along a guest to the party, Dr. Oscar Janiger, the Los Angeles psychiatrist, who happened to be in town. Janiger, he reminded his sister, was the fellow who had introduced Connell to LSD. "Oscar probably knows as much about drugs as anybody in the country," he wrote, "and everyone was fascinated with him."[12]

More parties occurred around the time of *A Long Desire*'s arrival in June 1979. Ruth Costello, a former girlfriend of Calvin Kentfield's and one of Sausalito's better-known bohemian socialites, threw Connell a large shindig. After all, Connell had dedicated the book to her and her son Mark Costello, who was an aspiring actor in Hollywood. The celebration sprawled aboard the S.S. *Vallejo,* the converted ferryboat that once housed the merriment of the artist Jean Varda and also served as home and Zen activity center for Alan Watts. Writers from all over the Bay Area were there.

The public library also threw a party for local authors, including Connell, a few days earlier. Alice Adams complained to Max Steele that it was an exasperating affair spoiled by the presence of too many of the blowhard writers, some in Connell's circle, whom she just couldn't stand. Connell, she said, was "the only one with class among the regulars."[13] She once remarked a bit cattily that Connell spent too much time at such parties talking about print runs and publishers' advertising shortfalls. But Adams realized that after knowing each other for more than twenty years, she and Connell had become friends. "I guess after all these years," she wrote to Steele a year later, "he has worked it out that I am not sexually interested in him but do admire his work. . . . He is most polite, is he not. Needless to say he looks terrific."[14]

Connell sat still that year for an interview with a writer for the Dartmouth alumni magazine and shared his similar views on the dreariness of literary soirées. "Evan Connell has little gift for hype," Mary Ross wrote.

> He's not much for autographing parties or talk shows. He avoids the lecture circuit. He talks engagingly about books, but is discomfited by the sort of questions that 'usually occur at parties when you are backed into a corner and somebody asks if you write about real people or just make things up.' 'And what sort of stories do you write?—I mean detective stories or what?' And 'Have you written something I might have read?' And 'I've got this absolutely fabulous idea for a novel, so why don't you just write it down and we'll split 50–50?'[15]

Connell had already delivered a sardonic take on such matters in "The Mountains of Guatemala," and chatter much like he complained about here would become the running annoyance of a later story, "A Cottage at Twin Falls."

If Connell had any doubts about his turn to historical essays, they were allayed by some of the reviews that greeted *A Long Desire*. Granted, Connell was not a great admirer of book reviews, except on occasion when he found a useful observation worth remembering. He had said as much in response to a survey of writers conducted by Robert Kirsch of the *Los Angeles Times* shortly after *A Long Desire* came out. Most provincial reviewers, Connell said, didn't have the courage to say what they thought, and many waited for the *New York Times*'s reviews in order to gauge their own judgments. Still, there were moments worth savoring. "This is the way history should be written and almost never is," Grover Sales wrote in the *Los Angeles Times*, the *San Francisco Chronicle*, and other newspapers.[16] Another critic relished Connell's "treacherously seductive prose."[17]

Still, the practical matters of publishing raised Connell's hackles. Because of the good reviews, especially in the Bay Area, bookstores quickly sold out of *A Long Desire* and had trouble getting it back in stock. Connell was livid. He couldn't understand how the publisher, Holt, could have done such a wonderful job producing the book—great proofreading, lovely cover—then performed so badly in the distribution. "I am tired," he told Blaisdell, his New Mexico friend, "of people telling me they have tried everywhere to buy the book and can't find it."[18]

It was Holt's decision to chop the suite of Connell's essays into two books. Connell did not disagree with the plan and was grateful for the time to continue working on the seven essays that would appear in 1980 under the title *The White Lantern*. Amanda Vaill, then an editor at Viking, had tried to make a play for the second volume but was overruled by her bosses, who couldn't see the return in it. In his review, John Leonard called *The White Lantern* "a brilliant browse," a phrase that later morphed into a *New York Times* blurb: "pleasant browse in the attic of an intellectual antiquarian."[19] Not all readers were so moved. An anonymous critic in the *Chicago Tribune* called the book "a superficial hodgepodge. . . . Connell is too glib for his own good."[20] Still, Connell seemed mostly upbeat over the general reception.

A few months after *A Long Desire* came out, Connell's longtime California friend and *Contact* co-editor Ken Lamott died of cancer. He was only fifty-six, a year older than Connell. He was the son of Presbyterian missionaries and, like Connell, a navy veteran of the World War II era. Born in Japan, he had spent most of his life in California, save for his time in the navy; at Yale, where he studied engineering before earning an English degree; and a few years in Washington, D.C., while working for the State Department in the early 1950s. In the mid-1950s, he taught at the San Quentin Prison, the subject of his *Holiday* magazine essay in 1961, a book, and an experience he brought to the pages of *Contact*. (In 1971, he returned to San Quentin for a magazine piece that reported on conditions even as a riot broke out, resulting in the stabbings of numerous prisoners.) Lamott and his first wife, Dorothy, often had Connell over for dinner at their home in Tiburon, during which the handsome visitor caught the eye of the Lamotts' young daughter, Annie. She was maybe five or six when she would sit under the dinner table and imagine that she would like eventually to be married to Connell. By the time of her father's death, Anne Lamott had gone through some wrenching life challenges, including a stretch of drug and alcohol abuse. Nevertheless, after achieving sobriety and her own success as a writer, she maintained a lifelong friendship with Connell.

Although Connell was solidly on a nonfiction track, another book that came together in 1980 was a short-fiction collection. Called *Saint Augustine's Pigeon*, it felt like a gathering of greatest hits. Blaisdell had offered to edit a collection, but Connell confessed that he didn't have enough new stories to make a book. He sent Blaisdell a list of his previously published stories, and they spent months exchanging revisions and ideas. Blaisdell planned to wrap it up with a closing essay, though by publication that fell by the wayside. "My own feeling," Connell cautioned, "is that unadulterated praise is suspect. There's no such thing as a perfect painting or a perfect story."[21]

Along with the titular Muhlbach story the book included "Arcturus" and "Otto and the Magi." Other pieces dated back to the 1950s, such as "At the Crossroads," "The Yellow Raft," and "The Short Happy Life of Henrietta." Blaisdell knew most of the earlier stories from his first reading of Connell in the early 1960s. Another entry was the trio of Ruth Bridge vignettes under the collective title "Mademoiselle from Kansas City." Connell had once thought of pursuing a Ruth Bridge novel but, beyond the Ruth segments of the two Bridge novels, produced only these few fragments. Clearly a sly bit of ironic self-revelation was at play when Connell and Blaisdell selected the final story in the volume. "A Brief Essay on the Subject of Celebrity with Numerous Digressions and

Particular Attention to the Actress, Rita Hayworth" was actually Connell's nonfiction account of a Hollywood experience written originally for *Esquire* and here disguised as a work of fiction. The most recent story in the book, from 1972, was "The Palace of the Moorish Kings," a companion story to "The Walls of Ávila." Both sprung from Connell's loitering in Spain and shared a central, Connell-like traveling character named J. D. The *New Yorker* had rejected "The Palace of the Moorish Kings" a few years earlier, just as it had rejected "The Walls of Ávila" two decades before.

Although he had nothing new, Connell was eager to revise. As he learned from Wallace Stegner, "Revision is what separates the men from the boys."[22] And as Connell put it for his Dartmouth interviewer, "There are writers who never revise, who consider their first thought to be the consequence of a divine spark. I've always thought that was an absurd conceit."[23] (A subtle criticism here of Allen Ginsberg, most likely, whose mythic motto was "first thought, best thought.") Connell amassed four pages of edits to "The Yellow Raft." "It was written so long ago," he told Blaisdell, "so many inappropriate words, etc. I've brought the pilot just a bit more into focus."[24] In its original form, the story, placed last in *The Anatomy Lesson*, had a chilling aura, heightened by Connell's deliberate pace and immaculately present and precise details. Now, more than two decades later, "The Yellow Raft" became the lead story in *Saint Augustine's Pigeon*, as if to set a tone of stark contemplation of human fate. Connell's revisions, largely imperceptible, turnbuckled the prose even tighter. In the story's closing two sentences, for example, Connell shaved a total of eleven useless words out of the original thirty. Any student of writing could learn much by looking closely at how he did it. Connell had learned in middle age to "eliminate whatever was necessary. Hemingway sometimes wrote one sentence too many. Faulkner's stories are twice as long as they need to be."[25] Raymond Carver was inspired by Connell's technique, by his confession that he was done with a story when he started taking commas out then putting them back in. Carver observed, "I like that way of working on something. I respect that kind of care for what is being done. That's all we have, finally, the words, and they had better be the right ones, with the punctuation in the right places so that they can best say what they are meant to say."[26]

Although it countered Connell's new emphasis on nonfiction, *Saint Augustine's Pigeon* marked still another significant turning point. It came from a new, independent literary publisher, North Point Press, which had been founded in the Bay Area by William Turnbull, a wealthy real estate developer, and Jack Shoemaker, a former bookseller who had known Blaisdell years earlier. Shoemaker sought out Connell, whose work he had admired since *Notes from a Bottle* had taken up that whole issue of *Contact*. The match turned out to be the beginning of a long-term, mostly happy relationship. And it soon led to the biggest and most successful project of Connell's career.

The Custer Cornucopia
1981–1985

So, for the moment, Custer is again leading the charge. How far he will go before slowing down is impossible to say.

—Connell to Barbara Zimmermann, 1984

AS ANOTHER SUMMER settles onto the high plains—the summer of 2019—the softly crinkled hills above the Little Bighorn River in Montana are blanketed with mixed grasses, sagebrush, and huge helpings of yellow sweet clover. Against a blue or even a rain-threatening gray sky, the golden fleece, streaked with young seasonal green, presents a vast, otherworldly vista like something out of Van Gogh. As botanists have it, the pervasive clover is a European import, having begun to invade the High Plains landscape in the late seventeenth century. There's no telling how much of the yellow plant stood here when another kind of invasion played out violently, tragically, and forever dramatically. As a park ranger puts it at the Little Bighorn Battlefield National Monument, there are ghosts in these folded, mesmerizing hills, and visitors would do well to listen to what they have to say. One can't ever get the full story of what happened here in the early summer of 1876 by reading books, the ranger says. One must feel it by being here.

Connell first sensed the deep tragedy of history that took place on this land while trekking through the West one spring in the mid-1950s, just a year and a half after returning from his postwar rambles in Europe. Connell never saw battle in World War II, never directly experienced the kinds of psychological traumas he depicted in his early war-spawned stories such as "A Cross to Bear," "The Yellow Raft," and "The Marine." So traveling in the West and contemplating the Little Bighorn can't really be thought of in the same terms as the healing pilgrimage in a natural landscape that Hemingway's Nick Adams made in "Big Two-Hearted River." Still, Connell had an idea to write about the battlefield, to wrestle with American historical myths and legacies, as early as 1962. This was in the aftermath of *The Patriot*, the not-so-successful novel that drew from his Naval Air Corps experience. His agent found the idea interesting, but it went dormant. It would be two more decades before he began stirring his memories of western figures (Billy the Kid, for one) and writing what he figured would be an essay about General George Armstrong Custer. Custer's checkered career came to its end in these western hills on June 25, 1876. Connell, like many an American schoolboy in the first half of the twentieth century, would have been introduced to a Custer generally portrayed as a fearless military hero. His "Last Stand" was a glorious fable about giving one's all for his country and fighting bravely against hostile forces until the end. Custer was painted in golden light all the way down to the mythically golden tresses that flowed like a holy aura beneath his government-issued hat. And Connell, while a college senior in Kansas, stood with great curiosity—if not undergraduate mockery, as he wrote—before Comanche, the taxidermied bay horse in the college's Natural History Museum. The steed had ridden into battle with Custer's ill-fated troops under Captain Myles Keogh.

Comanche, it was often said, was the U.S. military's sole surviving creature of the Little Bighorn battle, and his final resting place was on the Kansas campus. The wounded horse was treated after the battle and transported downriver, then recovered and appeared on ceremonious occasions from time to time. Comanche died in 1891, fifteen years after the Last Stand. A naturalist named L. L. Dyche, on behalf of the memory of the Seventh Cavalry, gathered his skin and bones and recreated him for long-term exhibit in Lawrence. The college resisted frequent requests to loan the preserved horse. In fact, Connell was at Kansas the year (1946) that university officials rebuffed General Jonathan Wainwright, who asked that Comanche be returned to Fort Riley, about eighty-five miles west.[1] Connell once told his sister that he was trying to learn more about a small yellow bulldog known to be on the battlefield—whose was it, what happened to it?[2] The pursuit of that fragment came up empty. "The other horses are gone," Connell writes, "and the mysterious yellow bulldog is gone, which means that in a sense the legend is true. Comanche alone survived."[3]

Fig. 30. *Ashes, Ashes, We All Fall Down*, from Paul Pletka's series of Custer portraits, c. 1985, inspired by *Son of the Morning Star*. From the book *Paul Pletka: Imagined Wests*, by Amy Scott, courtesy of the University of Oklahoma Press.

Custer and 260 of his men perished on that distant warm afternoon. Their names are listed on a memorial obelisk atop Last Stand Hill in the park. They succumbed to an unexpected assault by perhaps as many as 1,500 (and likely more) Indian warriors—Lakota and Hunkpapa Sioux, Cheyenne, Arapaho, and members of several other tribes. Estimates have been wildly varied about Native American casualties, though one highly regarded study puts them at thirty and sorted out the confusing record to account for each name—Cut Belly and Black Bear of the Cheyenne, for example, and Red Face and White Bull of the Hunkpapa.[4] A Native American memorial was commissioned for the park in 1997. Built down the hill from the cavalry marker, a circular stone wall rises from the earth, topped by a black, open-work bronze sculpture of warriors on horseback (by Colleen Cutschall, an Oglala Sioux artist). On the wall's interior surfaces visitors can view the names of the fallen and read tribal accounts of their lives.

To this day, 144 years later, as I write, the events of June 25 and June 26, 1876, remain matters not fully resolved or understood. Historians of Custer, the Little Bighorn, and famed Indian leaders such as Sitting Bull and Crazy Horse have analyzed, argued, mythologized, and calmly presented their evidence in what amounts to an industry of book production and history conferences. Facts and speculations continue to evolve.

Americans can thank Connell, at least in part, for the revival of interest in the Little Bighorn battle and the revision of our understanding of Custer and his adversaries. Connell's projected essay about Custer grew beyond his expectations. He traveled to sites and libraries throughout the West to gather fragments—always more fragments—and soon had hundreds of pages of a manuscript that he would eventually title *Son of the Morning Star*. The book was published in 1984 and became a surprising literary sensation. In the end, its commercial success exceeded even that of *Mrs. Bridge*. And its wide readership, accelerated a few years later by a television production, helped generate new interest among writers, educators, and even reenactors.

Sandy Barnard, who has been writing and publishing on various aspects of Custer and Little Bighorn history since the late 1970s, put that in perspective for me when we met, almost by chance, in Sheridan, Wyoming, in June 2019. I had visited the Little Bighorn Battlefield National Monument in Montana, about an hour north of Sheridan, on June 26. Barnard and fellow members of the Little Big Horn Associates were gathering in a Sheridan hotel for their annual conference. Barnard sat in the conference book room, tending to several tables covered with titles by him and others. He was not the first to tell me that many historians were disappointed that Connell's *Son of the Morning Star* appeared without footnotes. (Nevertheless, the organization gave Connell its literary award for best book on the subject in 1985.) They believed that the small North Point Press had stripped them out as economically unfeasible, though the truth was simpler: Connell didn't want to use them. "Evan hated footnotes," his editor Jack Shoemaker said, "and thought any question of using them might cast a negative light on the 'creative' aspect of his histories."[5] One historian, Elizabeth Atwood Lawrence, wrote to Connell to ask for his citations on eleven points. Connell's response itemized his notes for all but one that he couldn't locate.[6]

Despite the historians' arguments, Barnard acknowledged that Connell "basically revived interest in Custer." In doing so he moved the major general to more of a "middle ground" between his extreme detractors (see Thomas Berger's novel *Little Big Man* and the subsequent movie, directed by Arthur Penn, which presents a wildly debased caricature of Custer) and those who reveled only in Custer's glory.[7]

The Custer legacy, the Little Bighorn battle, and the ghostly voices of soldiers and tribal warriors permeate the cultural space of the present-day region. Bookshelves are packed with ever-new titles exploring the lives, trials, and deaths of battle participants. The artifact-covered walls of the Mint Bar in Sheridan, a watering hole that dates to 1906, includes a framed replica of the first newspaper account of the Little Bighorn bloodbath—the Bismarck, North

Dakota, *Tribune* of July 6, 1876: "Massacred! . . . No Officer or Man of 5 Companies Left to Tell the Tale." At the handsomely expanded Brinton Museum in Big Horn, Wyoming, visitors can encounter Frederic Remington's striking portrayal of the battle, a grisaille painting that foregrounds the Sioux warriors and puts Custer's dwindling troops on a faint hilltop, their demise certain and imminent. In another room at the Brinton, in the Native American collection, there's a painting on muslin (1899) depicting the battle and other important events in the life of Standing Bear, a Minneconjou Lakota who took part in the conquest of June 25, 1876. Standing Bear created at least a half-dozen versions of the pictorial narrative, sketching a history in images, from Sitting Bull's prophetic Sun Dance to the carnage and triumph on the battlefield three weeks later.

In the years he was compiling his Custer research, Connell moved twice in Sausalito, both times displaced when apartment buildings were converted to condominiums. He ultimately took an apartment in a hilltop complex at 487 Sherwood, on the town's northern fringe. The view was similar to what he'd had at the Eden Roc place but from a higher vantage point. It was a wide and long vista. Ships moved slowly through the harbor. He could watch the wind ruffling the edges of the Tiburon hills across Richardson Bay. Connell was becoming increasingly frustrated by Sausalito's churning real estate market and the overbearing freeway traffic. He had a passing thought about what it might be like to live in Santa Fe. But for now this new book project was all-consuming, and a stack of pink typing paper began growing in his closet as Connell worked through his constant revisions. Connell soon learned that his new publisher was all in.

"I didn't know him to sit down and talk with until about 1979," Shoemaker told me during our first meeting about Connell, over lunch at a restaurant near his office in Berkeley.[8]

Shoemaker once ran a bookshop in Santa Barbara, California, where he first met Gus Blaisdell, who had come in with a mutual friend. They remained good friends ever after. As Shoemaker and Bill Turnbull began creating North Point, Shoemaker added Connell to the list of writers he wanted to publish. "Gus said, 'we'll go over there together. I can introduce you to Evan.' So he did." Blaisdell had hoped to join the North Point partnership, but despite their friendship, Shoemaker didn't think the chemistry was right. Blaisdell and Turnbull wouldn't get along, he figured, and he gently let Blaisdell down by inviting him to suggest projects. *Saint Augustine's Pigeon* was one result, and the connection with Connell proved exceptional. As Shoemaker put it, "Evan became a very close friend of the press and of mine and brought other writers to us."[9]

Turnbull and Shoemaker set up shop in a former Nazarene church in Albany, California, just next door to Berkeley and across the street from a bookstore Shoemaker owned. They put out North Point's first books in the fall of 1980. The imprint's image as a literary publisher was burnished by its initial list. Along with *Saint Augustine's Pigeon* it included poetry by the essayist Wendell Berry (*The Part*), a novel by the poet Galway Kinnell (*Black Light*), and translations of Jean Giono's rustic French novel *Joy of Man's Desiring* and Ovid's *Metamorphoses*. Berry became a perennial author in North Point's stable. By the following spring, the literary critic Guy Davenport, who had reviewed two of Connell's novels, joined the lineup, as did M. F. K. Fisher, the California food historian; Gina Berriault; and other Bay Area notables. Part of North Point's popularity stemmed from its commitment to literary quality and the elegant, quality design it brought to its books, including acid-free paper and softcover editions that sported jackets with flaps. The press announced its philosophy in its first seasonal catalogue: "North Point Press is dedicated to the task of filling the growing gap between the small, fine press and the large commercial publisher; borrowing from the former a commitment to excellence in design and format, and from the latter, a distribution system to reach the wider audience our books deserve."

Connell's avowed resistance to the New York publishing cabal certainly fed his interest in North Point. But Turnbull and Shoemaker were not defiant about their place on the West Coast.

They soon forged a sales and distribution deal with a New York publisher, which helped their books gain better access to libraries and foreign markets.

After *Saint Augustine's Pigeon*, North Point built a campaign to reintroduce *Mrs. Bridge* and *Mr. Bridge*. In the fall of 1981, it landed window displays for the Bridge novels at B. Dalton stores—the largest chain in the business at the time—in shopping malls across the country. North Point promoted the reprints at the annual convention of the American Booksellers Association, held that year in Anaheim, California, just down the road from Disneyland. Out of that highly influential conclave, a British publisher acquired the rights to put out paperback editions of four of Connell's books, including the Bridge novels. "I must say," Connell told his sister, "that NP seems to be accomplishing quite a lot, one way or another."[10]

When it came time to shop the Custer manuscript, Connell's agent tried several New York publishers. Connell's ally William Abrahams, who edited *A Long Desire* and *The White Lantern* at Holt, wasn't interested, but others were. In the end, North Point came in with the best offer. More important, Turnbull and Shoemaker were enthusiastic about it. For a young publishing house, they were making a significant investment. They sensed something special.

"I remember sitting with Evan," Shoemaker told me,

and knowing that this book was out at a couple of other places and wondering could North Point compete. Were we going to be able to come up with an advance and win the day? And Bill Turnbull was at the table with me . . . desperate to get this book. . . . I remember saying to Evan something like, "in this negotiation what is loyalty worth?" And Evan said, "About seventeen thousand dollars." So, I knew that that would be our bid. Our bid would be seventeen thousand dollars less than the highest bid and we'd get it. I think he was kidding, I think he was joking, but there was an element of truth to it and that book made Evan a fortune. It made North Point a fortune.[11]

The deeper Connell got into the Custer story, the less intrigued he became by the man who had taken up so much figurative acreage and the more he explored the grand sweep of history and the tragic collision of American cultures. Of Custer, Connell said, "he himself, as an individual, is not all that interesting—he wasn't terribly complex, I think. In fact, he was predictable. One of his subordinates, Capt. Benteen, is much more interesting. What has sustained my interest is the wild cast of characters, not just Custer himself, and a truckload of bizarre, unexpected details which make the whole thing altogether human."[12] Connell's book thus traces, necessarily, the history of American and Indian relations both before and after the Little Bighorn. You can follow the lives of many of the principal actors and find digressions into weaponry, cultural traditions, and even a history of scalping that Connell traces as far back as Herodotus. Connell conceded the book "meanders around like a golf course."[13]

His brushes with Custer are telling, though, and indicative of the "bizarre, unexpected details" Connell exploited. "From the moment of Custer's arrival in Dakota Territory," he writes, "the explosive chronicle of his life seems preordained. In July of 1873 somewhere along the Yellowstone he shot an antelope whose carcass dripped blood on a package of doughnuts he meant to have for lunch. He noted the incident briefly in a letter to Elizabeth—he thought nothing of it—yet the queer misfortune reverberates like an Etruscan augury."[14]

Despite his aversion to footnotes, Connell included a bibliography that lists, in a relatively careful count, 229 books (plus dozens of articles) about Custer and his compatriots, about the battle and its consequences, and about tribal chiefs, warriors, and others whose lives intersected with Little Bighorn history. Surely he read them all, mined them for the choice pieces of his narrative puzzle. The bibliography includes the works of many formidable authors—Mari Sandoz, Paul Wellman, Stanley Vestal, Stephen Ambrose—on whose shoulders Connell stood while leaping off into his own creation.

Connell's take begins not at the beginning, or at some point along the gathering storm, but at the end. A soldier makes a grim discovery. Columns of "hostiles" wearing cavalry uniforms ride in something like a two-by-two formation. Custer's name is mentioned only in passing. His fate is implied, but he remains offstage for many pages. Connell in essence is crafting an overture, accented with a seductive flute and a rumbling, rising percussion.

But this is not a biography of Custer anyway. Connell, in his mosaic-making, is wrestling with America's sorry and murderous history of Indian relations. General William Tecumseh Sherman "thought there could be no peace until the Indians were removed, one way or another." Connell calls on the *Topeka Weekly-Leader* to capture the ugly spirit of *vox populi*: "a set of miserable, dirty, lousy, blanketed, thieving, lying, sneaking, murdering, graceless, faithless, gut-eating skunks as the Lord ever permitted to infect the earth, and whose immediate and final extermination all men, except Indian agents and traders should pray for."[15] As usual, Connell does not scold. He does not directly comment on such rants. He lets the harsh rhetoric ring in his readers' modern ears.

The Little Bighorn was the climactic result of an aggression that began two years earlier. Connell had noted it even in the pages of *Mrs. Bridge* when Grace Barron, the woman who "read books no one else had heard of," mentioned at a cocktail party "Custer's deliberate violation of the treaty of eighteen-sixty-eight."[16] In July 1874, the army sent Custer and the Seventh Cavalry into the Dakota Territory in order to gauge the mood of the Sioux, many of whom had settled there peacefully on a government-approved reservation, and, more importantly, to make the Black Hills safe for gold prospecting. This was the eastern boundary of the Powder River lands, which, under the Fort Laramie Treaty of 1868, were supposed to comprise "unceded" Indian territory. White settlement was not allowed. But gold had been discovered, and the United States was feebly unable or brazenly unwilling to stop another inevitable rush of fortune-seekers. Sioux anger began to rise over the trespassing. Here was yet another lie from Washington: "This invasion of the sacred Black Hills by a creaking, jingling, clanking train of canvas-topped wagons and malodorous cavalrymen displeased the Sioux, not just that tiny community of five lodges but hundreds more who looked down from remote, pine-covered slopes." The stage was set. Indian removal and expropriation had become the dominant national practice. Connell put a bow on the theme when writing about the death of Sitting Bull fourteen years after the Last Stand. In effect an assassination, Sitting Bull's killing earned the government "a further degree in militant stupidity."[17]

Custer had hoped to be in Philadelphia by July 4, 1876, to celebrate the nation's centennial. This bit of vainglory—imagine the hero on such a patriotic stage—helps explain Custer's reckless advance toward the Sioux villages along the Little Bighorn River two weeks earlier. "He and his friends would get to the fair on time," Connell writes, "if the power of the Sioux could be broken quickly. Such an explanation of the forced march, however absurd, might be true. Not only was 1876 the centennial, it was an election year and the Democratic convention was just about to open in St. Louis. A messenger could ride from the Little Bighorn to the Bozeman telegraph office in two days, which meant that news of a victory would reach the delegates while presidential nominees were being selected."[18] Certainly, Connell suggests, it wouldn't be beyond Custer's ego to imagine himself a candidate for president.

Instead, the news was horrible.

Like virtually every writer who has examined the battle of June 25, Connell is forced to leave Custer's actions that day an unsolved mystery: "Why he thought he could accomplish with a single regiment what would have been a difficult job for the entire army— why he thought he could pull it off is a puzzle that fascinates every student of this campaign. He had listened to knowledgeable scouts and he had read their faces. Bloody Knife understood beyond doubt that this would be the end of the trail. Mitch Bouyer, too, had made things quite clear. Maybe he felt no plan was necessary because of 'Custer's luck.' He was known to his officers and to the public as a lucky man."[19]

One of the achievements of *Son of the Morning Star* is the measured balance Connell brings to the multiple voices and threads in the story. He understood that human behavior comes from a place deeper than skin and culture. Custer was not the only player who operated on self-identified luck: "Crazy Horse called it something else. Crazy Horse tied a red-backed hawk on his head, wore magic pebbles, painted hailstones on his chest, and sprinkled his pony with dust, but it was all the same. Luck. Medicine. They were hatched in the same nest, these two."[20]

One foreboding thing that Custer heard before the end stands out among the many poignant lines in the history of the debacle. It was the prophesy of a Crow scout, Half Yellow Face: "You and I are both going home today by a road that we do not know."[21]

Connell's passion for the quirky, vibrating detail can be found from beginning to end. Here's a favorite among the many examples that made its way into my reading notes:

An old Cheyenne, who undoubtedly was present, told Frank Linderman in 1877 that the fight took about as long as it took the sun to travel the width of a lodge pole.

"How thick is a lodge pole? Three inches, four inches, five inches.

"How long does it take the sun to travel that far? Fifteen minutes. Twenty minutes."[22]

In the annals of power, one can find reverberations of the Custer story throughout American history ever since. Connell had a long-running argument with the U.S. government of his time. He bristled over the foreign-policy dealings of the administration of Ronald Reagan, the onetime actor and California governor who ascended to the White House in the election of 1980, as Connell was beginning to think about Custer. Connell recognized the fatal flaw of arrogance: "Custer's logic is inscrutable. One military analyst said he seemed to reach decisions according to the striding of his mount. Very seldom did he discuss a problem with subordinates; he preferred to give orders."[23]

Connell gave himself plenty of time to meditate in the battlefield landscape. He also made firsthand observations at other historic sites. Several miles south of Sheridan another hilltop monument memorializes another failure of the U.S. military, another massacre of blue-uniformed soldiers by tribal warriors. The Natives were led by the Sioux hero Red Cloud and included the up-and-coming star warrior Crazy Horse. This was the Fetterman Massacre of December 1866. It was named for U.S. Army captain William Fetterman, who, in a Custer-like surge of reckless bravado, failed to follow orders and charged past a ridgetop with his company of eighty men. All of them succumbed to a Sioux decoy-and-ambush operation, a military tactic, Connell writes, that predated the Punic Wars. The debacle led to the peace treaty, signed at Fort Laramie in 1868, which acknowledged the sovereignty of the Sioux Reservation in and around the Black Hills. Connell's account of the present-day Fetterman site describes it as a forlorn, perhaps forgotten piece of ground, much less traveled since the interstate highway system supplanted U.S. 87 and kept most nearby motorists blissfully unaware of its presence. Nearly four decades after Connell, I found the site to be somewhat more popular and clearly well-maintained as part of a state historic site that includes the recreated Fort Phil Kearny a couple of miles away. A half-dozen vehicles—cars, motorcycles, a bicycle—sat in the parking lot by the memorial's stone shaft, and pairs of people could be seen walking the trail along the ridgetop.

What becomes clear from the Fetterman history is the tragedy of U.S. military overconfidence and arrogance that led to the soldiers' slaughter. It was a lesson not much on Custer's mind just ten years later and less than a hundred miles away.

As Connell was finishing his manuscript, he without doubt became aware of a wildfire, started by a careless smoker, that blackened the entire expanse of the Little Bighorn battlefield. The National Park Service's main building near the monument was spared. What Connell might not have come to appreciate, until after his book appeared, were the extraordinary consequences of the fire. In the wake of the fire's destruction, the land gave up hundreds of artifacts—shell casings, bones, arrowheads, and much more. The discoveries set off a series of archaeological digs, which in turn added to the body of knowledge battle historians continue to study and helped to fuel new theories and conclusions about the movements of troops and warriors. Connell never faced a question about these new finds, at least according to the available record. It's doubtful, however, that his book would have been altered significantly. He might have sifted the findings for the odd surprise, for the details laden with irony or new insight. Still, the vast majority of his existing fragments would have remained intact.

After tuck-pointing the manuscript in March 1984, Connell took a breather. And another long journey. He booked a trip to the South Pacific. Why there? In part it was unfinished business. He felt a need to connect with the naval history he had not experienced for himself. At least one friend from his Naval Air Corps days, Blossom Williams, flew missions in the South Pacific. Connell never left the country during the war. With a stop at Honolulu, his ticket to Guam and beyond got him on an island-hopping cargo plane. His itinerary included Ponape (now Pohnpei), Truk—where an American assault on a Japanese naval base in World War II sunk dozens of enemy ships—Saipan, and, if things worked out, Manila.

After Honolulu the first three stops were coral atolls, a couple with U.S. naval bases—Johnston, Majuro, Kwajalein—all blasted by unchanging light. Guam and Saipan were nothing much. No beach hotels, little comfort in the worn, remote motels in which he was stuck. Connell contemplated the concrete rubble of World War II–era buildings being swallowed up by the jungle. And he wondered about the fate of the lost aviator Amelia Earhart and her co-pilot Fred Noonan, whom he'd heard had been imprisoned by Japanese military and subsequently died in a hospital on Saipan. (Earhart's fate, even today, remains unresolved.) Guam seemed like one long, dull commercial district, so Saipan, where he saw "chunks of corroding iron on the coast, a camouflaged tank on the beach," was more agreeable. Connell gave his sister a detailed travelogue, full of the kind of closely observed details and wry observations that typically elevate his published prose:

> I got off at Ponape, which is mountainous and thick jungle—wandered around and tried to imagine how those people can live like that all their lives, dozing in that steamy heat, doing almost nothing. My hotel room was like a $10 room in Fresno—linoleum curling off the floor, huge water stain on the sagging ceiling. Spent most of my time loitering at the Cliff Rainbow hotel just around the bend—it's like something out of Somerset Maugham, managed by a woman named Dusty, palm leaf bar outside. I met an elderly German and his wife who had been Everywhere. He was an authority on megalithic cultures of the South Pacific, so we took a rough one-hour motorboat ride to the ruins of Nan Madol, which was built about the 11th century and is now completely lost in the jungle except for one great ugly black basalt fortress, which was the palace. Those are places worth seeing once, but not twice. The Mayan ruins are elegant. Nan Madol is just grim.[24]

A clear highlight for Connell was what he learned on Truk. He had hoped to get a glimpse of the Japanese fleet. Sixty or seventy ships and a submarine, which sank because a crewman forgot to close a hatch, rested far below the lavender-hued surface. Instead, he could only hear about the sights from a documentary film and divers who had descended 160 or more. "There is so little oxygen at that depth that the skeletons have not disintegrated—untouched since '44."[25]

On the Truk beach, as at Saipan, Connell came across metal fragments of ships that crumbled like shale in his hands. And outside a swank hotel, he saw a concrete Japanese pillbox that had been punched thirty degrees into the air by a palm tree growing underneath it.

As it happened, Connell's letter turned out to be a mini-rehearsal. When he got back to writing short fiction in the early 1990s, he turned his mind back to the excursion in Micronesia.

Connell had nothing but good things to say about North Point. He liked the restraint it used in designing the cover of *Son of the Morning Star*. No attention-begging "lurid colors." The Leonard Baskin illustrations, including the cover portrait of Custer, were just right. Bill Turnbull, though not a designer, had a good eye, and so far all of Connell's North Point books had been quite handsome. Connell told his sister, "Everybody there is intelligent and courteous and they all seem to know what they're doing—which is not at all true of some people I've met in the NY industry."[26]

In the pre-publication downtime following his three-week sojourn to the South Pacific, Connell read a considerable amount. He was still reviewing books for several newspapers. He read another forthcoming North Point reprint, *Being Geniuses Together*, the memoir of 1920s Paris by Robert McAlmon and Kay Boyle. He had gotten to know Boyle, a literary pal of Ernest Hemingway and Gertrude Stein, on her annual trips to San Francisco from her Oregon home. There was always a lunch with George Gutekunst, a socially prominent Sausalito friend, at his waterfront restaurant, Ondine. Connell was pleased that *Son of the Morning Star* seemed to be well received at the annual American Booksellers Association convention. Gathering that spring in Washington, D.C., booksellers buzzed over the likes of Raquel Welch, Lee Iacocca, Studs Terkel, and Umberto Eco, the Italian semiotics professor whose *Name of the Rose* was a surprise bestseller and now moving up the charts in paperback. Lisa Ross, North Point's publicist and rights director, was not so happy when Connell declined a radio interview. Still, lots of publicity was planned for the fall: a press reception at North Point and abundant media coverage. The PBS news program *MacNeil/Lehrer Report* had planned to do something but backed away, and Ross worked to get its producers interested again. (She succeeded.)

Six weeks before publication, Connell reported to his sister that the first printing of ten thousand books was about to come off the press, and North Point already had orders for six thousand. His friend Don Carpenter was going to interview him for a Sunday feature in the *San Francisco Chronicle*, and *USA Today* was also planning an interview. Curt Gentry, the writer to whom Connell dedicated the book, had now read it three times. "So, for the moment, Custer is again leading the charge," Connell told Bobs. "How far he will go before slowing down is impossible to say."[27]

Connell also took a late summer drive through Wyoming: "Wort hotel in Jackson Hole has dancing every weekend, music provided by Custer's Last Band."[28]

Connell got an early sense that reviews of *Son of the Morning Star* would generally be good. He seemingly kept track of each and every one. There were thumbs up from the *Christian Science Monitor* and *Smithsonian* magazine. John Hanchette's admiring combination of review and interview ran in Gannett newspapers across the country. The *San Francisco Examiner* pronounced Connell a great writer who had fashioned the Custer story "as Flaubert would have written it."[29] And the *Washington Post* served up what Connell thought was the ideal reading of the book: "This is a vast mural of finely executed details," its critic wrote, adding that Connell included details that most dull standard histories leave out. "This one is never dull."[30]

In the *New York Times*, Page Stegner, son of Connell's early mentor, recognized that the power of the book lay in the author's craftsmanship: "Whether or not one cares about Custer, *Son of the Morning Star* makes good reading—its prose is elegant, its tone the voice of dry wit, its meandering narrative skillfully crafted."[31]

Dee Brown, the author of another important book of Native American history, *Bury My Heart at Wounded Knee*, took on *Son of the Morning Star* for the *Chicago Tribune*. Although he too griped about the lack of notes, Brown summed up what might be the most important insight about Connell's book—its singular style and point of view: "America tends to typecast its authors into categories, and it is encouraging to see one spread his loop—as writers do in other countries—to bring fresh viewpoints to an overspent subject. *Son of the Morning Star* fits into none of the classifications of books about Custer. It is unique and for that reason it should endure. Although Custer addicts may not learn many new facts here, they'll certainly see them in a different light."[32]

Barbara Zimmermann was distraught that the hometown Kansas City newspaper, so supportive of Connell in the past, published a pan. Her brother was not much put out by it, mostly just annoyed that the reviewer had gotten so many facts wrong. Most egregious, he felt, was an ignorant reference to Peter Matthiessen's recent book on the 1973 Native American uprising at Wounded Knee, *In the Spirit of Crazy Horse*. The reviewer, a college English teacher, implied that Matthiessen's book, like Connell's, was about Custer, which of course meant she hadn't read it.[33] "Anyway," Connell replied, "the response thus far has been remarkably good, so you shouldn't feel disturbed about the *Star*. If somebody says yahyah! Just show him/her the *Washington Post*."[34]

One day, while stopping in at the North Point office in Berkeley, Connell was charmed by the presence of a Japanese poet, Shuntaro Tanikawa. North Point had published Tanikawa's *Selected Poems* the year before, and he was visiting the offices accompanied by his translator. Tanikawa had no problem understanding English, given that he had the enviable job of translating the Peanuts comic strip for a Japanese news organization. Connell learned that Tanikawa was greatly influenced by American westerns. "So," he told his sister, "Jack gave him Custer and I got a signed copy of Tanikawa's selected poems."[35]

Connell that season processed disturbing news about two acquaintances. William Abrahams, his editor friend, jumped from Henry Holt, after a change in ownership, to E. P. Dutton. As he explained to Bobs, "I come across this situation more and more frequently—the squeezing out of anything that won't show a big profit." People he knew could not get published by New York firms anymore. "North Point was enthusiastic from the start, not because they thought it would sell, but because they liked it. That's what book publishing was all about once upon a time."[36]

Then there was the suicide of Richard Brautigan, the counter-culture satirist and poet. His best-known book was *Trout Fishing in America*, a novella that caught fire with the flower children and seeker-dreamers of the late 1960s. Connell was not much of a fan, though he regretted Brautigan's decline. The columnist Herb Caen once captured Connell and Brautigan sharing, in a way, the scene at Enrico's, the North Beach bar and writer hangout favored by Don Carpenter and his circle.[37] Caen reported on a "typical day" when Barnaby Conrad argued with Mel Tormé about movies at the bar; Herb Gold, newly bearded after a trip to Haiti, worked on a plate of eggs; and Brautigan sat on the sidewalk terrace "scribbling poetry on an old envelope" while Connell was off at another table, "staring into space."[38]

Brautigan had been a close friend of Carpenter's, and the latter was taking it hard. Another mutual friend, William Hamilton, memorialized Brautigan in the *New Yorker* in December. Connell found a disturbing thread in the Brautigan story: "He was one of those writers who had been quite successful, but his audience declined and the NY firms therefore rejected him."[39] Connell seemed to harbor a long resentment. Three decades later he said, "Brautigan and I had nothing to say to each other. He was an ugly guy. He came up to me one time at a party and said, 'Ain't never read anything you've ever written, but I like the fact that you keep at it.' Yeah, that was Brautigan. He finally shot himself."[40] Still, the tragedies of fame and its disappearance were not lost on Connell.

The Christmas season brought word of two award nominations for *Son of the Morning Star* (from the National Book Award and the National Book Critics Circle) and gifts from the family. His sister renewed Connell's subscription to *Arizona Highways*, which he said always gave him an itch to head out on the road in his Honda. And he also appreciated the belt buckle made of silver and Cripple Creek turquoise. One wholly unexpected gift came from his Sausalito friend Ruth Costello. She had crafted a booklet of fourteen poems inspired by Connell's own writings, one for each book to date.[41]

By the end of the year, there were 86,000 copies of *Son of the Morning Star* in print. This posed a philosophical struggle for Connell. On the one hand, he certainly craved the kind of attention that literary success brings. On the other, there was a kind of paradoxical sting that Connell had satirized in print more than once. It involved the rather elitist notion that commercial triumphs couldn't possibly be literary.

"That was during that time," Shoemaker told me, "when anybody who had broad success was thought of as a sellout. No matter what, they can still be singing the same song, but if it appealed to too many people, they were a sellout. And Evan was vulnerable to that, but Evan also was somebody who looked at his own royalty statements on a regular basis. He was very careful laundering everything. His father taught him about that kind of stuff and he emulated that. As I say, he was tight. He was somebody who didn't like spending money, didn't like to spend cash."[42]

Nevertheless, there was a lot to be grateful for. "Well," Connell told his sister, "we had a one-week break in the rainstorms and the 49ers are going to the superbowl so things could be worse."[43] (While Connell's optimism proved correct, in reality San Francisco's NFL team, led by quarterback Joe Montana, still had two playoff games to contend with. The dominant 49ers indeed went on to win Super Bowl XIX in a game against the Miami Dolphins that happened to be played at Connell's grad-school alma mater, Stanford.)

As the success of *Son of the Morning Star* snowballed, Connell was besieged. A handful of letters arrived each week from readers who wanted to lather him with praise or correct him on minor facts. Hollywood came calling, but Connell and his agent rebuffed the earliest inquiries. Newspapers wanted interviews. One winter day, *People* magazine flew Connell to Montana for a photo shoot at the Little Bighorn battlefield site. The park superintendent opened the gate to Custer's symbolic grave marker, and later that Monday joined Connell and the photographer at the Merry Mixer restaurant in Hardin, Montana, which wasn't so merry, he reported, but served up pretty good steaks. Connell was back home the next day. The *Washington Post* sent him two books for review, both with western themes, though when asked to review a seven-hundred-page novel by John Hersey (*The Call*), he passed. That would take a week, he told his sister.

North Point's Lisa Ross called Connell weekly to report on the book's slow climb up the bestseller lists. No. 13, No. 11, soon No. 6, then No. 5. It landed higher than anyone expected. The publisher's print runs could hardly keep up. The Book of the Month Club sold out as fast as it restocked.

When North Point began, its founders knew they hadn't built it to make bestsellers. Its books were quiet, literary. They would find their readers. A bestseller could ruin a publisher, first by raising expectations and then by overspending and expanding. North Point preferred slow and steady. Now, nearly five years into it and with a runaway hit on their hands, they were better equipped, especially having offloaded distribution to New York houses—first Scribner's, then Farrar, Straus and Giroux. "Having a bestseller may mean a few more staff parties," Shoemaker once said, "but the work doesn't let up."[44]

North Point auctioned the paperback rights in February. It had already turned down an offer of $150,000, so Shoemaker and Turnbull were feeling good about the prospects. When the auction was over, Harper and Row topped out at $210,000 (equivalent to more than $500,000 today; a paperback sale typically is split 50–50 between publisher and author). Harper planned to revive a long-dormant imprint, Perennial, with an aggressive marketing campaign and an initial print run of 100,000 books.

Connell was also responsible, at least in part, for another North Point mega-bestseller. It was the revival of a long-out-of-print memoir by Beryl Markham, a British aviator and bush pilot in Kenya who had accomplished the first solo trans-Atlantic flight moving east to west. The story of the arrival of *West with the Night* at

North Point, in 1983, goes something like this: George Gutekunst was a longtime fishing buddy of Jack Hemingway, the first-born son of Ernest Hemingway. On a fly-fishing excursion in Idaho, where Hemingway *fils* lived, Gutekunst began to ask a question he'd long avoided, something about Hemingway's father. Jack shut him down and recommended that he read Hemingway's letters. An edition of his selected correspondence, edited by Hemingway biographer Carlos Baker, had come out in 1981. Gutekunst took the recommendation seriously. Deep into the book, he encountered Hemingway's mention of Markham in a letter to his editor, Max Perkins. Hemingway, in short, was bowled over by her book, which had been published in 1942 but quickly faded from view. "But she can write rings around all of us who consider ourselves as writers," Hemingway commented. "I wish you would get it and read it because it is really a bloody, wonderful book." Given Hemingway's flinty reputation when it came to handing out literary praise, Gutekunst was stunned. It took a while for the Sausalito library to track down a copy of Markham's book. It took him no time to read it—a single sitting. When he finished, he gave the book to Connell.[45]

"George Gutekunst and I share three great loves: food, books and arguing," Connell told the *Chicago Tribune*. After reading Markham's book, Connell, in turn, raved about it to Bill Turnbull. Turnbull read it while flying to New York for a meeting, then pressed it on Shoemaker at their hotel.

"Over breakfast the next morning we agreed it was a minor masterpiece that should be back in print," Shoemaker recalled. Shoemaker knew they'd be taking a risk. Maybe it would find new readers, maybe it would "sink like a stone again."[46]

In the coming years Markham's book would far outsell even *Son of the Morning Star*. And its author, still alive for a few more years, was able to revel in her new success.

"The book is doing splendidly," Connell told his sister. "I'm told that Ms. Markham, who is now in her eighties and lives in Nairobi, feels much better about the world these days. She was in poor health, I think, feeling old and ignored, but now is receiving quite a lot of attention."[47]

The Indian Wars, the Little Bighorn, and Custer continue to attract attention from historians, writers and readers. Connell's book remains required reading, at least in part because of how he helped to bring Native American accounts of the battle and its aftermath into the historical mainstream. As an admiring reviewer for the *American Indian Quarterly* once put it, "He misses very little in winding his way through the astounding density of material that purports to account for seemingly every individual with any connection to what happened before, during, or after the battle."[48] And it remains immensely influential. "If ever I could write a history book," Lewis Lapham told me, "the model would be *Son of the Morning Star*."[49] John M. Carroll, a western historian with whom Connell consulted, credited him with raising "the art form of history to the art form of literature. And that I think is one of the best things that ever happened to us in a long long time."[50]

Twenty-five years after Connell's book began making waves, James Donovan took a new, deep look in *A Terrible Glory: Custer and the Little Bighorn—The Last Great Battle of the American West* (2008). In a published interview, Donovan paid respects to Connell. Although Donovan too lamented the lack of footnotes in *Son of the Morning Star*, he credited Connell for bringing to light "a good deal of original material" and for writing like a dream. "I'd pay to read Connell's grocery lists," Donovan said. "It's more a grand meditation on the American psyche and character presented through the prism of one of the great battles in our history and its participants. It's anything but a straightforward account of the battle, as mine is."[51]

Readers can still be divided by its spiraling style. While historians sometimes grouse about its nonlinear construction, the loop-de-loop arrangement of fragments and threads repays patience and reveals the book's internal logic as Connell proceeds. No less a master of nonfiction narrative than John McPhee would use *Son of the Morning Star* in his writing classes. McPhee once wrote to Connell to ask about his methods. How did he organize his research, what sort of computer tricks did he use? Connell's response: Computer? He had never touched one, then or ever.

According to Connell's correspondence, Stanley Crouch, a writer in the 1980s for the *Village Voice*, planned to publish a lengthy review of the book. Crouch, who died in 2020, apparently never finished it, and if the piece exists it never appeared in various collections of his essays. But he did discuss Connell's opus in a couple of paragraphs: "Probably the single event of prose writing that has most impressed me over the last decade or so is what Evan Connell did in *Son of the Morning Star*, where he used a digressive, Melvillian technique to tell a story we thought we knew. . . . The book is perhaps a masterpiece of form and originality, gallows humor, and eloquence, which is why so many historians hate it." Crouch said that Connell used Custer the way Melville used Ahab, "when that great New Englander decided to write about both America and the whole wide world." Crouch took from the book a sense of what even an essay like his own work could do, which is to "have the poetic power capable of summoning and projecting a larger feeling and a greater sense of information and engagement than the number of pages would suggest."[52]

Years later, Larry McMurtry, one of the most successful writers of the American West, gave a testament to Connell's legacy. McMurtry considered *Son of the Morning Star* to be one of the three best books on the subject.[53] "Three times in the past twenty years, I've been asked to write a book about Custer and the Little Bighorn," McMurtry wrote, "and each time I've pointed to *Son of the Morning Star* and asked why."[54]

That's Show Biz
1985–1989

"We are entering the realm of sweet talk, back-stabbing, and moonbeams."

—Connell to Gus Blaisdell, 1985

HOLLYWOOD HAD NOT been kind to Connell. There was the undocumented early flirt with Los Angeles when he tried selling western stories to the studios. There was the undocumented summer he spent, apparently at Warner Brothers, drafting a screenplay based on *The Diary of a Rapist*. If that were indeed a real project for a brief Hollywood moment, it went nowhere. Connell once said that producer Stuart Rosenberg tried to shop it, but the studios were put off by the subject. And who could forget the tease-and-toss maneuver from producer Abby Mann? He so much wanted to make a *Mrs. Bridge* movie, though, alas, that dream too evaporated. Connell could also recall at least two failed encounters with the New York theater scene, including a Broadway production based on *Mrs. Bridge* that flamed out before it got going. So here he was again. The actress Joanne Woodward, whom Abby Mann had identified as a possible India Bridge in 1971, came sniffing around the novel again, ten years later, at the time North Point Press was giving it new life. Yet, Connell and his agent weren't interested in her lowball offer for an option.

Connell knew the game and its disappointments at least in part through Calvin Kentfield and Don Carpenter, each of whom had dalliances, if not minor successes, with the movies. Carpenter, for example, had scored with the screenplay for *Payday* (1973), in which Rip Torn played an uncontrollable country music singer. Ruth Costello's son Mark was an aspiring actor in Hollywood. Connell had gotten to know Tony Bill, an actor-turned director who once optioned *The Patriot*, and the actor Sterling Hayden, a No Name regular. The director Philip Kaufman was another No Name acquaintance from the mid-1970s. Connell had attended a cast party in San Francisco for Miloš Forman's *Amadeus,* where he chatted with the screenwriter Niven Busch and met the movie's star, F. Murray Abraham. And Gale Garnett had spent plenty of time in Hollywood, playing bit parts in television shows and movies. She'd taken Connell to soirées—a New Year's Eve party at Pamela Mason's!—and introduced him to John Huston and others. Nevertheless, all of those connections never led anywhere productive.

Then came the unexpected. With the great success of *Son of the Morning Star*—more than 100,000 copies in print and No. 4 on the *Times* bestseller list by mid-February 1985—Connell was now a hot property. Woodward knocked on the door again, yet her offer for a Bridge option was still too low. And others were lining up to put the Custer project on screens large and small. Connell's agent wanted to sign something while the Custer fire was hot, she told him. The CBS television network was dangling the idea of a mini-series, maybe six or eight hours. A network executive even called Connell to praise the book, talk up the project, and express hope that something could be worked out. As Connell told his sister, Elizabeth McKee "reasons that the book is rising on the best seller list and we shouldn't wait too long. I reason that, while this is true, Custer has been around quite a while and isn't going to be forgotten."[1] He figured something would develop soon.

Arthur Axelman of the William Morris Agency got in the middle of negotiations. As he once described the action, he'd had lunch with McKee at the Algonquin Hotel and knew her reputation as a solid and candid agent. An NBC executive shared Axelman's enthusiasm for Connell's book and promised to buy it if a deal made sense. CBS had offered Connell $25,000 for an option. Axelman proposed

$60,000, with a two-year option, against a purchase of $150,000 for a two-hour production, plus $50,000 for each additional hour. McKee went for it.

Axelman soon pulled in Thom Mount, a former Hollywood studio executive, who wanted to produce, and Viacom, a former CBS unit but now independent, as a corporate backer. Mount, in a long, rambling, but convivial phone conversation, told Connell that he was a longtime Custer buff and wanted to run the project if Viacom were to land it. A contract had not yet been signed, but Connell was on board. Little did he realize, as Tony Bill told him, that these things take time. Under the contract, Connell would become a paid consultant, "so," he told Gus Blaisdell, "I may get to spend a couple of months in south Babylon tripping over electrical cables and saying things like, Hey, boss, order a couple dozen more Cheyennes." Connell, of course, knew enough to be realistic: "We are entering the realm of sweet talk, back-stabbing, and moonbeams."[2]

Connell was energized that an experienced scriptwriter had been signed for the Custer project. Mount had enlisted Melissa Mathison, whose recent projects included Steven Spielberg's crowd-pleaser *E.T.* and a popular new version of a children's classic, *The Black Stallion*. She usually got half a million dollars or more for a picture, Mount told him, but agreed to a discount because this one seemed so promising. She had read *The White Lantern* and "seems to like the Custer book a lot," Connell told his sister.[3] Mathison, who happened to be married to the actor Harrison Ford, called Connell and said she hoped to draft a script over the summer.

In June 1985, Connell made another promotional appearance at the American Booksellers Association (ABA) annual convention. *Son of the Morning Star* was still riding high, and Harper and Row had the paperback edition on deck for the fall. Harper and Row had been beefing up its presence in the quality paperback business. It had 100,000 copies of Milan Kundera's *Unbearable Lightness of Being* in print and was planning even more for the paperback launch of *Son of the Morning Star*, to be buttressed by a $75,000 advertising budget. That would be something—bigger than most hardcover ad buys. Also at the ABA convention, conveniently held that year in San Francisco, Connell sat down for a couple of media interviews. ("I don't enjoy answering questions but can endure a certain amount of it."[4]) One was with Robert Taylor of the *Boston Globe*, whose review of the Custer book had impressed Connell earlier in the year. Taylor had made a startling comparison: "Dry, laconic and rueful, that voice, in the tradition of Mark Twain, questions separate versions of historical events."[5] In addition to the invocation of Twain, Connell was pleased that Taylor was the rare reviewer to have noticed the subtle humor in his narrative.

Connell's sister and brother-in-law had come to town earlier that month. His local tour included dinner with George Gutekunst at Ondine, gatherings with Anne Lamott and Don Carpenter, and a visit to the North Point offices, though both Turnbull and Shoemaker were away on business. He regretted that Barbara and Matt Zimmermann couldn't return for the ABA weekend, because North Point was throwing a fifth anniversary party, which was destined to be a blowout affair. As it happened, some five hundred book people celebrated North Point on the *Balclutha,* a restored nineteenth-century global cargo ship.

The soft crunch of footsteps in a western meadow provided the soundtrack for Connell's first in-person meeting with Mathison. She had told him that the NBC executives liked her forty-page outline and gave her the green light to proceed. Connell ventured out in his Honda to see her in Jackson, Wyoming—a thousand-mile drive from Sausalito. After meeting with her, he planned to drive down to Colorado and New Mexico. Mathison and Ford had acquired eight hundred acres of mostly untouched wild land near the Snake River south of Jackson. They put Connell up for a night at their in-town apartment, and the three of them dined on elk at a quiet place away from the Jackson Hole tourist crowds. Mathison invited him out to their property to talk about the project. Connell liked what she was doing with his version of the Custer story, but there was much to discuss. On this day, she had another mission on their walkabout. She was on the lookout for a stray, banded eaglet, so she carried a radar device as they walked and talked under the big blue morning sky. Connell thought it was a bit odd, but Custer and company occupied most of their mental space. They ended up talking for hours.

Mathison had traveled to the Little Bighorn battlefield site. She'd met with the National Park historian Neil Mangum, who was something of a nemesis for Connell. Mangum despised his book, largely because of Connell's critical portrayal of Custer, and at first prevented it from being sold at the park gift shop. But Mathison and Mangum got along. "He never will become reconciled to the book," Connell said, "but I'm at least happy to hear that he is being cooperative about the film." At this point, Mathison planned to frame the book just as Connell had in its opening and closing passages: "Insofar as possible I think she will try for historical accuracy. She sounds excited about it and says 'experts are lined up at the door'—meaning that quite a few people want to become involved."[6] It was encouraging, if not unusual for Hollywood, that Mathison had been told not to worry about money, to just write the script as she saw it.

Connell pointed his Honda southward and drove through the Rockies to Aspen, Colorado. There was a gallery opening for an exhibit of the western-inspired paintings of a Santa Fe artist, Paul Pletka, and Connell was invited. The gallery was owned by a couple with Kansas City connections, so there was plenty of small talk about Connell's hometown. George Gutekunst, who was visiting friends in Colorado, was at the affair, along with many of Aspen's well-to-do residents. Pletka's show, titled "Custer and the Indians," sprang directly from Connell's book. The gallery owner, Joanne Lyon, had bought copies of *Son of the Morning Star* as Christmas presents for her husband, Lee Lyon, and Pletka. Lee Lyon realized he'd gone to high school with Connell nearly fifty years earlier, and Pletka was so wowed by the book he headed straight to his studio. His exhibit featured ten portrait paintings, several showing Custer in unusual, reflective moods. The paintings sold out even before the opening. Two of the largest pieces went to a Tulsa collector for $35,000 each. Pletka also produced two limited-edition lithographs, one of Custer and one of the Lakota Sioux warrior Gall.

Connell agreed to sign copies of *Son of the Morning Star* for gallery patrons. Pletka, meanwhile, drew sketches in the books Connell signed, adding one-of-a-kind artworks to the volumes that had until then sported only Leonard Baskin's images of Custer.

Mathison kept in touch with Connell about her progress on the script. Connell had connected her with John Carroll, a Custer historian he'd consulted with and befriended. Like Connell, he was a bit of a rebel, but he had studied the Custer saga for decades. Carroll's reputation among Custer historians was mixed, but he didn't much care and was pleased to stand in for Connell and accept his best-history award that summer from the Little Big Horn Associates. Connell was happy that Mathison and the producers actually listened to and even adopted some of his own suggestions. He was hearing from historians who expressed hope that finally Hollywood seemed to care about treating the Custer story right.

Connell drove down to "Lotusland" for a couple of days of script meetings in September. He recommended that everyone watch a twenty-year-old western movie, *The Stalking Moon* (1968), in which Gregory Peck played a U.S. Cavalry scout. The Mounts— Thom and Nikki—liked it enough to consider approaching its director, Robert Mulligan. Mathison also enlisted the aid of her former colleague Steven Spielberg. Spielberg wanted to read the script, as if to dangle the possibility of becoming involved. Eventually he offered an effective structural idea, suggesting that Libbie Custer be used as a narrator for some scenes, joining the Cheyenne woman Kate Bighead as another female voice in the forefront of the story. Connell thought the dual voices might well be worth trying.

Connell took a break from his writing desk one morning to help celebrate an old friend in San Francisco. Roger Barr, the artist he roomed with for a while in Barcelona, had been living in Santa Rosa in recent years. He made art and taught life drawing, and now one of his creations was an object of attention in San Francisco. Barr had been selected to produce a public sculpture, a tribute to the longshoreman philosopher Eric Hoffer. The stainless steel sculpture, combining an arch and a snaking, triple helix, stood twenty-six feet tall on a stretch of waterfront green space. Newsman Eric Sevareid, who had profiled Hoffer for CBS, was on hand to help dedicate the piece, along with Dianne Feinstein, then the city's mayor. Connell, the onetime sculpture student and longtime life-drawing sketcher, watched the ceremony and admired Barr's work, his most successful piece to date. "It was Roger's 64th birthday, so he looked very happy about the whole thing."[7]

Connell received a revised draft of Mathison's script by mid-October. Two of the weaker sections had been overhauled, which was good. But the presence of a few historical inaccuracies, nothing too serious, continued to bother him, and he vowed to keep after Mathison to fix them. "On the whole," he told Gus Blaisdell, "I'm pleased with it. I think it may be much closer to the facts than any previous Custer film."[8] Connell also suggested that Mathison reach out to a Native American consultant, someone like the writer Scott Momaday. She asked how to get hold of him.

Connell returned to Los Angeles later that month to accept another book award, this one best history from the *Los Angeles Times*. There was a lunch for booksellers the next day, and he had dinner with the Mounts. Nikki Mount told him that Spielberg wanted to direct the production, but her husband turned him down. "Nikki suspects it's the first time anybody has said no to Spielberg."[9] Other A-list names they were batting around included Francis Ford Coppola, of the *Godfather* movies, and Bruce Beresford, the Australian director of the memorably sophisticated war movie *Breaker Morant* (1980).

All the movie madness caused Connell's friend Annie Lamott to wonder whether Hollywood was going to his head. "I'm afraid you are going to forget WHO YOUR FRIENDS REALLY ARE," she wrote (her caps).[10] She hoped they would get together soon with Don Carpenter. Lamott and Carpenter were among those who knew the real Connell, the one that few others saw. "He sang the first stanza of a country western song to a group of us in Sonoma not long ago. (I am not making this up.),” Lamott would say. Connell could be kind of “goofy-ducky” when he's in a good mood, she observed, putting on accents around the dinner table, and he was secure enough to put up with endless teasing.[11]

Before the end of the year, Mathison sent Connell another version of the script, and he replied with six pages of notes, complaints, and compliments. He was encouraged by what felt like the show's sense of authenticity. He knew that John Carroll had been working on Mathison to treat the military more favorably. “I myself don't feel at all protective of the military,” he told Bobs. “I think she has been perfectly fair.”[12]

As if Connell's movie project weren't enough to excite Sausalito's cultural circles, another film was roaring ahead. George Gutekunst, the restaurateur who'd ignited the revival of Beryl Markham's *West with the Night*, was now involved in a documentary film about the legendary aviator. Gutekunst had acquired the rights to Markham's life story with an investor. Gutekunst had traveled to Kenya to meet Markham and collaborated with a reporter/producer from KQED, San Francisco's PBS station.

Robert Redford happened to drop into Gutekunst's restaurant, Ondine, one night when Connell was having dinner with William Hamilton, the cartoonist. They all sat around after hours to continue the good cheer. Redford was a big fan of Connell's Bridge novels. “Redford is friendly, intelligent, and rather quiet—though it is difficult for anybody to say much when George is present.”[13] Redford had recently returned from Kenya where production was wrapping up on *Out of Africa,* the film based on the life of the Danish writer Karen Blixen (Isak Dinesen). Redford naturally became interested in the Markham documentary, and Gutekunst spared few details.

Connell saw a preview screening of the documentary, *World without Walls,* at Gutekunst's house in October 1985, two months before KQED planned to air it. He pronounced it excellent. The film soared on Beryl Markham's words, and its success was due in no small part to her present-day appearance on film. Producers had interviewed her in Kenya; poignantly, she came down with pneumonia and died, at age eighty-three, in August 1986, just weeks before PBS broadcast the documentary nationwide. Herbert Mitgang, a culture writer at the *New York Times*, called the movie "beautifully crafted."[14] Gutekunst ended up in a messy legal battle over the rights to *West with the Night*. He eventually prevailed and sold the memoir rights to the actress Diane Baker and partners, one of two or three more film projects spawned by the rediscovered literary sensation.[15]

Connell's own TV project was dragging out, but he could take comfort in Melissa Mathison's comment that she and he were "the hot item" in Hollywood.[16]

The 1980s provided Connell with a new line of political commentary. His letters to Barbara often ended with his brief complaints about President Ronald Reagan. They traded news clippings and op-ed columns, each trying to convince the other of their understanding of current events. Neither succeeded in changing minds, but for Connell, he was happy to have the outlet for venting:

November 22, 1983, two days after millions of Americans watched *The Day After* on television, a movie about nuclear war set in Kansas City and Lawrence, Kansas, where Connell went to college: "I hope desperately that Reagan can be removed from office before he kills everybody. I hope that TV disaster film increases the resistance to his insane policy. I think he is the most dangerous and violent simpleton ever to get into the White House."

March 10, 1984: "I think if Reagan gets another four years he will attack Central America. He might even do it before the election, manipulating it as Nixon manipulated the Vietnam war to assure his reelection. I dare say there is only one thing about Reagan on which we could agree: he is dividing this country as it has not been divided for many years."

March 2, 1985, in a letter accompanied by a newspaper clipping of books about the Vietnam War: "I have a feeling you agree with Reagan that it was a 'noble cause' and that we should do it again in Central America, which he quite unmistakably advocates. It is a terrible idea."

September 19, 1986: "He tried to assassinate Khadafi and succeeded in murdering about sixty innocent people, many of them children. Now the level of Moslem terrorism has risen, which was easily predictable. What next?"

July 16, 1988, four months before George H. W. Bush, Reagan's vice president, was elected to succeed him: "Does it make any difference to you that Reagan has been condemned by an international court? . . . I think that if the U.S. continues to behave this way it will become the most despised nation on earth. You think very differently. So it goes."

If Connell was not rehearsing contextual outbursts for another volume of "Notes," he certainly was building up a storehouse of seething commentary that would prove useful in short stories and at least two book projects to come.

More than a year into it, the Custer television project had slowed down. NBC's enthusiasm waned. Connell's passing comment: "Mysterious business."[17] He remained busy. He was reviewing books for the *New York Times* and the *Boston Globe*. He had spent weeks off and on reading thousands of manuscript pages for a National Endowment for the Arts panel granting literary fellowships. He had hastily agreed to serve and, amid all the reading, soon regretted it. Still, he spent a couple of days in Washington, D.C., meeting with seven other judges, who ended up handing out about a million dollars to four dozen writers. Then he took an excursion to Europe.

When he got back he found a long letter from Mathison. She was outraged over the "stupidity and rudeness" of the NBC execs.[18] But now CBS had bought the rights—a rare move for one network to sell to another. CBS liked Mathison's script. Everything seemed to be back on track. The Mounts had set a budget at $8 million for a four-hour series tentatively to be shot and shown in 1987. Columbia Pictures replaced Viacom as a production partner. Kevin

Costner was angling to play Custer. Connell remained bemused but optimistic.

Aside from brooding over politics, Connell's other diversion from writing was travel. In August 1986, around the time of his sixty-second birthday, he took a jaunt to Mexico. He spent a week exploring and relaxing in Mazatlán and Puerto Vallarta. His travel report to Barbara included practical information in case she and her husband could use them: "Both places are steamy hot, which I don't enjoy, otherwise it was fun. Good food, beach, swimming pools, margaritas. Hotels are 50% gringo, Mexico still a bargain—Mazatlan bus is 8 [cents], and a good meal in a luxury hotel on the beach is six or eight dollars."[19]

After the literary business in Washington, Connell's excursion to Europe was fraught with mishaps. He hadn't been to France and Spain in nine years, and he had hoped to be exhilarated again by some of his favorite places. A railroad strike two days after he landed in France disrupted his plan to visit Mont-Saint-Michel and the Bayeux Tapestry in Normandy. Paris was expensive and crowded, and he had trouble finding a room. His travelogue is one sadness after another: "I walked around in the rain for almost two hours with my suitcase asking at one hotel after another, finally was allowed to stay two nights in 4th floor walkup the size of a closet, spent most of the next day sloshing around asking for a place to stay another four days. Rained for about 18 days out of the 21 in Europe." A missing bus left him stranded in Zaragoza. A train got him to "grimy" Bilbao in the rain, before moving on to San Sebastian. "Not the best of trips."[20]

Still, responding to his sister's uneasiness about going to Europe after a recent bombing, he noted, "Believe me, you are in much more danger any day of the week, any week, in Kansas City, than you would be anywhere in Europe. The level of violence in America is astounding. I noticed it as soon as I returned."[21]

While he was in Europe, John Dodds, an editor who had acquired Connell's *Double Honeymoon* for G. P. Putnam's Sons, died of cancer. And Bill Ryan, the founder of *Contact* magazine in Sausalito, took the same exit from life as his friend Calvin Kentfield had eleven years earlier. Ryan drove off a cliff, two hundred feet high, south of Stinson Beach. His departure place was not far from where Kentfield jumped to his death. Ryan, age fifty-eight, had been suffering from emphysema, bronchitis, and asthma. His family indicated he was despondent over his health. Ruth Costello threw a party in his honor on her houseboat. Connell commiserated with the writer Oakley Hall and numerous other friends. Anne Lamott eulogized Ryan in *California* magazine, where he'd become editor-at-large the year before. "He was a flamboyant man," she wrote, "insane, brilliant, wildly funny, sometimes a royal pain in the neck, and just about the most loyal friend any of us have ever had."[22]

Even as Connell was called to Hollywood to meet with Mathison and the Custer producers in January 1987, negotiations about a Bridge movie began picking up again. Joanne Woodward had made another offer a few months earlier but Connell again turned it down. McKee was now in discussions with the producer Robert Halmi, not a big surprise given that Halmi had worked in the past with Woodward. Soon, as Connell put it, "Elizabeth stuck a gun in Robt. Halmi's ribs and demanded a better offer for Mrs. B, so he agreed, and a contract is being drawn up."[23] Connell thought it was odd that Halmi said *Mr. Bridge* would remain Evan's property, because earlier Woodward had requested rights to both books. A few months later, the parties were still talking, and Halmi wound up making a new offer for both of the Bridge books.

In May, Connell sat on stage in the revered hall of the American Academy and Institute of Arts and Letters, a cultural outpost in Washington Heights in the far reaches of upper Manhattan. He was among the recipients of the academy's annual arts and letters awards in literature. His fellow awardees included the novelist Ernest J. Gaines (*The Autobiography of Miss Jane Pittman*) and Steven Millhauser, the fiction writer whose debut novel Connell had panned during judging for the National Book Award fourteen years earlier. Connell did not look happy. Gale Garnett, who joined him in New York for a few days, could see that from her seat in the audience. But she knew the look. Earlier that day at lunch, a woman had asked her whether Connell was depressed. Or angry. "No, not at all," she said.[24] But despite his mood, Connell gamely got up and received his award from Irving Howe, who pronounced, "In each case the form is reinvigorated, the work splendidly achieved."[25] A couple of nights later, Connell and Garnett got some together time away from the literary gatherings. They dined out on Indian food. A bout of humorous teasing erupted into a cascade of laughter. This was the side of Connell that almost no one ever saw.

Connell had also begun another project, a work of fiction but one rooted deeply in medieval history. He was slowly piecing together a narrative about alchemists, the intellectuals and natural philosophers of their day, who sought to transmute lead into gold and mundane aspects of life into perfection. He wasn't sure how long it would take, and the movie business and travels didn't give him much concentrated time to work on it: "There is a lot of reading, and the style I've used is rather knotty, archaic, difficult, so I can't work rapidly."[26] His mind had returned in other words to the territory of his "Notes" books but in a new, or rather quite old, way.

The book would be less fun than working on Custer, Connell told his niece Janet. The source materials were much drier and lacking in the kind of peculiar details he dredged up in the Custer story. "Alchemy is so much smoke and mirrors," he told her. He planned seven sections, "seven being a mystical number, each segment concluding with a reference to the fabulous serpent Ourobouros swallowing itself."[27]

Leave it to Connell to follow a commercial victory with a determined march into the arcane. "Evan did the ordinarily perverse thing that he always did," Jack Shoemaker said, "by following a bestselling book . . . with a book that he damn well knew, and I knew, would never sell a copy."[28] One day that summer Connell explained the project to a journalist. They sat by the bay in a San Francisco park. "Do you know what one of the most useful skills is? It's magic. If you're a magician you can drift around the world, and wherever you are you can stop in a town square, do a few tricks that people enjoy, collect a few coins, and feed yourself. You don't have to say a word."[29] Surely Connell knew in that moment, as the breeze wrinkled the water in his gaze, that he had just described the life of a writer as he lived it.

Connell got a taste that year of another writer's Hollywood escapade. Norman Mailer had adapted his own novel for the film *Tough Guys Don't Dance*. Ryan O'Neal starred as an alcoholic writer on the run from any number of wild complications in a kind of partly comic noir thriller. His co-star was the up-and-coming Isabella Rossellini. Connell didn't know Mailer well but liked him. Mailer had rented a place in San Francisco, and Connell saw him at a party for the first time in fifteen years. "He's very mild among friends, quite unlike his public image of a wild man."[30] A few months later, Connell and Don Carpenter were invited to a San Francisco preview of Mailer's movie. Mailer held Carpenter's Hollywood novel *A Couple of Comedians* in high regard. Connell wanted to like *Tough Guys Don't Dance* and hoped for Mailer's sake that it would succeed. To his sister his review amounted to one word: "Dreadful."[31] This seemed to be a pattern. A couple of years earlier, Connell went to see a Clint Eastwood western, *Pale Rider,* with high hopes because of its good press. "It's a waste of time—all clichés," he told Barbara.[32] He added that Eastwood had offered Sterling Hayden a role and good money, but Hayden turned it down because he thought the script was terrible.

CBS renewed its Custer option in the fall of 1987. Kevin Costner's name was still attached to the project, but Mathison was hitting roadblocks as she tried to finish the script. Connell had gotten her to discard several pages he disliked. There were hints that filming might start in the coming year. Connell tried to be patient.

The Bridge movie was also in a quiet period as Ruth Jhabvala was months away from completing a draft of the screenplay. Still, Connell had been told that production might begin the following year. "The schedule changes every time I hear from them," he reported to Bobs. "I told Don [Carpenter] and he laughed and said it'll be like that till the film is done."[33]

Early in the new year, Connell received a "final" script from Mathison, but she couldn't get the CBS executives to read it. And CBS staffers evidently were tinkering with it, which didn't bode well for its authenticity.

If that weren't enough disappointment, in March 1988 the Writer's Guild voted to go on strike against film and television producers large and small. The work stoppage waylaid both of Connell's projects.

Connell was back at the Audubon Terrace headquarters of the American Academy and Institute of Arts and Letters in May. This time, he had been elected a member, one of a handful of writers who had gained entry to the academy, taking spots left vacant by others who had died. John Updike, whom he had met during the academy festivities a year earlier, offered up Connell's name for membership. His fellow inductees this year included some familiar names, including John McPhee; Leslie Fiedler, with whom he'd sparred on the jury panel for the National Book Awards in 1973; and Raymond Carver. This was the occasion that led to the dinner hosted by Jack Shoemaker, its table enlivened by the presence of William and Rose Styron and Allen Ginsberg. On another night Connell had dinner with Garnett and Elizabeth McKee, and one morning he joined Ruth Jhabvala for breakfast. From Jhabvala, Connell learned that her script for the Bridges project would amount to a two-hour movie and scenes would be shot in Paris and Kansas City. She had just finished a draft, but with the Writer's Guild strike underway, she couldn't share it with him or anyone else.

Connell was surprised to learn that in addition to Joanne Woodward, her husband, Paul Newman, was also interested in becoming involved in the Bridge production. Connell was confident that, despite the strike, both Hollywood projects were secure.

He also shared some observations with his niece Janet. Merchant Ivory, he said, has "a reputation for sticking close to the book on which a film is based, rather than inventing a lot. I think Ruth J has chosen incidents that she thinks are graphic and will try to weave them into something continuous. In other words, I don't expect car chases, drug busts, etc."[34]

James Ivory had proposed filming *Mrs. Bridge* twenty years earlier but, Ismail Merchant once recalled, other projects got in the way. After Merchant Ivory's *Room with a View* won much acclaim in 1985, Joanne Woodward approached Ivory and talked up *Mrs. Bridge* as one of the best novels she'd ever read. She told him that Robert Halmi had the option, and a producing team was born. Paul Newman eventually read the script and couldn't resist. "One couldn't find a better couple than the quintessential Mr. Newman and Ms. Woodward," Merchant said at the time.[35] Newman's general feeling, expressed in interviews, was that good, substantial scripts were rare and when one came along it ought to be taken.

A copy of the screenplay made its way to Connell in July, shortly after the Writer's Guild settled with a large group of small and independent producers. "The script," he said, "is ok for a first draft— nothing really grossly wrong. Characters are basically true, most of the scenes are taken almost verbatim from the books."[36] In other words, close but nothing to get excited about.

Connell's response to Jhabvala's first draft was a twenty-two-page letter of suggestions and corrections. (Don't think he was being overly critical, he told producer Robert Halmi. If he were responding to his own first draft, he would've written more.)[37] He didn't like the ending, which had Mr. Bridge rescuing his wife from her existential limbo in the garage. He thought there was too much sexual anxiety, and he reminded the team that the characters were austere Midwesterners who had a hard time expressing their feelings. "These are the people Grant Wood painted in *American Gothic*," he wrote. He elaborated on one small point and asked his sister for advice: "Do you ever remember the expression 'yard-boy' for somebody who worked around the house or yard, such as the black man Jones in Mrs. B? That phrase occurs in the script, I think it's wrong. Ivory and I discussed it and I said I'd ask you. It seems to me that 'handyman' or 'gardener' or maybe 'yard-man' would be all right."[38] He also wondered whether there were chipmunks in Kansas City, as Jhabvala had mentioned in one scene. Certainly there were squirrels (still lots of them), but he couldn't remember chipmunks. He also suggested that Jhabvala add a scene about Douglas's junk tower. Ivory approved. Overall, Connell felt as if his feedback were appreciated.

Connell's time in Sausalito came to an end. He made good on his longtime desire to live in Santa Fe. That high-desert city was far less crowded. The scenic vistas and the opportunity for a quiet writing life were ultimately alluring. As at least one account had it, he was also escaping the clutches of Ruth Costello, who seemed to be coming on strong. Connell's art-dealer friends Charlotte and Bob Kornstein, owners of the Bellas Artes Gallery in Santa Fe's Canyon Road district, had lined him up with a real estate agent. She had a list of places to show him. After the first stop, in a condo compound called Fort Marcy, Connell said he'd take it. The agent told him he had to wait, she had more to show him. They drove. They looked. Connell mostly kept quiet. In the end he said he wanted the one at Fort Marcy, at 320 Artist Road, a short walk from Santa Fe's central plaza. "It's a two-story place," he told his sister, "five blocks from the plaza, solar heating unit on the roof, two bedroom, 2½ bath, a plum tree and an apricot tree in front, on a hillside overlooking Santa Fe, splendid view south and west, and it's a corner unit—which I like."[39]

He left Sausalito on April 30 and moved in on May 4, 1989, just as the *Son of the Morning Star* proceedings were becoming more complicated. First, CBS liked the script, and "two weeks later decided not to do the show. Ted Turner appeared, 'loves the book,' wants to discuss the show. Then just today ABC called. . . . Tune in next week."[40]

On the other hand, the Bridge production was rolling. Connell had written a synopsis of the movie for Paul Newman. James Ivory made a scouting trip to Kansas City in May with the team's art director. Connell told his sister that if Ivory got in touch she should show him photos of their parents. He wanted Ivory to see Dr. Connell's "severe withdrawn expression, the eyeglasses, and you might tell Ivory how you remember them. I expect any details you can think of—gestures, habits, attitudes—might help a director."[41]

Fig. 31. Connell with sister Barbara Zimmermann and nephew Matthew Zimmermann on the Kansas City set of the Bridge family home as used in *Mr. and Mrs. Bridge*. © Mikki Ansin.

Filming would begin in Paris in August. There the crew would gather scenes of the Bridges' European travels, which, as depicted in *Mrs. Bridge*, occurred exactly fifty years earlier, on the eve of Germany's invasion of Poland on September 1, 1939. Connell had hoped to go along for the Paris scenes but remained in Santa Fe. One thing he missed, as he told his niece, was a rehearsal by "sixteen can-can dancers, so maybe I should have gone over to supervise."[42]

The budget was announced at $7 million. Merchant, the team's financial overseer, had a well-earned reputation as a penny-pincher in service of authenticity and style. "Ismail rarely asks me to do for the sake of dollars anything I feel is artistically suspect," Ivory told the local newspaper after the Kansas City production had begun. They had become experts at economizing and the production values of their films were generally so well regarded, everyone wanted to work with them. The consequences of a tight budget meant there was a heightened sense of controlled urgency on the set. One scene was shot in a county courthouse on a holiday and there would be no question about returning a second day. "You work really hard on the main scenes, the ones that advance the story, giving them as much energy as you can," Ivory said. "Less important scenes sometimes fall through the cracks—you may not get around to them."[43]

Kansas City stepped up in a big way and embraced Hollywood's arrival, beginning in early September and lasting more than ten weeks. Local big-money supporters helped to open doors, to provide key locations and office space, and otherwise to stretch the budget. There were Newman and Woodward sightings all over town. Bookshops had trouble keeping the Bridge novels in stock. The Tivoli Theatre showed a Merchant Ivory retrospective of seventeen movies. The local theater and film community was robust enough to provide tech crew members, actors for speaking roles, and hundreds of extras. Costumers and set designers scoured local antique shops and flea markets for the kinds of period details a Merchant Ivory production prized. High-society households handed over family heirlooms—silver candlesticks here, armchairs and a buffet table there.

Kansas City's mayor, Richard Berkley, appears in one scene in the movie—as Kansas City's mayor handing Douglas Bridge (Robert Sean Leonard) an Eagle Scout medal. Douglas's mother (Woodward) stands beside him on the dais and receives a pin. For Berkley and 220 other extras, it turned out to be a fourteen-hour day as the filmmakers produced the single scene from multiple angles. Berkley missed a City Council meeting. Like everyone else, he collected twenty-five dollars in cash on the way out.[44] Alas, like so many moments in the history of filmdom, Berkley's star turn didn't make the final cut.

Despite Connell's mixed feelings for Kansas City, he was moved by moments of nostalgia and unexpected feelings of a homecoming. That Eagle Scout medal someone found was just like the one he had. Connell had fond memories of his scouting experience, one of

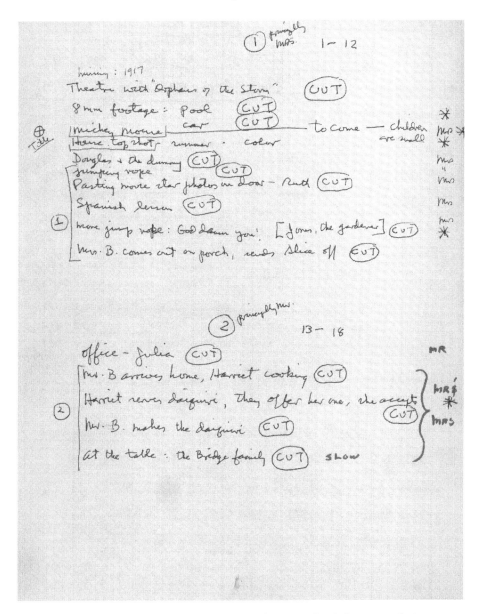

Fig. 32. A page from director James Ivory's editing notebook for *Mr. and Mrs. Bridge*, which includes a reel-by-reel listing of scenes. Courtesy of James Ivory, editing notebook for the film *Mr. and Mrs. Bridge,* autograph manuscript. New York, New York, and Kansas City, Missouri, 1989–90, p. [4], MA 9285. The Morgan Library & Museum, New York.

the few things he liked about his high school years. He had handed over his own merit badge sash for use in the movie. He saved his *Boy Scout Handbook* for posterity and it sits among his papers at Stanford, his name and Drury Lane address written inside. One day on the set, Connell chatted with Merchant about scouting, which was also big in India. "The Boy Scout salute was more important than the passage of prime ministers," Merchant, who had grown up in Bombay, told him.[45]

Merchant and Ivory were ideal teammates for Connell. They shared his independent spirit and his literary values. Their movies owed more to atmospherics and the subtleties of character than the average Hollywood product. As the deal for the Bridge novels was coming together, the company was just coming off their most commercially successful film in a quarter century, *A Room with a View,* their adaptation of the E. M. Forster novel. Hollywood was shoveling money at them, offering chances to make star vehicles, but Merchant and Ivory, sounding much like Connell, declined: "We see things differently. We like to work independently. We have never worked in a corporate structure. What's the use? . . . 'I made $2 million!' So what?"[46] That summer, their most recent release was *Slaves of New York,* a comedy based on the edgy short stories of the downtown art and fashion scenes by Tama Janowitz. Given some of its outré characters, Janowitz's book could be seen as a distant literary cousin of "Saint Augustine's Pigeon" and *Double Honeymoon.* Despite the filmmakers' reputation, the movie was a critical and box-office flop. And, as Connell frequently did, the team moved on to its next project, this one, undeterred.

Connell hadn't been back to Kansas City since his father had died fifteen years earlier. He told a reporter that the city felt different: "Things have changed for the better. When I was a boy there there was nothing to do." One day while walking near a group of onlookers, Connell heard someone yell out his first name and he stopped. "I haven't seen that man since I was fourteen."[47]

Shooting began on September 9. It was raining, so instead of the scheduled exterior shots, the production moved indoors.

At least two houses had been lined up to stand in for the Bridge home. Merchant one day led Connell on a tour of the main location. Connell sensed a familiarity with the patterned wallpaper and noticed a bell pull, just like his family had. "You're satisfied," Merchant said. "I don't see a thing wrong," Connell replied, even offering a smile and a brief chuckle.[48]

Connell spent much of the shooting schedule watching from the sidelines and often contributing rewrites and suggestions as scenes developed or came into play. When Newman was instructed to blow the foam off the top of a glass of beer, Connell counseled Ivory that Mr. Bridge "would never have done that." Connell also offered some character insights to Robert Sean Leonard, who was playing Douglas. Connell gave him tips "about how he spent his evenings in Kansas City, where he took a girl, how he draped a keychain from his belt, little things like that."[49]

Connell's own version of the movie script had opened with the death of Walter Bridge as he sat at the desk in his law office, his secretary at his side. It ended with the unforgettable closing scene of *Mrs. Bridge*, the title character in her wintry, garage-bound entrapment. Paul Newman had argued against focusing on the depressing fate of the character he played. In fact, as he read the novels and prepared for the role, he had begun to emphasize a more sympathetic version of the character than many readers see in Walter Bridge. Newman just didn't see the dark side of the character, said Richard Rhodes, a Kansas City–bred writer who got to know the Newmans as neighbors in Connecticut and saw them during the filming. "I thought *Mr. Bridge* was a portrait in acid," Rhodes told me. "I remember that he was surprised when I mentioned it and disagreed. Maybe Connell was too subtle."[50] Newman's instincts carried the day in the finished product, as producers also wanted to avoid the downers of death, despair, and ambiguity. The movie begins with a backyard barbecue scene and ends on a note of uplift wholly inconsistent with Connell's original vision. Still, as Ivory put it at the time, "It's a film without a plot as we know. You just start at the beginning and go on to the end. It's like life. There are scenes . . . but there's no plot as such, no really dramatic twists and turns, and yet it is dramatic."[51] Ivory sensed a deep connection with the film and Connell's two books. As the movie came together, he felt that it had become a representation of his own boyhood in Klamath Falls, Oregon. "In no other film," he told a Merchant Ivory chronicler, "have I been drawing directly out of my early years."[52]

Gale Garnett landed a supporting role—Connell insisted on it, his writer friend Herbert Gold told me, though Garnett said Elizabeth McKee had arranged her audition without Connell's knowledge. She played Mabel Ong, one of India Bridge's society friends, and appears in a handful of scenes. Notations accompanying a piece of the script in Connell's papers indicate that he contributed a rewrite of one scene involving Mrs. Bridge and Mabel, who had just returned from a scenic trip to Canada.

Fig. 33. Gale Garnett played the role of Mabel Ong, a friend of India Bridge, in *Mr. and Mrs. Bridge* and joined Connell for a gala Kansas City premiere of the Merchant Ivory movie in 1990. Courtesy of Janet Zimmermann and the Literary Estate of Evan Shelby Connell Jr.

Connell had envisioned Mabel as mannish and a dreadful poet. "Jim Ivory was in love with the character of Mabel Ong," Garnett recalled. "He was in love with the name but not the character. And I thought I would play this dyke. And that's how she was in the book, but he just wanted random lines that didn't belong to any-body to be put together in the film."[53]

In between shots one day near the end of the Kansas City stretch of the project, Newman got expressive with a reporter in his mo-bile dressing room. While changing suits for an unexpected scene, Newman almost erupted in joy over the news that Germans were dancing atop the Berlin Wall. He used Europe's transformation to make a point about "the flatfootedness" of the George H. W. Bush administration and "emotional Republicans" in general. (Connell most definitely would have agreed.) Not lost on Newman was the connection to Walter Bridge. "Mr. Bridge is a classic example of this personality," he said. "Two massive social upheavals occur during the years covered in *Mrs. Bridge*. There's the Depression and World War II. And yet in the Bridge household the Depression is almost never mentioned. And there's only a glancing mention of the war when their son, Douglas, comes home in a uniform. This is not a family that talks about major events." The movie, of course, was not intended to be a political statement, but it makes one "by omission," Newman said. "This was a family insulated from the realities of the world. It was a family that had the security of definition. You know who you were in the order of things. It's the same serenity religion gives some people. But what do you sacrifice for that serenity?"[54]

Off the set, Newman and Woodward proved to be relatively approachable and gracious. Connell's sister hosted a dinner par-ty for them. "They got along real well," Connell said a couple of years later. "She and Woodward were exchanging recipes. Newman would come up to me on the set after filming a scene and he'd salute and call me 'Mon capitaine!' What was I supposed to say to *that*?"[55] Connell was always cautious around gatherings with his sister. As a committed, born-again evangelical Christian, Barbara Zimmermann had a tendency to proselytize. If Connell was within earshot, as occurred during the making of the movie, he would stay quiet but "do his fist balling-up thing," said his niece Janet.[56]

By Thanksgiving, the Merchant Ivory production had wrapped in Kansas City and its principals departed. Connell would spend his favorite holiday without the great cheer of his Sausalito friends for the first time in a quarter century. Instead, he began another holiday tradition, visiting with Gus Blaisdell and his family in Albuquerque. Along with the good feelings that accompanied Connell's first successful Hollywood experience, there was another thing he was grateful for that season. Word had arrived from his agent that a deal had finally been signed to film *Son of the Morning Star.* The production was now in the hands of its third television network, ABC.

British journalist and film critic John Pym took the occasion of that news to catch Connell in a bit of humorous reflection. "I once imagined myself an actor in a Western," Connell told him. "The cowboy at the bar who says, 'They went thataway.'"[57]

Before the year was out, Connell was bracing to learn the implications of another piece of news. As a *New York Times* headline put it: "North Point Seeks Buyer."[58]

Sweet Smell of Success
1990–1995

"I say he that observes, studies, and learns during his tenure on earth shall be dressed with gold during the Resurrection, while not one that has loitered should aspire to superiority. This is because exploration leads upward."

—*The Alchymist's Journal*

Connell's move to Santa Fe was motivated, at least in part, by financial stability. His Hollywood projects, the great reception of the Custer book, the revival and reprinting of the Bridge novels and his other works—all meant Connell, at age sixty-five and counting, four decades into a writing career, had now come into his own. For the first time in his life he was a homeowner not a renter. "It finally happened," Anne Lamott once said. "He's finally getting the success he deserves. . . . Everyone was just so happy for him, and that must have made his heart feel soft and large."[1] Gale Garnett affirmed the idea that Connell was pleased. "Here's a man who has worked his buns off at a craft since the '40s," she told a writer for *People* magazine, one of several popular media outlets that took a new celebrity interest in Connell. "I think he's enjoying what has happened enormously."[2] Connell knew not to take success too seriously or to raise his expectations. In his experience of fleeting success and long neglect, "You finish one thing and go on to the next, and whatever happens, happens."[3]

The Merchant Ivory crew had an idea to stretch their involvement with Connell by assigning a producer, Donald Rosenfeld, to make a documentary about the writer. Footage was shot in

Kansas City, including interviews with the movie's stars on the set, and a crew was lined up to focus in on Connell in Santa Fe. The British film writer John Pym conducted the interviews. He had been a longtime chronicler of Merchant Ivory movies. Now, John Carroll was in town, and Connell enlisted him to talk about Custer for the film. A day of shooting was planned at Paul Pletka's place. "He remained mute through the entire filming at my studio," Pletka said.[4]

Connell and Garnett sat on a couch and watched as Carroll and Pletka spoke in front of one the latter's large, expressive portraits of Custer and the cameras rolled. Elsewhere, the producers interviewed Connell at his writing desk and got him to venture outdoors, to walk along some railroad tracks near the mountain town of Madrid, and to sit with Pym overlooking the desert landscape like a wizened oracle in an explorer's hat (borrowed from the local production coordinator). They also staged a scene outside a church near Madrid where Garnett read a dramatic passage from *Points for a Compass Rose*, which Connell had dedicated to her, as he walked up slowly to sit and listen. "He remains a mystery," Pym declared in conclusion, "even to those who know him well."[5] The reputation had become a cliché.

A few months after the Kansas City production wrapped, Connell received a rough cut of *Mr. and Mrs. Bridge*. He wasn't sure what to do with it. He called Pletka and told him he might have to drive up to Colorado, because he thought George Gutekunst, who vacationed there, would have the right piece of equipment with which to watch it. "I don't know," Connell said. "This is a real puzzle. I need to access something called a vee-cee-arr." "Evan," Pletka replied, "I've got one." Connell soon drove out to Pletka's new home and studio in a desert development on the western edge of Santa Fe. With the tape running in the videocassette device, Connell and Pletka watched the whole long movie. "He had no reaction," Pletka recalled thirty years later. "He didn't have that much to say, if I remember correctly."[6] It would be several more months before the public saw the movie and Connell would take it in again at a world premiere in Kansas City. For now, he could think about how his quasi-autobiographical novels had been reinterpreted for film. And he could concentrate on other projects and other interruptions in his daily routines.

A year after buying his condo, he had settled into his local habits. He had the essential books, pictures, and ceramics that he'd hauled from Sausalito. He bought a writing desk to add to the spare pieces of furniture the condo's previous owner had left. He even did some touching up, painting a balcony door the requisite Santa Fe turquoise. He could walk to the post office, the bank, and any number of restaurants in Santa Fe's plaza district. He was a morning regular at the Burrito Company, where he drank coffee, ate breakfast, and read the Albuquerque newspaper. Early on he found a classical music station on the radio, "with plenty of Mozart, so I haven't touched the dial since moving in."[7] He loved seeing the mountains in the distance. He loved the rice and beans, the simple comfort food of Mexican and southwestern cuisine. There was a quiet, ambling pace to Santa Fe living, far different from what he left behind in San Francisco. As Herbert Gold put it, "I'm trying not to catch your disease of finding San Francisco too nervous. . . . This place was a world away from New York when I got here; not any longer."[8]

Melissa Mathison was still tinkering with the script for *Son of the Morning Star* and Connell was still offering revisions. In April 1990 alone he compiled two stacks of pages with new comments and suggestions. The producers were still looking for a lead actor. Kevin Costner had veered off into another western history project. *Dances with Wolves,* which Costner co-produced, directed, and starred in, was a period piece with resonant parallels to the Custer project. The producers then dangled the Custer role before Tom Berenger, but his agent discouraged his participation in a TV project. Finally they signed Gary Cole, who starred in an ABC crime series set in San Francisco, *Midnight Caller.* Connell had

275

never seen it, but it wasn't his call anyway, and now production seemed to be set, after all these years, with a filming schedule beginning in late May.

Connell sent the manuscript of *The Alchymist's Journal*, his latest experiment in channeling arcane voices, to Elizabeth McKee in March. In the midst of writing, he described it as having the form of the two epic "Notes" projects. Rather than verse-like fragments, however, it progressed in paragraph-long segments filled with medieval language. It certainly can remind one of various voices heard in *Notes from a Bottle* and *Points for a Compass Rose*. He described its central figure as a fictional alchemist dating to the fifteenth and sixteenth centuries. Paracelsus, an historical figure—a "celebrated magus" who produced a huge book of "superstitions and beliefs, occult sciences, salvation and related matters," as Connell had written in *Points*—served as a model.[9] Connell invented narratives of six other alchemists to form his seven-part book. "I'm not so much interested in alchemy as I am in the lives of the alchemists," Connell said at the time. "What they were looking for when they turned lead into gold relates symbolically to so much that's happening today. At the present time, atomic physicists are alchemists. When Oppenheimer and those people set off the bomb in New Mexico, they were doing something the alchemists were trying to do. It resonates. I can't explain the relationship really."[10] As with all of his books, he wrote it without having a contract or an advance in hand. "No one looking over his shoulder that way . . . no feeling of obligation to a particular publishing house, beyond the fulfillment of a first-refusal option."[11]

By summer, North Point gave Connell $15,000 for the book and put it in the pipeline for publication in spring of 1991. The state of North Point remained uncertain, however. Don Carpenter reminded Connell of that. The press was still for sale, and Carpenter had no inkling when it might, if ever, reprint a book of his that Shoemaker had bought three years earlier. Still, Connell was happy about the new covers North Point was planning for the movie tie-in editions of the Bridge novels. Having Woodward and Newman on them couldn't hurt. He also began to get good signals on *The Alchymist's Journal.* "A magnificent book," wrote Ross Feld, a North Point contributing editor. Feld's one-page internal memo was so effusive Connell shared a copy of it with his sister. Feld rang out phrases like "richness of prose," "remarkable rhythms of its sections," "work of high art and uncompromised." Connell would have smiled, at least internally, when Feld mentioned the book's "Pythagorean musicality" because, he would say sometime later, he really was concentrating on turning the often-difficult language into a kind of music. Feld concluded with an expressive summation of the book's challenges and rewards: "I think it can be marketed a little like an oyster: magnificent hard shell—its great artfulness and literary curiosity—but sweet soft meat—a range of philosophies and alternations between despair and hope—within." Feld suggested that ideal reviewers might be "William Gass or Paul West for its prose" or "Bill Moyers for its 'spirituality.'"[12]

Two months later, Connell heard from Barbara Ras at North Point. She forwarded a manuscript containing numerous flags to alert Connell to mostly small questions, many about apparent anachronisms. If Connell meant to "borrow freely in historical time," Ras said, that could be dealt with in jacket copy, to alert close, perhaps science-oriented readers that he was intentionally playing with facts. She enclosed a green pencil to use for changes, the old-school equivalent of digital word processing's comments and change-tracking tools. She closed with more words of comfort: "This is a remarkable book, and I'm delighted to have the chance to work with you on it."[13]

Filming of *Son of the Morning Star* began in mid-May. Connell headed to Billings, Montana, and spent about ten days on the set in early June. He apparently didn't listen to Don Carpenter's advice to let John Carroll "be the one to go crazy while the director and the actors sit up all night rewriting the script, heh heh."[14] A private river valley near Billings stood in quite well for the Little Bighorn battlefield site. The schedule was intense. Nikki Mount had been enthusiastic, "said everybody was working above and beyond the call of duty."[15] Cathy Smith, a costume designer from Santa Fe, recalled twenty-hour days in a six-week span before and during the shooting to create hundreds of tribal costumes. While many civilian and military costumes could be rented, Native American costumes had to be made from scratch, as Smith learned earlier while making wardrobes for *Dances with Wolves*. On this project, she had even less time to supervise her crew of family and friends, including one whose sole job was cutting fringe. "We were making costumes every single day of shooting."[16]

As Connell viewed script revisions, he got the impression that things were going fairly well: "There is some historical distortion, and they are afraid of offending anybody, but it could have been worse." Generally, though, based on some of the daily rushes he'd seen, Connell thought the departures from history were small and inconsequential. John Carroll, for instance, got wound up one day when he noticed during a battle scene that two warriors were wearing Hidatsa headdresses, not Sioux, a detail, Connell said, "that would escape 99.9% of the audience."[17] He was encouraged that the director, Mike Robe, a latecomer to the project and a Kansas grad like himself, was sticking closely to Mathison's script.

Patricia Nelson Limerick, a historian at the University of Colorado, had a vantage point on the set. She sensed the possibility that the project, following the success of *Dances with Wolves*, represented some kind of historical and social progress. Her observation of "cross-cultural film making" led her to imagine a "cheerful fantasy," an improbable scenario that perhaps suggested "at the end of the 20th century, the epic of the conquest of Western America has taken an unexpected turn. After all the bitterness, injury, lost territory and lost morale, maybe Indians and whites have at last found a common ground—in the making of films." Limerick called Connell's book "an unlikely text to provide the occasion for pipe dreams of reconciliation." "Hypnotic" and unflinching, *Son of the Morning Star* diminished the "romance of the 'colorful Indian wars'" in repeated encounters with the facts of what happens to human bodies under the pressure of bullets or knives, as well as what happens to human minds in contact with a brutal reality." She added that Connell "was a commanding presence on the set."[18]

In chatting with Connell, Limerick learned of his hope that the story would come across as he intended it, as a critique of American power and the folly of war. "I hope the movie is controversial," he said. "It would be disappointing for people to say, 'So what.'"[19]

In private, Connell complained that one executive was squeezing the budget and giving off an attitude that he couldn't "understand why anybody would want to see an honest Western."[20] Still, ABC was upbeat and planned a robust advertising campaign.

Not long after the shooting wrapped up, John Carroll died, succumbing to heart disease at age sixty-two. Carroll had been a champion for the book and television project, as well as an official advisor. Connell was pleased that Carroll had at least gotten a feel for the final product during the filming. He told his sister that Carroll had been quoted enthusiastically in the local paper. He praised Gary Cole's performance, which Connell knew was "a bit of a fib."[21]

Carroll left an essay about the film production, which was published by the British Film Institute a few months later, on the eve of the television broadcast. In it, he wrote about his affinity for movies and how his professional studies in western history and Custer stemmed from the fact that his own father had joined the Seventh Cavalry in 1918 and had heard tales directly from two officers who had survived the Little Bighorn campaign. Carroll shared a story from the project's process. As the network and studio reviewed the final script, a staffer who happened to be Native American "challenged every little detail" and concluded that the creators of the teleplay had over-glamorized Custer. Carroll wrote back to say that "if it appeared that way it was because the truth was being told for the first time. And that has been the tempo for the entire project."[22] Carroll had nits to pick, but in essence he concluded that this would be the best Custer movie ever made. It certainly might have been the most expensive. Republic Pictures eventually reported that production costs totaled $18.2 million, and the cumulative net deficit amounted to $8.4 million.[23] At the time, the typical TV network movie budget was closer to $2.5 million.[24]

Mr. and Mrs. Bridge debuted at the Tribeca Film Center in New York in late August 1990 and the Venice Film Festival shortly thereafter. One press account noted the Venice audience loved it. Connell saved a Venice clip from the *Financial Times*: "Just when we thought Ivory had shut himself up forever in the E. M. Forster Institute for Demure Period-pieces (with occasional unhappy breakouts like 'Slaves of New York'), we find him inching forward in time while losing none of his flair for period nuance and sly social comedy." The critic admired the movie's sense of "irony and affection," its depth, and the acting chops of the Newmans.[25] *Variety* agreed, stamping the film as "a potent arthouse entry" and its main and supporting actors as top-notch across the board.[26]

Gale Garnett, now going by her middle name, Zoe, joined Connell in Kansas City for the premiere of *Mr. and Mrs. Bridge* in November. They dressed to the nines and stood for a snapshot at Barbara and Matt Zimmermann's house, a Thomas Hart Benton print of a Midwestern farm scene hanging behind them on a wood-paneled wall. For the premiere event, the Kansas City community commandeered the Midland Theater, an opulent, 1920s-era house that hadn't shown a movie in a decade. It was outfitted with properly up-to-date projection equipment, and its gala decorations gave the showing a sense of stylish sizzle. Nearly one thousand people paid at least $150 apiece to attend. The event was a benefit for the Variety Club, an organization devoted to supporting children's charities. Kansas City's high-society and philanthropic crowd turned out in black tie, formal gowns, and bejeweled finery. There were cocktails for VIPs beforehand, and after the showing another reception took place a block away at the Starlight Roof atop the Kansas City Club, a pinnacle of blue-blood elitism. Connell and Garnett joined the swirl, she always expressive and lively while he remained his taciturn and awkward social self. Woodward also attended the opening events and brought along her aunt in her husband's absence. Connell told a local reporter that the movie was "photographically very good and Joanne Woodward and Paul Newman did a very good job."[27] To *People* magazine, he was a little less polite. Although Woodward embodied his mother's essence, he said, her portrayal was a "little bit different than I imagined it in the book."[28]

Sometime after viewing the raw cut of *Mr. and Mrs. Bridge* earlier in the year, Connell acquired his own video cassette player. When he received a preview copy of *Son of the Morning Star*, he invited Cathy Smith to join him for a showing in his living room. They had beers, and Connell hauled his rarely used television out of the closet and fired it up. "We were sitting in his living room, thinking oh, no, why'd they do it that way, and oh, God, they cut that . . . and oh my God. It was crazy." Still, she said, "I think he was generally pleased. It was such a massive undertaking. It was an enormous undertaking."[29]

North Point was in its last months. Bill Turnbull, who had signed up Connell a decade earlier and brought *Son of the Morning Star* to market, couldn't find a buyer for the press and announced plans to shut down. Without any warning sign, Turnbull had been diagnosed with a virulent stomach cancer. Connell and his friends were grieving. In a letter, Don Carpenter, who had been treated for tuberculosis, said he couldn't even talk about Turnbull. Anne Lamott, already reeling because of a close friend's current bout with breast cancer, was also thrown by Turnbull's diagnosis. She talked to him frequently. "Just devastating," she told Connell. Turnbull and Mary Hall, the Mill Valley bookseller and Turnbull's longtime companion, were married in Lamott's house in January. "Mary seems to be holding on okay; of course she is just beside herself with fear and impending loss but at the same time she's pretty strong, and coping beautifully."[30]

Turnbull and Connell could take a certain pride that the project they both believed in had become something even bigger. ABC aired *Son of the Morning Star* over two nights, a Sunday and Monday, in early February. An ad for it had run during the Super Bowl broad-cast a week earlier. For all the anticipation, the first part of the show came in a distant third in the ratings—back when the three major networks vied for eyeballs and ad dollars in a far less fragmented media world than exists today. Still, Connell's towering work of narrative history was further burnished as a book for the ages.

Connell went for a run one winter day in Santa Fe and came down with what he thought was a cold. He ignored it for a while but it soon erupted into double pneumonia. Armed with a prescription for penicillin, he took off anyway for a journey in his Honda. He was bound for a short trip to San Francisco, where North Point would be throwing a party for Turnbull. He stopped at a motel in Phoenix and holed up for two days with a fever. When he recounted this story just a few weeks later, still hampered by a nagging cough, it came out as something of "an adventure, an accomplishment, not unlike surviving Barcelona," according to reporter Barry Siegel. The image of Connell suffering by himself in that motel room prompted Siegel to wonder about the author's life of loneliness. "Sure I get lonely," Connell told him. "You get accustomed to yourself as you go on, though. You don't feel that piercing loneliness as you did when young. I couldn't marry because then I'd have to support a wife and family, and I never wanted to take a job I hated. I always feared that. Sure, you miss something. Sure, you give up stuff. But I don't like things hanging around my neck. I like always having time to myself."[31]

Bill Turnbull died barely three months after his diagnosis, in March 1991, at age sixty-four. A few weeks before his death, Turnbull had looked at the sand and the ocean near his home in Stinson Beach and delivered what seemed like a soliloquy on publishing and the principles and ideals of North Point. His interlocutor was Patricia Holt, the book review editor of the *San Francisco Chronicle*. He'd made lots of money as a real estate developer, then set out to make his mark as a literary publisher, as a promoter of fine literature in the tradition of Alfred A. Knopf. Soon he was in debt for a million dollars. He noted, "We've been accused of being a little too prideful in what we were doing. We had some esoteric stuff on the list, still do." For one thing, the backlist didn't earn as much as he had hoped. For another, "we were hampered in the long run without a bestseller every couple of years, or some profitable sideline like Norton's academic books or other publishers' children's books." And it was just tough to sell even three thousand copies of a literary novel when television and other social forces dominated the cultural marketplace and made reading less essential: "Today we all seem fond of saying that winning the battle isn't important as long as we win the war. In publishing, in its fight for literacy and the love of books, I believe the war is lost, which makes it all the more important to win the battles. That I believe North Point has done. We won one small skirmish that did make one small difference."[32]

Rather than stick to its original principle of staying a moderate course, Turnbull and Shoemaker allowed the press to grow staff and expand its list in the hopes that another Markham or Custer would come along.

"I will miss North Point," Connell told Siegel a week after Turnbull's death. His analysis echoed Turnbull's. "If they could only have sold six or seven thousand copies of each book they released, they could have survived, but they couldn't even do that. I'm resigned to it. This is a TV culture. You can't change that."[33] Another observer, lamenting the publisher's demise, correctly concluded that "Connell, in a sense, is the human personification of North Point."[34] As North Point followed its gut instincts, so did Connell write what he wanted, unconcerned with the commercial consequences.

A Connell acquaintance from the *Paris Review* days, Peter Matthiessen, traveled to Santa Fe for a talk that same month, a Tuesday evening in March. Connell stood in a slow-moving ticket line, according to Siegel's account, and bolted from the theater when the post-lecture reception became too unbearable. "Nothing infuriates me more than stupidity," he said. Connell was turned off when Matthiessen, who read a bit from *The Snow Leopard*, yielded the stage to a Native American activist who rambled on about freeing Leonard Peltier. Peltier had been imprisoned for nearly twenty years for the deaths of two federal agents during a shootout at the Pine Ridge Indian reservation near Wounded Knee, South Dakota. Matthiessen's book *In the Spirit of Crazy Horse* (1981) had prompted a lawsuit and a rare publisher's recall over whether he had unfairly maligned FBI agents and other government officials involved in the case. Now, ten years later, the book was about to be reissued, with Matthiessen clarifying his argument that Peltier had been wrongly convicted because of tainted testimony by a Sioux woman who had been a witness for the FBI. Peltier had been in the vicinity of the shootings but did not pull the trigger, Matthiessen maintained. In fact, another man, whom he did not identify, confessed to the killing. There is no record that Connell and Matthiessen conversed about any of this during the reception or elsewhere that day. Connell's escape from the event landed him on a bar stool near Santa Fe's Plaza, alongside Siegel, who was spending a few days in town to profile the reluctantly visible writer. Connell did not have to say a word or make a gesture before the bartender delivered him a gin martini. Connell told Siegel about an unnerving encounter with a rickshaw attendant in Calcutta.[35]

Kevin Costner and *Dances with Wolves* cleaned up at the Academy Awards that season. *Mr. and Mrs. Bridge* earned a sole nomination, for Joanne Woodward as best actress. Alas, she and three others lost out to Kathy Bates, who starred in *Misery,* a thriller based on a novel by Stephen King. One is forced to only imagine how Connell reacted to that moment of book-to-film history.[36] But he did send a note of disappointment to Joanne Woodward. She agreed that the movie, her husband, and Blythe Danner all should have been treated better by the academy voters. "I wish I could have won for all of us," she replied. "However, that's show business and it doesn't erase the fact that I am so grateful to you for having written the books and creating the character which gave me more pleasure than almost any part I've played."[37]

North Point was able to sell its three hundred or so titles to Farrar, Straus, and Giroux, which maintained its distribution arrangement for the small publisher's list. As the press's staff shrunk and scattered, Shoemaker became West Coast editor for Pantheon Books.

But *The Alchymist's Journal* did appear on schedule in May, one of the last books issued under North Point's imprint. Connell dedicated it to Turnbull. San Francisco writer Don Skiles greeted it with a glowing review in the *Examiner* ("the true alchemical master here is Connell himself").[38] Skiles reveled in Connell's archaic language and correctly recognized the portrayal of Paracelsus as a further imagining of the material Connell explored in the closing essay of *A Long Desire*. Elsewhere there was a mixed bag of head-scratching and restrained praise. As Connell noted in a letter to Max Steele, Albert Manguel's review in the *Washington Post* began, "I am uncertain as to how to read this book."[39] The critic Sven Birkerts recognized how the unsuspecting reader, going on Connell's reputation, could become hopelessly baffled by the book. "Mr. Connell has here dared the unfashionable," Birkerts wrote, "a work that concedes nothing to the reader's appetite for dramatic structure or vivid historical tableaux." But Birkerts also recognized the pleasure and deep connections a willing and attentive reader could make: "We may get an inkling of what the world felt like some centuries before it assumed its modern contours. Here is existence haunted by demons and possibilities; we walk among long angular shadows and random scatterings of light. In moments of absorption we might even shed the reflexive skepticism and condescension with which denizens of any present tend to regard the benighted past."[40] In his *Washington Post* book column, David Streitfeld called it "a dense, difficult book" and added that it made Umberto Eco's medieval mystery *The Name of the Rose* "look like Danielle Steel."[41]

An interview with Connell published that year belies the idea that he was incapable of conversational engagement. To many interviewers, Connell could be terse and minimally responsive. But Melody Sumner (later Carnahan), a writer and avant-garde publisher in New Mexico, was able to extract what remain some of Connell's most cogent mutterings about *The Alchymist's Journal.* Sumner brought a well-prepared intelligence to the table, which helped her cause. She found the new book was "in the tradition of prolonged ecstatic utterance" of *Notes* and *Points* but "more tightly metaphorical." Sumner might have gotten Connell primed by asking whether the book was "an invitation to begin to think independently." Perhaps that was her reading of Connell's entire career. "I'd like to think so, though I hadn't thought of it consciously," he told her. "It's flattering to think so." Sumner gave him an opportunity to speak about his use of rich, elevated language and sometimes obscure words and phrases. This was not mere rhetoric. Connell agreed that a key element of the book was the music created by its language. "My sister complains that she spends all her time at the dictionary, but I don't think it should be taken so seriously. The sound can carry you along."[42]

On a night when the Emmy Awards broadcast honored forty years of television comedy and *Cheers* rang up more of its usual awards for the show's barroom antics, *Son of the Morning Star* took home a single Emmy—for costuming. Cathy Smith, who had overseen the frantic production of indigenous costumes, shared the award with two others, who handled military and civilian wardrobes respectively. "Evan was very proud of it," Smith said of the honor.[43]

Hollywood was now out of his system. (Forever, as it turned out. Paul Newman had been eager to see galleys of *The Alchymist's Journal,* prodding Connell with the idea that perhaps there was a movie in it. "I told him it was not likely."[44]) And with *The Alchymist's Journal* now past him, Connell got back to writing. May Castleberry, an editor at the Whitney Museum of American Art, invited him to consider writing an essay about the Southwest for a future book and exhibit that paired writers with photographers.

Connell began tinkering with a piece about Mesa Verde, a prehistoric site in southwestern Colorado where remains of ancient cliff dwellings held the legacy of the mysteriously vanished Anasazi people.

He also was tapped to deliver an introductory essay for a Library of America edition of William Dean Howells's quintessentially American novel *The Rise of Silas Lapham*. To read that piece is to encounter Connell in his comfort zone, extracting odd and enlightening nuggets from Howells's half-century of fame, which preceded his descent in the early twentieth century into literary obscurity. On the other hand, if Connell's flat-voiced summary of the novel's story leaves one less inclined to dig in, then so be it.

And always there were new pots to covet. He took a drive up to Colorado to see an exhibit and got a glimpse of a Kayente piece he might like to have, though he thought it was overpriced.

Forays into short fiction also came back to his Olympia typewriter in the fall of 1991 for the first time since the 1970s. "I'm working on a story," he told his sister, "which seems like a frivolous occupation."[45] Two stories that Connell produced in this period took his mind back to the Bay Area. In "Acedia," the narrator, Crawford, thinks he's suffering from an endless bout of listlessness, as the title suggests. He is soon lured, reluctantly, to a party on a Sausalito houseboat. The party unfolds in a series of ever-more slapstick scenes. The second Sausalito story, titled "Marla" at the time but later published as "Hooker," involved Bill Koerner, Connell's Muhlbachian stand-in. Koerner has a random barroom encounter with a turquoise-eyed temptress, whose name was maybe Marla or Maria or Mikki or something else. He remembers that they'd once spent a drunken evening together in Taos. She disappears, and Koerner, much like Muhlbach on the prowl in New York, goes off on an irrational, desire-fueled quest into the wilds of North Beach taverns and bookstores.

Koerner is also the implied narrator of "Nan Madol," from 1992, which Connell based on his journey to the South Pacific of eight years earlier. In it, the narrator, William, hosts a brief visit in San Francisco from his odd and cranky Uncle Gates, who hails from Springfield, Missouri. (Connell once conceded he was thinking of his father here, who made such a visit to San Francisco after remarrying in 1963. Uncle Gates turns out to be even more overtly and bitterly racist than even Walter Bridge.) Connell hands over to Gates the South Pacific experience and the character describes it as they drive through Marin County. "The humidity of those tropic islands—Lord, I could have been mistaken for a wet sponge," Uncle Gates says. "Those islands are worse than Springfield in August." Of Nan Madol, Gates haltingly recounts what he learned about the ruins of the huge basalt fortress. Its construction remains a mystery: "Oh, another thing. The walls of Nan Madol are alive with lizards." At one point before Uncle Gates gets rolling, William thinks to himself, much as a reader might when encountering the story title for the first time, "Nan Madol. Nan Madol. . . . It could be something spoken in a dream."[46]

As Connell turned out more stories in subsequent months, he began to think that he would have enough for another collection. After more than forty years with Elizabeth McKee and her successors at the Harold Matson Company, Connell had signed on with a new agent, Don Congdon, in 1994. (Connell and Shoemaker began to sour on McKee a decade earlier when she fumbled the rollout of *Son of the Morning Star*. For one thing, she missed out on the opportunity for key first-serial excerpts.) Connell was pleased that Congdon seemed more engaged and responsive than McKee had been in recent years. Congdon suggested making another run at Hollywood with *The Diary of a Rapist* and possibly *The Connoisseur*. He sold the *Diary* translation rights to a Japanese publisher for $3,000. And he welcomed Connell's plan for a story collection, sending out some of Connell's latest offerings and making suggestions about possible weaknesses. Connell began revising a handful of earlier stories to go along with the newly crafted ones and soon had a dozen pulled together for a book he thought could be called *Noah's Ark*, the title of the lead story.

Some of the new stories got Connell back in print in the literary magazines. *Antaeus* took "Au Lapin Gros," about a Muhlbach-worthy *pas de deux* in a Paris restaurant. The *Threepenny Review* published "Bowen," the first of two stories based on Calvin Kentfield and the *Contact* period, and got it into the annual Pushcart Prize small-press anthology for 1993. And *Glimmer Train* accepted "Mrs. Proctor Bemis," a sly satire of another buttoned-up, conservative Kansas City matron that Connell knew would hit much too close to home for his Kansas City sister.

Congdon maneuvered to have multiple copies made of the collection manuscript, in order to set off a bidding war among publishers. In the end, Farrar, Straus, and Giroux wanted it, but Jack Shoemaker, now attached to a new publishing house funded by a lawyer and investment banker in Washington, D.C., came in with a higher offer and landed it for Counterpoint's first seasonal catalogue.

Shoemaker also had a better idea. Instead of a small story collection, why not publish all of Connell's short fiction to date? The result, *The Collected Stories of Evan S. Connell*, served to remind readers of his formidable range and longevity—nearly fifty years—as a literary talent.

The writer Bruce Bawer described Connell, as he found him in the volume, as someone who constantly defied expectations, one of "those intrepid, maddening souls who, never attempting the same thing twice, single-mindedly pursue their idiosyncratic visions down paths that sometimes lead to gold mines, sometimes to dead ends, and occasionally to the literary equivalent of one of those cliffs that Wile E. Coyote finds himself speeding off of in Warner Brothers cartoons." Bawer was not exactly correct about Connell not trying "the same thing twice," if one considers the two Bridge novels, the two Muhlbach novels, the two "Notes" books, and a handful of story sequences featuring recurring characters. Moreover, Bawer was not generally enamored of Connell's stories, thinking many of them thin and populated by clichéd characters. Connell was at his best, he thought, in the deeply human story "Arcturus," which "quietly and deliberately captures something of the uneasiness of people in their frail bodies, in the great world where they find themselves, and in the company of fellow human beings to whom they are tied."[47]

In Kansas City, reviewer Conger Beasley repeated the age-old mantra about Connell, that he was likely "the least-known, least-appreciated major writer working in America today." Beasley also recognized the weak tea in the collection but celebrated the strong stuff—"Saint Augustine's Pigeon," "Puig's Wife," "Mrs. Proctor Bemis," "The Yellow Raft" ("a little masterpiece")—and Connell's "pitch-perfect prose" and "mordant and grim" humor.[48]

The story collection showed readers what Webster Schott had noticed as early as 1957, that "the range of his stories, moving from upper-class to lower-class society, from East to West and settling several times on gritty Kansas, suggests a writer who is not comfortable in one place or one state of mind."[49]

Connell's state of mind took another blow when Don Carpenter, in constant poor health and writer's despair, committed suicide, by handgun, in July 1995. It was at least the fourth suicide in Connell's world, following Bill Ryan, Calvin Kentfield, and Carpenter's close friend Richard Brautigan. "It would be my suspicion that Richard's suicide weighed on Don," Connell told the *New York Times*. Anne Lamott, who lived near Carpenter in Mill Valley, confirmed the feeling: "Noting that Mr. Brautigan's body had not been found for weeks she said Mr. Carpenter had been haunted 'by the really chilling specter' of Mr. Brautigan's final isolation from his friends."[50] Lamott, Connell, and Carpenter had often formed a self-protective triumvirate during Connell's Bay Area years, going to dinner parties and literary events together and otherwise hanging out. The writer Jane Vandenburgh later recalled Carpenter as a friend to whom you could spill your secrets. "Don was magic on the phone, the most incisive gossip, brilliant conversationalist, magpie sharer of news, mischief maker," she wrote.[51] Carpenter had been just the right kind of large personality to neatly complement Connell's reserve.

Connell often used travel and the attraction of the Southwest's wide-open roads as a way to get in touch with his own sense of isolation. This loneliness was not debilitating, it was the life he chose.

And once again he had work to do. He had libraries to visit. And he had the beginnings of another deep historical plunge. "In some respects," he told Web Schott, "similar to the Custer business."[52]

Disorder, Liberation, and Human Sorrow
1996–2008

"Each journey is the consequence of unbearable longing."

—*Notes from a Bottle Found on the Beach at Carmel*

IN THE MID-1990S, Connell followed his obsession with the human tragedy into deep medieval history. He had ventured in that direction frequently over the years. He drew from ancient texts and philosophers to darken the imagery in the *Notes* and *Points* projects. He explored historical violence in his essays and, of course, *Son of the Morning Star*. But now, again, the subject came back to him in high relief and in Connell's typically obsessive long view. As so often happened, his new project began with someone else's book. He was thinking about the Crusades and scouring a bookstore in Tucson, Arizona, when he found a paperback volume that combined two contemporaneous accounts of the Christian campaigns of centuries ago. One was by Jean de Joinville, the other by Geoffrey de Villehardouin.[1] Connell was especially impressed by Joinville's attention to detail. The Frenchman had gone along with Louis IX on the Seventh Crusade in the thirteenth century. (Villehardouin chronicled the Fourth Crusade.) In one scene, Joinville urged Louis not to abandon the Holy Land and disputed another nobleman arguing the opposite. Joinville wandered off to a window to calm down. Soon, someone came up behind him and startled him with a gentle hand to his head. Joinville recognized the king by his emerald ring and was relieved it was not the nobleman with whom he had been verbally jousting. "This moment brought these people back for me," Connell once explained. Academic historians don't usually pay attention to such intimate experiences or details that have nothing to do with "the social climate of the day and the economic motives."[2]

Connell went on to search library catalogues throughout the region for more musty books and translations of medieval accounts of the Crusades. Much as he did with the Custer book, he extracted a multigenerational sequence of bloody episodes to animate history. Gus Blaisdell had found some resources for him at the University of New Mexico library and also on "the Internet—whatever that is," Connell told his sister.[3] (He never owned a computer and would never learn firsthand about the potential bounty and certain annoyances of the wired world.)

Fig. 34. Connell with Gus Blaisdell, an Albuquerque writer, editor, and bookseller. Janet Maher, courtesy of Maher and Nicole Blaisdell Ivey.

In January 1997, he motored to Texas for more research. In the library at Texas Christian University in Fort Worth he found enough books to keep him busy for a week. He filled the days "skimming thousands of pages and Xeroxing what I wanted." He was particularly happy with a mid-nineteenth-century British volume that included translations of three medieval chronicles: "Also found the two-volume 1100 page chronicle of William of Tyre (1130–1184), which has all sorts of wonderful details. So I came back with hundreds of Xerox pages, enough to keep me busy all year."[4] A few months later he made the rounds of university libraries in Utah and Arizona and amassed three hundred more pages of copied material. "This is the first time I've depended on translations," he told his sister, "and only now appreciate what a difference it can make. A dull translation all but ruins the original."[5] He wrote for weeks at a time, then headed out on further library adventures. With each successive haul of material, Connell glued new paragraphs into his ever-bulging manuscript.

Connell loved to dig into the weeds in search of glittery nuggets. He also knew that his obsessive interests might not match the tastes of the reading public, but so be it. "I'm now in the midst of writing about an exchange of letters between Saladin and Frederick Barbarossa in 1188," he told Barbara. "How many readers may care about that is something else."[6]

The first draft of Connell's Crusades book, which he completed in October 1997, came in at about 450 pages. But he was nowhere near done. He had more research to conduct, more libraries to visit, more massaging of the narrative to perform. Over the next year and a half, there would be hundreds more pages of notes. There would be many more productive, meditative moments of silent writing in his head as he went on his five-mile walks around Santa Fe. And there would be two more complete drafts.

Gale Garnett visited Connell in Santa Fe for the second straight summer in 1999. This time she was "running on all 19 cylinders" and "higher than usual."[7] Her first novel was about to be published in Canada, and Connell had given it a blurb: "Bawdy, funny, sometimes desperate and moon-struck." "I'm a book!" she crowed. Called *Visible Amazement*, the novel (published a year later in the United States) followed the itinerant, sexually active life of fourteen-year-old Roane Chappell. Garnett said she had been working on it for seven years. She channeled the voice of a character very much like her younger self, who saw positive growth opportunities in teenage relationships with older men. Her view was unlike the typical fictional portrayals of young women as "victims and vamps," as she told a Canadian journalist. "So-called intergenerational sex is actually, if you're going to have sex, a far safer choice, in my mind, than peer sex," she said. "Adults behave much better than boys do and if you live through your teens it's mostly luck."[8]

Garnett was proud of her accomplishment. She told Connell she had commissioned a medallion from a Toronto jeweler engraved with her first ISBN number—that unique, thirteen-digit identifier attached to each and every published book.

And she was still keeping Connell clueless about her age. Ostensibly she was celebrating her fiftieth birthday on July 23, Connell told his sister. Fifty? That would put her birth year at 1949, and, well, see chapter 7 for the contrary details. (Garnett that summer also led the Canadian reporter to believe that she had just turned fifty, was a teenager throughout the 1960s in California, and was nineteen when she returned to Toronto, which she did in 1969.[9]) So, more like fifty-seven or fifty-nine. But so what? On her previous trip to Santa Fe, Garnett and Connell took a ride out to Jemez Springs in the mountains west of Santa Fe. And they always wandered through some of the Canyon Road galleries in search of new finds, new messages from the distant past in baked clay and stone. Not long before, Connell had come up with a little stone torso, perhaps a thousand years old, that came from India. He bought it because it reminded him of the Khajuraho temples he'd been awed by more than thirty years earlier.

Even before he finished the third draft of the Crusades manuscript, *Deus lo Volt!*, Connell sent the first fifty pages to Jack Shoemaker. Shoemaker, indeed, wanted the book for Counterpoint. As was his practice, though, Connell had no contract and wouldn't consider one until he finished. He and his agent Don Congdon also wanted to test the market, which Congdon did after receiving the manuscript in June. Within a month, Knopf and Houghton Mifflin passed and

Jack Macrae at Holt offered $135,000. In the end, Shoemaker offered 10 percent more, $148,500, and won the day.[10] Connell once again appreciated his enthusiasm and stuck with his loyal, longtime editor and publisher.

Before the book came out, Connell wrote a three-page essay for Counterpoint, a primer intended to give context and talking points to the publisher's sales reps. He recounted his library finds and emphasized his delight with the odd personal detail revealed in old documents. His process was similar to how he researched *Son of the Morning Star*. For one thing, never trust the stories told by descendants of those involved: "Musty archives, too, yield absurdities, so it becomes a matter of judgment when poking through the past." Connell also discussed his approach to language while voicing the narrative of medieval figures. "Should everything be modernized?" He confessed to using here and there unfamiliar or obsolete words ("sumpterbeast," for example, referring to a pack animal). "Again, it's a matter of judgment, of sensibility, a test of the ear. . . . It seemed to me that a measure of archaic usage might bring up the flavor of the Middle Ages, like seasoning in soup." He also explained why he thought *Deus lo Volt!* was not a historical novel, because, other than employing Joinville as a witness who spanned two centuries, he invented nothing that he hadn't found, adapted, and condensed from medieval sources. Still, Shoemaker clearly believed that the project was indeed a novel, and ultimately it was labeled as such on the cover. Shoemaker crafted his own supportive letter to booksellers in which he expounded a rare kind of "admiration and astonishment" for Connell's accomplishment. He suggested there was little else like it in American literature. "Perhaps the only book that even begins to compare in its strangeness and beauty and towering presence," Shoemaker wrote, possibly echoing Stanley Crouch, "is, to my mind, *Moby-Dick*." Connell sent a copy of Shoemaker's tout sheet to Webster Schott, who replied that in his fifty years as a book critic, he'd never seen such a high-flying testimonial from a publisher.[11]

"Some day," Schott wrote to his friend, "someone will try to figure out what took you from *Mrs. Bridge* to these distant other worlds. If you can ever bring yourself to dwell on that journey you may be rewarded with a more secure position in American literary history."[12] Save for the occasional interview in subsequent years and the introduction to his last book of stories, published eight years after *Deus lo Volt!*, Connell never did attempt to dwell publicly on his long literary journey.

Connell was pleased to hear from Max Steele that "Ah think you've got a classic," and passed on the remark to both his sister and Shoemaker.[13] Foreign publishers were already buying rights, and an audiobook company was planning unabridged and abridged recordings. Schott, who had been vacationing with his wife for a couple of months, returned home and found an inscribed copy of the book in his accumulated mail. Connell had dedicated it to the Schotts. "It's a work that figuratively takes my breath away," Schott wrote back. "You create a world. It exists. You have made a wondrous fiction that becomes truth."[14]

Connell had fretted over the title, which combines Latin and a variation on a medieval French word. As he explained to his sister, it came from the launch of the Crusades: "Pope Urban II gave an incendiary speech on Nov. 27, 1095 at Clermont in central France. He urged the Franks, and others, to liberate Jerusalem from the Muslims. The people responded by shouting 'God wills it!' in various dialects, such as Deus lo volt! Dieu livolt! Diex le volt! Dieu le vault! In modern French it would be Dieu le veut!" Connell, in fact, had used the phrase *dieu le veut* at least once before. It appears as a passing emphatic expression in *Notes from a Bottle Found on the Beach at Carmel*. This time Connell consulted a French historian's list of spellings in a book on the Crusades he found in the public library in Santa Fe. He ultimately decided that *Deus lo Volt!* would be "fairly easy for Americans to pronounce. Easier than Dieux le Veult."[15]

As usual he also aimed to micromanage the packaging. At his suggestion, Counterpoint's designers included an endpaper map, complete with a sea serpent afloat in the Mediterranean Sea, and incorporated decorative crosses in the cover imagery and fancy, medieval-looking drop capitals throughout the text.

Deus lo Volt!, with its formal, ancient-sounding language and its woven threads—Joinville's voice amid recounted historical testimony by churchmen, pilgrims, Muslim historians, and others—has the same kind of mesmerizing mosaic rhythms that characterize *Son of the Morning Star* and the two "Notes" books. At the end of many episodes of horrific violence and Christian triumph, the omniscient narrator interjects a chorus-like reminder of God's power, will, and grace. Often left unstated is what reverberates in the heads of modern readers: *the arrogance, the folly, the tragedy of human failure.* Connell saw the Crusades less in those academically economic terms and more as a "religious frenzy" stirred by a church leader calling for the liberation of Jerusalem and a popular "fury at the tales of the atrocities that got back to Europe about the way Christian pilgrims were being treated."[16]

Shoemaker convinced Connell to make a handful of publicity appearances. A couple of them started out shakily. Connell was booked on Diane Rehm's talk show at WAMU, an NPR station in Washington, D.C. He insisted that Shoemaker join him in the studio. As Shoemaker told the story years later, not without laughter, Connell responded to the first long question with a nod of the head. That's it. He had to be reminded he was on the radio. To Shoemaker, it was vintage Connell. Yet, if Connell's silent answer occurred while on the air, it has been edited out of the archived interview. Instead, for nearly fifty minutes Connell responded in his softly voiced way to substitute host Steve Roberts's questions, as well as those from a variety of callers, mostly with a kind of polite engagement.[17] "Evan was a nervous wreck before we got there," Shoemaker told me after I updated him with the evidence. "But he always was good at hiding how nervous he was."[18]

Another rough spot, as Shoemaker tells it, was the bookstore visit planned for a Barnes and Noble in New York one day. This was supposed to be a sign-stock-only appearance, but when Shoemaker and Connell stepped out of a cab, Connell rebelled at the store's entrance. Someone had put up a sign announcing his appearance. That wasn't supposed to happen. No way was he going to glad-hand and chit-chat with prospective readers. Shoemaker took Connell to a nearby coffee shop to talk him down. The store employees were reminded of the guidelines. Connell agreed to go back to the store, where, with a young woman attendant opening books for him, he signed dozens of copies.

The *San Francisco Chronicle* called *Deus lo Volt!* a "masterpiece," though Connell was always suspicious of such effusive judgments.[19] A writer for the online journal *Salon* said the book "rewards those who hang on to the end of its nearly 500 pages with stately prose and lofty, captivating ambition."[20] Reviewing the British edition that summer, Emily Wilson, a classicist, not a medievalist, lamented that Connell's chronicle offered no solution or explanation for the fundamental question, "Why did thousands upon thousands of people, from all over Christendom, flock towards Jerusalem to kill and be killed." As she concluded, "This is a book about the incomprehensibility both of the original Crusades, and, by implication, the modern wars of religion, such as the struggle for Jerusalem. . . . One may suspect it of implicit satire on Christian savagery; but the book ends with the Muslim devastation of 'Beyrouth,' suggesting that neither side has a monopoly on meaningless violence. God may have wanted the Crusades, but *Deus lo Volt!* does not presume why."[21] Connell penciled in a note to himself on his copy of the review: "London, circ. 34,329." Maybe, one can imagine him thinking, such comments would not achieve much traction.

James Reston Jr., who would soon publish his own book about the Third Crusade pitting Richard the Lionhearted and Saladin, the hallowed Sultan of Egypt and Syria, was dismissive of Connell's strategy. He complained, among other things, that Connell overlooked "the Muslim perspective."[22] Steele counseled Connell to ignore Reston's review, suggesting, based on his experience with

Reston at the University of North Carolina, that he possibly hadn't even read the book.[23]

Connell found a sympathetic reader in Greg Bottoms, whose essay for *Salon* opened with the startling line: "I knew a guy who lost his mind reading Evan S. Connell." So began Bottoms's graduate school experience with Connell, which continued over the years and now culminated in the arrival of *Deus lo Volt!* The book, Bottoms wrote, was "a perfect summation of his career. Taking all the early concerns and aesthetic shape-shifting and funneling them into what may be, if we're still allowed to use such words without undercutting their authority in the next sentence, a masterpiece." There it is again, though with the self-conscious caveat and a wider sense of context. Bottoms added, "Once you realize it is like no other novel written, its remarkable and subtle intelligence is awe-inspiring." Bottoms placed *Deus lo Volt!* within the continuum of Connell's work—from the Bridges and the rapist Earl Summerfield to everything in between. It advanced his obsession with exploring how the "roots of our civilization are soaked in blood."[24] Bottoms did not yet know how Connell bristled over such unrestrained praise.

Then again, maybe Connell was softening. In the fall of 2000, Connell seemed agreeable when the Lannan Foundation, a literary philanthropy based in Santa Fe, gave him its Lifetime Achievement Award. He was more than a bit pleased when he learned that the prize came with $100,000. "It's certainly a nice surprise," he told an Albuquerque reporter. "It isn't anything I desperately need or want. I don't have any great plans. I don't know what I'll do."[25] Connell also must have been doubly pleased that he didn't have to do a thing: no cocktail reception, no award ceremony. There was nothing but a simple, understated announcement and the cutting of a check.

Connell's political sparring with his sister continued long after the "Reaganbush" years. The Clinton presidency, intern scandal, and impeachment provided running fodder for snipes and retorts. As another presidential election approached in 2000, Connell took the opportunity to skewer Barbara's viewpoint once again in a public way. His character Marguerite Bemis, a second-generation India Bridge, had already appeared in two short stories ("Proctor Bemis," "Mrs. Proctor Bemis"). Now she came around again, in a story that brought some of Connell's political angst to the surface. Curiously, Proctor Bemis, though a successful financier, was an "apostate Republican," while his wife clung to a sometimes virulent brand of conservative uptightness and xenophobia.[26]

Connell expressed his displeasure when his sister sent him a right-wing newsletter boiling with conspiracy theories and revolting opinions. He turned around and dished it back in "Election Eve," a story that would be published first in the *Threepenny Review*, a literary journal based in Berkeley, California. The story begins with Proctor Bemis imagining a getaway to Costa Rica and channeling a Connell checklist of warped American life as it had recently been playing out: "No winter storm watch. No schoolboys in black trenchcoats gunning down classmates. No lunatics blowing up federal buildings. No hillbilly militia. No politicians braying platitudes." His wife drags Proctor to a costume party the night before an election, where many of their acquaintances would be wearing presidential costumes. "Some jackass will do Nixon," Bemis complains. On the way, he recalls how much (like Connell) he despised Reagan and reflects on his wife's mindset: "She hated Kennedys, all Kennedys . . . and thought they contaminated whatever they touched. She disapproved of modern art and welfare and foreign aid. She did not like immigrants. She subscribed to newsletters warning that liberals had weakened the armed forces. The United States could be destroyed at any moment. Crazed, malignant letters oozing poison. Absurd theories. Libelous charges. Implausible conspiracies. Rhetorical questions. Secret societies. Jewish bankers. Communist armies in Montana. Letters concocted of hate and fear. Doomsday letters. Nourishment for the paranoid."[27] Mrs. Bemis's brand of pointed conservatism was the kind fanned nightly on right-wing radio shows.

Her husband embarrasses her when during the party he stands up and delivers a rant about Reagan and the state of the nation.

People elsewhere look at America and "see a nation steeped in righteousness where guns are as easy to buy as lollipops. A nation that executes criminals without spilling one drop of blood. A nation of hypocritical preachers with the brains of pterodactyls and politicians who would sell their daughters for a vote."[28] Bemis (and Connell) is just warming up, and the chauffeured drive home settles into chilly back-and-forth volleys between him and his wife. Connell earned another small comfort when editor Laura Furman selected "Election Eve" for the O. Henry Prize anthology for 2003, his first appearance in that annual in more than fifty years. The story also landed in the leadoff spot of the 2004 Pushcart Prize anthology, which highlights the best of small-press publishing. Connell was happy for the endorsements and happy he got a chance to air his political gripes in the inventive medium of fiction.

Greg Bottoms got another bite of the Connell apple that summer when he successfully convinced the writer to participate in an interview by mail. Bottoms wondered whether Connell felt he was writing a subversive kind of history and noted that some critics of *Son of the Morning Star*, for example, had accused its author of being a "liberal crank." Connell's response clearly applies to his efforts to capture the social and political zeitgeist in his fiction as well.

"'Liberal crank' isn't much of an epithet," Connell replied.

Anyway, I've never decided to debunk or subvert, not unless that means pointing out lies and hypocrisy. Montesquieu said one must be truthful in all things, even when they concern one's own country. I do believe that. Our nineteenth-century campaign to suppress or exterminate Indian tribes, undertaken with the best of nineteenth-century intentions, was not altogether noble. We should understand this. Our esteemed ex-president Bush [George H. W. Bush] repeatedly said that he supported America, never mind the facts. I disrespectfully disagree. And surely Montesquieu's wisdom extends to religion. We should understand that crusaders invading the Middle East with God's name on their lips were not immaculate knights in gleaming armor.[29]

If the disturbing relevance of the Vietnam War had long been on Connell's mind, an even older conflict had been in the air for years and erupted with unprecedented force eighteen months after the appearance of *Deus lo Volt!* On September 11, 2001, terrorists aligned with the Al-Qaeda network of Islamic militants and funded by an expatriate Saudi rebel named Osama bin Laden commandeered four commercial aircraft and fatally attacked the United States in an acceleration of a modern-day holy war.

Connell was asked to reflect on the attack a year later, and he delivered an essay to his original hometown newspaper and its fellow members of the Knight-Ridder News Service. He began by recalling H. G. Wells, whose *Outline of History* he'd read fifty years earlier. One line in it stayed with him, at least in paraphrase: "If you make men sufficiently angry or fearful the hot red eyes of cavemen will glare out at you." While Americans had no idea that the legacy of the Crusades remained with us, the mindset of the Muslim world included the still-relevant idea of "legitimate vengeance." Connell was not a pessimist but a realist, delivering the same prophesy he channeled as far back as *Notes from a Bottle.* As he wrote now:

> Another year has come and gone. We are frightened, angry, thirsty for blood, glaring out at the world with hot red eyes. Although terrorists have declared holy war against the United States, we know nothing about a legacy of hatred bequeathed to the Muslim world centuries ago by Frankish Crusaders.
>
> President [George W.] Bush vows to rid the world of evil. Nonsense. Nothing will accomplish that, neither fatuous rhetoric nor hydrogen bombs. Malevolence is built into the human structure and we must live with this ugly fact.[30]

Jack Shoemaker dialed up another Connell title for Counterpoint. *The Aztec Treasure House* repackaged the essays of *A Long Desire* and *The White Lantern* and added two more recent pieces. The new essays came from the Southwest—"Mesa Verde" and "Messages from a Sandstone Bluff"—and carried on Connell's explorations in history. The volume made the American Library Association's Notable Book List for 2002, a compendium of only twenty-six exceptional works of fiction, nonfiction, and poetry.

And Connell was well along the way toward his next new project. In further travels to libraries in the region, he was researching the life and work of Francisco Goya, the Spanish artist who first captivated Connell's interest decades earlier in Europe. During one journey through Arizona and southern New Mexico, Connell inexplicably suffered an infection in his index finger. The ailment hampered his usual two-fingered typing for a few weeks, slowing the production of a clean manuscript. "It's not quite 300 pages," he told Web Schott in a flurry of understatement. "I like it, but what does that mean? People who ask what I'm doing seem interested in the subject."[31]

Shoemaker was certainly interested, but his benefactor at the Perseus Group, Frank Pearl, decided that Counterpoint wasn't making enough money and tried to reassign him. Shoemaker left and started his own house, Shoemaker and Hoard. He bid on the Goya book after Don Congdon sent it out. Shoemaker surely winced when his former colleagues at Counterpoint offered three times more money. But he soon put into motion plans to publish new editions of the Bridge novels, *The Connoisseur*, and even *The Alchymist's Journal* (retitled as *Alchymic Journals*), which had been a commercial failure a decade earlier but was likely to resonate in the current environment, Shoemaker told Connell.

As a full-life portrait, *Francisco Goya* is relatively brief, not much more than two hundred pages. Yet, as with so much of Connell's work, it is brimming with enjoyable nuggets of historical irony, unpredictable human nature, unspeakable violence, and cultural glory. It is not surprising to encounter Connell digressing from the first page onward. He begins not with, say, the birth of his subject but rather with some delicious dish about a secondary character, the racy Duchess of Alba, who was the subject of Goya portraits and no small amount of Spanish gossip. Her story would in time present Connell with a portal to the titular subject. All of that—the themes, the nuggets, the digressions—just about covers the gamut of Connell's singular enterprise as a writer.

In another carefully chosen epigraph, Connell connected his Goya to the sober themes that run throughout his work. The quote came from a French writer and art critic, Jean-François Chabrun, author of a book about Goya in the 1960s: "As in all the turbulent periods which have foreshadowed crucial and violent phases in the history of mankind, many writers and artists tended to translate into their own idiom the repugnance they felt for an established but tottering order from which they wanted to dissociate themselves at all costs." Chabrun may just as well have been describing Connell's career-long enterprise.

Given their lack of personal contact, Connell may or may not have been aware that Lawrence Ferlinghetti, the bard of San Francisco, had anointed Francisco Goya as a moral and cultural force in the opening poem of an early collection. But Ferlinghetti's evocation of Goya certainly aligns with Connell's last book-length project: "In Goya's greatest scenes we seem to see / the people of the world / exactly at the moment when / they first attained the title of / 'suffering humanity.'" Goya's wretched masses are still with us, Ferlinghetti writes, on wide highways, "illustrating imbecile illusions of happiness."[32]

Harper's published a piece of *Francisco Goya* in the fall of 2003. A senior editor there was overjoyed with it and fretted over cutting it down to a manageable size. But he seemed to know exactly how to play to Connell's sensibilities. He said he was aiming to focus the excerpts on Goya's portrayals of political power. "I thought the similarities to our own situation in the United States were irresistible," wrote Luke Mitchell. "And I liked that Goya's droll subversiveness in many ways recapitulated your own."[33]

The published excerpt set off an exchange of letters from an unhappy reader. Angus Trumble, an art curator at Yale, thought Connell was too hard on the family of Charles IV. Connell told his sister it was hardly worth a response. But he did write back, and *Harper's* published both letters in a subsequent issue. The exchange presented a revealing example of Connell's curt certainty that he had done his homework and had represented his research well.

Unraveled and braided together as if a dialogue, the exchange of letters becomes a microstudy of historical and writerly bickering:

Trumble: "Connell fails to mention that with the Spanish throne came another, far less enjoyable inheritance. Charles II passed on a genetic predisposition to a disorder known as mandibular prognathism, or Class II skeletal malocclusion. The disfiguring effects of this condition . . . are clearly visible in several of the faces in Goya's portrait, particularly that of the Infanta María Josefa, the king's unfortunate sister."

Connell: "Mr. Trumble states that I failed to mention the Bourbon genetic inheritance. True. I failed to mention a number of things."

Trumble: "It seems unnecessarily cruel to call her 'demented' . . ."

Connell: "He states that it is unnecessarily cruel to call María Josefa 'demented.' I wrote that she had a 'demented expression.'"

Trumble: ". . . to ridicule her use of cosmetics . . ."

Connell: "Aside from mentioning her beauty patch, 'which fashionable ladies have employed for a long time,' I said nothing about María Josefa's cosmetics . . ."

Trumble: ". . . to characterize the rest of the family as 'sluggish,' 'feebleminded,' or 'poached.'"

Connell: ". . . nor did I characterize the rest of the family as sluggish, feebleminded, and poached. I described King Charles as sluggish; by most accounts, he was. I noted that Don Antonio Pascual was feebleminded; beyond doubt, he was. Charles Poore commented that Velázquez gave all his Philips a look of poached nobility; in my opinion, Charles looks equally poached."

Trumble: "Leaving aside the question as to whether Queen María Luisa was a nymphomaniac, I do not see in her face 'a look of gastric malevolence.' Nor can she be blamed for losing her teeth, one of the relatively few things she actually had in common with many of her husband's subjects."

Connell: "Mr. Trumble implies that I blame María Luisa for losing her teeth—a non sequitur that leaves me completely baffled."[34]

Connell was in the midst of reading page proofs for the book and complained about a fussy copy editor's compulsion for commas and attempts to revise every sentence. His reference to Picasso, for example, needed a "Pablo." There was far too much of that sort of thing. "I believe all copy editors are former high school teachers," he told Web Schott.[35]

Connell was unshaken when he learned that another Goya book had come to market just months before his. That one was by Robert Hughes, the prominent art critic. His *Goya* got a glowing review in the *New York Times*, and Connell agreed that it was a fine book. But Connell's book was his own. His Goya was guaranteed to be distinct from Hughes's expansive study. Counterpoint planned a first edition of thirty thousand copies, and at one point Connell learned there were advance orders of thirteen thousand. "If Stephen King's publishers gave him such numbers he would jump off a bridge," Connell told Schott, "but I'm rather pleased."[36] Connell also began to hear nice things from early readers, including Alexander Theroux and James Ivory. And *Publishers Weekly*'s advance review found the book to be a "rousing history" and suggested that readers of Hughes's book "will want Connell's cultural reportage as a counterpoint."[37]

As the book was hitting the stands, Connell had to explain to his sister that the figures in the Goya painting on its cover were not "girls dancing," as she supposed, but "men in drag." As he wrote, "This was, as you know from the book, one day of the year when celebrants could be whatever they wanted to be."[38]

After Web Schott caught up to *Francisco Goya*, he sent Connell a congratulatory letter. He applauded the book's "circular and discursive" exploration of "Goya, Spanish decadence, religious madness, hypocrisy—the total human comedy." Schott suggested that if some reviewers didn't quite get what Connell was after, the "people who count will."[39]

The art critic Arthur Danto took up Connell's book along with Hughes's and a third recent study of Goya in a group review that focused largely on how little we can really know for certain about the artist and how much biographers can disagree. "His is not an easy mind to penetrate," Danto writes of the artist, "as these biographies attest."[40] Such a judgment seems to make the general case for the common argument in the field of biography that Connell's Goya is his own construction, and one, I might add, that we can read with pleasure along with a certain skepticism.

Connell turned eighty the year that his *Francisco Goya* appeared. His family gathered in Santa Fe and threw him a party. After decades of running, he was beginning to feel his age. His knees were acting up. In order to forestall and, he hoped, avoid surgery, he began a series of shots. The Euflexxa seemed to work for a while, alleviating the worst of the pain.

But he continued to write. He couldn't really not write. It was so much a part of his daily existence. It was as natural a physical ritual as his in-town breakfast and the nightly cocktails and dinner on a barstool at the Santa Fe Bar and Grill.

After the historical canvases of *Deus lo Volt!* and *Francisco Goya*, Connell returned somewhat to the present, or at least to the kinds of intimate, contemporary fictional worlds he'd been erecting for more than half a century. One new story was triggered by memories of Connell's travels through India four decades earlier, though he transposed some of his own experiences onto a character unlike himself. Another was set around a dinner table—not dissimilar to the frequent social settings Connell experienced among friends in Sausalito—with a boisterous and opinionated blowhard named Wigglesworth dominating the room. Wigglesworth is a former merchant marine and owned a restaurant, just like the voluble George Gutekunst, who, as it happened, had died in 2002. The story is not warm enough to be an elegy for his friend; Connell instead seemed more interested in exorcising a kind of irritating truth.[41] Connell unsuccessfully shopped the story for a while as "Mr. Wigglesworth." Eventually he changed the title, almost inexplicably, to "The Land Where Lemon Trees Bloom," a passing nod to Goethe.

In 2005, Jack Shoemaker moved his publishing concern back to the West Coast, first setting up shop in Emeryville, next door to Berkeley. Shoemaker managed to survive a rocky two years of transition. His distributor had gone bankrupt, owing Shoemaker and Hoard $260,000, he told Connell. Then, the Avalon Publishing Group, his corporate ally when leaving Frank Pearl's Counterpoint and the Perseus Group, sold itself back to Perseus. "You can barely imagine my shock," he said. But he had a buyback option, and spent more than a year raising the money to do that and keep Shoemaker and Hoard independent and out of Pearl's clutches. Shoemaker also eventually managed to retrieve and resurrect the Counterpoint imprint from Perseus. And soon he was encouraging a new collection of Connell's stories, which took its title, *Lost in Uttar Pradesh*, from the new India story. "I wish Gus was around to help with the selection," Shoemaker said of their mutual friend, Gus Blaisdell, who'd edited *Saint Augustine's Pigeon* and died a few years earlier. "He was always so *certain* about these sorts of things."[42] As an afterthought, Shoemaker wrote a note on his typed letter, telling Connell that he'd just ordered a thousand-copy reprint of *Mrs. Bridge*.

When *Lost in Uttar Pradesh* appeared in 2008, it included a preface from Connell that gave readers a rare and revealing idea of how his fictive imagination operated. His stories came from momentary impulses, experiences, passing thoughts, and often inexplicable sources. In describing the origin of his story "Ancient Musik," which he elsewhere called a "second cousin" to the two "Notes" books, Connell presents a quintessentially lyrical account of the writer's mind at work: "It grew briskly as a starfish from Robert Burton's sui genesis book *The Anatomy of Melancholy*, from Herodotus' account of Greco-Persian wars, fabulous monsters of the Middle Ages, alchemic mysteries, tales of phantom islands, the trial of Boethius, the arrogance of emperors, from this or that, a mosaic, a quilt of conflicting colors, perhaps a psychotic collation or recollection distorted by rage at the descent of the United States. It ends with a parable that may or may not seem relevant, depending on the reader."[43]

Connell, it has become obvious, didn't really care what we thought, but he did hope in the end that we might find something relevant—or irrelevant, or even irreverent—in his work. And in the midst of his erudite wanderings, he reminded his readers of the simplicity with which he approached his art, making it "from this or that."[44]

Trying to explain his retitling of the Wigglesworth story, he concludes, "Poets, painters, sculptors, musicians, dancers, novelists, and other members of that bedraggled fraternity live forever in a madhouse, one reason being that their problems have no solution. Next time, they think, next time I'll get it right."[45]

In the preface, Connell does not mention Flaubert's "Simple Heart" as the inspiration for "Noah's Ark," though he does so elsewhere. The story of a farm-bred housemaid under the spell of a radio preacher carries some superficial echoes of its predecessor, though Connell's version comes off more as a pale caricature. Nevertheless the story, written in 1993, dislodged a memory that meant enough to Connell to use more than once. As he wrote *Francisco Goya*, he found a contextual moment to recall a childhood housekeeper in the Connells' home who reminded him of the artist's wife, Josefa: "a placid, expressionless, devout, overweight farm girl. Not once did I see her angry, excited, depressed, or amused. Day after day, month after month, heavy on her feet, she cleaned house, prepared meals. Sunday morning she dressed up to attend church. Wednesday night she attended Bible class. Life being what it was, she acquiesced."[46] So Flaubert through an autobiographical filter—the stuff of fiction, the useful fragments of personal history.

Lost in Uttar Pradesh presented a career-long view of Connell's fictional talent. It includes some of his earliest, polished, and sparely crafted triumphs—"The Yellow Raft" and "The Marine," now retitled "Guadalcanal." Connell expressed his surprise that the latter had been long ignored, but he thought it carried an important theme of men degraded by war. And there were three Muhlbach stories—"Arcturus," "Saint Augustine's Pigeon," and "Puig's Wife," which brimmed with sexual anxieties and the straightlaced insurance man's search for connection, wildness, and meaning in life. Once again, in the preface, Connell pays homage to the influence of Thomas Mann's great story "Disorder and Early Sorrow," which had sat on his desktop as he wrote "Arcturus" in the mid-1950s.

The more recent stories in the collection include several with another recurring character and Connell stand-in, William Koerner, and the three politically inspired encounters with Proctor Bemis and his ultra-conservative wife. One atmospheric and psychologically intense story—the volume opener, "Lion"—owes an obvious though unacknowledged debt to Connell's early mentor Walter Van Tilburg Clark. Connell writes that he had heard such a tale of a mountain lion pursuing a cow from a Colorado woman, but he also would have recalled Clark's celebrated western novel *The Track of the Cat* (1949).

In a preparatory note to Jack Shoemaker, Connell identified the six new stories and sixteen previously collected as his favorites among nearly sixty years of writing short fiction. He also pointed out that, ever the revisionist, he dropped the article "The" from a few of the titles ("Assassin," for instance), crediting Occam's razor (he misspelled it "Ockham's") for the guidance to "eliminate whatever is unnecessary."[47]

What few reviews *Lost in Uttar Pradesh* received—it arrived as the U.S. economy was plunging into the financial meltdown of 2008—were polite if not universally approving. One critic complained that the book had no apparently rational organization, and if anyone cared about chronological development, he or she would have to turn back to the *Collected Stories*, which included the years of composition. Fair point. Writing in the *Los Angeles Times*, David Ulin had a smarter take on the book, for better and for worse. He seemed to appreciate the unexpected rhythms produced by the dispersal of the connected stories throughout the book. And he found a centrally located, thematically important pivot point in a line from Muhlbach: "There are times a man must liberate his soul, otherwise he's in for trouble." Ulin correctly recognized that the "tension between the rebel and straight society is a key motif, as it is in much of Connell's work." And he offered an intriguing and thoughtful observation that Connell is at his weakest when attempting to mine the inner lives of his characters, at least in these stories. Some circumstances felt contrived and psychologically inexplicable, Ulin said. "The trouble is that Connell is not a psychological writer." This seems, however, an odd criticism in light of Connell's major successes with interior portraits. Still, it gave Ulin ballast for his conclusion that the collection was both brilliant and frustrating, "enigmatic in both content and conception," and "a vivid metaphor for Connell's career."[48]

Connell may well have taken stock of his literary footprint as he chose the contents of his last book. He'd had brief and meaningful brushes with popularity, but for the most part his variegated body of work mainly satisfied his own curiosity and his own intellectual self-interest. *Son of the Morning Star* was the only one of his books that he felt generally comfortable with. ("I can open that book and read almost any page without flinching," he told a reporter.[49]) If writers and faithful readers came along with him, Connell appreciated that but he never much expected a crowd. He once embedded a projection of his own fate in a book review of all places. The assignment involved two biographies of notable but, to most, obscure archaeologists, the German Heinrich Schliemann and Sir Aurel Stein, a Londoner in Central Asia. Connell writes of them, and perhaps of himself, that "both achieved what they set out to do and their accomplishments, however meaningless to the great treacle-eating public, will not be forgotten by other archaeologists or by four-tenths of one percent of the citizenry."[50]

Ulin noted too that "Connell remains on the periphery of our literary consciousness, marginalized by his eclecticism, his inability to be pinned down."[51] But there was more to it than that. As Web Schott put it to me, "Evan's career could have been grander had he been more of an engaging personality."[52]

Desert Solitaire
2009–2013

"If once you have performed brilliantly, people remember."

—Connell, "Girl Crazy," *New York Times,* November 23,
1980, reviewing a novel by Thomas Rogers

CONNELL HAD NOT yet moved to Santa Fe when he expressed a regret that he hadn't taken up residence in the Southwest much earlier. He'd had a short stint in Albuquerque during his Naval Air Corps days, taking in the subtly majestic sights of the Sandia Mountains and the desert mesas in winter. But much earlier, even before he was born, there was a missed opportunity. After his father graduated from Tulane's medical school, early in the twentieth century, he'd had a choice of establishing a medical practice in Kansas City or Albuquerque. "I wish he'd chosen Albuquerque," Connell said. It was yet another denunciation of his Kansas City roots.[1] It was also a harmless lamentation along the lines of the one where he wished he'd gotten to Paris sooner and stayed longer.[2]

Except for the icy cold winters in the high desert, Santa Fe for two decades mostly suited Connell's desires for isolation, routine, simple food, comforting landscape, and scenic wanderings. Connell lived a ritualized existence, Gale Zoe Garnett once said, one day's activities very much like the next. "Late summer is quite pleasant here," he wrote to Max Steele, "big big sky of great cumulus, cool nights, distant lightning storms, much better than June which is the hottest and emptiest month."[3]

Connell maneuvered to get out of town when the annual Zozobra gathering erupted on Santa Fe's plaza in early September. It was a festival-launching debauch that featured the ritual burning of a gloomy spirit figure meant to wipe away the past year's troubles of the party-going souls. More to his liking were the annual outdoor markets in August, where thousands of people flocked to buy antiquities and Native American artworks. When he strolled through the crowds and browsed the stalls, he certainly could sense what the historian David Treuer has written, that "to be in the Southwest is to feel the continued lived presence of Native America to a degree not found in most other homelands in the United States."[4]

When Connell's niece Janet Zimmermann was in town for her annual visit, they would walk all day. There were galleries near the plaza to check out. Maybe they'd have lunch at the historic La Fonda Hotel, with its warm wood-accented lobby. Then it was over to Canyon Road and a hike up to more galleries on that famous shopping strip. In the winter, they would stop to have a drink or a meal at the swank Inn of the Anasazi, because Connell loved to sit around its fireplace. The cold got to him, Zimmermann told me, just like with her mother, Barbara.

Max Steele had a place in Santa Fe for a while, and they would get together when he was in town. Steele died in 2005, a passing that went unremarked in any of Connell's letters I turned up. Several years later, Connell expressed a bit of guilt about his friend. Every Christmas season, Connell would take an aimless drive around the region. One year Steele subtly hinted that he'd like to go along: "Max was getting old. He wanted to tell me about his life, I think. He was about three years older than I. I thought about it later. I thought, why didn't I invite Max? I was being selfish."[5]

Connell would have learned much about Steele's life had he read a personal essay published in the *Washington Post* in 2004. Steele's piece left me wondering whether the conversation Connell wanted to avoid was about fathers. Unlike Connell's fictional renderings of the father figure, Steele laid bare his own experiences and the still-raw memories from which he wanted to learn something about himself. He began, "My own father died in 1939. Now, in 2004, I am an old man, by any reckoning: 82 and not given to memory, except as a strict discipline, when I am trying to see what went right, what went wrong." Steele continued,

> Freud said, in effect, that the greatest loss in any man's life is the loss of his father. Freud seems less important these days. Yet I still lie in bed each morning remembering my dreams to stay in touch with myself, and then I spend a luxurious few minutes of memory and reflection to prepare for living the rest of the day: Here and Now. During that time I am often gazing at the portrait of my father on the wall beyond the foot of my bed, and wondering why I did not know him better.[6]

How would Connell have felt about Freud's definition of a man's great loss? It seems obvious that he would beg to differ, but even this late in his life, those feelings about his father—the silent estrangement and the ultimate loss—remained unresolved and in a kind of flux.

Connell took pleasure in his occasional jaunts down to Albuquerque, which almost always involved a visit with Gus Blaisdell at his Living Batch Bookstore on Central Avenue and over lunch at the Frontier Café next door. But Gus too had died, two years before Max, and the loss of two of Connell's closest friends weighed on him.

Connell had attended a memorial for Blaisdell a week after his death in September 2003. Blaisdell was the critic who once said of Connell that he was "both Kansas and Dostoevski."[7] The Alumni Chapel on the University of New Mexico campus was filled to overflowing with friends and former students of Blaisdell's. Connell couldn't bring himself to speak. He left a card. A few weeks later, Blaisdell's daughter, Nicole Blaisdell Ivey, pored over the condolences and came to Connell's. Fronting the card was a photograph of a New Mexico wilderness scene "dominated by a cloud-filled darkening sky," she told me. "I opened the card and there were no words. It was a blank white page with his signature at the bottom, 'Evan.' The writer had no words."[8] Still, to her, it was a moving gesture.

A few years later Ivey asked Connell to write a tribute, which she wanted to include in a book of her father's collected essays. Connell demurred, saying he didn't know how to write such a thing. Yet, he went on to deliver at least a short version of a eulogy in his response to her:

Gus and I were friends for quite a good many years. I always looked forward to seeing him, no matter how outrageous he might be, and just about anybody who knew him probably would testify that he was less than altogether civilized. Who would expect anything else? It is impossible to imagine Gus behaving like ordinary people. One time we went to the museum for an exhibit of Japanese woodblock prints. He talked steadily and I wished he would go on forever. I knew quite well that he knew a lot about this, that, any number of things, but somehow his understanding of those prints impressed me. There were other times, many other times. You are by no means alone in your loss.[9]

Another New Mexico writer, Geary Hobson, memorialized Blaisdell in similar terms on a local blog, giving more clues to the intellectual bonds that Connell had long felt with his friend: "Gus was one of the few real geniuses that I have been fortunate to meet. I used to sit in the Batch, behind the checkout counter, and listen to him talk about poetry, fiction writing, history, films, math, the military, political affairs, publishing—you name it—and his mind, revealed and displayed in his absolutely individualized style of discourse, leaping from idea to idea, example to example, book title to film scene to historical event to personal commentary on all matters thus mentioned."[10] As with George Gutekunst, Bill Ryan, Don Carpenter, and even Gale Zoe Garnett, Connell felt some sort of magnetic pull toward the large, opinionated personalities in his small circle as if they filled his life with something he knew that he himself lacked.

The Blaisdell essay collection was published in 2012 without any honoring words from Connell. Praise flowed the other way, however, in an excerpt about the first "vatic" project, *Notes from a Bottle*, from Blaisdell's landmark, mid-1960s assessment of Connell's talent.

Mostly, in Santa Fe, Connell kept to himself. Acquaintances—gallery owners, his tax accountants—might see him around town once or twice a year but knew he'd prefer sitting alone if he were, say, bellied up at the Santa Fe Bar and Grill. Curiously, another writer-recluse, Cormac McCarthy, was known to frequent the same place and also sit alone. There's no evidence they ever communicated. By one account Connell's lawyer once wrote to McCarthy saying he and Connell should get together for dinner. McCarthy never replied. Another curious lacuna: The writer J. R. Humphreys, who was one of Connell's teachers at Columbia circa 1949, had retired to Santa Fe the year before Connell got there. I've found nothing to indicate any connection between the two writers even after Humphreys published a novel partly based on his interest in ancient Mayan culture and received local publicity.

Connell had a long though little-documented friendship with Nancy Wood, a poet, novelist, and much-accomplished photographer. Connell had been among the literary jurors who granted Wood a National Endowment for the Arts fellowship in the late 1980s, and later, as friends in Santa Fe, he read parts of her novel in progress *The Soledad Crucifixion*. Their friendship remains mostly in the shadows.

Jack Shoemaker had visited with Connell in Santa Fe in 1991 and met Wood over dinner at La Fonda. Recently divorced, Shoemaker brought along a new friend, a writer and teacher named Jane Vandenburgh (they would marry within a few years). Connell was droll and fun to be with, Vandenburgh recalled of her first encounter with him. She could sense that Wood, a widow, was making a play for Connell and maybe even for Shoemaker, given that she had a novel to pitch. Connell later told Shoemaker that Wood often asked about him.

Eight years later, in November 1999, Shoemaker and Vandenburgh, now married and living in Washington, D.C., visited with Connell again in Santa Fe. Two of Shoemaker's North Point writers, Wendell Berry and Gary Snyder, were featured in a public program put on by the Lannan Foundation. Connell attended the event, during which Shoemaker moderated a discussion with the two writers on stage at Santa Fe's Lensic Theater. Connell, Berry, and Snyder were the seasoned anchors of North Point, each esteemed, intelligent, and accomplished in very different ways. Anne Lamott also traveled to Santa Fe to join them, and during the post-talk dinner, she and Vandenburgh book-ended Connell at the table. This was an ideal social situation. Vandenburgh knew that Connell was always happy to yield the conversational lead to a lively, engaging woman, and here he was surrounded by two good friends with whom he could be comfortable. Vandenburgh recalled that Berry's wife explicitly expressed hope not to sit next to Connell. Their mutual shyness might prove excruciating. But here were the ebullient Lamott and friendly Vandenburgh to the rescue, lifting Connell's spirits with their good humor.[11]

For the most part, few people have vivid memories of their Santa Fe time with Connell. "If you tried to talk to him at the bar, forget it," the artist Paul Pletka said. "How you doing? Fine. No elaboration. He'd go back to his drink, nursing it." Pletka and his wife, Nancy Benkof, once invited Connell to join them and an old friend at a restaurant. The friend had lived in Santa Fe since the 1930s and was said to be a great storyteller. "He [Connell] was so mute," Benkof said. "He never said a word."[12]

Art dealer Charlotte Kornstein said that at one dinner out with Connell he talked constantly. But another time Connell showed up at her gallery for an opening during which he sat by himself and just looked at people, to the point some began to feel a little unnerved. "We never invited him again," she said. "What would be the point?"[13]

Kornstein observed that Connell was never happier than when Garnett came to town. Or one time when she ran into him on the plaza. He'd just returned from an excursion to Albuquerque, where he'd managed to find the right typewriter ribbons for his fifty-year-old Olympia and bought enough to last the rest of his life.

Not long after *Lost in Uttar Pradesh* came out, Connell's version of Santa Fe came to a halt and his life changed completely. The pain in his legs had become unbearable. Anyone who had visited him at home could detect the accumulation of his handprints on the stairway walls, marking the struggles he had going up to his writing lair and bedroom, the pain only partly dulled by the evening's cocktails. (Now here, the grime on his walls, was the kind of small, human, character-shaping detail Connell would have zeroed in on if he were sifting through the makings of his own life. Could it dredge up references to prehistoric cave paintings or messages from the past he once wrote about at Inscription Rock?)

Connell finally decided that knee surgery was the answer. He went along with a plan to replace both knees at the same time, hoping to get it over with. But the short version of the sad tale: it didn't go well. The problems evidently were largely of his own doing. Connell's sister and niece were in New Mexico for the surgery and for the immediate recovery at a rehab clinic. Connell was despondent. And he had no interest in or real understanding of the demands of rehab or even of going through the restorative motions that routinely follow knee surgery. It typically could take three months of learning to walk again. He sat glumly in his wheelchair and resisted. He complained that the physical therapy, or his therapist, was ineffective. The situation became even more dire when the stress led to heart fibrillations and he was fitted with a pacemaker. Soon it became clear, at least to his family, that he wouldn't be able to return to his two-story condominium and pick up where he left off.

By early 2009, his sister and niece found him an apartment at an assisted living complex, the Ponce de Leon, at 640 Alta Vista in Santa Fe. They spent days cleaning his condo, scrubbing the stairway walls, and ridding every surface of the dust that Connell apparently never cared about.

Some people in contact with Connell that winter—notably Susan Ramer, his agent at Congdon, and Jack Shoemaker—had noticed his pronounced weakness in phone conversations. He hardly perked up when told he'd made the long list for the Man Booker international prize for lifetime achievement that year (ultimately won by Alice Munro). Shoemaker, though, got him laughing on the phone, "which is a good sign," he told Ramer in an email. He reported that Connell "spoke positively about the place he's in (except for the quality of the food and the company he now has to keep)." And Connell also bought a new television to occupy his time.[14]

Garnett came to town that spring. Along with reviving Connell's spirits, she helped move some of his belongings from the condo before it went on the market.

A few months later, on the morning of August 1, 2009, Connell received a couple of visitors from San Francisco. Andrew Hoyem, the fine-press publisher, and his wife, Diana Ketcham, arrived on a mission. Hoyem's Arion Press, producer of deluxe, letterpress editions of classic books, was soon to issue a fiftieth-anniversary edition of *Mrs. Bridge*, and he wanted Connell to sign the books— all 326 copies of the run. To make the task more manageable, Hoyem brought along just the title-page sheets on which to capture Connell's signature.

The blue New Mexico sky was bright and the temperature was relatively cool for an August day, in the seventies. Connell's two-room suite at Ponce de Leon was still filled with unpacked boxes, though he had retrieved and installed some of his cherished objects on shelves. After the last signature, they all went out to a Santa Fe lunch. One can even catch Connell on the verge of a rare smile in the photograph Hoyem took that day in a restaurant's patio garden. Connell surely was happy that fifty years on, his first great literary success still had life, still had readers, still felt worthy of this high-art production of a book.

With nineteen distinct books behind him, the one that essentially had ensured Connell's career—*Mrs. Bridge*, the intimate novel that could stir the blood of anyone who would read it—once again felt like a resonant presence in the forefront of his consciousness.

For Connell, life had been a long stream filled with shadows, an image he had projected in *Notes from a Bottle* and used in a story ("Assassin") collected in his last book. His purposeful intellectual pursuits had been punctuated by an immense personal reserve and only fleeting joy. He never wanted much attention. He professed to prefer anonymity.

Evan who? In my unscientific experience, it is not at all unusual to encounter people who had never heard of him but who fondly recalled his most famous novel. Connell deliberately left few footprints. He lived a quiet and mostly private life. He was not fully ascetic. He loved to gather among friends, especially other writers, at this bar or that one. He played chess and blackjack. He traveled extensively, though mostly by himself. He was committed to his work. He wrote and published what he wanted and accepted the consequences. He suffered interviews from time to time, and a few of those even developed into meaningful and rewarding conversations. He loved women but somewhat in light of the family experience he revealed in the Bridge novels he never wanted to marry. For one thing, there was the fear of failure at relationships, the sense that he didn't want to find himself in the sort of emotionally vacant reality he saw in his own parents and wrote about in his books. And so many of his friends had gone through divorce. He didn't want to risk that. But more important, he recognized that his life as a writer was all-consuming, a full-time commitment that wouldn't be fair either to a family, to children if he had them. Again, he could recall his father, gone from morning to night, not having the proper time or inclination for nurturing connections. He might have even thought of William Carlos Williams, the New Jersey doctor, great American writer, and patron saint of Connell's *Contact* magazine, who burrowed into his library each evening after a long day of seeing patients, shutting out his family in order to write his poems.

When Hoyem and Ketcham left Santa Fe that weekend in 2009, they had little indication of the psychic turbulence Connell's last chapter would present as a result of his move to the nursing home. But they—and he—had something to celebrate. And they would soon honor him and his legacy with Arion's commemorative *Mrs. Bridge* ($500 or more a copy). In a sense, Connell's first novel would be his final book. Jack Shoemaker also took the opportunity to bring fresh light to *Mrs. Bridge* that season. Counterpoint issued a fiftieth-anniversary edition, in a paperback with more of a consumer-friendly price. "The struggles and sorrows in it are timeless," James Salter stated in an afterword for that edition.[15] And in introducing a British reissue the following year, the American novelist Joshua Ferris asserted the novel's lasting appeal in its central character's standing as "a reflection of you and me, an exemplar of our shared humanity and all the terror and opportunity it so briefly provides."[16]

Connell found laughter rarely in those last years. Garnett could bring it out of him. She couldn't afford to visit often, but she called from her part-time residence in Visby, Sweden, where she kept a sculpture studio. After a few minutes of small talk, Connell revived from whatever funk he'd put himself into and they'd banter for hours as if the years and distance didn't matter at all.

Jean Cantú, Connell's tax accountant, became fond of her visits with him: "One of the absolute joys in my life was getting him to laugh. On Thursdays or Fridays they had cocktail hour. I would go over, the two of us we would sit, and other people would approach him to sign books, oh, no, no. We'd sit and I'd get him to laugh at silly jokes."[17]

What Cantú describes, as anyone who has watched an aging parent on the decline can recognize, is a sense of resignation, the slow sap of entropy in action.

Connell could do nothing about his circumstances. He complained about the lack of light in his apartment. Because of it, the typewriter sat unused on his desk. He could no longer write, no longer tap out a story that tried to emerge in his mind. The quaint mania had ceased to operate. The literary alchemist had closed his practice.

Connell's last couple of years at Ponce de Leon were brightened by the presence of an employee who took interest in him and broke through his shell. Linda Carfagno, a photographer and filmmaker, had taken a job in the facility's dining room. One day at breakfast, she noticed the "elegant handsome man" for the first time. He sat alone. Carfagno brought him the extra butter she heard that he liked and started talking to him about movies. Her father had been in the business as an art director and production designer for MGM—the first film he worked on was *The Wizard of Oz*—and Connell seemed interested in her stories. Soon she invited an artist friend, Linda Hunsaker, to join her in visits with Connell, and together they managed to keep him comfortable and engaged.

Another female visitor got Connell talking a bit in those last years. Gemma Sieff, a young writer, spent time with him in 2011 to produce an interview for the *Paris Review*. In several meetings over four days Sieff was able to extract from Connell a few intimate and revealing memories. She read his quietude as "equal parts reticence and modesty," she wrote. "He had a wonderful laugh, a huh-huh-huh, gentle and self-deprecating. You could tell he was accustomed to downplaying his erudition. But he clearly wanted to communicate what he considered important."[18] Sieff got Connell to reflect on the absence of love in his family, though only briefly.

Carfagno's tenure at Ponce de Leon came to an end in 2012 as a result of an act of kindness on Connell's part. She needed a car, and he gave her his. He wasn't driving any more. By that point, it had sat unused in the parking lot for two years. "It's a cute little Honda Civic," he told her. "Linda, I want you to have it. I don't want your money. Check the battery." Management did not approve, but Carfagno didn't care. "Every time I got in that car, it was as if I was driving him around." After losing her job over accepting the gift she often would sneak back into the facility to see him.[19]

Annie Lamott visited Connell in the fall of 2012. She was the friend who relentlessly teased Connell in private and in public. Once, in a restaurant review, she nicknamed him Scoots. The irony would not have been lost on either of them now that his mobility was limited to wheelchair, walker, and cane. Lamott sat with him and held his hand. She easily could recall how she felt about the gravity and innocence with which he'd managed to greet life. There was a kind of perpetual, earnest boyishness about him. "Sometimes," she once wrote, "he will be talking about a childhood book, or a movie he saw a few years ago, or a memory from long ago, and he'll be telling it so intently, with such seriousness, that his eyes get hooded over with concentration, and you can see exactly what he looked like at six years old."[20]

Web Schott and his wife also visited Connell in late summer that year. They took him out to dinner. Back at Ponce de Leon, Nan went inside to wait for a cab. "Evan and I were sitting on a bench outside," Schott recalled. "He was physically frail, he had his walker and a cane. I raised the question about the disparate nature of what he did—*Notes* to *Compass* to *Mrs. Bridge* to *Deus lo Volt!* to *Goya*. I was fishing for a motive, a driving force, and what he said was that he got interested in somebody and he wanted to know what he thought about him, and he wrote a book about them. He told me essentially, he wanted to know himself."[21]

Schott's anecdote made me think about that old photograph of Connell, at age twenty-five, sitting atop Long's Peak like Rodin's *Thinker,* surrounded by air amid the vastness of the universe. And of James Joyce's line about "silence, exile and cunning."

"Life passes into pages if it passes into anything," James Salter once wrote. Salter and Connell had a mutual admiration if not a close friendship. Katie Roiphe quoted that line from Salter's *Burning the Days* in a book about writers facing death, *The Violet Hour*. She was lucky to have had a conversation with Salter, at age eighty-nine, the year before he died. If Roiphe had thought to examine Connell on the topic, she might have found him ruminating in print: "When hate and love together have exhausted the soul, the body seldom endures for long."[22]

Connell died in the early morning hours of January 10, 2013. The death certificate listed causes as cardiovascular disease and atrial fibrillation. He was alone in his apartment, save for the silent murmur of voices across time captured in ceramic and enlivening the shelves against his walls.

"Connell was and is a hero among writers," Lorin Stein wrote on the *Paris Review*'s website that day. The Bridge novels, he said, "have been cited as a crucial influence by authors as different as Lydia Davis, Jonathan Franzen, and Zadie Smith." Stein noted that his historical works "sang the glories of lost civilizations and pointed to the ruins at our feet," and added, "Connell loved any tale of doomed experiments, he delighted in waste and folly, but his own experiments bore fruit, and no two of the same kind."[23]

A Sausalito writer remembered Connell as "Smilin' Jack," a moniker foisted on him by some wag at the No Name Bar, possibly Calvin Kentfield, because he shared the mustache and the flight jacket of a comic-strip character by that name. "Those of us who knew Evan accepted his taciturnity as who he was and treasured his friendship," said the Sausalito newsletter.[24]

"In my view he's one of the very best American writers of his generation," Lewis Lapham, once *Harper*'s editor and now principal editor of his namesake *Lapham's Quarterly*, told me a few years later. With its amalgam of historical readings, nuggets, and unburied wisdom from the past, Lapham's journal, in fact, represents a kind of tribute to Connell. He and Montaigne were the quarterly's intellectual pillars, Lapham said. "You know, he was enigmatic, not easy to approach, not a glad-handing, little friend of all the world. It was the same kind of quality I came to regard in Thelonious Monk, one of my other heroes."[25]

Connell was no jazz fan, but I am, and as someone who has tried to incorporate Monk into my late-life piano noodlings, along with my deep study of Connell, I can appreciate Lapham's sentiment. Both were what we like to refer to as American originals. Both danced, in their respective ways, to different drummers. Both created in rather rule-breaking, improvisational ways. Both would recognize what William Carlos Williams wrote in his early volume of "improvisations," *Kora in Hell*: "I'll write whatever I damn please, whenever I damn please and it'll be good if the authentic spirit of change is on it."[26]

A. M. Homes, who introduced a new edition of *The Diary of a Rapist* in 2004, saddled Connell, as many have, with the "writer's writer" syndrome: "One of the things that has kept Connell less known than he should be is that his oeuvre isn't easily described: his territory shifts with each volume, absenting him from categorization. Eccentric, idiosyncratic, he writes what he wants. Throughout his body of work there is a consistent clarity, an unblinking authorial eye that doesn't render judgment but simply presents his characters real and imagined, writ large and small, leaving room for the reader to participate in the creation of the narrative."[27]

The clarity, the eccentricity—yes, and to which I would add the inner, manic light of adventure and discovery.

Gerald Howard, the longtime New York editor, published an essay in praise of Don DeLillo in early 2020, suggesting that he would be a formidable candidate among American writers for a Nobel Prize. "By every metric," Howard wrote, "that we use to measure literary greatness—including overall achievement, scope and variety of subject matter, striking and fully realized style, duration of career, originality and formal innovation, widespread influence here and abroad, production of masterpieces, consistency of excellence, pertinence of themes, density of critical commentary, and dignity in the conduct of a literary career—Don DeLillo, now eighty-three, scores in the highest possible percentile."[28]

I couldn't help but think favorably of Connell at just about every tick along Howard's list of metrics.

Howard once asked DeLillo about the contrast between the image of powerless writers found in his books and the high repute with which others held him. Howard said DeLillo's response was unforgettable:

The writer has lost a great deal of his influence, and he is situated now, if anywhere, on the margins of the culture. But isn't this where he belongs? How could it be any other way? And in my personal view this is a perfect place to observe what's happening at the dead center of things. . . . I am not particularly distressed by the state of fiction or the role of the writer. The more marginal, perhaps ultimately the more trenchant and observant and finally necessary he'll become.[29]

Again, few important American writers remained as marginal as Connell throughout most of his career, let alone his last days.

After Connell's death, Nancy Benkof couldn't believe no memorial had been planned for him, so she set out to create one in Santa Fe. Patrick Lannan at the Lannan Foundation, which had bestowed its achievement award on Connell three years earlier, agreed to host a luncheon gathering. A couple of dozen people looked at photos and heard stories. Garnett sent a video in which she shared an account of their long friendship. Jack Shoemaker told his story about Connell's mute moment on the Diane Rehm radio show.

Web and Nan Schott did not attend. But as someone who knew Connell for more than sixty years, Schott remained grateful for what he learned from Connell. It wasn't so much that there was a close bond. In his memory, Connell never once picked up a tab or asked about Schott's children. He had little empathy for people in that way. What Connell and Schott shared was a commitment to writing, art, and literature, a commitment to craft and an unwillingness to compromise.

"The essential Evan Connell was an extraordinarily talented, somewhat psychologically isolated and extremely sensitive writer," Schott said one late winter day as we sat around a table in his spacious kitchen on an exurban edge of Kansas City. "From our point of view, he was a loner. From his point of view, I don't believe he suffered from it. From his point of view, nothing was more important than that, than writing."[30]

Five years after Connell's death I traveled to Santa Fe as part of my quest to know his life better. It was early autumn. Before leaving the city on a Saturday morning, I had a decision to make. Turn left out of the motel parking lot and head straight to the airport in Albuquerque or turn right and make another attempt to find Connell's final resting place. His ashes had been laid near a tree.

I could've gone either way, I told myself. What would this really accomplish? What would I get out of it? Researching and writing a biography of a deliberately elusive subject was a risky project to begin with. What difference would it make if I skipped this— what?—wild ash chase? Then again, reporting a life means turning over every stone, tracing every thread that might lead to a mote of meaning. Robert Caro's great advice, learned as an investigative reporter before becoming one of our supreme biographers, was "turn every page." Sure, I could save the task for another trip. But why not here and now? The silly, scolding things we do to our inner selves in a decisive moment.

So, in a split second, propelled by a sense that I would regret it if I left that part of this journey on the table, I turned right. And soon I was heading up Canyon Road to try again.

Two days earlier, I had passed through the tourist-choked street, lined with art galleries and restaurants, on the way to a couple of possible memorial spots. But I never located a tree that looked like the one in a picture Janet Zimmermann had sent me. This was where she had poured his ashes. Her directions were unclear. I drove on a bit longer and eventually gave up and turned around. Later, I realized that I should've driven just a little farther.

So, after a breakfast burrito at Café Pasqual's, I set out again on a crisp and bright weekend morning. It was one of those early fall days Connell himself might have been thinking about when he wrote to Steele of the "big big sky of great cumulus." The drive took little more than five minutes. I got out at a parking lot—maybe the one mentioned by Janet—but again, saw nothing like the tree I thought I was looking for. Oh, well, I was prepared just to offer a generic gesture: *Peace, Evan. I'll try to do you right.*

Throughout this excursion, I could appreciate the empathy with which Jean Cantú regarded Connell's last wish, which was to be connected to the land: "I think he was so enthralled with that whole thing, how old this land is, how much has gone on in this area, how many different kinds of people, that combination. I think he fell hook, line, and sinker, and wanted eventually to be part of that landscape. My husband said the dirt got in his blood, and that's it. That's all it takes."[31]

I got back in the car and within a few seconds spotted a turnout at the edge of the dirt road that I'd missed earlier. Right next to it and down a slight incline stood a pine tree that may or may not have resembled the one in the photo. I walked over and took a couple of steps into the brush- and branch-covered slope. At the base of the tree was a patch of light-colored dirt that just might have once held the layer of dust and bones I saw in Zimmermann's picture. Or not. I have no idea. Nevertheless, surely by now the ashes would have washed away.

Still, as everyone knows, life is all about the journey not the destination. And, at the least, this pilgrimage gave me something important. A sense of the finality—dust to dust—of a man who ventured through the physical and intellectual worlds on his own terms. From Connell: "As Horace wrote, we're dust and shadow. *Pulvis et umbra sumus.*"[32] And as Connell also wrote, some artists are like onions, layer upon layer of membranes: "If you continue peeling in hopes of catching him you end up with nothing in your hand."[33] Such is the writer's dilemma.

I had spent the previous few days talking with people who knew him, loved him, and made him happy in those protected moments when he let others into his space. Connell's anonymity in death is unsurprising. That's certainly how he had wanted it. But it doesn't change the breadth and depth of the work he left behind, a collection of ordered intelligence in words that as often as not are breathtaking. This is what we expect of writers and the literature they leave behind.

In 2001, seven decades after discovering the inspirational adventures of Richard Halliburton and twenty years after remembering him in an essay in *A Long Desire*, Connell returned again to the spirit with which his "astonishing journeys" amounted to an unparalleled existence. Connell recognized that Halliburton's writing often left something to be desired, but that hardly mattered: "His name is not apt to be mentioned alongside Melville, James, Faulkner, Hemingway. . . . Still, if there are thirteen ways of looking at a blackbird, there must be several ways of measuring the value of a writer."[34]

Connell's detractors point to his inconsistencies in style and substance, his willful disregard for convention, his self-involved and aimless meditations. Well, right there are three ways of measuring his value, and, in my mind, each can be massaged into a positive attribute. I was taken aback while reading Mark Oppenheimer's generally praiseworthy essay on Connell for *The Believer*, that bastion of literary irony, by his dismissal of the late 1970s essays of *A Long Desire* and *The White Lantern*. Some readers—Lewis Lapham, for one—count these armchair excursions into history as among Connell's most memorable works. Oppenheimer could only manage a swipe at Connell and his penchant for research—never, he wrote, had anyone read so many books about so little. There's a whiff of anti-intellectual pomposity in that.

Yet reading, as we know, is a matter of taste. The ever-shifting "canon" of American literature is no longer the museum of white male creation. We can still celebrate, debate, and/or reexamine Melville and Hemingway, but we also make room for James Baldwin and Toni Morrison. Don DeLillo will surely last, alongside Joan Didion, and, in our current generation of writers, Colson Whitehead.

But any discussion of the most memorable and long-lasting American literature must reckon with Evan S. Connell—the Bridge novels, *Son of the Morning Star*, *Notes*, *Points*, and some of the best of his short stories and essays. He cast a wise eye over the span of human history and the troubles of American life. He transmuted it all into entertainments, screeds, indelible portraits, and boundless insights into our existence.

I've been a reader all of my life, sometimes focused but more often a free-ranging, undisciplined explorer. Call it loitering through books and life, as Connell might have put it. And these last few years of journeying through Connell's territory has both widened my

Fig. 35. Last portrait, c. 2011. Courtesy of Linda Carfagno.

horizons and deepened my appreciation for his contributions. His example of living with the quaint mania of writing and of choosing to work above all else in life may not present the ideal template for an aspiring author today. But his commitment, principles, and arduous dedication remain inspiring. His mission to write in order to know himself, perhaps to drive away his personal anxieties and to swim in the shadow stream, is not uncommon. But the products of his alchemical efforts certainly are.

Connell's portraits of filial rebellion (hello, Douglas Bridge, my friend) certainly resonate for me. And I can identify with his penchant for the "long desire," the soul-burning, quixotic obsession for the new, the hidden, the unattainable. I regret I never had the chance to tell Connell—I spoke with him once only briefly on the phone—that I was intimately familiar with his first boyhood home. A good friend owned the wood-framed colonial on 66th Street for many years. It was the site of frequent gatherings, and I'm sure we spoke about Connell from time to time because we were writers and critics and book readers. At the time, generally in the 1970s, 1980s, and 1990s, I knew little of his life, or his work for that matter, except the slight details that most Kansas City literati might have known. Now, of course, I know a bit more.

As Connell's centenary approaches (2024), we'll have an opportunity to bring more fresh light on him and his contributions to American literature. Perhaps that will spark new interest among readers, critics, and scholars. Connell may only have written for himself but it cannot be denied that he also wrote for the ages.

Acknowledgments

WHILE THIS PROJECT was not "authorized" per se, I am grateful for the patience, interest, and help given by Evan Connell's family, including his sister, Barbara Zimmermann; his cousin Bill Bolin; and especially his niece Janet Zimmermann. Thanks also to Mike and Donna (Zimmermann) Waller and Matthew Zimmermann, who, along with an early interview, gave me my first glimpse of his uncle's pre-Columbian collection and one of his oil paintings. Jack Shoemaker, Connell's longtime editor and publisher, who now serves as trustee of the Literary Estate of Evan S. Connell Jr., has been an invaluable connection and graciously fielded nearly four years of questions.

Gale Zoe Garnett, Anne Lamott, Herbert Gold, Jane Vandenburgh, Neil Davis, and other remaining members of Connell's circle of friends offered important insights and memories. In Santa Fe, Jean Cantú, Linda Carfagno, Charlotte Kornstein, and Paul Pletka and Nancy Benkof were particularly helpful. Maria Finn gave me a good tour of Sausalito, and Bart Schneider provided hospitality and literary conversation while I researched in the Bay Area. Nicole Blaisdell Ivey kindly shared Connell's letters to her father, the editor and critic Gus Blaisdell, and pointed me to other pertinent material. Quite significantly, Ivey also introduced me to the Frontier Café in Albuquerque, where many of Connell and Blaisdell's intellectual bull sessions took place. Sally Deskins, Bill Ryan's granddaughter, turned me onto some pertinent material regarding *Contact*.

Thanks also to the family of Max Steele, including his ex-wife Diana, son Oliver Steele, and daughter-in-law Margaret Minsky. I learned from Carol Sklenicka, author of an inspiring biography of Alice Adams (as well as one about Raymond Carver), that she had helped the Steele family deposit Max's papers in the Wilson Library. In them, along with Steele and Adams's correspondence, I discovered a trove of dozens of letters from Connell, which proved to be invaluable for illuminating long periods of his work and life.

Webster Schott, who first mentioned Connell in print in 1949, met him two years later, and wrote about him and his books several times over the years, welcomed me into his home to share stories and his personal collection of Connell letters, clips, and other material. Schott also offered insightful challenges and his eagle editor's eye in an early reading of my manuscript. His enthusiasm for this project was both humbling and essential. I was saddened to learn of his death in late December 2020, at age ninety-three, but moved by his daughter Marya's comment about how our connection via the manuscript had stimulated him and given him purpose so late in life.

Mary Dearborn, another early reader, helped me detonate rough edges and useless digressions and otherwise provided encouragement and confidence-building comments when they were most needed. If potholes remain, they are entirely of my own doing.

In the depths of my research I made a mental note to create a "Librarian and Archivists Hall of Fame" in honor of the great help delivered by devoted staffers at institutions across the country. Jacquelyn K. Sundstrand at the University of Nevada–Reno library was an early anointee for her help in transcribing an important but nearly illegible handwritten note to Connell from Walter Van Tilburg Clark. Staffers at the Santa Cruz, California, Public Library could not uncover much but shared an image from a patent application that had turned up with the name of Evan S. Connell Jr., though they suggested that couldn't possibly be the Evan S. Connell Jr. I was looking for. Archivists at the Library of Congress and the Veterans of Foreign Wars headquarters in Kansas City excavated one of Connell's earliest published stories in a magazine that had long eluded me. Elspeth Healey at the Spencer Library of the University of Kansas retrieved a motherlode of material—issues of *The Bitter Bird*, a campus humor magazine containing the extracurricular record of Connell's college career as a writer and illustrator. Dani Wellemeyer (quoted anonymously in the preface) and others on the reference desk at the University of Missouri–Kansas City's Miller Nichols Library helped retrieve several useful publications.

Tim Noakes and colleagues in special collections at Stanford University's Cecil Green Library helped me navigate Connell's papers during an onsite week and later remotely, even as the Covid-19 pandemic put first a halt then a slow crawl to library activities. Similarly, Nora Dolliver at the New York Public Library found important and previously hard to find material as special collections archivists tiptoed back into action in 2020. The San Francisco Public Library came to my aid remotely more than once; I am also indebted to that library for its deaccessioned stash of about half the issues of *Contact*, which I acquired online, completing my collection. Before his recent retirement, Bill Van Niekerken, a history columnist for the *San Francisco Chronicle*, dove into the newspaper's archives to find an elusive book review by Connell and other material I was unable to locate otherwise. Rudi Keller gave me guidance on Civil War history in Missouri.

I am, of course, extremely grateful to Gary Kass, the former acquiring editor at the University of Missouri Press, who first saw the potential of this book, and to Mary Conley, my editor, who inherited the project and enthusiastically carried it to fruition along with the press' production staff. Margaret Hogan's sharp copy editing saved me from a few embarrassing gaffes and schooled me in the intricacies of the scholarly publishing apparatus.

ArtsKC, a vital piece of the local cultural ecosystem, gave me an early boost in the form of an Inspiration Grant, which subsidized some research travel in 2018.

Sharon Dynak, executive director of the Ucross Foundation, kindly provided a base of operations as I explored the Little Bighorn territory. And I am ever grateful for the inspiration and encouragement from my writer friends in Kansas City and elsewhere. Robert Stewart, for example, published my early essay about this project in *New Letters*. Other sounding boards and cheerleaders included my late friend Lawrence Alton and his sister, Joanne Riordan (also

RIP), who long lived in Connell's boyhood home in Kansas City. I regret they won't be here to read this. Also Thomas Stroik, Michael Pritchett (and his modern American literature class at UMKC), Lisa D. Stewart, Karla Deel, José Faus, Rick Serrano, Candice Millard, Donna Seaman, Susan Whitmore, Pete Dulin, Scott Ditzler (who interviewed Connell in 2010 as an intern working with me at the *Kansas City Star*), Tom Averill, Jeffrey Ann Goudie, Whitney Terrell, Hadara Bar-Nadav, Christie Hodgen, Phong Nguyen, Helen Ashmore, Darren Sextro, Liz Cook, Scott Wilson, Alice Thorson, Heather Paxton, Gloria Vando Hickok, Mike Lankford, Tracy and Marjorie Daugherty, Meg Wolitzer, Laurie Hertzel, the late Scott Donaldson, Nick Reynolds, and fellow members of the Biographers International Organization, including Linda Leavell, Amanda Vaill, Carol Sklenicka, William Souder, Carl Rollyson, Timothy Christian, James McGrath Morris, and members of our discussion groups on literary biography.

As always, Carol Zastoupil never really complained about all those hours I vanished into my home office or buried my nose endlessly in books or took off for research trips and library visits or yammered about exciting (to me) discoveries.

Abbreviations

Works of Evan S. Connell

AL	*The Anatomy Lesson and Other Stories*
ALD	*A Long Desire*
ATC	*At the Crossroads: Stories*
ATH	*The Aztec Treasure House: New and Selected Essays*
CAAS	*Contemporary Authors Autobiography Series*, vol. 2
CS	*The Collected Stories of Evan S. Connell*
DH	*Double Honeymoon*
DR	*The Diary of a Rapist*
DV	*Deus lo Volt!*
FG	*Francisco Goya: A Life*
LIUP	*Lost in Uttar Pradesh: New and Selected Stories*
MrB	*Mr. Bridge*
MrsB	*Mrs. Bridge*
PCR	*Points for a Compass Rose*
SAP	*Saint Augustine's Pigeon: Selected Stories*
SOMS	*Son of the Morning Star: Custer and the Little Bighorn*
TC	*The Connoisseur*
TP	*The Patriot*

Other Abbreviations

AL	Anne Lamott
BZ	Barbara Zimmermann (sister)
EM	Elizabeth McKee
ESC	Evan S. Connell
EW	Eugene Walter
GB	Gus Blaisdell

Abbreviations

GZG	Gale Zoe Garnett
JS	Jack Shoemaker
JZ	Janet Zimmermann (niece)
RG	Robert Gottlieb
MS	Max Steele
WS	Webster Schott

Sources and Credits

Evan S. Connell's papers are housed in the Special Collections department of the Cecil H. Green Library at Stanford University, Stanford, California (abbreviated "Stanford" in the notes). Some correspondence and other items remain with family members. The Stanford collection includes nearly two hundred letters from Connell to his sister, Barbara Zimmermann, and hundreds of pages of incoming letters as well as manuscript drafts, periodical publications, news clippings, ephemera, a family scrapbook, and personal items. Unpublished letters and manuscript material are copyright by the Literary Estate of Evan Shelby Connell Jr. and are used by permission.

Stanford's Special Collections also contain papers of Jack Shoemaker, Connell's longtime editor and publisher. Letters to Shoemaker cited in the notes are from the Shoemaker Papers unless otherwise noted. Letters from Shoemaker to Connell are in the Connell Papers unless otherwise noted.

Connell always typed his letters and never included the year when dating them. When postmarks were unavailable, in most cases dates were determined by internal evidence.

Letters from Connell to friends and other correspondents also exist in numerous archives elsewhere, which are cited in the endnotes with shorthand references as follows:

Letters to Max Steele and other documents are in Max Steele's papers in the Southern Historical Collection, Louis Round Wilson Special Collections Library, University of North Carolina–Chapel Hill (Wilson).

Letters to Jonathan Yardley and other records from the National Book Awards panel Yardley chaired in 1973 come from the Jonathan Yardley Papers, also at the Wilson Library.

The papers of Eugene Walter and Gordon Lish (in the Genesis West Collection), containing letters and other materials, are at the Harry Ransom Center, University of Texas, Austin (Ransom).

Connell's letters to Robert Gottlieb and his colleagues come from the Alfred A. Knopf Inc. Records, also at the Ransom Center. Letters between Max Steele and Alice Adams appear in their respective collections at Wilson and Ransom, though some copies exist in both places.

Some of Connell's letters and other documents appear in records of his agents, Elizabeth McKee, Harold Matson and Company, and Donald Congdon, housed at the Rare Book and Manuscript Library, Butler Library, Columbia University, New York (Butler). McKee's documents prior to her agency's merger with the Matson Company in 1965 have not been located.

Letters from Gale Garnett to John Huston are located at the Margaret Herrick Library of the American Academy of Motion Pictures Arts and Sciences in Beverly Hills, California (Herrick).

Material collected by Connell's alma mater Dartmouth College comes from the Rauner Special Collections Library, Hanover, New Hampshire (Rauner).

Writings and drawings from Connell's period at the University of Kansas were accessed at the Kenneth Spencer Research Library Special Collections, Lawrence, Kansas (Spencer).

Paris Review records, including correspondence with George Plimpton, are located at the Morgan Library, New York (Morgan).

Correspondence with *New Yorker* editors comes from the *New Yorker* Collection at the New York Public Library (NYPL).

Connell items of local interest are deposited in the Missouri Valley Room of the Kansas City Public Library (KCPL) and the archives of the Jackson County Historical Society in Independence, Missouri (JCHS).

Connell's letters to Gus Blaisdell remain in the private collection of his daughter, Nicole Blaisdell Ivey, in Albuquerque, New

Mexico. Other scattered letters remain in private hands and are noted as such.

Many of Connell's letters to Webster Schott are in Schott's private collection. A collection of Schott's earlier papers at the Howard Gotlieb Library, Boston University, came to my attention belatedly.

Also useful were the papers of Don Carpenter at the Bancroft Library, University of California, Berkeley; John Barth's papers in the Special Collections division of the Johns Hopkins University Sheridan Libraries; the archives of Walter Van Tilburg Clark at the University of Nevada-Reno; Gordon Lish's papers at the Lilly Library, University of Indiana, Bloomington; the George Hitchcock Kayak Collection in Special Collections at the State University of New York at Buffalo; some *Contact* material in the Howard Gotlieb Library, Boston University; Annie Dillard's papers at the Beinecke Library, Yale University, New Haven, Connecticut; James Ivory's papers at the University of Oregon, Special Collections and Archives, and other Ivory items at the Morgan Library; the Ka Rose Collection in Special Collections, Archives and Preservation, University of Colorado Boulder Libraries; and Connell's Naval Air Corps records from the National Personnel Records Center of the National Archives, St. Louis, Missouri.

Many newspaper articles (and some magazine pieces) have become increasingly accessible in digital form from various sources, including the major papers' and periodicals' own archives as well as those made available by third-party sources, such as newspapers. com, ProQuest, and others. A tradeoff of having the convenience of such access is the loss of accurate page numbers for citations. As a result, many citations appear without them. Some clippings in various archival collections also exist shorn of some publication details. In addition, wire service material, such as dispatches by the Associated Press and shared content from chain newspaper providers, might be cited as appearing in publications where they were found rather than where they might have originated.

Dozens of interviews with friends, acquaintances, and others in Connell's various worlds were conducted in person, by phone, and by email and are usually cited as such in the text or notes.

Notes

Preface

1. AL to Gerald Shapiro, copied to "Bobs," the nickname Connell used in letters to his sister, Barbara Zimmermann (BZ), April 16, 1986, Evan Shelby Connell Papers M1961, Department of Special Collections and University Archives, Stanford University Libraries, Stanford, California (hereafter "Stanford").

2. WS, interview with author, February 20, 2020.

3. Connell, "Beginnings," 9.

4. Storr, *Solitude*, 98.

5. Alice Adams to MS, January 22, 1974, Max Steele Papers, Southern Historical Collection, Louis Round Wilson Special Collections Library, University of North Carolina, Chapel Hill (hereafter "Wilson"), box 17, folder 127.

6. Shapiro, "Evan S. Connell."

7. Jack Shoemaker, interview with author, May 22, 2018.

8. Pickus, "On Being Out of Touch."

Chapter 1

1. Connell, "Notes from a Bottle Found on the Beach at Carmel," *Contact*, no. 3, 1959, 136.

2. ESC to BZ, December 3, 1988, Stanford.

3. Eve Crane to Toinette Rees, June 21, 1968, Alfred A. Knopf Inc. Records, 1873-1966, Harry Ransom Center, University of Texas at Austin (hereafter "Ransom"), box 814, folder 14.

4. *MrsB*, 9.

5. "John I. Williamson," *Independent* (Kansas City society magazine), April 14, 1917, 1. Reprinted in Katherine Baxter, ed., *Notable Kansas Citians of 1915-1916-1917-1918* (privately printed, 1925), 163-64, Local History Collection, Missouri Valley Room, Kansas City Public Library (hereafter "KCPL").

6. Connell, "Evan S. Connell," in *CAAS*, 100.

7. Connell, "Evan S. Connell," in *CAAS*, 101.

8. *TP*, 65.

9. *TP*, 65.

10. *TP*, 66, 69.

11. Hugh P. Williamson, "Missouri Soldier's Widow Went through Winter and Wilderness to His Grave," *Kansas City Times*, March 18, 1952, 26.

12. Connell, "Evan S. Connell," in *CAAS*, 97.

13. "A Dish My Friends Praised," *Kansas City Star*, July 23, 1928, 9.

14. *CS*, 5.

15. "Every Week Is Book Week at Border Star School," *Kansas City Star*, October 19, 1930, 6C.

16. *ALD*, 240–41; *ATH*, 408–9.

17. Penny Ice Fund reports, *Kansas City Times*, July 1, 1930, 1; June 30, 1933, 3; *Kansas City Star*, June 25, 1935, 3.

18. Connell, "Crash Landing," *Esquire*, February 1958, 60; *CS*, 586.

19. *MrB*, 140.

20. Bill Bolin, interview with author, February 14, 2018.

21. Connell, "Evan S. Connell," in *CAAS*, 99.

22. *MrsB*, 11.

23. See Gary M. Pomerantz, *The Devil's Tickets: A Night of Bridge, a Fatal Hand, and a New American Age* (New York: Crown, 2009).

24. John Brady, "An Independent Sort," *The Writer*, March 2011. Part of the quotation comes from a draft of the interview that Brady shared with the author.

25. Presson, *New Letters on the Air*.

26. *MrsB*, 20.

27. The record of his high school classes and grades appears with his University of Kansas transcript.

28. *LIUP*, 354.

29. William LaVarre, "All the GOLD in Yucatan," *Kansas City Star*, January 10, 1937, 1–2C.

30. ESC to MS, October 26, [1957], Wilson, box 28, folder 214.

31. Richard Halliburton, "Cairo: The World Capital of Sin," *Kansas City Star*, June 2, 1935, 1C, 4C.

32. Quoted in Greg Daugherty, "The Last Adventure of Richard Halliburton, the Forgotten Hero of 1930s America," *Smithsonian Magazine,* March 25, 2014, https://www.smithsonianmag.com/history/last-adventure-richard -halliburton-forgotten-hero-1930s-america-180950164/.

33. E. B. Garnett, "Silence after a Storm at Sea Causes Fear That Halliburton Has Found His 'Great Adventure,'" *Kansas City Star*, May 21, 1939, 1-2C.

34. Quoted in Daugherty, "The Last Adventure of Richard Halliburton."

35. Connell, "The Last Great Traveler," 129.

36. *DH*, 233.

37. *ATH*, 252.

38. Connell, "A Cookbook That Leaves You with a Sense of Wonder," *San Francisco Chronicle*, December 12, 1961, Stanford, box 41, folder 5.

39. *ATH*, 253.

40. Connell, "Evan S. Connell," in *CAAS*, 97.

41. *CS*, 14.

42. Connell," Evan S. Connell," in *CAAS*, 99.

43. Jean Cantú, interview with author, October 8, 2018.

44. Connell, "Evan S. Connell," in *CAAS*, 100.

45. Connell, "Evan S. Connell," in *CAAS*, 100.

46. *MrsB*, 32–33.

47. *MrsB*, 54.

48. *MrsB*, 191, 196, 195, 76.

49. *MrB*, 168.

50. Connell, "Evan S. Connell," in *CAAS*, 101.

51. P. L. Byers, "Dartmouth College: Alumni Council Rating Blank," February 6, 1941, Evan Connell Alumni File, Rauner Special Collections Library, Dartmouth College, Hanover, New Hampshire (hereafter "Rauner").

52. Marisa Agha, "Warm Memories of a Big Brother," *Kansas City Star*, July 17, 1996, Johnson County/Shawnee Mission section, 8.

53. *PCR*, 3.

Chapter 2

1. Connell, "Evan S. Connell," in *CAAS*, 102.

2. "Bébert's Nephew," in *ATC*, 228; *CS*, 313.

3. Marisa Agha, "Warm Memories of a Big Brother," *Kansas City Star*, July 17, 1996, 1, 8.

4. Connell, "Evan S. Connell," in *CAAS*, 102.

5. Connell, "Evan S. Connell," in *CAAS*, 102.

6. Miles C. Thomas to Naval Aviation Cadet Selection Board, April 29, 1943, U.S. Navy Records, National Personnel Records Center, St. Louis. Many details of Connell's service, as well as school transcripts and other personal information, are contained in his navy file.

7. J. M. Ranney, "Report of Naval Aviation Cadet Selection Board," May 4, 1943, U.S. Navy Records, National Personnel Records Center.

8. Connell, "Evan S. Connell," in *CAAS*, 102.

9. *TP*, 286.

10. *TP*, 290.

11. Brady, "An Independent Sort," 20-55.

12. Connell, "Evan S. Connell," in *CAAS*, 103.

13. Connell, "Crash Landing," *Esquire*, February 1958, 59. Connell would rewrite the story substantially before it ended up in *The Patriot*. The original magazine version also appears in *CS*, 582–95.

14. Connell, "Evan S. Connell," in *CAAS*, 104.

15. Connell, "Evan S. Connell," in *CAAS*, 104.

16. Connell, "Evan S. Connell," in *CAAS*, 104-5.

17. Connell, "Evan S. Connell," in *CAAS*, 105.

18. Connell, "Evan S. Connell," in *CAAS*, 105.

19. Connell, "Evan S. Connell," in *CAAS*, 105-6.

20. *TP*, 250–51.

21. Connell, "Evan S. Connell," in *CAAS*, 106.

22. Connell, "Evan S. Connell," in *CAAS*, 106.

23. Matthew Zimmermann, interview with author, July 24, 2017.

24. ESC to MS, July 31, [1958], Wilson, box 28, folder 214.

25. *TP*, 3, 4.

26. *TP*, 6.

Chapter 3

1. Connell, "Bitter Bird's Week," *Bitter Bird* 1, no. 2 (June 1946), Kenneth Spencer Research Library Special Collections, University of Kansas, Lawrence (hereafter "Spencer").

2. *Bitter Bird* 2, no. 1 (October 1946): 17, Spencer.

3. *Bitter Bird* 2, no. 2 (November 1946), Spencer.

4. Connell, "Dogface," *Bitter Bird* 2, no. 4 (Spring 1947), Spencer.

5. Byron Shutz, "Evan S. Connell Jr.—A Recollection," revised January 1986, Byron Shutz Collection, Jackson County Historical Society, Independence, Missouri, folder 275.02 F16 2004-102.

6. *TP*, 297.

7. "Evan Connell," *Bitter Bird* 2, no. 4 (Spring 1947), Spencer.

8. Connell and Glenn Williams, "Flaw on the Kaw," *Bitter Bird* 2, no. 3 (December 1946): 17, Spencer.

9. Connell, "Medical Ethics," *Bitter Bird* 2, no. 1 (October 1946): 5, 23, Spencer. Connell's father was of the generation greatly influenced by William Osler's essay "Aequanimitas" (1889), which was required reading in medical schools.

10. West, *A Country in the Mind*, vii.

11. Connell, "A Cross to Bear," *Foreign Service*, April 1947, 13. Archivists at the Library of Congress and the Veterans of Foreign Wars headquarters in Kansas City, Missouri, unearthed copies.

12. Holt, "Evan S. Connell," 13.

13. Camelia Uzzell to ESC, October 8, 1946, Stanford, box 39, folder 1.

14. Camelia Uzzell to ESC, July 25, 1947, Stanford, box 39, folder 1.

15. Camelia Uzzell to ESC, July 25, 1947, Stanford, box 39, folder 1.

16. "Evan Shelby Connell," transcript, Office of the University Registrar, University of Kansas, Lawrence.

17. Fradkin, *Wallace Stegner and the American West*, 117.

18. Scott Meredith to ESC, February 10, 1948, Stanford, box 39, folder 1.

19. Scott Meredith to ESC, April 2, 1948, Stanford, box 39, folder 1.

20. *CS*, 513-22.

21. Scott Meredith to ESC, April 2, 1948, Stanford, box 39, folder 1.

22. Scott Meredith to ESC, April 16, 1948, Stanford, box 39, folder 1.

23. Scott Meredith, introduction, in P. G. Wodehouse, *The Best of Wodehouse* (New York: Pocket Books, 1949), i.

24. Elizabeth Lawrence to ESC, August 6, 1948, Stanford, box 39, folder 1.

25. Charles Humboldt to ESC, February 15, 1949, Stanford, box 39, folder 1.

26. Wallace Stegner to ESC, June 2, 1949, Stanford, box 39, folder 1.

27. Elaine (Mrs. Robert) Shaplen to ESC, August 19, 1949, Alfred A. Knopf Inc. Records, Ransom, box 814, folder 45.9.

28. Brady, "An Independent Sort." When writing his southern stories, "I was faking it," Connell told Tooker and Hofheins in *Fiction!*, 63.

29. EM to ESC, June 22, 1949, Stanford, box 39, folder 1.

30. Holt, "Evan S. Connell," 13.

31. Connell, "Evan S. Connell," in *CAAS*, 107.

32. EM to ESC, April 27, 1950, Stanford, box 39, folder 1.

33. *TP*, 358.

34. Evan S. Connell Jr., Bicycle Attached Toy Machine Gun, U.S. Patent Office, no. 2,667,720, application filed September 18, 1951; patented February 2, 1954.

35. Webster Schott, "Kansas Citians in Prize Stories," *Kansas City Star*, September 14, 1951, 14. Copy in family scrapbook, Stanford.

36. Webster Schott, interviews with author, February 2020.

37. Connell, "Evan S. Connell," in *CAAS*, 108.

38. William Styron to EM, April 20, 1952, Harold Matson Company Inc. Records, 1937-80, Butler Rare Book and Manuscript Library, Columbia University, New York, series J: Box cataloged 6, folder 1952.

39. Sieff, "A Visit with Evan Connell," 260.

40. Sterling North, "A Story of Permanent Childhood," *Washington Post*, March 19, 1950, B7.

41. MS to Minnie Russell Steele, September 9, 1952, Wilson, box 9, folder 61.

42. MS to Minnie Russell Steele, December 8, 1952, Wilson, box 9, folder 61.

43. Connell, "Beginnings," 10.

44. ESC to Eugene F. Saxton Memorial Trust, December 7, [1952], Stanford, box 39, folder 1.

45. ESC to Saxton Memorial Trust, March 12, [1953], Stanford, box 39, folder 1.

46. Connell, "Evan S. Connell," in *CAAS*, 108.

47. Connell, "Evan S. Connell," in *CAAS*, 108.

48. ESC to MS, March 8, [1953], Wilson, box 9, folder 62.

49. Connell, "Evan S. Connell," in *CAAS*, 109.

50. Connell, "Evan S. Connell," in *CAAS*, 109.
51. Simon Michael Bessie to Mavis McIntosh, undated memo, probably 1953, Stanford, box 39, folder 1.
52. ESC to MS, June [1953], Wilson, box 28, folder 216.
53. ESC to MS, March 8, [1953], Wilson, box 9, folder 62.
54. *AL*, 6; *CS*, 525.
55. *CS*, 536.
56. Lloyd Maffitt, "Smorgasbord," *Burlington [IA] Hawkeye Gazette*, August 19, 1953, 11.
57. ESC to MS, March 8, [1953], Wilson, box 9, folder 62.
58. ESC to EW, January 9, [1956], Eugene Walter Collection, Ransom, box 5, folder 11.
59. *LIUP*, 79.
60. ESC to MS, June [1953], Wilson, box 28, folder 216.
61. ESC to MS, June [1953], Wilson, box 28, folder 216.
62. ESC to MS, Wednesday, c. July [1953], Wilson, box 28, folder 216.
63. ESC to MS, Wednesday, c. July [1953], Wilson, box 28, folder 216.
64. ESC to MS, Wednesday, c. July [1953], Wilson, box 28, folder 216.

Chapter 4

1. William Styron, "Letter to an Editor," *Paris Review* 1, no. 1 (1953), https://www.theparisreview.org/letters-essays/5220/letter-to-an-editor-william-styron.
2. Sawyer-Lauçanno, *Continual Pilgrimage*, 152–53.
3. Jack Massee, "Work of Kansas City Writer Appears in Paris English-Language Review," *Kansas City Times*, March 22, 1955, 28.
4. George Plimpton to William Styron, September 22, 1953, *Paris Review* Papers, Morgan Library, New York (hereafter "Morgan"), box 8, folder: Editorial Correspondence: Plimpton, George: 1953. The plan evolved and largely dissolved over the next five years, save for an extended interview Plimpton famously published in 1958.
5. George Plimpton to MS, September 10, 1953, Morgan, box 8, folder: Editorial Correspondence: Plimpton, George: 1953.
6. George Plimpton, interview in "Evan S. Connell: Aspects of an American Writer."
7. "Advance-Guard Advance," *Newsweek*, March 30, 1953, 94.
8. *CS*, 544.
9. *CS*, 544.
10. *AL*, 56-58; *CS*, 69-71.
11. *CS*, 261.
12. Tooker and Hofheins, *Fiction!* 67.
13. *ATC*, 162; *CS*, 267.
14. *ATC*, 163; *CS*, 268.
15. *ATC*, 167; *CS*, 271.

16. "Christopher Logue: The Art of Poetry LXVI," *Paris Review* 127 (Summer 1993): 248.

17. Connell, "Evan S. Connell," in *CAAS*, 108.

18. Sawyer-Lauçanno, *Continual Pilgrimage*, 153.

19. ESC to MS, November 16, [1953], Wilson, box 28, folder 216. No such movie project is documented in the Circle in the Square Papers at the New York Public Library for the Performing Arts, Billy Rose Theatre Division.

20. ESC to MS, November 16, [1953], Wilson, box 28, folder 216.

21. ESC to MS, April 7, [1954], Wilson, box 28, folder 216.

22. ESC to MS, August 19, [1954], Wilson, box 28, folder 216.

23. ESC to EW, July 23, [1954], Eugene Walter Collection, Ransom, box 5, folder 11.

24. Connell subverts the experience in a later short story, "The Voyeur," by channeling the model's point of view.

25. No evidence of an early, conventional version of the novel exists in Connell's papers.

26. Brady, "An Independent Sort."

27. ESC to MS, November 16, [1953], Wilson, box 28, folder 216.

28. ESC to MS, April 7, [1954], Wilson, box 28, folder 216.

29. ESC to EW, July 23, [1954], Eugene Walter Collection, Ransom, box 5, folder 11.

30. EM to ESC, April 20, 22, 1954, Stanford, box 39, folder 1.

31. Joe Fox to McIntosh McKee (EM's partner in the agency was Mavis McIntosh), January 10, 1955, Stanford, box 39, folder 1.

32. Peter Davison to ESC, June 17, 1954, Stanford, box 39, folder 1.

33. Robert Loomis to Mavis McIntosh, November 2, 1954, Stanford, box 39, folder 1.

34. Cass Canfield Jr. to EM, November 11, 1955, annotated copy in Stanford, box 39, folder 1.

35. ESC to MS, August 19, [1954], Wilson, box 28, folder 216.

36. ESC to MS, December 15, [1954], Wilson, box 28, folder 216.

37. George Plimpton to multiple recipients, April 25, 1955, Morgan, box 8, folder: Editorial Correspondence: Plimpton, George, 1955.

38. George Plimpton to ESC, February 22, 1955, Morgan, box 2, folder: Editorial Correspondence: Connell, Evan.

39. ESC to MS, June 6, [1955], Wilson, box 28, folder 216.

40. ESC to MS, June 6, [1955], Wilson, box 28, folder 216.

41. Connell, "Evan S. Connell," in *CAAS*, 112.

42. Joe Fox to EM, November 16, 1955, Stanford, box 39, folder 1.

43. ESC to EW, May 29, [1956], Eugene Walter Collection, Ransom, box 5, folder 11.

44. ESC to EW, January 9, 1956, Eugene Walter Collection, Ransom, box 5, folder 11.

45. EM to ESC, June 29, [1956], Stanford, box 39, folder 1.

46. ESC to EW, January 29, [1954], Eugene Walter Collection, Ransom, box 5, folder 11.

47. Connell, untitled article manuscript, Genesis West Collection, Ransom, box 3, folder 4.

48. Candida Donadio to ESC, October 4, 1956, Stanford, box 39, folder 1.

49. EM to ESC, October 10, 1956, Stanford, box 39, folder 1.

50. EM to ESC, October 8, 1956, Stanford, box 39, folder 1.

51. ESC to EW, January 9, [1956], Eugene Walter Collection, Ransom, box 5, folder 11.

52. ESC to MS, April 12, [1957], Wilson, box 28, folder 216.

53. ESC to MS, November 16, [1953], Wilson, box 28, folder 216.

54. Connell, "Evan S. Connell," in *CAAS*, 109.

55. Benson, *The Ox-Bow Man*, 294.

56. Carpenter, *Fridays at Enrico's*, 12.

57. Connell, "Evan S. Connell," in *CAAS*, 109.

58. Connell, "Westward to Elusive Eden," review of Stegner's *Where the Bluebird Sings to the Lemonade Springs*, *Tampa [FL] Tribune*, May 3, 1992, 116.

59. ESC, interview with Patrick Lannan, March 29, 2010, Lannan Foundation Archives, Santa Fe, NM.

60. Viking Press spring books advertisement, *Publishers Weekly*, January 7, 1957, 7.

61. Siegfried Mandel, "In the Secrecy of the Heart," *New York Times*, May 19, 1957, T3.

62. ESC to Walter Clark, undated, spring 1958, Stanford, box 39, folder 1.

63. I once wrote a brief essay for the Biographers International Organization newsletter about the enormous challenge of reading Clark's handwriting. I'm grateful for the deciphering help given to me by Jacquelyn K. Sundstrand, an archivist at the University of Nevada-Reno library, where Clark's papers are deposited.

64. Undated response written on ESC's letter to Clark of spring 1958, Stanford, box 39, folder 1.

65. C. M. Newman to Candida Donadio, July 22, 1957, *New Yorker* Collection, New York Public Library (hereafter "NYPL"), box 750, folder 16.

66. Helen Taylor to ESC, April 16, 1958, Stanford, box 39, folder 1.

67. Helen Taylor to ESC, April 16, 1958, Stanford, box 39, folder 1.

68. ESC to MS, July 31, [1958], Wilson, box 28, folder 214.

69. Editor's note, *Contact*, no. 1, 1958, 1.

70. William Carlos Williams, "The Contact Story," *Contact*, no. 1, 1958, 75-77.

71. "Mrs. Bridge and the Ruined City," *Contact*, no. 1, 1958, 110.

72. Connell, "Mademoiselle from Kansas City," *Contact*, no. 1, 1958, 111.

73. Connell, "Mademoiselle from Kansas City," 123.

74. "Mrs. Evan S. Connell," *Kansas City Star*, July 9, 1958, 40.

75. Brady, "An Independent Sort."

76. Rebecca Christian, "Mrs. Bridge," *Kansas City Magazine*, December 1988, 13.

77. Christian, "Mrs. Bridge," 16.

78. ESC to MS, July 31, [1958], Wilson, box 28, folder 214.

Chapter 5

1. Wallace Stegner to ESC, December 20, 1958, Stanford, box 39, folder 1.

2. Helen Hull to ESC, December 24, 1958, Stanford, box 39, folder 1.

3. Helen Taylor to ESC, December 11, 1958, Stanford, box 39, folder 1.

4. Helen Taylor to ESC, January 15, 1959, Stanford, box 39, folder 2.

5. Thorpe Menn, "More about Books and Authors," *Kansas City Star*, January 17, 1959, 6.

6. ESC to MS, October 26, [1958], Wilson, box 28, folder 214.

7. Viking publicity sheet, Stanford, box 39, folder 1.

8. Charles Poore, "Books of the Times," review of *Mrs. Bridge*, *New York Times*, February 7, 1959, 17.

9. Dudley Fitts, "A Masterpiece from Brazil," *New York Times Book Review*, July 13, 1952, 4.

10. In June 2020, Penguin Classics published a new edition of the Machado novel under its original title (in English), *The Posthumous Diary of Brás Cubas*, translated by Flora Thompson-DeVeaux and with an introduction by Dave Eggers, who called it the wittiest book ever written. A second translation, by Margaret Jull Costa and Robin Patterson, was also published in 2020 by Liveright. One reviewer preferred the latter. See Parul Sehgal, "Crossing Over to the Other Side on a Hippo," *New York Times*, June 17, 2020, C5.

11. The Pacifica Radio Archives include the recording of a reading of the entire novel, by Rella Lossy, a Bay Area poet and theater critic, dated 1962; see https://www.pacificaradioarchives.org/recording/bb1107. The recordings have not been digitized.

12. ESC to MS, December 17, [1958], Wilson, box 28, folder 214.

13. ESC to MS, November 23, [1958], Wilson, box 10, folder 72.

14. Luther Nichols, "Dissecting the Mink Brigade," *San Francisco Examiner*, January 18, 1959, 108.

15. William Hogan, "A Striking New Novel: Connell's 'Mrs. Bridge,'" *San Francisco Chronicle*, January 19, 1959, 29.

16. ESC to MS, January 20, [1959], Wilson, box 28, folder 214.

17. Webster Schott, "Kansas City Society Life Is Subject of Major Novel," *Kansas City Star*, January 10, 1959, 1, 16.

18. Florence Crowther, "Stranded Matriarch," *New York Times*, February 1, 1959, 30.

19. Charles Poore, "Books of the Times," *New York Times*, February 7, 1959, 17.

20. Fanny Butcher, "Portrait of Womanhood?" *Chicago Tribune*, January 25, 1959, 178.

21. Dorothy Parker, "Book Reviews: An End to Beating about the Bush," *Esquire*, March 1959, 20.

22. ESC to MS, March 15, [1959], Wilson, box 28, folder 214.

23. Polsgrove, *It Wasn't Pretty, Folks*, 52.

24. ESC to MS, March 15, [1959], Wilson, box 28, folder 214.

25. ESC to MS, January 20, [1958], Wilson, box 28, folder 214.

26. My efforts to find Shaber's papers were unsuccessful. EM to ESC, July 26, 1961, Stanford, box 39, folder 2.

27. John Updike to ESC, March 16, [1959], Stanford, box 39, folder 2.

28. ESC to MS, August 17, [1957], Wilson, box 28, folder 214.

29. ESC to MS, February 16, [1959], Wilson, box 28, folder 214.

30. ESC to MS, March 15, [1959], Wilson, box 28, folder 214. Sexual double entendres appear with some frequency in Connell's letters to Steele. The two men seemed to have shared an interest in soft-porn postcards, though none exists in Connell's papers.

31. ESC to MS, December 13, [1959], Wilson, box 10, folder 72.

32. ESC to MS, December 13, [1959], Wilson, box 10, folder 72.

33. ESC to Byron Shutz, October 31, [1957], Jackson County Historical Society, Independence, MO.

34. ESC to George Plimpton, June 15, [1959], Morgan, box 8, folder: Editorial Correspondence: Plimpton, George: 1959.

35. Gold, *Fiction of the Fifties*, 9.

36. Gold, *Fiction of the Fifties*, 19.

37. Gold, *Fiction of the Fifties*, 21.

38. "*Fiction of the Fifties*," *Kirkus*, November 1, 1959, https://www.kirkus reviews.com/book-reviews/herbert-ed-gold/fiction-of-the-fifties/.

39. A few years later, nevertheless, Connell found himself surrounded by some Beats and other rebellious writers in another anthology. His story "The Fisherman from Chihuahua" appeared in *Writers in Revolt*, a collection of "the most controversial writing in the world today," edited by Terry Southern, Richard Seaver, and Alexander Trocchi (New York: Berkley Medallion, 1965). Seaver and Trocchi probably knew Connell from the *Paris Review* days and Café Tournon.

40. Roy Perrott, "Big Strange Writing," *Guardian*, March 11, 1960, 7.

41. ESC to MS, April 1, [1959], Wilson, box 28, folder 214.

42. William Styron to ESC, January 3, 1961, Stanford, box 39, folder 2.

43. *Best Short Stories from* The Paris Review, 15.

44. Neal Morgan, "WLB Biography: Evan S. Connell Jr." *Wilson Quarterly Bulletin*, April 1965, 695, quoted in Blaisdell, "After Ground Zero," 186. Blaisdell mistakenly dated the citation as 1963.

45. Plutarch, *Parallel Lives*, quoted in "Introduction to the Work of Plutarch," Great Thinkers, https://thegreatthinkers.org/plutarch/introduction/.

46. *MrsB*, 239.
47. Blaisdell, "After Ground Zero," 187.
48. Blaisdell, "After Ground Zero," 187.
49. *Mrs. B*, 102-3.
50. Blaisdell, "After Ground Zero," 188.
51. Oppenheimer, "An Era of Awkward Obsession."
52. Meg Wolitzer, interview with author, May 29, 2019.
53. Meg Wolitzer, "In Praise of Evan S. Connell," *New York Times*, January 25, 2018, https://www.nytimes.com/2018/01/25/books/evan-s-connell-mrs-bridge.html.
54. Meg Wolitzer, email with author, June 28, 2020. For a fully feminist reading of India Bridge, see Dana Heller, "The Culture of 'Momism,'" in *Family Plots: The De-Oedipalization of Popular Culture* (Philadelphia: University of Pennsylvania Press, 1995), 60-76.
55. Oppenheimer, "An Era of Awkward Obsession."

Chapter 6

1. ESC to MS, November 30, [1959], Wilson, box 10, folder 75.
2. Norman Mailer, "The Mind of an Outlaw," *Esquire*, November 1, 1959, https://classic.esquire.com/article/1959/11/1/the-mind-of-an-outlaw.
3. ESC to MS, November 30, [1959], Wilson, box 28, folder 214.
4. MS to ESC, January 2, [1960], attached to ESC to MS, December 13, [1959], Wilson, box 10, folder 72. Steele dated his letter 1959, but it is clear from internal evidence that he overlooked the turning of a new year.
5. ESC to MS, February 18, [1960], marked "copy," Wilson, box 11, folder 76.
6. Luther Nichols, quoted in an advertisement in *Contact 3*, 1959, 156.
7. ESC to MS, December 17, [1958], Wilson, box 28, folder 214.
8. Walter Van Tilburg Clark, "A Timely Coming—WR and RW," *Contact 3*, 1959, 53.
9. ESC to MS, July 4, [1959], Wilson, box 28, folder 214.
10. Thorpe Menn, "Books of the Day," *Kansas City Star*, September 9, 1959, 20, quoted in "Contributors," *Contact 3*, 1959, 151.
11. Phoebe Lou Adams to EM, July 15, 1958, Stanford, box 39, folder 1.
12. Connell, "Notes from a Bottle Found on the Beach at Carmel," *Contact 3*, 1959, 135.
13. Connell, "Notes from a Bottle," 136.
14. Whatever remained of Connell's library after his death ended up mostly in his family's hands. A niece's daughter shared with me Connell's copy of an edition of Hemingway's short stories, which he had filled with light pencil marks though no annotations.
15. Connolly's book contains several superficial connections to Connell's interests in *Notes from a Bottle*, beginning with the pseudonymous narrator, Palinurus, who in Virgil's *Aeneid* was the ill-fated helmsman. It is possible, though

unsubstantiated, that Connell borrowed the device of the navigator, who addresses readers in *Notes*. Other subjects Connolly touches on and Connell explores in varying ways include love and decaying marriage, natural science, alchemy, and specifically the alchemist Paracelsus, who plays a leading role in future Connell books. The French essayist Montaigne may provide an intellectual bridge between the two writers. Elsewhere in this book, Lewis Lapham equates Connell with Montaigne. Here is a piece of William Boyd's assessment of Connolly in *The Unquiet Grave*: "Connolly is no Montaigne, he has none of his calm, resigned sagacity (though Montaigne is one of the presiding spirits of the book), but Connolly captures something ineffably present in the human spirit." Boyd, "Lessons in the Art of Living." If Connell and Connolly never crossed paths, they certainly shared a sense of the human and literary spirit.

16. Myers, "Notes from a Bottle," 64.

17. ESC to MS, October 27, [1959], Wilson, box 28, folder 214.

18. Connell, "In a Strange World with Amazing New Drug," *Kansas City Times*, June 14, 1962, 10F, clipping at Stanford.

19. ESC to David Streitfeld, March 30, [probably 2008], private collection. Connell professed to enjoying Denham's 2006 memoir ("compulsively readable"), though he said she mostly misquoted him and erred in the majority of details. He never met Alpert, for instance, or Timothy Leary, and the chronology of their careers would seem to back him up.

20. Denham, *Sleeping with Bad Boys*, 170–72.

21. Spurred by an article he had read recently and aware of Connell's experience, Thorpe Menn, the Kansas City book critic, speculated in print about whether Connell was offering "the literary equivalent of the chemical LSD." See Menn, "Books of the Day," *Kansas City Star*, May 19, 1963, 13D.

22. See E. T. Guidotti, "Una Limpia de Bruja," and Dr. J. L. D. Lamm, "Through a Mushroom Darkly," *Contact 18,* 4, no. 4, April–May 1964, 11-15.

23. ESC to MS, April 1, [1960], Wilson, box 28, folder 214.

24. Stoll, *I Am a Lover*, 1.

25. The record of Jill Strohn in Connell's life remains thin, but she appears like a wisp in a couple of letters I retrieved late in my research. She was "beautiful and very sweet," and they dated for a few years. Connell mentions "my lady" Jill in a letter to Max Steele as early as July 31, 1958. Once, when she moved into an apartment off a shady North Beach alley, Connell "delivered my Dutch Uncle lecture" and told her she shouldn't stay there. The episode clearly inspired Connell's story "Valentine's Day." It begins with a line reflecting Strohn's actual art practice at the time: "McCrae looked at the delicate tissue paper collages Julie had pinned to a slab of cork above the sink." *CS*, 406; ESC to David Streitfeld, undated, c. 1990s, and March 30, [probably 2008], private collection.

26. Barr and Sachs, *The Artists' and Writers' Cookbook*, 105. Thirty-five years later, Connell was asked to contribute to a new edition of *The Great American Writers' Cookbook*. He confessed that he didn't cook and added

an interest in a previous entry: "'The Career-Woman's Meal' by Joyce Carol Oates, which involves opening a can, sounds impossibly difficult," he wrote. "I will study it." ESC to Dean Faulkner Wells, November 22, [1996], Stanford, box 41, folder 2.

27. ESC to MS, May 24, [1960], Wilson, box 28, folder 214.

28. *TP*, 32.

29. *TP*, 82.

30. *TP*, 332-43.

31. Nolte, "Evan S. Connell, Jr.," 101.

32. *TP*, 258-63.

33. Jonathan Quandt, a Barr stepson, interview with author, November 23, 2020.

34. Jack C. Botts, "Bare Unrealities of Today," *Lincoln [NE] Star Journal*, September 25, 1960, 37.

35. ESC to MS, November 28, [1960], Wilson, box 28, folder 214.

36. Granville Hicks, "Flyer Out of Formation," *Saturday Review of Literature*, September 24, 1960, 16.

37. Webster Schott, "The Trouble Is the Hero Is Negative," *Kansas City Star*, September 24, 1960, 9.

38. ESC to MS, November 28, [1960], Wilson, box 28, folder 214.

39. Connell, "San Francisco: The Golden Gate," 18.

40. Connell, "San Francisco: The Golden Gate," 25, 18.

41. Lamott, "San Francisco: San Quentin," 25-31.

42. Kentfield, "San Francisco: The Waterfront," 104.

43. Thorpe Menn, "Books of the Day," *Kansas City Star*, July 21, 1963, 107.

44. Richard G. Hubler, "Variations on the Flying Dutchman," *Los Angeles Times*, May 19, 1963, 485.

45. Kenneth Lamott, "The Spirit of Man," *Contact 13*, 3, no. 5, December 1962, 1.

46. Helen Taylor to ESC, May 17, 1962, Stanford, box 39, folder 2. Connell's likely response to Taylor has not been located.

47. Richard Barker, "Gingerbread in a Bottle," *San Francisco Examiner*, May 12, 1963, 161.

48. Hubler, "Variations on the Flying Dutchman," 485.

49. Quoted in Mark Oppenheimer, "Searching for Evan S. Connell's Bohemian Sausalito," *New York Times*, March 25, 2015, TR10.

50. ESC to GB, December 5, [1966], private collection.

Chapter 7

1. Robert Sylvester, "Dream Street," *New York Daily News*, October 11, 1957, 72; Cholly Knickerbocker, "The Smart Set," *Shamokin [PA] News Dispatch*, December 5, 1957, 6; Earl Wilson, "It Happened Last Night," *The Tribune* [Scranton, PA], December 14, 1957, 13 (syndicated); Charles McHarry,

"On the Town," *New York Daily News*, October 3, 1958, 56; Earl Wilson, "Maui Girl in New York Gets Touch of Stardust," *Honolulu Star-Bulletin*, November 12, 1958, 22.

2. A *New York Times* review from that year confirms the production though does not list Garnett as an opening cast member. Brooks Atkinson, "Theatre: Two by Ionesco," *New York Times,* June 4, 1958, 39. Still, it is conceivable she understudied.

3. Earl Wilson, "Maui Girl in New York Gets Touch of Stardust," *Honolulu Star Bulletin*, November 12, 1958, 24.

4. Mary Campbell, "Young Actress Also Writes, Sings," *Rocky Mount [NC] Telegram*, January 13, 1965, 3A, and other newspapers around the same time.

5. Mary Campbell, "Gale Garnett: Rural Sound," *Sunday News* (Lancaster, PA), May 10, 1964, 28.

6. GZG to John Huston, undated [November-December 1965]; Gladys Hill to GZG, January 4, 1966, John Huston Collection, Margaret Herrick Library, Academy of Motion Pictures Arts and Sciences, Beverly Hills, California (hereafter "Herrick").

7. GZG, interview with author, October 25-26, 2017.

8. Curt Gentry to ESC, quoting Dave Deck, July 25, 1966, Stanford, box 39, folder 3.

9. Connell, "New Titles from the Creative Publishing House across the Bay," *San Francisco Sunday Chronicle*, October 7, 1962, 34.

10. C. M. Newman to EM, February 7, 1963, *New Yorker* Collection, NYPL, box 798, folder: Connell, Evan Editorial Correspondence, Fiction 1963. The story has never turned up under that name, and indeed rare is the extant manuscript of an unpublished Connell story. His papers include a list of thirty odd titles labeled "Unpublished Stories," circa 1963. Most of those probably existed in his agent Elizabeth McKee's files, before her firm's merger with the Harold Matson agency in 1965. But those documents, if they exist, appear to be lost. Ben Camardi of the Matson Company reported in an email (with author, January 4, 2018) that after McKee's death in 1996 only her Flannery O'Connor files were salvaged.

11. MS to EM, August 27, 1963, Wilson, box 12, folder 88.

12. George P. Elliott, "Why Are They Driving Me Crazy?" *Contact 14,* 3, no. 6, April 1963, 46-48.

13. Kenneth Lamott, "California! California!" *Contact 14,* 3, no. 6, April 1963, 63-68.

14. "With Blank and Blank for Blank," *Contact 14,* 3, no. 6, April 1963, 88. In December 2020, the *Kansas City Star* prominently investigated and apologized for its own history of ignoring and poorly covering the Black community.

15. Connell's interest in racial strife in the United States extended to a subsequent issue of *Contact*. Issue 20 (4, no. 6), in October–November 1964,

included the transcript of an interview with the comedian and activist Dick Gregory entitled "Jim Crow's Funeral." Among other topics, which may resonate with readers today, the piece covered the police killing that year of James Powell, a Black teenager, which was followed by demonstrations in Harlem that turned violent.

16. Grover Sales, "Presenting . . . the Kornfelds," *San Francisco Sunday Examiner and Chronicle*, July 9, 1972, 16-21.

17. Anita Clay Johnson, "Where the Beat and the Neat Folk Meet," *Kansas City Star*, September 29, 1963, 17E.

18. Ken Lamott, "Two Reviews," *Contact 11*, 3, no. 3, August 1962, 68.

19. Ken Lamott, "The Warriors," *Contact 16*, 4, no. 2, October–November 1963, 72.

20. Richard Harrity, "Bohemia on the Bay," *Cosmopolitan*, December 1963, 22-27.

21. Untitled editor's note, *California Magazine*, February 1985, 5.

22. John Clellon Holmes, "The Philosophy of the Beat Generation," *Esquire*, February 1958, https://classic.esquire.com/article/1958/2/1/the-philosophy-of-the-beat-generation.

23. ESC to David Streitfeld, March 30, [probably 2008], private collection.

24. Linda Carfagno, email with author, January 28, 2021.

25. GZG to ESC, January 12–13, 1965, Stanford, box 39, folder 2.

26. GZG to John Huston, December 29, 1965, Herrick.

27. "Is Anybody Listening?" *Contact 15*, 4, no. 1, July 1963, 3.

28. Max Steele, "The Most Exciting Magazine," *San Francisco Examiner*, November 17, 1963, Book Week 26.

29. Quoted in Steele, "Most Exciting Magazine."

30. ESC to David [Stacton], June 26, [1963], Stanford.

31. Steele, "Most Exciting Magazine," 27.

32. ESC to Gordon Lish, undated, c. 1965, Genesis West Collection, Ransom, box 3, folder 4.

33. ESC to Wallace Stegner, undated, Stegner Papers, Stanford.

34. Ellen Bry, "Erratic Marin-Based Magazine Has Most Status in Far Climes," *San Rafael [CA] Daily Independent Journal*, June 11, 1965, 18.

35. William Hogan, "Books," *San Francisco Sunday Examiner and Chronicle*, December 12, 1965, 219.

36. Ken Lamott to Gordon Lish, August 5, [1965], and August 16, 1965, Genesis West Collection, Ransom, box 4, folder 1.

37. *LIUP*, 149, 150, 210.

38. *LIUP*, x–xi.

39. Harold Gratzmacher, "At the Crossroads," *Chicago Tribune*, July 11, 1965, 211.

40. Irwin Gold, "Connell's Skills in 12 Vignettes," *Los Angeles Times*, July 18, 1965, Calendar 3.

41. Donald Stanley, "First-Rate Fiction," *San Francisco Examiner*, June 22, 1965, 33.

42. Prescott, "The Satirical Comedy of Evan S. Connell."

43. *ATC*, 19, 14, 55; *CS*, 333, 329, 355.

44. *ATC*, 57, 66–67; *CS*, 155, 161.

45. Carl Rollyson, *The Last Days of Sylvia Plath* (Jackson: University Press of Mississippi, 2020), 112.

46. Prescott, "The Satirical Comedy of Evan S. Connell."

47. Auchincloss, "The World Is Not a Wedding."

48. Siegel, "The Iconoclastic Mr. Connell."

49. The story appeared fifteen years later in *Saint Augustine's Pigeon*, ostensibly a collection of short fiction. Quotes come from that edition. Connell's editor at North Point, now at Counterpoint, Jack Shoemaker, told me that he always understood the encounter occurred: "Evan did make the visit relayed in the *Esquire* piece, or so I was always told, and we were quite aware we were inserting a nonfiction piece into a collection that otherwise contained only fiction. Gus Blaisdell did that on purpose, saying he thought it was one of the best things Evan had ever written." Shoemaker, email with author, December 19, 2019.

50. Siegel, "The Iconoclastic Mr. Connell."

51. *SAP*, 282, 287; Connell, "A Brief Essay on the Subject of Celebrity with Numerous Digressions and Particular Attention to the Actress, Rita Hayworth," *Esquire,* March 1, 1965, https://classic.esquire.com/article/1965/3/1/a-brief-essay-on-the-subject-of-celebrity.

52. Shapiro, *The Bourgeois Poet*, 89.

53. Harold Matson Company Records, Rare Book and Manuscript Library, Butler Library, Columbia University, New York (hereafter "Butler"), box 62, folder McIntosh McKee and Dodds, 1965. In 1965, Elizabeth McKee merged her firm into the Harold Matson Company, whose records, unlike McKee's, remain largely accessible, though incomplete in Connell's case.

Chapter 8

1. Associated Press, "Beauty Queen Assaulted; Fiance Captures Assailant," *San Francisco Examiner*, January 12, 1956, 5.

2. *Contact 6*, 2, no. 6, October 1960, 1.

3. *SAP*, 210.

4. Bensky, "Meet Evan Connell."

5. ESC to GB, October 1, [1966], private collection.

6. Tooker and Hofheins, *Fiction!* 59.

7. *DR*, 5.

8. Thomas Hardy, "In Tenebris II," quoted in "Thomas Hardy," Poetry Foundation, https://www.poetryfoundation.org/poets/thomas-hardy.

9. GZG, interview with author, October 25-26, 2017.

10. Eliot Fremont-Smith, "'In Cold Blood' Success," *Herald Magazine* (Calgary, AB), February 18, 1966, 7.

11. Connell, "'In Cold Blood': A Dissenting Voice," *San Francisco Chronicle*, January 16, 1966, 32.

12. Marjorie Driscoll, "Diary of Disintegration," *Los Angeles Times*, May 1, 1966, Calendar section, 12.

13. Roger Shattuck, "Fiction à la Mode," *New York Review of Books*, June 23, 1966, https://www.nybooks.com/articles/1966/06/23/fiction-a-la-mode/.

14. MS to Pat McNees (of Harper and Row), May 10, 1966, Wilson, box 13, folder 99.

15. Bottoms, "Interview."

16. Homes, Introduction, xii.

17. ESC to MS, June 17, [1966], Wilson, box 28, folder 214.

18. Blaisdell, "After Ground Zero," 181.

19. Blaisdell, "After Ground Zero," 183.

20. Blaisdell, "After Ground Zero," 191, 199.

21. Blaisdell, "After Ground Zero," 202

22. Leiris, *Manhood*, 103.

23. Leiris, *Manhood*, 4.

24. Blaisdell, "After Ground Zero," 205.

25. ESC to GB, September 13, [1966], private collection.

26. Evan Connell Sr. to GB, October 3, 1966, private collection.

27. ESC to GB, September 13, [1966], private collection.

28. ESC to GB, September 13, [1966], private collection.

29. ESC to GB, October 1, [1966], private collection.

30. Matthiessen, *At Play in the Fields of the Lord*, 2.

Chapter 9

1. Draft of *Mr. Bridge*, Stanford, box 3, folder 1.

2. Presson, *New Letters on the Air.*

3. *LIUP,* xv.

4. Jean Cantú, interview with author, October 8, 2018.

5. Bensky, "Meet Evan Connell."

6. Albert Morch, "Views from Builder of 'Bridges,'" *San Francisco Examiner*, April 20, 1969, 89.

7. Bensky, "Meet Evan Connell."

8. ESC to RG, January 5, [1968], Alfred A. Knopf Inc. Records, Ransom, box 814, folder 14.

9. ESC to RG, March 30, [1968], Knopf Records, Ransom, box 814, folder 14.

10. *MrB*, 79.

11. Bensky, "Meet Evan Connell."

12. ESC to Toinette Rees, June 21, [1968], Knopf Records, Ransom, box 814, folder 14.

13. ESC to Toinette Rees, June 21, [1968], Knopf Records, Ransom, box 814, folder 14.

14. Calvin Trillin, another product of Kansas City's Southwest High School, wrote a memoir about his father that referenced the social standing of Jews in the WASP world of the Country Club Plaza area and developer J. C. Nichols during the period that parallels the Bridges' fictional era: "Although there were eventually plenty of Jews in the Country Club District, there was a widespread feeling in the late thirties that its developer held the prevailing country club views on how few Jews it took to be too many." Trillin, *Messages from My Father* (New York: Farrar, Straus and Giroux, 1996), 54.

15. *MrB*, 241, 363, 365.

16. *MrB*, 127.

17. Connell, *Mr. Bridge* drafts, Stanford, box 3, folders 1-2.

18. Connell, *Mr. Bridge* drafts, Stanford, box 3, folders 1-2.

19. A *Billboard* review, July 9, 1966, 36, concluded that the highlight was her version of George Gershwin's "It Ain't Necessarily So."

20. ESC to RG, January 5, [1968], Knopf Records, Ransom, box 814, folder 14.

21. ESC to RG, March 30, [1968], Knopf Records, Ransom, box 814, folder 14.

22. Connell, "Forget Me Not."

23. *CS*, 558, 580.

24. Connell, "Threads and Feathers from Everywhere," *New York Times Book Review*, March 3, 1968, 4.

25. ESC to GB, May 9, [1968], private collection.

26. Connell, "A Man's Woman," *New York Times Book Review*, June 23, 1968, 4.

27. Bensky, "Meet Evan Connell."

28. EM to RG, April 26, 1968, Knopf Records, Ransom, box 814, folder 14.

29. ESC to MS, May 21, [1968], Wilson, box 28, folder 220.

30. ESC to MS, May 21, [1968], Wilson, box 28, folder 220.

31. ESC to MS, May 21, [1968], Wilson, box 28, folder 220.

32. *CS*, 477.

33. Siegel, "The Iconoclastic Mr. Connell."

34. Herb Caen, "The Stewardess Joke," *Santa Maria [CA] Times* (syndicated column), November 4, 1968, 24.

35. Blanche Streeter, interview with author, December 12, 2019; Anne Lamott interview with author, December 16, 2019.

36. ESC to RG, Tuesday [undated, 1969], Knopf Records, Ransom, box 814, folder 14.

37. *LIUP*, 73.

38. Albert Morch, "Views from Builder of 'Bridges,'" *San Francisco Examiner*, April 20, 1969, 89.

39. Webster Schott, "The Roundest Square in American Letters," *Life,* October 3, 1969. The article, according to correspondence, appeared only in a San Francisco regional edition and an international edition of *Life*, not the national edition. A clipping, without page numbers, exists in the Max Steele Papers, Wilson, box 28, folder 214. Another clipping and a copy of the international edition article, dated October 13, 1969, can be found in Schott's papers at the Gotlieb Library, Boston University.

40. Webster Schott, interview with author, February 19-20, 2020, and subsequent phone calls.

41. Internal memo to RG from an unidentified colleague, undated [probably May 1968], Knopf Records, Ransom, box 814, folder 14.

42. RG to ESC, May 22, 1968. A version on Knopf letterhead appears in Connell's papers at Stanford, box 39, folder 4; an identical unsigned typescript appears in Gottlieb's papers in the Knopf Records at Ransom, box 814, folder 14.

43. ESC to RG, Friday [undated, May 1968], Knopf Records, Ransom, box 814, folder 14.

44. ESC to RG, June 11, [1968], Knopf Records, Ransom, box 814, folder 14.

45. RG to ESC, May 22, 1968, Stanford, box 39, folder 4.

46. *SAP,* 274–79; see the "Messalina" section, with Ruth as a prostitute. The vignette's title references an ancient Roman royal woman known for her sexual appetite.

47. Wallace Stevens, *Harmonium* (1923), 64, http://wallacestevens.com/wp-content/uploads/2019/01/HARMONIUM-1923-WALLACE-STEVENS.pdf.

48. ESC to RG, January 5, [1968], Knopf Records, Ransom, box 814, folder 14.

49. Connell, "Speaking of Books: 'The Warriors,'" *New York Times Book Review*, December 15, 1968, 2.

50. Connell, "Speaking of Books: 'The Warriors.'"

51. Connell, "From Notes 2," *New Mexico Quarterly* 38, no. 4 (November 1968): 57.

52. Carroll Newman to EM, July 5, 1968, *New Yorker* Records, NYPL, box 835, folder 4.

53. ESC to Toinette Rees, Friday [undated; late November 1968], and December 11, [1968], Knopf Records, Ransom, box 814, folder 14.

54. *Woman by Three.*

55. ESC to Toinette Rees, December 11, 1968, Knopf Records, Ransom, box 814, folder 14.

56. Bensky, "Meet Evan Connell."

57. I am indebted to Carol Sklenicka's *Raymond Carver: A Writer's Life* for some of these details.

58. Sklenicka, *Raymond Carver*, 170.

59. Douglas Unger, "A Woman Who Touches Fame," http://www.doug lasunger.com/Writings-AWomanWhoTouchesFame.html.

60. Lehmann-Haupt, "One Man Who Is an Island."

61. Guy Davenport, "The Dilemmas of a Solid Citizen of Kansas City, Who Had Everything and Nothing," *New York Times Book Review*, April 4, 1969, 1, 30.

62. Webster Schott, "Last Half a Superb American Saga," *Life*, April 25, 1969, 8.

63. Richard Rhodes, "Life of a Kansas City Puritan," *Chicago Tribune*, April 20, 1969, 317.

64. MS to EM, June 3, 1969, Wilson, box 15, folder 111.

65. Schott, "The Roundest Square in U.S. Letters."

66. GZG to ESC, October 23, 1969, Stanford, box 39, folder 4.

67. Gale Zoe Garnett, interview with author, October 25, 2017.

68. GZG to ESC, January 7, 1970, Stanford, box 39, folder 4.

69. Blake Bailey, email with author, January 7, 2020.

70. Connell's niece Janet Zimmermann shared a photograph of the inscription in the family copy of *Mr. Bridge*. Janet Zimmermann, interview with author, October 17, 2018, and subsequent emails; Schott, "The Roundest Square in U.S. Letters."

71. Schott, "The Roundest Square in U.S. Letters."

Chapter 10

1. Dennis Stack, "Kansas City Setting for Movie Next Year," *Kansas City Star*, August 19, 1971, 7.

2. Janet Zimmermann, email with author, September 2, 2020. In fact, Dr. Connell expressly excluded Janet from his will, dated June 15, 1972. Two years later, he restored her as a beneficiary in a codicil written less than two weeks before he died. Probate Court of Jackson County, Missouri, case K119927.

3. ESC to George Hitchcock, October 13, 1971, Kayak Collection, University at Buffalo, State University of New York.

4. Connell, "From Notes 2," *New Mexico Quarterly* 38, no. 4 (1968), http://digitalrepository.unm.edu/nmq/vol38/iss4/26.

5. ESC to MS, July 14, [1973], Wilson, box 28, folder 219.

6. Carpenter, *Fridays at Enrico's*, 151.

7. ESC to MS, July 14, [1973], Wilson, box 28, folder 219.

8. ESC to GB, July 9, [1973], private collection.

9. Myers, "Notes from a Bottle," 65.

10. Holt, "Evan S. Connell."

11. ESC to MS, Saturday [May 10, 1969], Wilson, box 28, folder 220.

12. Connell, "Preface," viii.

13. ESC to MS, Friday [c. October 10, 1969], Wilson, box 28, folder 220.

14. *ATC*, 13; *CS*, 329.

15. Connell, "Legacy of a Maya Lord."

16. "Evan S. Connell: Aspects of an American Writer."

17. Sale, *On Not Being Good Enough*, 146.

18. Details from Pace, "The National Book Award in Fiction." A rather complete record of the National Book Award fiction panel that season also exists in the papers of Jonathan Yardley, longtime book critic and panel chair that year, at the Wilson Library in Chapel Hill, NC.

19. Pace, "The National Book Award in Fiction."

20. ESC to Jonathan Yardley, March 23, [1973], Yardley Papers, Wilson.

21. Leonard, "One Cranberry's Predictions," 39.

22. Pace, "The National Book Award in Fiction."

23. ESC to MS, July 14, [1973], Wilson, box 28, folder 219.

24. ESC to Jonathan Yardley, June 14, [1973], Yardley Papers, Wilson.

25. John Barth to ESC, December 22, 2000, Stanford, box 41, folder 3; ESC to John Barth, January 5, [2001], John Barth Collection, Sheridan Libraries, Johns Hopkins University, Baltimore, Maryland.

26. ESC to GB, July 9, [1973], private collection.

27. Paul West, "Points for a Compass Rose," *New York Times Book Review*, April 29, 1973, 7.

28. ESC to GB, July 9, [1973], private collection.

29. Herbert Mitgang, "Prose Candles for Mankind," *New York Times*, June 30, 1973, 31.

30. Annie Dillard, "Winter Melons," *Harper's*, January 1974, 87, 89.

31. Dillard, "Winter Melons," 89.

32. ESC to Annie Dillard, January 6, [1974], Annie Dillard Papers, Beinecke Rare Book and Manuscript Library, Yale University, New Haven, Connecticut.

33. Annie Dillard to ESC, January 12, 1974, Stanford, box 39, folder 5.

34. RG to ESC, November 5, 1973, Stanford, box 39, folder 5.

35. Undated enclosure with RG to ESC, November 5, 1973, Stanford, box 39, folder 5.

36. RG to ESC, December 11, 1973, Alfred A. Knopf Inc. Records, Ransom, box 814, folder 12.

37. ESC to MS, December 17, [1973], Wilson, box 28, folder 219.

38. *TC*, 168.

39. Adams, "Evan Connell, Connoisseur."

40. "Evan S. Connell: Aspects of an American Writer."

41. Sieff, "A Visit with Evan Connell."

42. Ana Pacheco, "Passion over Practicality," *Santa Fe New Mexican*, May 1, 2011, C7.

43. Edward Weeks, "The Peripatetic Review," *Atlantic Monthly*, September 1974, 102.

44. Guy Davenport, "The Hero Is an Idea, the Setting a Man's Mind," *New York Times Book Review*, September 1, 1974, 4.

45. MS to Alice Adams, September 1, 1974, Alice Adams Papers, Ransom, box 24, folder 3.

46. Alice Adams to MS, September 10, 1974, Alice Adams Papers, Ransom, box 24, folder 3.

47. RG to ESC, November 23, 1974, Knopf Records, Ransom, box 814, folder 12. Gottlieb enclosed a copy of Nina Bourne's memo.

48. ESC to RG, December 11, [1974], Knopf Records, Ransom, box 814, folder 12.

49. ESC to RG, December 11, [1974], Knopf Records, Ransom, box 814, folder 12.

50. Mary B. Ross, "Writer Possessed," *Dartmouth Alumni Magazine*, January–February 1979, 35.

51. Gottlieb, *Avid Reader*, 177.

Chapter 11

1. *ALD*, 162; *ATH*, 346.

2. ESC to MS, undated, c. 1975–76, Wilson, box 28, folder 219.

3. Mary B. Ross, "Writer Possessed," *Dartmouth Alumni Magazine*, January–February 1979, 35.

4. *ALD*, 6; *ATH*, 223.

5. Ross, "Writer Possessed."

6. Lewis Lapham, interview with author, 2018. This is no idle quotation. Connell used Montaigne's motto, *Que sais-je?* as the epigraph to *The White Lantern*, a second volume of essays, which soon followed *A Long Desire*.

7. *MrsB*, 214.

8. Ross, "Writer Possessed."

9. ESC to MS, December 19, [1979], Wilson, box 19, folder 145.

10. Quoted in Lapham, "The Enchanted Loom."

11. *ALD*, 241; *ATH*, 409.

12. ESC to BZ, December 18, [1978], Stanford. All of ESC's letters to his sister were uncatalogued when I saw them.

13. Alice Adams to MS, June 6, 1979, Wilson, box 18, folder 142.

14. Alice Adams to MS, July 23, 1980, Alice Adams Papers, Ransom, box 24, folder 4.

15. Ross, "Writer Possessed."

16. Grover Sales, "Compulsive Tourists Out of the Past in Colorful Living," *Los Angeles Times,* June 3, 1979, 10.

17. Edith Hamilton, "'A Long Desire': Cornucopia of Great Adventures," *Miami Herald*, August 5, 1979, 8DW.

18. ESC to GB, August 9, 1979, private collection.

19. John Leonard, "Celebrating the Scratchers: An Answer for the Itches Caused by an Acute Case of Curiosity," *Baltimore Sun,* June 3, 1980, 18.

20. "Browsing," *Chicago Tribune*, September 21, 1980, sec. 7, p. 6.

21. ESC to GB, February 15, [1980], private collection.

22. James P. Hepworth, "Wallace Stegner, The Art of Fiction No. 118," *Paris Review*, no. 115, Summer 1990, https://www.theparisreview.org/interviews/2314/wallace-stegner-the-art-of-fiction-no-118-wallace-stegner.

23. Ross, "Writer Possessed."

24. ESC to GB, August 6, [1980], private collection.

25. Sieff, "A Visit with Evan Connell."

26. Raymond Carver, "On Writing," *Mississippi Review* 14, no. 1–2 (Winter 1985): 48.

Chapter 12

1. *SOMS*, 297–98.

2. ESC to BZ, June 19, [1982], Stanford.

3. *SOMS*, 298.

4. Rodney G. Thomas, "Indian Casualties of the Little Big Horn," https://littlebighorn.info/Articles/IndianCasualties.pdf.

5. Jack Shoemaker, email with author, March 10, 2020.

6. Elizabeth Lawrence to ESC, February 12, 1987, and ESC to Lawrence, February 19, [1987], courtesy of Bruce Liddic. The original of Lawrence's letter also exists in Connell's papers at Stanford.

7. Sandy Barnard, interview with author, June 26, 2019.

8. Jack Shoemaker, interview with author, May 22, 2018.

9. Jack Shoemaker, interview with author, May 22, 2018, and subsequent emails.

10. ESC to BZ, July 24, [1981], Stanford.

11. Jack Shoemaker, interview with author, May 22, 2018.

12. ESC to BZ, January 3, [1983], Stanford.

13. Chris Goodrich, "Dealing with a Best-Seller," *Small Press* 2, no. 5 (May–June 1985), unpaginated photocopy accessed in Connell's uncatalogued papers, Stanford.

14. *SOMS*, 232.

15. *SOMS*, 148–49.

16. *MrsB*, 107.

17. *SOMS*, 238, 392.

18. *SOMS*, 272.

19. *SOMS*, 276.

20. *SOMS*, 276.

21. *SOMS*, 274.

22. *SOMS*, 303.

23. *SOMS*, 276.

24. ESC to BZ, May 7, [1984], Stanford.

25. ESC to BZ, May 7, [1984], Stanford.

26. ESC to BZ, March 10, [1984], Stanford.

27. ESC to BZ, September 1, [1984], Stanford.

28. ESC to BZ, October 6, [1984], Stanford.

29. Thomas D'Evelyn, "A Great Biography Demystifies Gen. Custer," *San Francisco Examiner,* November 7, 1984, E12.

30. Thom, "Custer Rides to the Little Big Horn."

31. Page Stegner, "General Custer, Immortal in Death," *New York Times Book Review,* January 20, 1985, 10. The *Times* and several other major review outlets did not get around to Connell's book until three months after publication. Most likely all were taken by surprise by its arrival on the widely watched *Times* bestseller list in late December.

32. Dee Brown, "Novelist Brings Custer to Life with Vivid Biography," *Chicago Tribune*, October 14, 1984, Book World, 37, 40.

33. Mary M. Reefer, "Custer and His Last Stand," *Kansas City Star,* November 18, 1984, 1F, 12F. A reader, Joel F. Snyder, objected to the "singularly unenlightened review" in the newspaper's letters column, November 30, 1984, 16A.

34. ESC to BZ, October 14, 1984, Stanford.

35. ESC to BZ, November 1–2, [1984], Stanford.

36. ESC to BZ, November 30, [1984], Stanford.

37. See Carpenter's novel *Fridays at Enrico's.*

38. Quoted in Hjortsberg, *Jubilee Hitchhiker*, 523.

39. ESC to BZ, December 15, [1984], Stanford.

40. Sieff, "A Visit with Evan Connell."

41. The chapbook *Poems for Evan Connell* was self-published. The cover also promised a "foreward" by Anne Lamott, though it's not there, and Lamott told me she didn't remember writing one. As it happens the copy I acquired was owned by Peter Matthiessen and includes a slipped-in typescript poem by Costello, "For Lama Anagarika Govinda." Costello might have known Lama Govinda when he lived in Marin County, California.

42. Jack Shoemaker, interview with author, May 22, 2018.

43. ESC to BZ, December 15, [1984], Stanford.

44. Goodrich, "Dealing with a Best-Seller."

45. Recounted in Grossman, "Literary Lifesaving."

46. Grossman, "Literary Lifesaving."

47. ESC to BZ, January 30, [1984], Stanford.

48. Clyde A. Milner II, "Book Reviews," *American Indian Quarterly* 10, no. 3 (Summer 1986): 246.

49. Lewis Lapham, interview with author, March 5, 2019.

50. "Evan S. Connell: Aspects of an American Writer."

51. Johnny D. Boggs, "Interview with George Custer Expert James Donovan," *Wild West*, April 2, 2009, https://www.historynet.com/interview-with -george-custer-expert-james-donovan.htm.

52. Crouch, *Always in Pursuit*, 7.

53. The other two were chapters in Richard Slotkin's *The Fatal Environment* (1985) and Michael A. Elliott's *Custerology* (2007), which McMurtry was in the process of reviewing.

54. Larry McMurtry, "He Went against the Peace Pipe," *New York Review of Books*, March 6, 2008, http://www.nybooks.com/articles/2008/03/06/he-went -against-the-peace-pipe/.

Chapter 13

1. ESC to BZ, February 17, [1985], Stanford.

2. ESC to GB, March 3, 1985, private collection.

3. ESC to BZ, undated [May 1985], Stanford.

4. ESC to BZ, undated [May 1985], Stanford.

5. Robert Taylor, "Riding with Those Who Rode to the Little Bighorn," *Boston Globe*, February 3, 1985, A10–11.

6. ESC to BZ, July 20, [1985], Stanford.

7. ESC to BZ, September 17, [1985], Stanford.

8. ESC to GB, October 13, 1985, private collection.

9. ESC to BZ, October 30, [1985], Stanford.

10. AL to ESC, August 15, 1985, Stanford.

11. AL to Gerald Shapiro, April 16, 1986, Stanford.

12. ESC to BZ, December 4, [1985], Stanford.

13. ESC to BZ, July 8, [1985], Stanford.

14. Herbert Mitgang, "'World without Walls,' about Beryl Markham," *New York Times,* October 8, 1986, C26.

15. Roderick Mann, "Beryl Markham's Amazing Life Captivates Three Actresses," *Los Angeles Times*, December 9, 1987, part 6, pp. 1, 4.

16. ESC to GB, October 28, 1985, private collection.

17. ESC to GB, October 28, 1985, private collection.

18. ESC to BZ, November 7, [1986], Stanford.

19. ESC to BZ, August 25, [1986], Stanford.

20. ESC to BZ, November 7, [1986], Stanford.

21. ESC to BZ, November 7, [1986], Stanford.

22. Lamott, "A Eulogy for Bill Ryan."

23. ESC to BZ, February 17, [1987], Stanford.

24. Popper, "The Alchemy of Evan Connell."

25. American Academy and Institute of Arts and Letters, Award Program booklet, May 20, 1987, Stanford. The institute dissolved in 1993, succeeded by the American Academy of Arts and Letters.

26. ESC to BZ, June 3, [1987], Stanford.

27. ESC to JZ, August 31, [probably 1986], private collection.

28. Jack Shoemaker, interview with author, 2018.

29. Popper, "The Alchemy of Evan Connell."

30. ESC to BZ, May 8, [1987], Stanford.

31. ESC to BZ, August 31, [1987], Stanford.

32. ESC to BZ, July 8, [1985], Stanford.

33. ESC to BZ, October 17, [1987], Stanford.

34. ESC to JZ, June 1, [1988], private collection.

35. Lawrence Van Gelder, "At the Movies," *New York Times*, January 20, 1989, C6.

36. ESC to BZ, July 15, [1988], Stanford.

37. ESC to Robert Halmi, July 23, 1988, James Ivory Papers, Coll 283, Special Collections and University Archives, University of Oregon Libraries, Eugene. Halmi forwarded the letter to Woodward, Newman, and Merchant.

38. ESC to BZ, August 22, [1988], Stanford.

39. ESC to BZ, April 21, [1989], Stanford.

40. ESC to BZ, April 21, [1989], Stanford.

41. ESC to BZ, May 20, [1989], Stanford.

42. ESC to JZ, August 25, [1989], private collection.

43. Robert W. Butler, "Steady in the Storm," *Kansas City Star*, October 29, 1989, 1, 3E.

44. Kansas City production details come from interviews by the author and the *Kansas City Star*'s robust coverage of the Merchant Ivory team in action from September 8 through November 1989. I was the newspaper's arts editor at the time.

45. Robert Trussell, "Ismail Merchant: Managing the Magic—and the Money for 'Mr. and Mrs. Bridge,'" *Kansas City Star*, October 13, 1989, 18D.

46. Trussell, "Ismail Merchant," 18D.

47. John Pym, "Evan S. Connell," *International Film Quarterly*, Winter 1989/1990, 20–21.

48. "Evan S. Connell: Aspects of An American Writer."

49. "Evan S. Connell: Aspects of An American Writer."

50. Richard Rhodes, email with author, February 12, 2020.

51. "Evan S. Connell: Aspects of An American Writer."

52. Long, *The Films of Merchant Ivory*, 174.

53. Gale Zoe Garnett, interview with author, October 25, 2017.

54. Robert W. Butler, "Paul Newman: Regular Guy," *Kansas City Star*, November 19, 1989, 1, 5D.

55. Sumner, "Evan S. Connell," 28.

56. Janet Zimmermann, email with author, September 2, 2020.

57. Pym, "Evan S. Connell."

58. "North Point Seeks Buyer," *New York Times*, December 18, 1989, 11.

Chapter 14

1. Popper, "The Alchemy of Evan Connell."

2. Wadler, "The Creator of Mr. and Mrs. Bridge."

3. Shapiro, "Evan S. Connell."

4. Paul Pletka, email with author, August 18, 2018; Pletka, interview with author, September 20, 2018.

5. "Evan S. Connell: Aspects of an American Writer."

6. Paul Pletka, interview with author, September 20, 2018.

7. ESC to BZ, May 20, [1989], Stanford.

8. Herbert Gold to ESC, February 18, 1990, Stanford.

9. *PCR*, 109.

10. Christian, "Mrs. Bridge."

11. Shapiro, "Evan S. Connell."

12. Ross Feld, "Evan Connell, The Alchemist's Journal," North Point Press memo, enclosure in ESC to BZ, July 19, [1990], Stanford.

13. Barbara Ras to ESC, September 11, 1990, Stanford, box 41, folder 1.

14. Don Carpenter to ESC, April 24, 1990, Stanford, box 41, folder 1.

15. ESC to JZ, May 30, [1990], private collection.

16. Cathy Smith, interview with author, April 7, 2020.

17. ESC to BZ, June 12, [1990], Stanford.

18. Limerick, "How the West Was (Almost) Lost."

19. Limerick, "How the West Was (Almost) Lost."

20. ESC to BZ, July 19 [1990], Stanford.

21. ESC to BZ, July 19, [1990], Stanford.

22. John M. Carroll, "Son of the Morning Star," *Monthly Film Bulletin,* Winter 1991, 27–29.

23. Republic Pictures Corp. Statement no. 25 for *Son of the Morning Star,* Connell Papers, Stanford, box 29, folder 2.

24. National Archives and Records Administration, *Federal Register, vol. 56, no. 109,* June 6, 1991, p. 26276, https://www.loc.gov/item/fr056109/. Report based on media accounts.

25. Nigel Andrews, "Multilingual Mayhem," *Weekend Financial Times*, September 9, 1990, clipping in Connell Papers, Stanford, box 27, folder 4.

26. "Mr. and Mrs. Bridge," *Variety*, September 10, 1990, clipping in Connell Papers, Stanford, box 1, folder 5.

27. Laura Rollins Hockaday and Robert W. Butler, "'Mr. and Mrs. Bridge' Fever Fills Midland with Applause," *Kansas City Star*, November 16, 1990, C1–2.

28. Wadler, "The Creator of Mr. and Mrs. Bridge."

29. Cathy Smith, interview with author, April 7, 2020.

30. AL to ESC, January 14, 1991, Stanford, box 41, folder 1.

31. Siegel, "The Iconoclastic Mr. Connell."

32. Patricia Holt, "Fighting the Good Fight," *San Francisco Sunday Examiner and Chronicle*, March 24, 1991, review 2.

33. Siegel, "The Iconoclastic Mr. Connell."

34. Streitfeld, "Book Report."

35. Siegel, "The Iconoclastic Mr. Connell." Some information for this account also comes from Katherine Saltzstein, "U.S. Court Clears Publication

of Indians' Side of Shoot-Out," *Albuquerque Journal*, March 17, 1991, 62.

36. Stephen King has long represented a flashpoint in the debate over the relative values of commercial and literary fiction. It is doubtful that Connell ever read him. In my days as book review editor at the *Kansas City Star*, I had to admit that I had never read King, but when *Misery* came out in 1987, I took it on. I wasn't totally sold, but I did experience a belated regard for King's brand of psychological thriller.

37. Joanne Woodward to ESC, April 10, 1991, Stanford, box 41, folder 1.

38. Don Skiles, "A Renaissance Medicine Man," *San Francisco Examiner*, May 12, 1991, review 7.

39. Quoted in ESC to MS, August 16, 1991, Wilson, box 24, folder 185.

40. Sven Birkerts, "A World Ripe with Magic," *New York Times Book Review*, May 12, 1991, 16.

41. Streitfeld, "Book Report."

42. Sumner, "Evan S. Connell: Gentleman or Joker?" 26–28. In recent correspondence, Sumner emphasized she had nothing to do with the headline.

43. Cathy Smith, interview with author, April 7, 2020.

44. Siegel, "The Iconoclastic Mr. Connell." Five years after Connell's death, Hollywood in fact caught up to his explorations into alchemy. *Lodge 49*, a quirky TV series for the AMC channel (later streaming on Hulu), pays a nuanced respect to Connell through an alchemy theme and quoting Paracelsus among others. In one episode, a character is seen holding a copy of *The White Lantern*. The show's creator, Jim Gavin, described his debt to Connell in emails to me, March 2021.

45. ESC to BZ, November 11, 1991, Stanford.

46. *CS*, 39, 40.

47. Bruce Bawer, "Tales of a Lifetime," *New York Times*, 1995, clipping in Evan Connell Alumni File, Rauner.

48. Conger Beasley, "Friends of Mrs. Bridge," *Kansas City Star*, November 19, 1995, J1, 10.

49. Webster Schott, "Captives within Themselves," *New Republic*, October 14, 1957, 20.

50. Robert McG. Thomas Jr., "Don Carpenter, 64, a Novelist Who Wrote about Bleak Lives," *New York Times*, July 30, 1995, 36.

51. Jane Vandenburgh, "Fridays at Enrico's, Don Carpenter's No-Longer-Lost Last Book," *Huffington Post*, April 28, 2014, https://www.huffpost.com/entry/don-carpenters-fridays-at_b_5206931.

52. ESC to WS, August 8, 1996, private collection.

Chapter 15

1. Republished in a single edition, *Joinville and Villehardouin: Chronicles of the Crusades*, translated by Caroline Smith (New York: Penguin, 2009).

2. Richard Benke, "Evan S. Connell's Heroes Ride in from the Crusades," *Associated Press*, January 26, 2000, photocopy of the typescript dispatch in Evan Connell Alumni File, Rauner.

3. ESC to BZ, January 3, [1997], Stanford.

4. ESC to BZ, January 31, [1997], Stanford.

5. ESC to BZ, May 31, [1997], Stanford.

6. ESC to BZ, July 9, [1997], Stanford.

7. ESC to Webster Schott, August 6, [1999], private collection.

8. Brad Fraser, "Garnett's Latest Role," *National Post* (Toronto), September 22, 1999, 28.

9. Fraser, "Garnett's Latest Role," 28.

10. JS, contract detail, photocopy shared in email with author, October 30, 2020.

11. ESC to MS, January 5, 2000, enclosures included a typescript of ESC's three-page essay, addressed to Jack Shoemaker; a Counterpoint press release for *Deus lo Volt!*; and a copy of Shoemaker's "Dear Bookseller" cover letter, Wilson, box 26, folder 201.

12. WS to ESC, January 5, [2000], Stanford, box 41, folder 3.

13. Quoted in ESC to MS, January 29, 2000, Wilson, box 26, folder 201.

14. WS to ESC, April 11, [2000], Stanford, box 41, folder 3.

15. ESC to BZ, undated, c. January 2000, Stanford.

16. Benke, "Evan S. Connell's Heroes Ride in from the Crusades."

17. Roberts, *Diane Rehm Show*. When I asked Diane Rehm about the interview, she had no memory of it, which made sense when I listened to the broadcast and heard it was conducted by a substitute host, Steve Roberts.

18. Jack Shoemaker, email with author, June 22, 2020.

19. Jim Paul, "Blood-Covered Glory," *San Francisco Chronicle Book Review*, April 16, 2000, 1, 6.

20. Marion Lignana Rosenberg, "A Masterly Novelist Re-Creates the Medieval Campaigns in All Their Depravity, Faith and Gore," *Salon*, June 7, 2000, https://www.salon.com/2000/06/07/connell_2/.

21. Emily Wilson, "Taking Jerusalem," *Times Literary Supplement*, August 18, 2000, 24.

22. James Reston Jr., "Onward, Christian Soldiers," *Washington Post Book World*, June 4, 2000, 3.

23. ESC related his phone conversation with MS in a letter to WS, June 7, [2000], private collection.

24. Bottoms, "Evan S. Connell."

25. Morgan Lee, "Writer Rewarded for Life's Work," *Albuquerque Journal*, September 27, 2000, 1.

26. *LIUP*, xx.

27. *LIUP*, 153, 156.

28. *LIUP*, 164.

29. Bottoms, "Interview."

30. Connell, "9/11," *Kansas City Star*, September 8, 2002, 27.

31. ESC to WS, January 28, 2003, private collection.

32. Ferlinghetti, *A Coney Island of the Mind*, 9.

33. Luke Mitchell to ESC, June 19, 2003, enclosure with a letter from ESC to MS, December 5, [2003], Wilson, box 26, folder 205.

34. Letters column, "Portrait of a Malady," *Harper's*, November 2003, 7.

35. ESC to WS, November 12, [2003], private collection.

36. ESC to WS, November 12, [2003], private collection.

37. *Publisher's Weekly*, December 1, 2003; full text reproduced in publicity material enclosed in ESC to MS, December 5, [2003], Wilson, box 26, folder 205.

38. ESC to BZ, February 27, [2004], Stanford.

39. WS to ESC, July 2, 2004, Stanford, box 41, folder 5.

40. Danto, "Shock of the Old," 52.

41. Connell wrote another story about Gutekunst, titled "Mr. Gutemusik," one that his friend had even read and criticized years earlier. Connell agreed that it was unsuccessful and never published it. A typescript copy of the story remains in his papers at Stanford, the only unpublished piece of Connell's short fiction that turned up in my research.

42. JS to ESC, February 9, 2007, courtesy of Janet Zimmermann.

43. *LIUP*, xii.

44. *LIUP*, xii.

45. *LIUP*, xiii.

46. *FG*, 27.

47. ESC to JS, May 16, [2007], Shoemaker Papers, Stanford.

48. David Ulin, "The Outsider," *Los Angeles Times*, July 27, 2008, R4.

49. Scott Ditzler, "Bridging Genres," *Kansas City Star*, April 18, 2010, G1, 10.

50. Connell, "Two Stalwarts among the Ruins," *Harper's*, July 1977, 76.

51. David Ulin, "The Outsider," *Los Angeles Times*, July 27, 2008, R4.

52. Webster Schott, interview with author, February 19, 2020.

Chapter 16

1. Robert Taylor, "Evoking the Legend of Custer's Last Stand," *Boston Globe*, June 27, 1985, 32.

2. "Evan S. Connell: Aspects of an American Author."

3. ESC to MS, August 16, 1991, Wilson, box 24, folder 185.

4. David Treuer, *The Heartbeat of Wounded Knee: Native America from 1890 to the Present* (New York: Riverhead Books, 2019), 62–63.

5. Sieff, "A Visit with Evan Connell," 264.

6. Steele, "My Father's Image."

7. Quoted in Siegel, "The Iconoclastic Mr. Connell."

8. Nicole Blaisdell Ivey, email to author, May 26, 2020.

9. ESC to Nicole Blaisdell Ivey, June 1, 2006, private collection.

10. Geary Hobson, "The Living Batch Bookstore," *Lotsa, Larry Goodell* (blog), December 10, 2012, https://larrygoodell.wordpress.com/2012/12/10/the-living-batch-bookstore-by-geary-hobson.

11. Jane Vandenburgh, interview and emails with author, October 2020.

12. Nancy Benkof and Paul Pletka, interview with author, September 20, 2018.

13. Charlotte Kornstein, interview with author, September 20, 2018.

14. JS to Susan Ramer, March 31, 2009, Donald Congdon Records, Butler, box 113, folder: Evan Connell 2009.

15. *MrsB*, 242.

16. Quoted in D. J. Taylor, "Classic Cases," *Times Literary Supplement*, August 17–24, 2010, 7.

17. Jean Cantú, interview with author, October 8, 2018.

18. Sieff, "A Visit with Evan S. Connell." A longer version of the interview appeared in the *Paris Review,* no. 208 (Spring 2014): 248-65.

19. Linda Carfagno, interview with author, September 21, 2018, and subsequent emails.

20. AL to Gerald Shapiro, April 16, 1986, copy at Stanford.

21. Webster Schott, interview with author, February 20, 2020.

22. Connell, "Genius Unobserved," review of Janet Lewis's *The Wife of Martin Guerre, Atlantic*, December 1969, 156.

23. Stein, "In Memoriam."

24. Richard Seymour, "We called Him Smilin' Jack," January 2013, https://shsociety.squarespace.com/2016-columns/2016/4/5/we-called-him-smilin-jack.

25. Lewis Lapham, interview with author, March 5, 2019.

26. Quoted in Williams, *Imaginations*, xii.

27. A. M. Homes, introduction, in *DR*, viii.

28. Gerald Howard, "Stockholm, Are You Listening?" *Bookforum*, April–May 2020, https://www.bookforum.com/print/2701/why-don-delillo-deserves-the-nobel-23926.

29. Quoted in Howard, "Stockholm, Are You Listening?"

30. Webster Schott, interview with author, February 20, 2020.

31. Jean Cantú, interview with author, October 8, 2018.

32. *PCR*, 29.

33. *FG,* 143.

34. Connell, "The Last Great Traveler," 129.

Bibliography

Primary Sources

Books by Connell

The Alchymist's Journal. San Francisco: North Point Press, 1991. Expanded and retitled edition: *Alchymic Journals.* Berkeley, CA: Counterpoint, 2005.

The Anatomy Lesson and Other Stories. New York: Viking Press, 1957.

At the Crossroads: Stories. New York: Simon and Schuster, 1965.

The Aztec Treasure House: New and Selected Essays. Washington, D.C.: Counterpoint. Includes contents of *A Long Desire* and *The White Lantern.*

The Collected Stories of Evan S. Connell. Washington, D.C.: Counterpoint, 1995.

The Connoisseur. New York: Knopf, 1974.

Deus lo Volt! Chronicle of the Crusades. Washington, D.C.: Counterpoint, 2000.

The Diary of a Rapist. New York: Simon and Schuster, 1966.

Double Honeymoon. New York: G. P. Putnam's Sons, 1976.

Francisco Goya: A Life. New York: Counterpoint/Perseus, 2004.

A Long Desire. New York: Holt, Rinehart and Winston, 1989.

Lost in Uttar Pradesh: New and Selected Stories. Berkeley, CA: Counterpoint, 2008.

Mr. Bridge. New York: Knopf, 1969.

Mrs. Bridge. New York: Viking Press, 1959.

Notes from a Bottle Found on the Beach at Carmel. New York: Viking Press, 1962.

The Patriot. New York: Viking Press, 1960.

Points for a Compass Rose. New York: Knopf, 1973.

Saint Augustine's Pigeon: Selected Stories. San Francisco: North Point Press, 1980.

Son of the Morning Star: Custer and the Little Bighorn. San Francisco: North Point Press, 1984.

The White Lantern. New York: Holt, Rinehart and Winston, 1980.

Uncollected Articles and Essays by Connell

"Beginnings." *The Writer* 83, no. 9 (September 1970): 9–11.

"Evan S. Connell." In *Contemporary Authors Autobiography Series*, 2:97–112. Detroit: Thomson Gale, 1985.

"Forget Me Not." *California Living Magazine*, February 13, 1983, 6–7.

"Introduction." In William Dean Howells, *The Rise of Silas Lapham*, xi–xx. New York: Vintage Books/Library of America, 1991.

"The Last Great Traveler" (profile of Richard Halliburton). *Oxford American* 38 (March–April 2001): 124–29.

"Legacy of a Maya Lord." *Art and Antiques* (January 1987): 75–79.

"Preface." In H. M. Tomlinson, *The Sea and the Jungle*, vii–x. Marlboro, VT: Marlboro Press, 1989.

"San Francisco: The Golden Gate." *Holiday*, San Francisco issue, 29, no. 4 (April 1961): 18, 22–25.

Connell wrote at least four dozen book reviews for the *New York Times, Harper's, Washington Post, Boston Globe, Los Angeles Times, Kansas City Star* (and *Times*), *Atlantic*, and other publications. Some are cited in the text. Articles and essays (other than book excerpts) for the *San Francisco Chronicle, The Writer, Family Weekly* magazine, and others are also cited where appropriate.

Interviews

Brady, John. "An Independent Sort." *The Writer* 124, no. 3 (March 2011): 20–55.

Ditzler, Scott. "Bridging Genres." *Kansas City Star*, April 18, 2010, G1, 10.

Holt, Patricia. "Evan S. Connell." *Publishers Weekly*, November 20, 1981, 12–13.

Lannan, Patrick. Video recording, March 29, 2010. Courtesy of the Lannan Foundation, Santa Fe, New Mexico.

Myers, Edward. "Notes from a Bottle Found on the Beach at Sausalito: An Interview with Evan S. Connell." *Literary Review* 35 (Fall 1991): 60–69. Reprinted in Sylvia Skaggs McTague, ed. *The Muse upon My Shoulder: Discussions of the Creative Process*. Madison, NJ: Fairleigh Dickinson University Press, 2004.

Presson, Rebekah. *New Letters on the Air*. Interview recorded 1989, aired 1991. https://beta.prx.org/stories/91222.

Roberts, Steve. *Diane Rehm Show*, WAMU-FM, April 27, 2000. https://dianerehm.org/audio/#/shows/2000-04-27/evan-connell-deus-lo-volt-counterpoint/104347/@00:00.

Sieff, Gemma. "A Visit with Evan Connell." *Paris Review* 208 (Spring 2014): 248–64.

Son of the Morning Star, addendum to the Recorded Books audio edition, 1984.

Tooker, Dan, and Roger Hofheins, eds. *Fiction! Interviews with Northern California Novelists*. New York: Harcourt Brace Jovanovich, 1976, 55–69.

Miscellany

Barr, Beryl, and Barbara Turner Sachs, eds. *The Artists' and Writers' Cookbook*. Sausalito, CA: Contact Editions, 1961, 105.

Connell, Evan. Self-Portrait. In *Self-Portrait: Book People Picture Themselves, from the Collection of Burt Britton*, 7. New York: Random House, 1976.

"Evan S. Connell: Aspects of an American Writer." Limited-distribution documentary film, made in conjunction with Merchant Ivory Productions, 1990. Associate producer: Donald Rosenfeld; written and narrated by John Pym.

Stoll, Jerry. *I Am a Lover*. Photographs by Jerry Stoll, texts selected by Evan S. Connell Jr. Sausalito, CA: Contact Editions/Angel Island Publications, 1961.

Woman by Three. Photographs by Joanne Leonard, Michael E. Bry, Barbara Cannon Myers. Prose and poetry selected by Evan S. Connell Jr. Menlo Park, CA: Pacific Coast/Farallon Book, 1969.

Secondary Sources

Adams, Gerald. "Evan Connell, Connoisseur." *San Francisco Sunday Examiner California Living Magazine*, February 2, 1975, 18–22.

Ashmore, Helen. "The Brave Old World of Evan S. Connell." *Chouteau Review* 4, no. 1 (1980): 76–88. Reprinted in *Chouteau Review: Selections from the First Ten Years*, edited by David Perkins, vol. 7, nos. 1–2 (1985): 118–27.

Auchincloss, Eve. "The World Is Not a Wedding." *New York Review of Books*, October 28, 1965. http://www.nybooks.com/articles/1965/10/28/the -world-is-not-a-wedding/.

Bailey, Blake. *Cheever: A Life*. New York: Knopf, 2009.

Barnes, Harper. "Kansas City Modern: Growing Pains and Pleasures," *Atlantic* 233, no. 2, (February 1974): 60–67.

Barth, Dan. "Don Carpenter's Last Laugh." *Literary Kicks*, August 28, 2014. https://www.litkicks.com/DonCarpenter.

Beasley, Conger. "Friends of Mrs. Bridge." *Kansas City Star*, November 19, 1995, J1, J10.

Bensky, Lawrence M. "Meet Evan Connell, Friend of Mr. and Mrs. Bridge." *New York Times Book Review*, April 21, 1969, 2.

Benson, Jackson J. *The Ox-Bow Man: A Biography of Walter Van Tilburg Clark*. Reno: University of Nevada Press, 2004.

Best Short Stories from The Paris Review. New York: E. P. Dutton, 1961.

Blaisdell, Gus. "After Ground Zero: The Writings of Evan S. Connell, Jr." *New Mexico Quarterly* 36, no. 2 (1966): 181–207.

Bottoms, Greg. "Evan S. Connell." *Salon*, July 18, 2000. https://www.salon.com /2000/07/18/connell_3/.

———. "Interview: Evan S. Connell." *Bookforum*, Winter 2001. https://www .bookforum.com/print/804/interview-evan-s-connell-21450.

Boyd, William. "Lessons in the Art of Living." *The Guardian*, October 26, 2002. https://www.theguardian.com/books/2002/oct/26/featuresreviews.gua rdianreview14.

Campbell, Mary. "Young Actress Also Writes, Sings." *Rocky Mount [NC] Telegram*, January 13, 1965, 3.

Carpenter, Don. *Fridays at Enrico's*. Berkeley, CA: Counterpoint, 2014.

Christian, Rebecca. "Mrs. Bridge: Evan Connell's Classic Novel of Kansas City Will Be Filmed by Oscar Winning Team." *Kansas City Magazine*, December 1988, 13–15, 61.

Clark, Walter Van Tilburg. "The Wind and the Snow of Winter." In *The Watchful Gods and Other Stories*, 33-50. Reno: University of Nevada Press, 2004.

Contact: The San Francisco Collection of New Writing, Art and Ideas, nos. 1–21 (1958–65).

Costello, Ruth. *Poems for Evan Connell*. Privately printed, n.d., c. 1984.

Crouch, Stanley. *Always in Pursuit: Fresh American Perspectives, 1995–1997*. New York: Pantheon, 1998.

Danto, Arthur. "Shock of the Old." *Artforum International* 42, no. 7 (March 2004): 49, 52.

Denham, Alice. *Sleeping with Bad Boys: A Juicy Tell-All of Literary New York in the 1950s and 1960s*. New York: Cardoza, 2006.

Dillard, Annie. *For the Time Being*. New York: Knopf, 1999.

———. "Winter Melons." *Harper's*, January 1974, 87–90.

Ferlinghetti, Lawrence. *A Coney Island of the Mind*. New York: New Directions, 1958.

Ferlinghetti, Lawrence, and Nancy J. Peters. *Literary San Francisco: A Pictorial History from Its Beginnings to the Present Day*. New York: Harper and Row; San Francisco: City Lights Books, 1980.

Fradkin, Philip L. *Wallace Stegner and the American West*. Berkeley: University of California Press, 2009.

Freedman, Samuel G. "Can This Man Save Publishing?" *New York*, March 2, 1998. https://nymag.com/nymetro/news/media/features/2305/.

Garnett, Gale Zoe. *Visible Amazement*. New York: Simon and Schuster, 2001.

Gilmore, Shawn. "The 'Double Exposure' of History in Evan S. Connell's *Mrs. Bridge* and *Mr. Bridge*." *Journal of American Studies* 42, no. 1 (April 2008): 67–87.

Gold, Herbert, ed. *Fiction of the Fifties: A Decade of American Writing*. New York: Doubleday, 1959.

Gottlieb, Robert. *Avid Reader: A Life*. New York: Farrar, Straus, and Giroux, 2016.

Gould, Anne H. "Custer Captured on Canvas: Gift of Book Fired Artist's Zeal." *Daily Sentinel* (Grand Junction, CO), August 6, 1985, 9.

Grossman, Ron. "Literary Lifesaving." *Chicago Tribune*, August 28, 1987, Tempo 1, 4.

Harrity, Richard. "Bohemia on the Bay." *Cosmopolitan*, December 1963, 22-27.

Hjortsberg, William. *Jubilee Hitchhiker: The Life and Times of Richard Brautigan*. Berkeley, CA: Counterpoint, 2012.

Hohn, Donovan. "Anatomy Lessons." *Harper's* 303, no. 1819 (December 2001): 79–83.

Holmes, John Clellon. "The Philosophy of the Beat Generation." *Esquire*, February 1958, 35–38.

Homes, A. M. Introduction. In Evan S. Connell, *The Diary of a Rapist*, vii–xii. New York: New York Review Books, 2004.

Huston, John. *An Open Book*. New York: Knopf, 1980.

Kentfield, Calvin. "San Francisco: The Waterfront." *Holiday*, San Francisco issue, 29, no. 4 (April 1961): 104–15, 197–200.

Klein, Melanie. "On the Sense of Loneliness." In *Envy and Gratitude and Other Works, 1946–1963*, 300-313. New York: Free Press, 1975. https://nonoedipal.files.wordpress.com/2009/10/on-the-sense-of-loneliness.pdf.

Lamott, Anne. "A Eulogy for Bill Ryan." *California*, December 1986, 136.

Lamott, Kenneth. "San Francisco: San Quentin." *Holiday*, San Francisco issue, 29, no. 4 (April 1961): 26–31.

———. "The Warriors." *Contact 16*, 4, no. 3, October–November 1963. 71–74.

Landon, Brooks. "Evan S. Connell, Jr." In *Dictionary of Literary Biography Yearbook: 1981*, edited by Karen Rood, Jean W. Ross, and Richard Ziegfeld, 30-34. Detroit: Thomson Gale, 1982.

Lapham, Lewis H. "The Enchanted Loom." *Lapham's Quarterly: States of Mind* 11, no. 1 (Winter 2018). https://www.laphamsquarterly.org/states-mind/enchanted-loom.

Lehmann-Haupt, Christopher. "One Man Who Is an Island." *New York Times*, April 23, 1969, 45.

Leiris, Michael. *Manhood: A Journey from Childhood into the Fierce Order of Virility*. Translated by Richard Howard. Chicago: University of Chicago Press, 1984.

Leonard, John. "One Cranberry's Predictions." *New York Times*, April 8, 1973.

Lewis, Janet. *The Wife of Martin Guerre*. Colt Press, 1941. Reprint, Denver: Alan Swallow, 1966.

Limerick, Patricia Nelson. "How the West Was (Almost) Lost." *New York Times*, January 27, 1991, sec. 2, 29.

Logue, Christopher. "The Art of Poetry LXVI." Interview by Susha Guppy. *Paris Review* 35, no. 127 (Summer 1993): 238–64.

Long, Robert Emmet. *The Films of Merchant Ivory.* Newly updated edition. New York: Harry N. Abrams, 1997.

Machado de Assis, Joaquim Maria. *Epitaph of a Small Winner.* Translated by William L. Grossman. New York: Farrar, Straus and Giroux, 2008. Reprinted as *The Posthumous Memoirs of Brás Cubas* in two separate translations: translated by Flora Thomson-DeVeaux (New York: Penguin Classics, 2020); translated by Margaret Jull Costa and Robin Patterson (New York: Liveright, 2020).

Mann, Thomas. "Disorder and Early Sorrow." 1925. https://literaturesave2.files.wordpress.com/2009/12/thomas-mann-disorder-and-early-sorrow.pdf.

Matthiessen, Peter. *At Play in the Fields of the Lord.* New York: Random House, 1965.

McGurl, Mark. *The Program Era: Postwar Fiction and the Rise of Creative Writing.* Cambridge, MA: Harvard University Press, 2009.

McMurtry, Larry. "He Went against the Peace Pipe." *New York Review of Books*, March 6, 2008. http://www.nybooks.com/articles/2008/03/06/he-went-against-the-peace-pipe/.

Medillín Zenil, Alfonso. "The Olmec Culture." In *The Olmec Tradition* (exhibition catalogue). Houston: Museum of Fine Arts, 1963.

Miller, John, ed. *San Francisco Stories: Great Writers on the City.* San Francisco: Chronicle Books, 1990.

Nolte, William H. "Evan S. Connell, Jr." In *Dictionary of Literary Biography: American Novelists since World War II*, edited by Jeffrey Helterman and Richard Layman, 2:100–105. Detroit: Thomson Gale, 1978.

North, Sterling. "A Story of Permanent Childhood." *Washington Post*, March 19, 1950, B7.

Oppenheimer, Mark. "An Era of Awkward Obsession." *Believer* 21 (February 1, 2005), https://believermag.com/an-era-of-awkward-obsession/. Originally published as "An Era of Awkward Repression."

———. "Searching for Evan S. Connell's Bohemian Sausalito." *New York Times*, March 25, 2015, TR10, https://www.nytimes.com/2015/03/29/travel/searching-for-evan-connells-bohemian-sausalito.html.

Pace, Eric. "The National Book Award in Fiction: A Curious Case." *New York Times Book Review*, May 6, 1973, 16-17.

Pickus, David. "On Being Out of Touch: Evan S. Connell and the Aesthetic of Social Oblivion." *South Central Review* 37, no. 1 (Spring 2020): 54–72.

Polsgrove, Carol. *It Wasn't Pretty, Folks, but Didn't We Have Fun? Esquire in the Sixties.* New York: Norton, 1995.

Popper, Joe. "The Alchemy of Evan Connell." *Kansas City Star Magazine*, June 28, 1987, 10–22.

Prescott, Orville. "The Satirical Comedy of Evan S. Connell." *New York Times*, June 25, 1965, 31.

Ryan, William H. Untitled self-introduction as editor at large. *California* 10, no. 2 (February 1985): 5.

Sale, Roger. *On Not Being Good Enough: Writings of a Working Critic*. New York: Oxford University Press, 1979.

Sawyer-Lauçanno, Christopher. *The Continual Pilgrimage: American Writers in Paris, 1944–1960*. San Francisco: City Lights Books, 1992.

Schott, Webster. "Captives within Themselves." *New Republic*, July 29, 1957, 20.

———. "Effective Stories by Native of Kansas City." *Kansas City Star*, May 18, 1957, 9.

———. "Kansas Citians in Prize Stories." *Kansas City Star*, September 14, 1951, 14.

———. "Kansas City Society Life Is Subject of Major Novel." *Kansas City Star*, January 10, 1959, 1, 16.

———. "Last Half of a Superb American Saga." *Life*, April 25, 1969, 8.

———. "The Roundest Square in U.S. Letters." *Life*, San Francisco regional edition, October 3, 1969.

———. "Testing the Dream." *Washington Post Book World*, June 6, 1976, H5.

Shapiro, Gerald. "Evan S. Connell: A Profile." *Ploughshares Online*, August 2, 2004. https://www.pshares.org/issues/fall-1987/evan-s-connell-profile.

Shapiro, Karl. *The Bourgeois Poet*. New York: Random House, 1964.

Siegel, Barry. "The Iconoclastic Mr. Connell." *Los Angeles Times*, June 9, 1991. https://www.latimes.com/archives/la-xpm-1991-06-09-tm-822-story.html.

Sklenicka, Carol. *Alice Adams: Portrait of a Writer*. New York: Scribner, 2019.

———. *Raymond Carver: A Writer's Life*. New York: Simon and Schuster, 2009.

Steele, Max. *Debby*. New York: Harper, 1950.

———. "The Most Exciting Magazine." *San Francisco Examiner*, November 17, 1963, Book Week section, 26–27.

———. "My Father's Image: A Portrait from Memory." *Washington Post Magazine*, June 20, 2004, 18-23.

Stegner, Wallace. *On Teaching and Writing Fiction*. New York: Penguin Books, 2002.

Stein, Lorin. "In Memoriam: Evan S. Connell, 1924–2013." *Paris Review* blog, January 10, 2013. https://www.theparisreview.org/blog/2013/01/10/in-memoriam-evan-s-connell/.

Storr, Anthony. *Solitude: A Return to the Self*. New York: Ballantine Books, 1988.

Streitfeld, David. "Book Report." *Washington Post*, August 25, 1991, 15.

Sumner, Melody. "Evan S. Connell: Gentleman or Joker?" *San Francisco Review of Books*, February 1991, 26–28.

Thom, James Alexander. "Custer Rides to the Little Big Horn." *Washington Post*, November 18, 1984. https://www.washingtonpost.com/archive/entertainment/books/1984/11/18/custer-rides-to-the-little-big-horn/d9c15b9b-203f-4d29-9fc2-f98bd4a0451e/.

Vandenburgh, Jane. "Fridays at Enrico's, Don Carpenter's No-Longer-Lost Last Book." *Huffington Post*, April 28, 2014. https://www.huffpost.com/entry/don-carpenters-fridays-at_b_5206931.

Wadler, Joyce. "The Creator of Mr. and Mrs. Bridge Goes Home Again—With Reluctance and No Thanks for the Memories." *People*, December 10, 1990. https://people.com/archive/the-creator-of-mr-and-mrs-bridge-goes-home-again-with-reluctance-and-no-thanks-for-the-memories-vol-34-no-23/.

Watts, Alan. *In My Own Way: An Autobiography*. New York: Vintage Books, 1973.

Weaver, John D., ed. *Glad Tidings: A Friendship in Letters: The Correspondence of John Cheever and John D. Weaver, 1945–1982*. New York: HarperCollins, 1993.

West, Raymond B., ed. *A Country in the Mind: An Anthology of Stories and Poems from* The Western Review. Sausalito, CA: Contact Editions, 1962.

Williams, William Carlos. *Imaginations*. Edited by Webster Schott. New York: New Directions, 1970.

Zengos, Hariclea. "Evan S. Connell." In *Dictionary of Literary Biography 335: American Short-Story Writers since World War II*, edited by Richard E. Lee and Patrick Meanor, 2:73–80. Detroit: Thomson Gale, 2007.

Index

Note: Page numbers in italics indicate illustrations.